Bitemporal Data

Bitemporal Data
Theory and Practice

Tom Johnston

AMSTERDAM • BOSTON • HEIDELBERG • LONDON
NEW YORK • OXFORD • PARIS • SAN DIEGO
SAN FRANCISCO • SINGAPORE • SYDNEY • TOKYO

Morgan Kaufmann is an imprint of Elsevier

Acquiring Editor: Steve Elliot
Editorial Project Manager: Kaitlin Herbert
Project Manager: Punithavathy Govindaradjane
Designer: Mark Rogers

Morgan Kaufmann is an imprint of Elsevier
225 Wyman Street, Waltham, MA, 02451, USA

Library of Congress Cataloging-in-Publication Data
Application submitted

British Library Cataloguing-in-Publication Data
A catalogue record for this book is available from the British Library

ISBN: 978-0-12-408067-6

For information on all Morgan Kaufmann publications
visit our website at www.mkp.com

This book has been manufactured using Print On Demand technology. Each copy is produced to order
and is limited to black ink. The online version of this book will show color figures where appropriate.

Working together
to grow libraries in
developing countries

www.elsevier.com • www.bookaid.org

I dedicate this book to my wife Trish, and to my sons Adrian and Ian.

Contents

Foreword

"It's about time," was my first thought when Tom Johnston asked me to review his manuscript. It is indeed about matters temporal. And it certainly is about time that we consider chronology as a key component of data. But it is about much more. Because in order to understand time and its relationship to data and, more importantly, to business, Tom has had to explore what stored data actually represents. It's in and through that exploration that the true, lasting value of this book emerges: a deep insight into the connections between the real, physically existing world and the representations we create in the data we record about that world. And although this book focuses on time and its relational representation, I believe that this insight will enable us to navigate the realm of so-called big data and its proper use in business.

If you think carefully about the concept of time as a dimension of data—and Tom has considered this in depth and at length prior to this book—you will likely conclude that it can be a maddeningly complex topic. You will probably come to realize that it is central to any representation of business information as computerized data. And I suspect that you may be disappointed when you openly and honestly review the temporal features provided by many of today's systems.

The majority of operational, run-the-business systems are essentially atemporal in nature; they exist in some existential Now as might be envisaged by Eckhart Tolle, largely oblivious of the past and indifferent to the future. We can trace this thinking to the original batch implementation of applications that ran overnight and basically summarized a day's business. Technological limitations also constrained early transaction systems, which relied on end-of-day reconciliation routines to integrate data across disparate systems. Today's technology is well capable of overcoming these limits. But a fundamental design aspect persists: the status of yesterday's business is overwritten by today's and will be again tomorrow (although there are, of course, exceptions, especially in particular industries).

Informational, understand-and-manage-the-business systems deal, by necessity, with time past, but mostly by means of incomplete and often awkward simplifications. Snapshots have been the basis of much of Inmon's thinking about the data warehouse since the 1990s. Slowly changing dimensions were added by Kimball to address time in his own architecture in the 2000s. Extensive computer science research on temporal databases through the 1980s and 1990s has had limited impact in the real world; TSQL2, proposed to the SQL Standards Committee in 1994, languished for years, eventually being implemented by Teradata in 2010 for data warehousing purposes, while formal adoption of an ISO Standard for (some) temporal characteristics only occurred in SQL:2011, implemented in DB2 by IBM in 2012.

You might imagine that a vast volcanic reservoir of frustration would have built up and erupted by now. A very simple example of business needs that cannot easily be implemented in the atemporal relational databases we've lived with since the 1980s follows. On Monday, the operational database contains a set of current product prices. On Tuesday, the prices of half the products are updated; Monday's prices are overwritten. On Wednesday, we try to roll back a number of the price changes, but where are the old prices? Fortunately, backed up and available for manual reentry, which overwrite Tuesday's values. On Thursday, we discover that a small number of prices reset on Wednesday were input incorrectly. We update them, but now there's no record of the incorrect prices on Wednesday that were used in invoices generated on that day. How will we deal with that? On Friday, a technical problem necessitates restoring some of the data from backups.

At this point, creating a true historical record of the week's prices is challenging, to say the least. The data warehouse may have it, although this was not its purpose, but it does depend on the design chosen. Different answers emerge depending on your choice of Inmon, Kimball or other approaches to history. The correctness and consistency of the restored data is heavily dependent on the timing and content of the extracts. None of this is new. Most IT shops and ERP vendors have been building workarounds for decades to deal with these situations. The unfortunate truth is that much of the bitemporal database theory needed to deal with such issues properly and in a consistent, comprehensive manner has been around since the early 1990s.

This book is, on the one hand, a primer in the theory and practice of bitemporal data: what the practitioner needs to understand before starting to use a database that incorporates the functionality, before attempting to design a temporal application. It can also be used, like its predecessor publication, *Managing Time in Relational Databases* by Tom Johnston and Randall Weis (Morgan Kaufmann, 2010), to design a framework to implement a bitemporal system on top of an atemporal DBMS. It will be invaluable to businesses who decide it's well past time to migrate to a bitemporal database. Tom explains the approach needed to simplify the transition, to ensure that prior applications still work as they did and that the new generic functionality really does what it says on the box.

On the other hand, this book is a critique of the bitemporal standards as currently defined and implemented. Unfortunately, as Tom explains, they are incomplete and what exists is not quite right. To understand the problem, we have to dig into the semantics of the naming of the bitemporal columns. I resisted at first; after all, what's in a name? Is it important that TSQ2 talks of valid and transaction times, whereas the ISO standard calls the equivalent columns application and system time? And why does Tom insist on state and assertion time? Roughly speaking, valid, application and state time are all described in terms of the business action. The others—transaction, system and assertion time—are in some way related to the technological action of writing into the database. I'm being deliberately vague, because the terms are subtly different, but it seems that few, other than Tom, have so far noted the importance of this difference.

Reading this book, it eventually came clear to me that the naming chosen in the standards either drove flawed thinking or resulted from it. This is a strong claim, and to decide if it is fair, we need to go all the way back to first principles and ask: what does it really *mean* to store data in a computer system. Tom takes us on a tour of logic, ontology and semantics to explain. Allow me to attempt a summary.

Business (and people) are interested in things in the real world, how they relate to one another, and any changes that take place in these things and relationships. For example, Mary buys a tablet for $500 on Wednesday. This is a fact. But, as far as the financial controller is concerned, it happens only when he sees this fact represented in the sales database on Thursday. The fact and the recording of it are different things. Furthermore, even recording a fact is not so semantically clear. Mary gave the salesperson a deposit of $250 on Monday, the last day of the quarter. In the salesperson's optimistic view—and aren't all salespeople optimistic?—the book was sold at that moment and he recorded it in his sales tracking system to push him over his quota. But will he get his bonus?

There is thus a meaning, and often several different meanings, implied and often unstated when data is recorded in a system. It is only when we carefully consider temporal aspects of reality that it becomes clear that facts, statements of those facts, and the inscriptions of those statements in databases are all very different things. Furthermore, they can, and do, happen at different times. This detailed thinking allows Tom to recognize a real flaw in the standards—the ability to correct data in state time tables—and to propose a valuable extension—the addition of future transaction time. And he opens up a thorny question: is bitemporal data the ultimate in time tracking, or should we consider the need for tritemporal database support. I consider that a topic worth serious consideration, and one that makes sense in the context of the understanding of what it really means to record and store business data.

This understanding is vital if we are to navigate the expanding world of big data. I will go further. I believe that, without such an understanding, we are destined to crash and burn. Much of our current approach to data meaning, storage and usage is based on thinking from the early days of computing, when data was designed for a particular purpose, and stored and used centrally for that purpose alone. We are moving rapidly into an era when the devices on the Internet of Things are generating data, the structure, meaning, and content of which are often beyond the knowledge and control of those who use it. Its reliability and timing is suspect. The intent of its producers may be unknowable.

Here, maybe more than in the field of relational databases, this book will be cited in the future as the starting point for a rational definition of an area loosely known today as big data. In this perhaps brave, and certainly new and uncertain world, Tom's thinking about the underlying logic, ontology and semantics of data provides, I believe, a firm foundation for future research and development. It will be used by technologies required to track the provenance of both human-sourced and machine-generated data as such data is moved and copied within and among enterprises. And it points the way to an integration of formal ontologies with relational databases and other data stores without which semantic interoperability across the Semantic Web will be a hollow claim.

In summary, this book makes an important contribution to our use and understanding of data in three areas. First, it provides solid guidance to practitioners who are implementing bitemporal data stores. Second, its careful analysis of the temporal nature of data shows how product developers and standards designers must correct and expand current implementations. Third, and perhaps most importantly, it creates a conceptual framework stretching from the real world through the statements we make about it to the inscriptions we place in data stores. This framework is vital if we are to untangle what we think we see in data, especially so-called big data, from what is, or is not, actually there.

Dr. Barry Devlin,
Cape Town, 27 January 2014

Preface

Time present and time past
Are both perhaps present in time future
And time future contained in time past.

T. S. Eliot, The Four Quartets: Burnt Norton

In this fragment from Burnt Norton, Eliot describes a Buddhist conception of time, one which encourages us to think of past time, present time and future time as interwoven with one another. This Buddhist concept is a useful counter-balance to our mechanistic notion of time as a linear sequence of moments which occur one after the other, and which constitute a series which can be traversed in one direction only.

Anything at all — you, or me, or any of the changeable objects around us — is at the present moment the latest stage in the history of what we are. With a different history, we would, at this present moment, be other than what we are now. In this sense, William Faulkner was correct when he wrote (in *Requiem for a Nun*), "The past is never dead. It's not even past."

It is perhaps with human beings, and the short-term and long-term projects and plans that inform their lives, that it is most obviously true that time present and time past are present in time future. Somewhere, a store manager is reviewing a history of product price changes and their effect on sales. She isn't doing this out of simple curiosity. She is doing it because she wants to maximize future profits for her store. Somewhere, an author is working on the Great American Novel. He isn't doing it just to pass the time. He imagines a future in which he has accomplished the great work of his life, in which accolades are heaped on him, and in which royalty checks are more than pittances. If and when either of those futures is achieved, it will be because of a history of present moments, each the culmination of a sequence of past moments during which those people worked towards those future goals.

So the intimate relationships of past, present and future manifest themselves in the changes that take place in the world. But they also manifest themselves in the changes that take place in what we say about the world.

This brings us to the subject of this book: temporal data and, in particular, bitemporal data. Bitemporal data is data that is associated with two kinds of time. One of these is the time in which things happen in the world; the other is the time in which descriptions of the world accumulate. The first kind of time is about when things were, are, or will be as the data which describes those things says they were, are, or will be. The second kind of time is about that data itself. It is about when we once thought, or still think, or may eventually come to think, that that data correctly describes what things were, are, or will be like; or at least when we once thought or still think that that data constitutes the best descriptions currently available to us.

This book is about bitemporal data that is persisted in relational databases, and about the information which that data provides. However, the extension to non-relational ways of persisting data is straightforward. I talk about data in relational databases, first of all, because that is the prevalent way of storing character set data, and because character set data is still the prevalent kind of data that describes the things an enterprise engages with, and the processes in which it engages with them.

I talk about data in relational databases, secondly, because the language of relational data and relational databases is a lingua franca among data management professionals. For example, we all know what tables, rows and columns are, and we all know what entity integrity and referential integrity are. Or, at least, we all should know these things.

But I also talk about data in relational databases, thirdly and most importantly, because relational theory is the richest and most mathematically informed of theories of data management. It is thus best suited to incorporate extensions needed to manage bitemporal data while itself remaining stable and well-grounded.

Relational theory also has both an ontology and a semantics, although neither are much discussed. To the best of my knowledge, little has been written about how the ontology and the semantics of the Relational Paradigm (as I will call the use of relational theory in data management) give meaning to the mathematical structures of sets, Cartesian Products and relations, and to their concrete manifestations as tables, columns and rows.

But in this book, I would like to say something about the ontology and the semantics of the Relational Paradigm — a set of concepts based on the relational theory invented by Dr. E. F. Codd, and on the implementation of that theory in the world's major Database Management Systems (DBMSs). In fact, I don't think that the Relational Paradigm can be correctly extended to accommodate bitemporal data unless these perspectives are understood and taken into consideration.

PERSPECTIVES ON THE RELATIONAL PARADIGM OF DATA

One of the distinctive features of this book is that it discusses relational concepts, and their extension into the realm of bitemporal data, from several perspectives. In these discussions, I try to avoid explanations which mix these perspectives because I think that when that happens, explanations become pseudo-explanations which in fact explain nothing at all. In these discussions, I will occasionally point out examples of perspectival confusion so the reader may be better prepared to recognize it when she encounters it in her own working environment.

One perspectival distinction is the distinction between *syntax* and *semantics*. This distinction will become clearer through repeated use, but this much can be said at the outset. The *syntax* of the Relational Paradigm describes relational data structures, instances of those structures, and transformations made to those instances. It's about the things that DBAs and programmers construct and manipulate. A Customer table is a data structure, for example, and one row in that table is an instance of that structure. An update to a row in that table is a transformation made to that instance. Syntax describes structures and their instances, and transformations on those instances. Those transformations add instances to a database, change instances in a database, and remove instances from a database. The instances have the structure described by their syntax. The transformations add and remove syntactically valid instances, and change valid instances into other valid instances.

The *semantics* of the Relational Paradigm is about the information expressed in those data structures and in their instances. Data is created and modified so that it accurately conveys information. If customer Smith changes her name to "Jones", then we change her name on her row in the Customer table to reflect that change.

The important point here is that what we do to data, we do in order to preserve its value as an embodiment of information. That is all too obvious, of course. But once we get deep into the syntax of data and its management, it is easy to lose sight of this important fact. Information is the master; data is the servant.

Here is a brief example. Relational entity integrity is often explained as the rule that no primary key in a table can be null, and that each primary key must be unique. That is a rule of syntax that a relational DBMS enforces.

Is the semantics of entity integrity left undescribed because it is too obvious to be worth mentioning? Well, consider the fact that the semantics of entity integrity is that a database may never contain contradictory statements. Is this so widely recognized and so obvious as to not be worth mentioning? I don't think so.

A consideration of contradictory statements is an entry into the realm of propositional logic and predicate logic. I discuss these perspectives on the Relational Paradigm in this book because we data management professionals should have some understanding of that logic, of how it is expressed in the Relational Paradigm, and of how it is used to manage data in relational databases.

We are all willing to do the hand-waving which acknowledges that relational theory is based on mathematics and logic. But if we can catch on to the trick of *seeing* mathematics and logic embedded in the data structures and transformations that we manage, then we will build better databases and better applications. In particular, we will be more likely to provide generalized solutions to specific problems. These solutions are always more stable in the face of changing requirements than point solutions to specific problems are. They are easier to code and to maintain because they express simpler and clearer patterns than do idiosyncratic implementations of solutions to narrowly conceptualized problems. They are always better solutions.

THE TEMPORAL SQL STANDARDS: ISO 9075:2011 AND TSQL2

In late 2011, the ISO published the latest release of its SQL standard, ISO 9075:2011. This was the first ISO release to include support for bitemporal data. Prior to that, in 1994, a group of computer scientists published the TSQL2 proposed standard for the management of bitemporal data, but this proposal was never accepted by the ISO. Nonetheless, I will refer to it as a standard because it is a draft standard which represented, at the time, a consensus among a significant part of the computer science community.

A current implementation of the ISO SQL standard can be found in IBM's DB2 10 DBMS and its successive releases, and a current implementation of the TSQL2 standard can be found in the Teradata 13 DBMS and its successive releases.[1]

This book is not an introduction to either of these standards, or to either of these families of products. For example, the insert, update and delete transactions that I describe in this book (in Chapter 11), and the queries that I also describe (in Chapters 12 and 13) use my own syntax. More

---

[1]However, I don't claim that these two commercial products are complete with respect to their regulating standards documents, or even that they are fully conformant with them. They may or may not be. I haven't looked into the issue closely enough to make that determination.

importantly, several of the types of transactions and types of queries that I describe will not be found in either the ISO or TSQL2 standard, or in DB2 10 or Teradata 13. They are types of transactions and queries that I believe will be useful in the management of commercial data, and I recommend them to the standards committees and vendors for inclusion in future releases.

In its emphasis on ontology and semantics, and in its presentation of novel types of transactions and queries, this book provides a unique perspective on the management of temporal data, and suggests useful extensions to the traditional scope of temporal data functionality. This book takes you "behind" the standards-defined and vendor-supported management of temporal data.

From this perspective, you will be better prepared to understand the good, the bad, and perhaps even the ugly, in the current temporal standards and in current vendor implementations of those standards. With that understanding, you will be better prepared to utilize those vendor implementations in a manner that maximizes their value to your enterprise, and minimizes the penalties of their shortcomings. You will also be in a better position to influence the evolution of those standards and those products.

AUDIENCE

The "Theory" chapters of this book contain material that may be unfamiliar to many IT professionals, while the "Practice" chapters of this book contain material that may be unfamiliar to many computer scientists. Not everyone will find every part of this book equally relevant to her work and to her interests. But theorists can always benefit from seeing how their theories are put to use, and practitioners can always benefit from understanding the theory behind the data constructs they build and maintain.

This suggests two different reading strategies. I recommend that both the theorist and the practitioner begin each chapter by reading the Glossary entry for each term in that chapter's Glossary List. Then, for the theorist, reading from Chapter 1 through to the end of the book is probably the best strategy. But for the practitioner, especially the IT professional who does not have a strong background in one or more of mathematics, logic, ontology or semantics, the better strategy might be to read Chapter 1 and then skip ahead to Part 2 and use the rest of Part 1 as reference material. Whenever the narrative in Part 2 is confusing, this reader should first identify unfamiliar technical terms and look up their definitions. The key technical terms which I have introduced are defined in the Glossary for this book (available at http://booksite.elsevier.com/9780124080676). The definitions of other important technical terms will be available from reliable sources on the internet.

If this review of definitions doesn't provide enough clarification, then this reader should go back to Part 1 and at least skim the relevant chapter or chapters there. After finishing the book by reading chapters in this sequence, the practitioner should be well-equipped to go back and study the chapters in Part 1.

All this theory and practice, of course, has a focus. That focus is bitemporal data. But this book is not for IT professionals whose only interest is in gaining proficiency in how bitemporal data is managed by a specific DBMS, or for those whose only interest is in a commentary on one or other of the temporal SQL standards. It is, rather, for IT professionals who will work with specific vendor support for bitemporal data, but who will benefit from understanding the theory behind the constructs and functions, behind the DDL and DML, of those specific vendor products. It is also for computer scientists and their students, not only those interested in the management of temporal data, but also those interested in formal ontologies and their role in expressing the semantics of data. So this audience includes:

- business analysts;
- enterprise data modelers;
- enterprise data architects;
- database, data warehouse and data mart developers;
- business ontologists;
- computer science students; and
- computer scientists.

BUSINESS ANALYSTS

The role of the business analyst is not a passive one. Subject matter experts can seldom express their requirements clearly enough that what they really want can be built from an initial statement of those requirements. Developing accurate requirements is an interactive process in which the business analyst must bring out distinctions that were "too obvious" to the experts to mention, and must describe relevant possibilities to those experts that exist because of the capabilities of DBMSs and of related hardware and software technologies.

When temporal requirements are the issue, it is especially easy for subject matter experts to fail to communicate what they really want. When the requirement is to "add history" to one or more tables, the business analyst will often write up requirements that developers will implement by adding a timestamp to the primary keys of those tables. After implementation, when the business users find that the "history" that is available does not allow them to rerun a report and get the same results as when the report was originally run, they will wonder what the business analyst meant when she promised them support for "as-was" as well as "as-is" reporting.

The as-was capabilities that she promised, in fact, were never anything more than the ability to report on the past, using *current* data. But if the data as originally entered was incorrect or incomplete, and was later corrected or completed, then that as-was reporting will not reproduce what was originally reported.

Occasionally, the business analyst is confronted with another important requirement which, in the absence of a yet-to-be-implemented feature of bitemporal data, cannot be fulfilled. That is the requirement to implement a go-live event for a very large number of rows in a set of database tables. This is a situation in which there are too many rows to load in one off-line session. But the business may be unhappy when IT tells them that it will take multiple off-line sessions to complete the load, the reason for their unhappiness being that when the database comes back up after each session, the results of that session immediately becomes visible in the database. And so there isn't one go-live event. There are as many events as there are batch load sessions.

The business analyst should understand that this problem is now solvable. The solution isn't to attach a future effectivity date to the data being loaded, because it may be that the data is a mix of rows which are to become immediately effective, rows which are to become effective on specified future dates, and even rows which became effective on specified past dates. It is all of these rows, those with past effectivity, those with future effectivity, and those with current effectivity, that the business wants to become available to database users at the same point in time, on the same go-live event.

Unfortunately, the solution to this problem is neither specified in the current SQL standards nor implemented in current DBMSs which support bitemporal data. The solution to this problem lies in an extension to current bitemporal theory which I first described, with my co-author Randy Weis, in our 2010 book *Managing Time in Relational Databases*, and which I describe in this book in Chapter 14. But when IT professionals understand that this solution has been defined, then together we may be able to encourage standards bodies and DBMS vendors to implement it.

This is another reason to understand more about bitemporal data than just how to code it. If we understand bitemporal data itself, we don't have to passively accept what standards bodies define and what vendors implement. We can have a say in the process because we will know what is possible, and we can prioritize what we want. Perhaps it is not customary for IT professionals in end-user organizations to attempt to influence standards committees or DBMS vendors in any serious way. But there is no reason why it shouldn't be done.

ENTERPRISE DATA MODELERS

Bitemporal requirements do not have to be hand-designed into data models. And they shouldn't be. A declarative specification of temporal requirements is far less costly than coding those requirements in data models. It is also a more reliable way of expressing those requirements.

One reason we can use a declarative approach is that, for a given DBMS, there will be no two ways about how to make tables bitemporal. The CREATE TABLE statements for bitemporal tables are well-defined in the standards. Unitemporal tables are also defined in the standards, and so there is a choice there for the modeler to express. But that choice, and all other choices whose end result is to define a set of one or more bitemporal or unitemporal tables, can easily be expressed in metadata by selecting options from a list from which temporal DDL is then generated.

Nonetheless, data modelers will have to specify those options, and so there will be something related to bitemporal data for the modeler to do. Also, although the bitemporal target of a table conversion will be well-defined, the source table will be as idiosyncratic as you care to imagine. The mapping from a non-bitemporal source table to a bitemporal target table will require a careful inventory and labelling of the components of the non-temporal table. For example, primary keys, foreign keys, surrogate keys, natural keys and non-keys will all have to be identified, because they must all be mapped onto corresponding components of the target bitemporal table. If the source table is the result of a prior attempt to "add history", the mapping will be even more complex.

There is also another major role for the data modeler that is on the horizon, and the chapter on the ontology of relational data (Chapter 5) introduces that role. The role is that of a business ontologist. Many major corporations do not yet have ontologists on their IT staffs. Others have ontologists, and employ them to develop ontologies for the information expressed in emails, documents, and other semi-structured data. But the most important ontology an enterprise can develop is the ontology that formalizes the types of which the rows in that enterprise's production tables are instances.

It is the enterprise data modelers of a company who are most familiar with that data and with those types, and it is those data modelers who are best qualified to become the ontologists of their companies' production databases. But for this role, the mathematics, logic, ontology, and semantics of relational databases are all important. Without some grounding in all four of these perspectives on relational databases, these IT professionals will be unable to take that considerable step from data modeler to data ontologist.

I hope this book will be useful as an introduction to enterprise data ontology and to related theoretical topics for those IT professionals who have the best understanding of an enterprise's core data—enterprise data modelers.

ENTERPRISE DATA ARCHITECTS

Enterprise data architecture, in some considerable part, is enterprise data modeling writ large. Of course, data architecture must consider data in motion as well as data at rest. But even with respect to data in motion, the structure of the data itself is important. For example, as I will describe in Chapter 17, the canonical message model in an SOA architecture can in large part replace an enterprise data model.

The ontologies discovered in semi-structured data will have much in common with the ontologies discovered in an enterprise's production databases. It is the natural role of the enterprise data architect to oversee the integration of these ontologies.

DATABASE, DATA WAREHOUSE, AND DATA MART DEVELOPERS

In this book, I will demonstrate that Inmon-style data warehouses and Kimball-style data marts are not able to provide the historical information that bitemporal data can provide. The accumulation of data in today's data warehouses does not distinguish between a history of what the data is about and a history of the data itself. Yet this distinction is vital to supporting the real requirements that business users have in mind when they request "historical data". The history provided by the slowly-changing dimensions of star schemas are also unable to make this distinction and provide this information.

This will change. The added information that becomes available only with bitemporal data is too important to ignore. Developers will have to make their databases, data warehouses, and data marts bitemporal, although this conversion to bitemporal data can take place gradually, one set of tables at a time. So when the first projects roll out to make these modifications, developers better have some understanding of what bitemporal structures look like, of the differences between entity integrity and temporal entity integrity and between referential integrity and temporal referential integrity. This book provides a DBMS-neutral description of these structures and these constraints.

BUSINESS ONTOLOGISTS

Many business ontologists will have some familiarity with semantics, and should have some familiarity with both classical and formal ontologies. If not, I discuss those topics in Chapters 5 and 6. But if the business ontologist has not been put to work developing ontologies for the entity, attribute and relationship types of the production data of the enterprise he works for, he may not be familiar with the mathematics of relational databases, or with the propositional and predicate logic used to access and manipulate those databases. If he is not, he should pay special attention to Chapters 3 and 4.

I especially recommend to the ontologist's attention the Relational Paradigm Ontology presented in Chapter 5. It is an upper-level ontology which is based on Aristotle's work. I present it, not as one more among several current upper-level ontologies, but rather as *the* ontology common to all relational databases.

This Relational Paradigm Ontology is not a carefully crafted prescriptive structured ontology, by which I mean one which formalizes someone's preferred theories of important concepts like space, time, matter, or mind. Nor is it a descriptive unstructured ontology, by which I mean an ontology based on translating general-purpose or subject-matter-specific dictionaries into an ontology management tool. Rather, it is a carefully selected, extensible, descriptive, structured ontology.

- It is *descriptive* rather than prescriptive because it expresses the ontology underlying our everyday experiences. It is a *folk ontology*. For that reason, as readers focus on Chapter 5, they will likely find the ontology described there to be familiar, even if the terminology used to describe it is not.
- It is *selective* rather than universal in scope because it expresses that part of this folk ontology which is implicit in the structures of relational databases. That part includes objects and how they are distinguished, properties and relationships of objects, and events that objects take part in. The expression of those ontological categories in the tables, rows, columns, primary keys and foreign keys of relational databases is straightforward, and constitutes an upper-level ontology common to all relational databases.
- It is *structured* rather than unstructured because its components are mapped onto the mathematical constructs of relational databases, expressing those upper-level ontological commitments common to all databases. Because of this mapping onto mathematical structures, formal logic can be used to express the ontology, and to do theorem-proving and other reasoning on it.
- It is *extensible* rather than static because by means of subtyping, middle-level and lower-level ontologies can be formalized which express the ontological commitments of an enterprise in greater and greater detail. With a rich set of distinctions mapped onto mathematical structures, semantic interoperability among databases can be expressed formally and verified across the Semantic Web. And this can be done automatically, i.e. by software. Databases will be able to talk to databases directly, and know when the same names of data objects mean the same thing and when they don't. Currently, OWL (WC3's Web Ontology Language) and RDF (WC3's Resource Description Framework) are the technologies in which these ontologies are most likely to be expressed. But enterprise-level ontologies themselves remain for the most part unformulated.

There is important ontology work to be done at the enterprise level.

COMPUTER SCIENCE STUDENTS

This book may also be useful to computer science students, especially at the graduate level. It shows how much work remains to be done after the mathematics of bitemporal data − its structures and algorithms − are fully defined. The best direction for any topic in computer science to evolve, of course, is towards reducing the additional useful work that always remains after current theory has straightened up what it can. Several of the advanced topics discussed in this book illustrate this point. I would mention, in particular, the distinction between the physical serialization of transactions and the semantic serialization of the statements they make, a topic discussed in Chapter 14.

COMPUTER SCIENTISTS

These advanced topics may also prove of interest to computer scientists working on bitemporal data. An example is the explicit representation of statements as managed objects in databases. The standard theory of bitemporal data does not distinguish between rows of data and the statements which they express. That theory defines the transaction time of a row as the time which begins when the row is physically created. In my previous book, I and my co-author replaced transaction time with assertion time, and defined assertion time as the time which begins when the owners of a database are ready to assign the status of making a true statement to a row. This point in time is normally identical to the point in time at which the row is physically created. But there is no reason why the statement-making status of a row cannot be postponed until some time *after* the row is physically created.

The issue here is simply that transaction time is a physical concept and assertion time is a semantic one. Transaction time is about rows of data. Assertion time is about statements expressed by those rows.

In this book, statements are explicitly represented as managed objects. Statements may be asserted to be true, or asserted to be false, by those who make them. Other people may assent to a statement, or dissent from it. Still others may take note of a statement, but withhold judgment as to its truth value. Thus, truth values are not inherent in statements. They are ascribed to statements by people. These different stances that different people may take to the same statement are *propositional attitudes* these people have to these statements. These propositional attitudes are expressed in *speech acts* made by people in which they indicate what they think about the possible truth of a statement. Speech act time is thus a period of time which relates a person or a group of persons to a statement. It is a generalization of the assertion time of my previous book, and a relativization of that time to one person's or one group's relationship to one statement.

Rows are different managed objects. They are not statements. They are physical inscriptions of statements. Hence the transaction time of the standard theory is called inscription time in this book. However, creating inscriptions, copying and/or moving inscriptions, and physically removing inscriptions, are also acts performed by people. Thus, in this book, different inscriptional actions are relationships between the people who perform those actions, and the rows which appear in and disappear from databases as a result of those actions.

Valid time was never in dispute. It is what, in this book, I call state time. So although most of this book is a description of bitemporal data, and specifically a vendor-neutral description of how the bitemporal data defined in the ISO and TSQL2 standards is managed in databases, I currently believe that the most complete and semantically consistent theory of temporal data is a *tritemporal* theory. The three temporal dimensions of this tritemporal theory of time are these:

- *State Time.* Statements are about what things are like at one or more times. Those times are intervals of state time or, as the standard theory calls it, valid time.

- *Speech Act Time*. Different people have different attitudes, at different times, about the truth value of different statements. The temporal intervals of these person-relative attitudes exist in a second temporal dimension which I call speech-act time.
- *Inscription Time*. Rows physically exist in a database from the moment they are created to the moment they are physically deleted from that database. The temporal intervals of these inscriptions exist in a third temporal dimension which I call inscription time.

This tritemporal theory of temporal data is described in Chapter 19 of this book.

A COMPANION VOLUME TO *MANAGING TIME IN RELATIONAL DATABASES*

Many of the concepts discussed in this book were also discussed in my earlier book *Managing Time in Relational Databases*, co-authored with Randy Weis. When referring to that book, I will use the abbreviation "*MTRD*". These two books can usefully be considered companion volumes. *MTRD* focused on the syntax of how bitemporal data is implemented, although it did not ignore the semantics of the information that bitemporal data alone can make available.

This book extends both discussions. It brings in concepts from logic, ontology and linguistics which deepen our understanding of the semantics of bitemporal data. Among implementation issues, it shows how bitemporal data can be used in star schema databases, and demonstrates that none of the varieties of slowly-changing dimensions can provide the information that bitemporal data provides.

These two books can also be usefully contrasted. In *MTRD*, my co-author and I essentially argued for replacing the standard theory's transaction time with our assertion time. In this book, I argue that we need to keep transaction time and add assertion time as a distinct temporal dimension. This gives us one temporal dimension for things (state time), one temporal dimension for statements (speech act time), and one temporal dimension for rows (inscription time).

AN EXTENSIVE GLOSSARY

As in *MTRD*, an extensive Glossary accompanies this book. Unlike *MTRD*, that Glossary is not contained in this book. Instead, it is available from Morgan-Kaufmann at (http://booksite.elsevier.com/9780124080676).

As in *MTRD*, there is also a Glossary List at the end of each chapter. These are lists of the most important of the temporal data technical terms introduced in this book that are used in the chapter. Each of these terms is defined in the Glossary.

A NOTE ON STYLE

Some people who come up with ideas like to publish their results, and nothing but those results. For them, the thought process which led to the results is a private matter. All that anyone else is entitled to know are those results. All that anyone else cares to know, perhaps they think, are those results. The mathematician Carl Friedrich Gauss put it this way: "One does not leave the scaffolding around the cathedral" (quoted in Rockmore, 2006, pp. 39-40).

For some topics, that's the right way to do things. In a manual for a programming language, for example, no one can reasonably be expected to be interested in what led the designers of the language to include the features they did. But in a book on how to design programming languages, how one thinks about designing a language is at least as important as a list of features that the author believes all programming languages should include.

So should a book on bitemporal data be more like a language manual, or more like a book on how to design a language? Should it be a book exclusively about bitemporal data structures and the algorithms that manipulate instances of those structures? Or should it be a book which explains those things in the context of why we are beginning to use bitemporal data, why the bitemporal structures of that data include the components they include, and why the algorithms that transform that data do what they do?

Most computer science publications about bitemporal data tend to follow Gauss' lead. They emphasize results, and they demonstrate the correctness of those results. They are not written, for the most part, to show the train of thought that led to those results. Temporal SQL standards documents, and the technical manuals for DBMSs which support bitemporal data, are also written without any mention of scaffolding.

My objective is to do both things. I have written to show both the cathedral and the scaffolding. I have attempted to show how I thought my way through to the conclusions I reached. That should make it easier for others to discover my mistakes, and to do better themselves.

I have written to show, for example, not only what temporal entity integrity and temporal referential integrity are, but in what sense they are temporal extensions of entity and referential integrity, and in what sense each form of the two constraints implements rules which give data its meaning, rules without which that data would not express information. Which, after all, is the reason we go to the expense of managing data in the first place.

This makes this book more discursive, more conversational, than most technical books. It is my sincere hope that, at the end of this book, readers will have gained insights into bitemporal data that they would not have gained from a book written more like a technical manual or a standards document.

LOOKING FORWARD

Bitemporal data provides a history, and a future. On one timeline, which I call *state time*, it is the history and future of the things data is about. On another timeline, which I call *assertion time*, it is the history and future of the data itself. Specifically, bitemporal data makes the following kinds of information available.[2]

---

[2]"State time" is my term for what computer scientists, vendors, and the SQL standards — i.e. pretty much everybody else — calls "valid time". "Assertion time", excluding its extension into future time, is my term for what nearly everybody else calls "transaction time". My reasons for being a terminological iconoclast will become clear as this book progresses. My basic reason is that bad terminology makes you think badly.

- <u>As-was states of things</u>. Past state time makes it possible for queries and reports to be run that show what the things we are interested in used to be like, based on any corrections that may have been made to the data in the meantime.
- <u>As-will-be states of things</u>. Future state time makes it possible for inserts, updates and deletes to be made proactively, to make information available about the anticipated future states of things.
- <u>As-was data about things</u>. Past assertion time makes it possible for queries and reports to be rerun that show what we used to say the things we are interested were like, are like, or will be like. It makes it possible to do this without restoring old data, without redirection to different table names, and it produces exactly the same results that appeared when the queries and reports were originally run — even if corrections to that data were later made.
- <u>As-will-be data about things</u>. Future assertion time — introduced in *MTRD* as part of the Asserted Versioning method of managing temporal data — makes it possible for staging areas and sandboxes to co-exist in the same tables as the production data they are about, and makes it possible to switch such data into production status instantaneously, without latency delays, and regardless of volume. It makes it possible to load a large volume of transactions over multiple update cycles, whose results must all become visible in the database at the same moment in time.

These capabilities are clearly useful in almost every industry and every subject area. So imagine that these capabilities are available in every database, that all existing transactions, queries and reports against those databases work correctly, without modification, and that all temporal updates and queries are seamlessly integrated with them.

This *is* possible. This is the future of relational databases. From this perspective, non-temporal tables in non-temporal databases are like a tiny moving window on this two-dimensional realm of data. This tiny window shows us, with each tick of the clock, what the things our data is about are like at that moment, based on what the data itself is like at that moment. This tiny window loses, with each tick of the clock, all information about the past. This tiny window is unable, at any tick of the clock, to show us what things may be like in the future.

Bitemporal data expands this tiny window to the infinite horizons of past and future, along both temporal dimensions.

Acknowledgments

My editors Steve Elliot, Kaitlin Herbert, and Punithavathy Govindaradjane, were helpful and supportive to me throughout a lengthy process which tested the patience of author and editors alike. I could recommend no better editors to any author of a technical book in any field.

My reviewers were Barry Devlin, Theo Gantos, Richard Hackathorn, Andy Hessey, Craig Mullins and Sergey Sviridyuk. To each I extend my thanks. Also, the reviewers of my original proposal made a number of careful comments which helped to set the direction for the book, and got me off to a good start. They were Michael Brackett, Daniel Fitzpatrick, Craig Mullins and Stan Muse. Needless to say, any mistakes in this book are entirely my own responsibility and none of theirs.

I would also like to thank Rick Snodgrass whose publications first introduced me to computer science work on bitemporal data, and whose encouragement led me to write my first book. My particular thanks go to my good friend and the co-author of my first book, Randy Weis. My early ideas on bitemporal data were developed in partnership with Randy, and I owe him a great deal. Finally, my ideas and beliefs about almost everything important were developed in partnership with my wife Trish, and what I owe her is beyond my ability to express.

Chapter 17 is adapted from a three-part article published in *Enterprise Systems Journal* in late 2011, by permission of the editor. Their URL is http://esj.com/home.aspx.

BITEMPORAL DATA: PRELIMINARIES

All things change.
Heraclitus.

Objects show up, change in various ways, and eventually go away. Sometimes the same object shows up again. *Events* happen and then they're over. An event shows up only once.

Objects come into and go out of existence. While they exist, some change frenetically, some change at a leisurely pace, and some change hardly at all.

Between these changes are the *states* of those objects. Objects are in different states at different times. The transition between two successive states of an object occurs during an event in which that object takes part.

Events happen either at moments in time, or within an *interval* of time. But either way, events don't change. Once they happen, they're over, and they fall immediately into the past.

The connection is this: objects change because they are affected by other objects, and events are the occasions on which objects affect and are affected by other objects. So there is only one way that events are, but there are many ways that objects are, those ways being the states of those objects.

The succession of states that an object moves through over time constitutes the *life history* of that object. The one state of an event is all there is to its life history.

The data we keep in our databases is in general data about contingent matters of fact. It's data about the things that are of interest to us, and the interesting things that happen to them. This data is the *inscription* of information about those things.

Transactions are what take place during events.[1] If we are interested in those events, we keep a record of those transactions in a transaction table, and we keep that transaction table available for querying. From this event-centric point of view, objects are temporally enduring threads that run through a succession of events. For example, a bank account is a temporally enduring thread that runs through a succession of deposit and withdrawal events. By starting with the creation event for any object, and then tracking that object through the succession of events in which it was/is/will be involved, we can recreate any state of that object, as of any point in time.

---

[1]There are two senses of the term "transaction". Here, it means what takes place during an event. For example, making a bank deposit is a transaction. The other sense of the term "transaction" is its technical sense, in which it refers to inserts, updates and deletes to data in databases. The connection is that transactions in this second sense modify a database in order to record transactions in the first sense.

That's one way to keep track of how objects change over time. Another way is to move events to the background, and track objects directly, state by state, from their initial states to their current and/or terminal states, and sometimes on to their anticipated future states as well. From this object-centric point of view, events are the occasions on which objects change state or cause other objects to change state. If we are interested in what happened to any object in any event in which it took part, that is simply the delta between its pre-event state and its post-event state, or else the continuance of its pre-event state through the event and out the other side.

But most of our tables about objects do not track multiple states of those objects. In these *object tables*, each object is represented by only one row, and that one row tells us, at all times, about the current state of that object. With every update, that data is overwritten; with every deletion, that data is removed. Nor do object tables tell us anything about future states.

Object tables tell us about objects, specifically about their current states. *State-time tables* tell us about states of objects, past, present and/or future. So in an object table, there is only one row for each object because only one state of each object is being kept track of. In a state-time table, many states of the same object may be kept track of, so there may be many rows for the same object, one for each state.

Also — and this limitation applies to *event tables* as well as to object tables — these tables only show us what we currently believe to be true. Over time, as we learn more about the states of objects or about the events they take part in, we may be able to fill in missing information about those states or about those events, or correct data that we later discover to be in error.

A series of such additions to information about a given state of an object, or to information about an event, may be worth keeping track of, and making available for querying. So too for a series of corrections. But we cannot keep either kind of series in object tables or in event tables.

State-time tables are the first step in removing these limitations. With state-time tables, we need not be limited to information about only the current states of objects. We can keep data about past states as well. This data will not be locked up in a difficult-to-access logfile, or segregated from current data in an historical data warehouse. With state-time tables, we can also keep a record of anticipated future states. In both cases, that data can be just as readily available and just as easily retrievable as current state data is.

Also, as we extend the concept of a state-time table, we will not be limited to the data about the current states of objects and events that we currently believe is correct. We will be able to keep track of a history of supplements and/or corrections to data we already have about the past, present or future states of objects, or about events.

I will need a term that covers both objects and events. I will use the term *referent* for this purpose, indicating something that can be referred to. It will also be convenient to have a more colloquial term to rely on and, for that purpose, I will occasionally use the term *thing*.

In ordinary language, the term "thing" usually designates some object that is being referred to, but it can be used in a more general sense as well. For example, in "That thing over there can be used as a hammer", "thing" refers to an object. But in "When the new immigration law is passed, three things will happen right away", "thing" refers to three events. So "thing" is indeed an adequate colloquialism for "referent", since it can be used to refer to either objects or events.

In summary: every object is a referent, and so is every event. Every referent is either an object or an event, and no referent is both. This important set of concepts will be developed more fully in later chapters, especially in Chapter 5.

NONTEMPORAL, UNITEMPORAL AND BITEMPORAL DATA

Bitemporal data is a special kind of temporal data, one in which there are two *time periods* which are part of the primary key of a table. The *version tables* most of us have worked with at one time or another are *unitemporal tables*. They are tables in which there is only one time period which is part of the primary key. And just as unitemporal tables are *nontemporal tables* whose primary keys have been supplemented with one time period, bitemporal tables are unitemporal tables whose primary keys have been supplemented with a second time period.

Figure 1.1 shows these three kinds of tables.

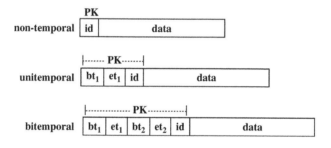

FIGURE 1.1

Nontemporal, Unitemporal and Bitemporal Tables.

In this Figure, "bt" stands for *begin time* and "et" stands for *end time*. "id" stands for the component of a primary key which identifies the referent that the row of data refers to and describes. I will hereafter refer to it as the *referent identifier*, or *RefId*.[2]

In a nontemporal table, no two rows have the same RefId, since a RefId, by itself, is a unique identifier of a row in the table. This is what we want, of course, because in a nontemporal table, if two rows could designate the same referent, then since both would be about the current state of that referent, they could say contradictory things. For example, in a Customer table, one row could say that a customer's current name is "Smith", and another row designating that same customer could say that her current name is "Jones".

In a unitemporal or a bitemporal table, however, several rows may have the same RefId without conflicting with one another, as long as each row is about a different state of that referent, or (in the case of a bitemporal table) a different description of a state. How this works is what temporal and bitemporal data is all about.

---

[2]Of course, there are many other ways of making temporal tables out of nontemporal ones, for example by adding only a begin time or an end time to a table's primary key, instead of adding both. These variations are categorized and analyzed in Chapter 4 of *MTRD*.

NONTEMPORAL TABLES

Unless otherwise noted, all tables used for examples in this book — temporal tables and nontemporal tables — are relational tables.[3] As relational tables, they are relations. As relations, they are sets. Their columns are sets. The set members of those tables are the rows they contain. Since the members of a set must be distinct from one another, nontemporal relational tables must satisfy the entity integrity constraint. The DBMS enforces this constraint by requiring that every primary key value be unique within its table.

To illustrate some notational conventions, four conventional tables are shown in Figure 1.2.

```
S-Cat
sc-id  sc-abbr  sc-desc
SC1    SCA      tier 1
SC2    SCB      tier 2
SC3    SCC      off contract


Supplier
s-id  s-nm      s-scfk  s-type
S1    Acme      SC1     T4
S2    Superior  SC3     T22


Part
p-id  p-nbr  p-nm     p-upr
P1    W45    wheel    $3.25
P2    A02    axle     $5.50
P3    C01    chassis  $13.25


Supplier-Part
sp-id  sp-sfk  sp-pfk
SP1    S1      P3
SP2    S2      P1
SP3    S1      P2
```

FIGURE 1.2

Four Conventional Tables.

Table Names

The name of each table is shown above the table. Here, there are four tables, whose names are S-Cat, Supplier, Part, and Supplier-Part. S-Cat is a table of supplier categories. Supplier-Part is an associative table which shows, for each supplier, the parts he is eligible to supply, and for each part, the suppliers who are eligible to supply it.

---

[3] I will also frequently refer to nontemporal tables as *conventional tables*.

Schema Rows

Next comes the schema row for the table. A *schema row* is a list of all the columns in the table. It is sometimes called the "header" of the table. Note that it is an abstraction from the table's full definition in the catalog of the database that contains it, or in the physical data model from which that catalog entry is generated. It is an abstraction because it doesn't contain all the information in the table's definition. For example, the schema row doesn't show the datatype of each column.

In the schema row, primary key columns are listed left-most, and their column headings are underlined. Foreign key column headings are italicized.

Foreign Keys and Primary Keys

Foreign keys may appear anywhere in a schema row. The Supplier table contains the foreign key *s-scfk* to the S-Cat table. The Supplier-Part table contains two foreign keys, *sp-sfk* and *sp-pfk* to, respectively, the Supplier and Part tables.[4]

In many databases, there are tables which include one or more foreign keys in their primary keys. But most of the nontemporal tables in this book use a single surrogate-valued column as the primary key, and so do not have foreign keys as part of their primary keys. For example, neither foreign key in the Supplier-Part table is part of the primary key of that table. Nor do the temporal tables in this book, in general, contain foreign keys as part of their primary keys.

Nothing in this book depends on this convention, however. Temporal tables, including bitemporal tables, may have foreign keys as part of their primary keys. Temporal tables, including bitemporal tables, may use multiple columns of business data instead of single surrogate-valued columns in their primary keys.

Data Model Diagrams

I don't show a data model diagram for any of the tables used as examples in this book. Instead, I use sample data tables. My examples require only a small number of tables in each case, and so the inter-table relationships should be easy to see. For example, there is a parent-child relationship from S-Cat to Supplier, and the Supplier-Part table is an associative table between the Supplier and Part tables.

Another reason for not using data model diagrams is that relationship lines drawn in data model diagrams always represent a relationship in which a row containing a foreign key – the child row – is related to exactly one other row – the parent row. But this is not necessarily the case with the temporal form of the relationship, in which a child row is more commonly related to several parent rows.

Stand-Alone Representation of Rows

Rows of tables are always shown in a non-proportionally-spaced font so that, when several of them are shown together, the columns of each row line up one under the other. Also, rows of tables are sometimes shown on their own, rather than as rows underneath a table name and a schema row.

---

[4]My foreign key naming convention is to indicate the related tables with a short abbreviation, separate the abbreviations with a dash, and append "fk" to the name. Thus, for example, in the foreign key name "sp-sfk", "sp" stands for "Supplier-Part", the "s" following the dash stands for "Supplier", and the suffix "fk" stands for "foreign key. I also italicize these foreign key names as they appear in the text, or else replace then with their expanded form.

In these cases, each row will be enclosed in braces, and its columns will be separated by a vertical bar. For example, the second row in the Part table in Figure 1.2 is:

[P2|A02|axle|$5.50]

and the third row in the Supplier-Part table is [SP3|S1|P2]. Note that these stand-alone rows may be either set apart on their own line of text, or included in-line as part of the narrative. Note also that the underlining and italicizing conventions used for schema rows are carried over to the data rows themselves when those data rows are shown in stand-alone mode or in-line with the text.

UNITEMPORAL TABLES

As well as conventional tables, there are also temporal tables. They are either unitemporal or bitemporal, containing either a single time period in their primary keys or containing two time periods in their primary keys.

One of the two temporal dimensions of bitemporal data is called *valid time* in the computer science literature. I used the term "effective time" for this temporal dimension in my first book, *MTRD*. In this book, I will use the term "state time" because it seems to me to be the least misleading term to apply to this concept. And this leads to my choice of the column headings *sbeg* and *send* to stand for, respectively, *state begin time* and *state end time*.[5,6]

All time periods used in the examples in this book are shown as a begin month and an end month. Each date is shown as a three-character month abbreviation together with two numerals representing a year. For example, "Nov15" represents the month of November 2015.

Figure 1.3 illustrates how time periods are shown in these tables. The state-time periods of these tables are shown as a begin time and an end time. So the time period for the second row in the Supplier-Part-S table, for example, extends from October 2014 up to January 2015. I use a "from" and "up to" terminology to emphasize that October 2014 is part of that time period, but that January 2015 is not, and is, rather, the first month after the last month of that time period. This way of representing time periods by means of a begin time and end time, in which the begin time is part of the time period but the end time is the next *clock tick* after the end of the time period, is called the *closed/open* convention for representing time periods by saying when they begin and when they end.[7]

---

[5]All column names (not just foreign key names) are represented in a proportional font in the text, or else replaced with the expanded version of those names. Thus "sbeg" and "state begin time" are equivalent expressions.

[6]I regret contributing to the profusion of terminology surrounding bitemporal data, a profusion, however, to which the computer science community, DBMS vendors, and standards committees have also contributed. I use a terminology of my own choosing because I think that terminology is important, that inappropriate terminology can persistently mislead those who use it, and that appropriate terminology can greatly enhance the clarity of an explanation. In fact, I originally wrote most of this book using the terminology standardized in the ISO 9075:2011 SQL standard, and only late in the project went back and substituted my own terms. The fact that there is now a de jure standard terminology, and that I have decided not to use it, indicates the importance I attach to terminology. I will, of course, describe a mapping among the different terminologies, which include the standard computer science terminology, DBMS vendor terminology, and the terminology used in the temporal SQL standards. For a summary of those mappings, see the end of this chapter. For details, see Chapter 2.

[7]Another way of representing time periods, for example, would be to say when they begin, and how long they last.

```
S-Cat-S
sbeg  send   sc-id sc-abbr sc-desc
Jan14 9999  SC1   SCA     tier 1
Jun14 9999  SC2   SCB     tier 2
May14 Jun15 SC3   NUC     off contract


Supplier-S
sbeg  send   s-id s-nm     s-scfk s-type
Feb14 9999  S1   Acme     SC1    T4
Aug14 Mar15 S2   Superior SC3    T22
Mar15 Nov15 S2   Superior SC3    T15


Part-S
sbeg  send   p-id p-nbr p-nm    p-upr
May14 9999  P1   W45   wheel   $3.25
Jul14 Mar16 P2   A02   axle    $5.50
Mar16 9999  P2   A02   axle    $6.25
Jun15 9999  P3   C01   chassis $13.25


Supplier-Part-S
sbeg  send   sp-id sp-sfk sp-pfk
Sep15 9999  SP1   S1     P3
Oct14 Jan15 SP2   S2     P1
Jan15 9999  SP3   S1     P2
```

FIGURE 1.3

Four State-Time Tables.

In reality, most time periods for real data will be specified at the level of dates or timestamps. The level at which time periods are specified is called the *granularity* of those time periods. I have chosen a granularity of months simply because it takes fewer characters to represent time periods this way, and this makes it easier to show each row of a table on one line across a page.

I use the special string *9999* to represent the latest point in time, at the chosen level of granularity, that a specific DBMS can represent. For example, in SQL Server, and for our level of granularity, that is December of the year 9999. For a date datatype, it is 12/31/9999. Time periods that end on the latest representable point in time are said to be *open time periods*, and all others *closed time periods*.

The semantics of an open time period is that it is one whose end point is unknown.[8] This unknown end point could be represented by a null. But for reasons that I will present later, most implementations of time periods use the highest value a specific DBMS can represent, at the chosen level of granularity, for these time periods, instead of a null. As far as the DBMS is concerned, a

---

[8] An open time period could also be one whose begin point is unknown. However, it could not be one in which both begin and end points are unknown.

time period ending on December 9999 is a time period that ends just under eight-thousand years from now. But as far as users of a database are concerned, it is a time period which does not yet have a determinate end point in time.

In Figure 1.3, begin and end times are underlined to show that they are part of the primary keys of their tables. Temporal columns which are not primary key or candidate key columns, as far as this book is concerned, are just like any other non-key columns. All non-key temporal columns describe something about whatever it is that each row represents. But primary and candidate key temporal columns do something quite different. They *change* what it is that each row represents.

For example, each row in the Supplier table of Figure 1.2 refers to a supplier. No two rows in that table refer to the same supplier. But in the Supplier-S table of Figure 1.3, two rows both refer to supplier S2. What distinguishes those two rows is their non-overlapping *state-time periods*. Each row refers to a different *state* of S2. In state-time tables, it is not referents that each row refers to. It is *states* of those referents. I shall also say that each row represents a *timeslice* from an *episode* in the life history of a referent.

Table Names

In Figure 1.3, there are four tables, whose names are S-Cat-S, Supplier-S, Part-S and Supplier-Part-S. "S" is a suffix standing for "state time".

These state-time tables are all unitemporal tables, utilizing only one of the two kinds of bitemporal time in their primary keys. For now, we can think of a unitemporal table as one that is created from a nontemporal table by adding one of the two temporal dimension time periods to the primary key of the nontemporal table.

Schema Rows

As shown in Figure 1.3, a unitemporal table contains both the begin time and end time of a time period as part of its primary key. But as I said before, that isn't necessary. A table is a state-time table if its rows represent state-time intervals in the life history of something that can exist over time, and can change while remaining that same thing — something such as a supplier, a supplier category, a part, or a relationship between a supplier and a part. Whatever column or columns function, in a state-time or bitemporal table, as a unique identifier of a state-time segment in an episode in the life history of a referent, I will call the *state identifier (StId)* of that table.

Temporal Foreign Keys and Temporal Primary Keys

A *temporal primary key* is a primary key of a temporal table in which the one or two time periods associated with the table are included in the primary key.[9] A *temporal foreign key* is a foreign key which points to a parent row (or rows!) that exists in a temporal table. For example, the `s-scfk` column of Supplier-S, and the `sp-sfk` and `sp-pfk` columns of Supplier-Part-S are not conventional foreign keys; they are temporal foreign keys. They are temporal foreign keys because the tables they reference — S-Cat-S for `s-scfk`, and Supplier-S and Part-S, respectively, for `sp-sfk` and `sp-pfk` — are temporal tables.

---

[9]For the most part, I will use temporal primary keys in my sample tables, because this emphasizes the point that they are the unique identifiers of those tables, and also because this helps to fit one row of data on one printed line. However, my preferred implementation would be to use a single surrogate-valued primary key, and change temporal primary keys into non-primary-key *temporal unique identifiers*.

Notice that *s-scfk* points to the RefId of the S-Cat-S table, and not to the full primary key of that table. Similarly, *sp-sfk* points to the RefId of the Supplier-S table, and *sp-pfk* points to the RefId of the Part-S table. Since there are two rows for the Superior company in the Supplier-S table, the *sp-sfk* temporal foreign key value of "S2" does not uniquely identify one parent row. By the same token, the *sp-pfk* temporal foreign key value of "P2" does not uniquely identify one parent row. It is only because RefIds are the sole components of the primary keys of nontemporal tables that nontemporal foreign keys uniquely identify single parent rows. Temporal and nontemporal foreign keys are both RefId pointers.

The temporally-extended constraints of entity integrity and referential integrity — which I call, respectively, *temporal entity integrity* and *temporal referential integrity*, apply to these temporal tables. If they did not, then temporal tables would not be relational tables, as I have said they are. As we will see later on, it is the temporal form of these constraints, not the conventional form, which is basic. Conventional entity integrity and conventional referential integrity are merely special cases of temporal entity integrity and temporal referential integrity.

Stand-Alone Representation of Temporal Rows

Sometimes rows of temporal tables are shown on their own rather than as rows underneath a table name and a schema row. In these cases, as with rows of nontemporal tables, each row is enclosed in braces. For example, the second row in the Part-S table in Figure 1.3 is:

$$[\text{Jul14} | \text{Mar16} | \text{P2} | \text{A02} | \text{axle} | \$5.50]$$

and the third row in the Supplier-Part-S table is [Jan15 | 9999 | SP3 | *S1* | *P2*] .

Note that these stand-alone rows may be either set apart on their own line of text, or included in-line as part of the narrative.

A Note on Assertion-Time Tables

State-time tables are one kind of unitemporal table. In the computer science literature, the term "transaction-time table" designates another kind of unitemporal table. But the term "transaction time", I believe, has and continues to be misleading. As I will explain later, that term is a *homonym*. As designating a physical feature of data, it means one thing. As designating the semantics supported by that physical feature, it means something different.

The best term for the semantics which this kind of time expresses is *assertion*, because these semantics are that these time periods mark the time during which a row of data is asserted to make a true statement. And so I will use the terms *assertion begin time* and *assertion end time* to mark the delimiters of these *assertion time periods*, and will use the abbreviations *abeg* and *aend* as the column names for these delimiters. I will also use "A" as the table-name suffix for these *assertion-time tables*. Except for those changes, these tables use the same names, the same schema row conventions, and the same conventions for stand-alone representations as do state-time tables.

A more detailed discussion of the difference between the physical and semantic senses of "transaction time" will be found in Chapter 14. The semantics of assertion time, as I will explain there, are an extension of the semantics of transaction time.[10] Assertion time is a proper superset of transaction time, both in its semantics and in its implementation. However, since those extensions will not be discussed until Chapter 14, the change in terminology, until then, is nothing more than that — a change in terminology.

One important difference between state time and (the pre-Chapter 14 concept of) assertion time is that only state time may be specified on *temporal transactions*. Furthermore, an insert, update or delete temporal transaction may specify a state-time period that ends in the past or begins in the future, and therefore is not restricted to state-time periods that include the current moment in time.

As for assertion time, all new rows added to a table by temporal transactions are assigned their assertion-time periods by the DBMS. This is the time period during which a row has the status of representing a statement which its authors assert to be true. Until Chapter 14, we will assume that this time period is identical to the time period delimited by the moment in time on which the transaction creating the row completes, to the moment in time at which another transaction (logically) deletes that row.

In Chapter 14, I will discuss how and why assertion time can be specified on temporal transactions, and how and why temporal transactions can add rows to temporal tables with a transaction-time period that begins and/or ends in the future. Clearly, if I kept the term "transaction time", the very term *future transaction time* would be an oxymoron. But a point about terminology is not an argument. For data that carries useful information, and that can be managed so as to preserve a consistent semantics, an oxymoronic label isn't an argument against it. It's an indication that the label was ill-chosen.

BITEMPORAL TABLES

Just as unitemporal tables are nontemporal tables with a time period added to their primary keys, bitemporal tables are unitemporal tables with a second time period added to their primary keys.

As indicated above, the second of the two temporal dimensions of bitemporal data is called *transaction time* in the computer science literature. I used the term *assertion time* for an extended form of this temporal dimension in *MTRD*, and will continue to use that term in this book.

Table Names

In Figure 1.4, there are four tables, whose names are S-Cat-B, Supplier-B, Part-B and Supplier-Part-B. "B" is a suffix standing for "bitemporal time".

Temporal Foreign Keys and Temporal Primary Keys

Like temporal primary keys in unitemporal tables, temporal primary keys in bitemporal tables contain a RefId. To be more precise, RefIds are components in non-surrogate candidate keys. For like any table, a temporal table may have a surrogate key as its primary key, and may indeed have a single-column surrogate key as its primary key. But for the most part, I will ignore this issue, and speak about temporal primary keys including RefIds. Most of the temporal

---

[10]I will use the term *standard theory* to refer to the theory of bitemporal data developed by computer scientists, implemented in several major DBMSs, and standardized in the ISO and TSQL2 standards. The extension to that theory, which I will describe in Chapter 14, I will refer to as the *Asserted Versioning theory* of bitemporal data. That is the theory which I originally developed with Randy Weis, the co-author of *MTRD*.

```
S-Cat-B
```

abeg	aend	sbeg	send	sc-id	sc-abbr	sc-desc
Jan14	9999	Jan14	9999	SC1	SCA	tier 1
Jun14	9999	Jun14	9999	SC2	SCB	tier 2
May14	9999	May14	Jun15	SC3	NUC	off contract

```
Supplier-B
```

abeg	aend	sbeg	send	s-id	s-nm	*s-scfk*	s-type
Feb14	9999	Feb14	9999	S1	Acme	SC1	T4
Aug14	9999	Aug14	Mar15	S2	Superior	SC3	T22
Mar15	9999	Mar15	Nov15	S2	Superior	SC3	T15

```
Part-B
```

abeg	aend	sbeg	send	p-id	p-nbr	p-nm	p-upr
May14	9999	May14	9999	P1	W45	wheel	$3.25
Mar16	9999	Jul14	Mar16	P2	A02	axle	$5.50
Mar16	9999	Mar16	9999	P2	A02	axle	$6.25
Jun15	9999	Jun15	9999	P3	C01	chassis	$13.25

```
Supplier-Part-B
```

abeg	aend	sbeg	send	sp-id	*sp-sfk*	*sp-pfk*
Sep15	9999	Sep15	9999	SP1	S1	P3
Oct14	9999	Oct14	Jan15	SP2	S2	P1
Jan15	9999	Jan15	9999	SP3	S1	P2

FIGURE 1.4

Four Bitemporal Tables.

tables used in the examples in this book will consist of a RefId plus additional columns to represent time periods.

SEMANTICS AND ITS IMPLEMENTATIONS

Data is *persisted* by means of database tables or software-specific file structures. Data is *transformed* by means of algorithms which exist as program code, macros, or scripts. Data is *moved* by means of messages, or by the physical movement of persisted copies of that data. Data is *presented* by means of screen displays, reports, and query result sets, or in various non-character-based forms such as graphs, charts and icons.

Throughout all these activities, the data itself is something physical. And yet these physical things carry information, and these physical activities preserve that information. In creating data, we encode information in a physical form. In updating data, we preserve that information.

In consuming data, we decode it. That is, we understand it, and in understanding it, we recover the information it contains.

All these things we do to and with data — creating it, persisting it, transforming it, presenting it, moving it, archiving it, and so on — are rule-governed. The rules align the data with what the data is about. The person creating the data follows those rules, and the person consuming that data understands those rules, and operates on the assumption that the person creating the data also understands those rules, and has followed those rules in creating that data. This is how data has meaning, how it is something more than vibrations in the air, marks on a page, or strings of zeroes and ones in a computer's storage.

The physical structures and instances that we manage, and the transformations we apply to those instances, constitute the *syntax* of data management. The rules by virtue of which data conveys information constitute the *semantics* of that data. Most books on information management focus on data, on algorithms, and on the technology by which data is created, persisted, transformed, presented, moved, and archived. That technology is the infrastructure; that data and those algorithms are the syntax. Semantics exists in the background, and little is said about it. Perhaps this is because the semantics of data seem so obvious.

A very simple set of transformations, for example, is this:

- At some point in time, a row is inserted into a database table.
- At various later points in time, one or more columns of that row are updated.
- At a yet later point in time, that row may be deleted from that database table.

The semantics implemented by these transformations is the semantics of keeping track of what happens to things. For example, one of the objects any company wants to keep track of is its employees. At some point in time, someone is hired as an employee. At later points in time, important things about that employee may change, such as the department she works in. And at a yet later point in time, that person may leave the company and cease being an employee.

Semantics are the rules for managing data so that the data provides us with information. In this example, one rule is that when a person is hired as an employee, a row is added to an Employee table. Another rule is that when something important about the employee changes, the row is updated to reflect that change. A third rule is that when the employee leaves the company, that row is deleted from the Employee table.

The real semantics of real data will be more detailed than these very basic correlations, of course. For example, there will be rules which associate each column of the Employee table with a property of an employee, or with a relationship an employee has with someone or something else.

I introduced the distinction between semantics and syntax in *MTRD*, and used it to structure the extensive Glossary in that book. Because data is the means by which we store information in databases, semantics and syntax run in parallel. Syntax is about the data. Semantics is about the information it carries.

The constraints imposed on introducing data into a database, altering data in a database, or removing data from a database, exist so that those transformations will reflect what is happening to what that data is about. In doing so, the syntax of those transformations preserve the semantics of that data. The constraints which every valid database state must conform to — such as entity integrity, referential integrity, domain integrity, and application-specific business rules — exist so that the data in the database will accurately and intelligibly describe what that data is about to those who query the database.

For any physical structures or processes dealing with data in databases, it should be possible to state the semantics supported by those structures or those processes. This is because the whole reason for having those structures and processes is to persist information about the objects we are interested in, and to make that information available on demand.

Conversely, for any semantic rule, it should be possible to describe the physical structures and processes that implement that rule. For example, the rule that at no time may a database contain contradictory statements is implemented by enforcing the relational constraint of entity integrity. That is what entity integrity is — a mechanism for keeping contradictory statements out of a database by permitting only one statement at a time in the database about any object, or any state of an object, represented in that database. The absence of contradictory statements in a database is a universal semantic requirement.

ASIDE

Many readers will be familiar with the standard terminology of "transaction time" and "valid time", especially those working with the releases of DB2 or of Teradata that support bitemporal data. For them, I note that the standard term "valid time" and my term "state time" are synonymous. Throughout this book, "state time" may be read as "valid time", as much as I advise against using the latter term.

As for the standard term "transaction time", it is only in Chapter 14 and in a few places downstream from that chapter, that transaction time and assertion time differ. So except for those places, "assertion time" may be read as "transaction time", albeit with the same caveat.

For those who read my earlier book *Managing Time in Relational Databases*, or who wish to consult it as they read this book, the terminological mappings are quite simple. Assertion time in this book is assertion time in that book. State time in this book is effective time in that book. Other terminological differences are insignificant.

GLOSSARY LIST

assertion time
assertion
assertion-time period
assertion-time table
bitemporal table
clock tick
closed time period
closed/open
conventional table
episode
event table
event
future transaction time
granularity
information
inscription

interval
life history
object table
object
open time period
referent identifier
referent
schema row
standard theory
state identifier
state time
state
state-time period
state-time table
temporal entity
  integrity

temporal foreign key
temporal primary key
temporal referential
  integrity
temporal transaction
temporal unique
  identifier
thing
time period
timeslice
transaction table
transaction time
transaction
unitemporal table
valid time

THEORY

1

Time is the heart of the matter. Chapter 2 discusses two interpretations of points in time, one treating them as *instants* that have no temporal extent, and the other treating them as *moments* that do have a temporal extent. It introduces the concepts of both physical and logical *clock ticks*, and explains the connection between them. It explains why the distinction between moments and instants is moot as far as the representation of time in databases is concerned. It introduces the four conventions for representing time periods by means of their start and end times. This chapter also discusses the various terminologies used to talk about bitemporal time, in particular the terminology used by the computer science community, the terminology used in the ISO and TSQL2 standards documents, and the terminology I introduced in 2010 and have adapted for this book.

The Relational Paradigm is in the process of being extended to manage temporal data and, in particular, bitemporal data. I think that if we develop a multi-perspectival view of time and its incorporation into relational theory and technology, one which goes beyond the well-known mathematics and logic of that theory to include its ontology and semantics as well, we will discover several mistakes and/or shortcomings in those extensions. We will also know what to do to correct those mistakes and to extend theory and implementation into hitherto unexplored temporal space.

By the "Relational Paradigm", I mean the relational theory of data originally developed by Dr. Edgar Codd, and its implementation in today's relational databases. The Relational Paradigm is implemented in the visible structures that are common to all relational databases, the integrity constraints that govern the processes that populate those structures, and the operations that are combined in queries to retrieve data from those structures. Those structures are tables, rows, columns, domains, primary keys, foreign keys and non-keys. Those constraints are entity integrity, referential integrity and domain integrity. Further constraints are usually called "business rules", and are application-specific and thus not part of the Relational Paradigm. Those operations are select, project, join, various logical operations such as conjunction and negation, and various set-theoretic operations such as union and intersection. How these operations are combined in specific queries is also application-specific and thus is also not part of the Relational Paradigm.

There are four perspectives on the Relational Paradigm which we need to integrate in order to more deeply understand how that paradigm manages databases that store, and that provide on demand, the information that we think is worth the cost of managing. Those perspectives are:

- The *mathematics* of sets, Cartesian Products, relations and functions.
- Formal *logic*, both propositional logic and typed predicate logic.
- An *ontology* of types, things, objects, events, attributes, properties, relationships and states.
- The *semantics* of inscriptions, statements and assertions.

In Chapter 3, I review the mathematical foundations of relational theory. The mathematics consists of sets, Cartesian Products, relations, tuples and functions. Their implementation in a relational database consists of tables, columns and a time-varying set of rows. This is something that C. J. Date has already explained very well. But I think that another attempt, on the part of someone who has spent his entire career doing hands-on work in end-user IT organizations, may still be worthwhile.

In Chapter 4, I review the logical foundations of relational theory. The logic consists of a subset of propositional logic, and a subset of typed predicate logic. It shows that table definitions in database catalogs are *statement schemas*, and that the rows of those tables are ordered sets of values which instantiate those schemas. Understood from this logical point of view, relational databases are mechanisms which manage sets of values which, when assigned to the variables in typed existentially-quantified statement schemas, result in true statements that provide information to the users of those databases.

In Chapter 5, I construct a high-level formal ontology which underlies the Relational Paradigm, and which also underlies much of our common-sense view of the world as well. This ontology consists of *types* and *instances* of objects and events, of states of objects and events, and of types and instances of the properties of these things and the relationships among them. These types and instances are the upper levels of an ontology which is applicable across all relational databases, each of whose more specific ontological categories are the types defined as tables and columns in those databases' catalogs.

Formal ontologies are beginning to move out of academia and into IT organizations. The tools available to the IT professional to manage formal ontologies are still pretty basic, but what ontology can do for data management is extremely important, and I consider it a given that it will become a permanent part of the IT landscape. If I'm right, then data architects, data modelers, and others with responsibility for an enterprise's data, will have to become conversant with this new perspective on the data they manage.

In Chapter 6, I discuss the semantics of the Relational Paradigm. To understand the semantics of how data in databases is used to make meaningful statements, we need to distinguish rows of relational tables as physical objects, those rows as instantiated statements, and the temporally-delimited acts of asserting that those statements are true and of withdrawing assertions that those statements are true. We need to understand:

- the distinctions among inscriptions, sentences, statements, and propositions;
- the speech acts of asserting a statement and withdrawing that assertion; and
- semantic anomalies including synonymy, homonymy, and ambiguity.

In Chapter 7, I describe the *Allen relationships*, which are a list of all possible positional relationships between two time periods located on a common timeline. I group the Allen relationships under the nodes of a six-level binary taxonomy, thereby demonstrating that the Allen relationships are a partitioning of those positional relationships.

In Chapter 8, I develop the concepts and notation required to discuss temporal entity integrity and temporal referential integrity, and I also introduce a graphic notation for representing temporal integrity constraints. One of the key concepts is that of a *bitemporal cell*, which is a pair of *clock ticks*, one from one temporal dimension and one from a second temporal dimension. The bitemporal cell is the most basic temporal extent within which entity and referential integrity are applicable.

Another key concept is the distinction between these two integrity constraints as applicable to physical rows of data, and as applicable to the objects and events which those rows represent.

A third important concept is the thesis that all data is bitemporal, and that the distinction between non-temporal, unitemporal and bitemporal data is a distinction based on whether or not transaction time and/or valid time — as these two temporal dimensions are usually called — are expressed implicitly or explicitly.[1]

In Chapter 9, I describe entity integrity as it applies to bitemporal tables and to valid-time tables, as well as to conventional tables. I describe *bitemporal entity integrity* as the constraint that no two rows in a bitemporal table that represent the same thing can include the same bitemporal cell in the bitemporal areas circumscribed by their transaction-time and valid-time periods, and I explain the semantics which are supported by this constraint. I provide similar explanations of valid-time and of conventional entity integrity, and of the semantics they support.

In Chapter 10, I describe referential integrity as it applies to bitemporal tables and valid-time tables, as well as to conventional tables. I describe *bitemporal referential integrity* as the constraint that the bitemporal area of any child row in a bitemporal referential integrity relationship must be fully contained within the bitemporal area of a set of parent rows, and explain the semantics which are supported by this constraint. I provide similar explanations of valid-time and of conventional referential integrity, and of the semantics they support.

At this point, our conceptual tool chest will be complete. Turning to the practice of managing temporal data, in Part 2, I will use the inter-related points of view of mathematics, logic, ontology and semantics to analyze issues arising in that practice. As for mistakes and/or shortcomings, this multi-perspective approach will lead us towards an analysis of root causes, and away from the impulse to fix things by applying patches. We will fix the problems we come across, to use an analogy, as automotive engineers of our trade rather than as neighborhood mechanics.

---

[1]In this introduction to Part 1, I use the well-known computer science terminology of "valid time" and "transaction time" for the two temporal dimensions of bitemporal data. In Chapter 2, I will discuss the different terminologies used to talk about bitemporal data, and introduce my own terminology, that of "state time" and "assertion time".

TIME AND TEMPORAL TERMINOLOGY

2

The management of time in databases is a challenging topic for several reasons. One is that the concepts involved, especially the concept of two temporal dimensions, are somewhat difficult. Those concepts are examined in the first section of this chapter. Another reason is that the structures and transformations that are integral to the management of bitemporal data do not fit smoothly with the structures and transformations that are integral to the management of conventional data by means of relational databases.

Each of the two standards documents define their own terminology for talking about time and, in particular, bitemporal time. The ISO 9075:2011 standard defines a set of terms which have been adopted, for the most part, by IBM. The TSQL2 standard terminology was defined in a computer science glossary (Jensen, Clifford et al., 1992), and again in a "consensus glossary" (Jensen and Dyreson, 1998), and this terminology has been adopted, for the most part, by Teradata. These terminologies overlap to some degree, but not completely.

Into this terminological mix, I introduce a third set of terms, ones that I will use throughout this book. It is adapted from terminology I developed, with my co-author Randy Weis, in *MTRD*. I would have preferred, of course, to use one of the two standard terminologies. I mentioned my reasons for not doing so in the Preface and in the previous chapter, and I will have more to say about these terminology issues later in this chapter.

TIME

With our commonsense notion of time, we think that, at least for some events, when they happen, they happen at a point in time. A decay event in an atomic nucleus, for example, might be such an event. Perhaps when a deposit hits a checking account, that happens at a point in time. Of course, that point in time exists within a nested set of intervals of time. For example, that deposit hit that account on some specific second, located within a specific minute of a specific day of a specific year.

But what is a point in time?

INSTANTS AND MOMENTS

One view is that a point in time is an extensionless location on a continuous timeline, one which takes up no time at all. Let's call this the *instant* interpretation of a point in time. This interpretation seems plausible when we consider that if a point in time took up some extent of time then there would be a first point in time within that point in time, a last point in time within that point in time, and possibly a succession of additional points in time between them. But if that were the case, then the point in time wouldn't be a point in time at all, because a point in time, like a point in space, is indivisible.

Neither will a series of successive instants, no matter how many instants there are in the series, serve as the time when something happened. For no matter how many successive instants we add together, they won't add up to any extent of time, no matter how small. Zero plus zero plus zero ....., no matter how many zeroes there are, always add up to zero.

A different view is that a point in time is some very short extent of time. Let's call this the *moment* interpretation of a point in time. This interpretation seems plausible when we consider that when anything happens, it takes up some amount of time, however brief that may be. Also, when anything happens, it begins and it ends, and it begins before it ends. And, however brief it may be, it takes time to complete. So when anything happens, it doesn't happen at an extensionless point in time. It doesn't happen in an instant.

But what separates one moment from the next? If nothing separates them, then we don't have distinct moments. Extensionless instants can't separate them because, on the moment interpretation, there are no instants. If it is very small moments that separate them, then what separates those very small moments from the moments on either side of them whose job it is for them to separate?

So our commonsense intuitions about time support both the instant and the moment interpretations, and are also somewhat uncomfortable with both interpretations. However, both interpretations can be formalized in axiomatic systems which are consistent and complete.

CLOCK TICKS

However, when it comes to recording points in time in a database, the distinction between the instant and the moment interpretations becomes unimportant, a distinction without a difference.

For example, it might seem that a table which contains a single timestamp in its primary key is a table that records instantaneous events. In a table of trading transactions on the stock market, timestamps must be extremely precise because no matter how close together in time two trades are, it is often important to know which one happened first. But if that timestamp marks a moment in time and not a point in time, and two trades happen on that same timestamp, then although one trade occurred earlier than the other, we are unable to tell which it was that happened first. So it would seem that the instant interpretation is required in order to guarantee that we can always sequence events that happen one before the other, no matter how close together in time they occur.

However, a timestamp, no matter what its level of precision, cannot represent an instant. It can only represent a moment, an extent of time having a duration. The reason is that timestamps are based on the computer's internal clock. That clock marks off time, as all clocks do, with clock ticks. A timestamp with maximum precision is either equivalent to a single physical clock tick, or is as close to it as the software which uses those timestamps can manage.

Consider two successive maximally precise timestamps. Whatever that level of precision is — say (as it eventually may be) that it's a nanosecond — it still represents an extent of time. So suppose that one nanosecond does elapse between every pair of successive clock ticks.

In that case, how long is each clock tick itself? Perhaps, the above arguments to the contrary, each clock tick is an instant, and moments — ones lasting a nanosecond in this case — are the elapsed times between instants. This would preserve the notion that there are instants in time, and that they take up no time at all.

But as far as databases and timestamps are concerned, it doesn't make anything any more precise than the moment interpretation of a point in time. Here's why.

Suppose we do interpret points in time as instants, and say that clock ticks mark off instants. And suppose we have a table of financial transactions, each one using a timestamp in its primary key. In that case, each transaction occurs at some instant, that instant being either the one that separates its timestamp from the previous timestamp, or the one that separates its timestamp from the next timestamp — one or the other, it doesn't matter which. It follows that if two transactions are given the same timestamp, we must say that they happen at the same time.

But if points in time are the instants between extents of time, then it shouldn't matter how long those extents are. So let's say that we use a timestamp whose precision is one second. Clearly, several financial transactions could take place in one second, on one machine, and so they would all be given the same timestamp. But on this interpretation, they would all occur at the same time because they all occur at the same moment. Yet, as taking place on the same machine, they clearly occur in some sequence. They clearly do not all occur at the same point in time. So preserving the instant interpretation of points in time by locating those dimension-less points *between* extents of time, however small, does not add any precision to our databases. On whichever interpretation of a point in time we use, if multiple events are tagged with the same timestamp, even events which we know must have occurred in a serial order, we can't tell in what sequence they occurred.

So database time is based on clocks which measure time as a sequence of physical clock ticks. And it doesn't matter whether we think of those clock ticks as the instants between the extents of time that elapse between them, or as those extents themselves. I choose the latter interpretation, and so will call a single clock tick a moment in time, not an instant in time.

Hardware Clock Ticks and DBMS Clock Ticks

A single hardware clock tick lasts as long as it takes until the next clock tick. The context in which we care about clock ticks, however, is a context provided by the software which mediates our readings of the computer's clock. And the software we are most concerned with is a DBMS. Let's call the most precise timestamp that a DBMS can represent an *atomic DBMS clock tick* or, for short, an *atomic clock tick*. So an atomic clock tick is not a physical clock tick; it is a maximally precise timestamp relative to some DBMS.

The clock that ticks off atomic clock ticks is not the computer's physical clock since atomic clock ticks are not physical clock ticks. It is a *logical clock*, ones whose ticks are the logical ticks I am calling atomic clock ticks. But a DBMS can recognize many different temporal extents, and may use any of those extents as the lowest level of granularity at which it will record time, for any given requirement. So there is a logical clock corresponding to each level of granularity used to mark off time relative to a given requirement, and each tick of that logical clock is one moment of time, at that level of granularity.

So at one extreme, we might want a clock that ticks once a decade or once a century (for historians) or even once every million years (for geologists). For some business purposes, we might want a clock which ticks once a month. For other business purposes, we might want a timestamp with microsecond precision. For transactional data, we will usually want an atomic clock tick.

DBMS Clock Ticks and Chronons

Not surprisingly, clock ticks are an important concept in the computer science literature as well, where the term for them is *chronon*.

Jensen and Clifford say "A *chronon* is the shortest duration of time supported by a temporal DBMS − it is a nondecomposable unit of time. A particular chronon is a subinterval of fixed duration on (sic) time-line." (Jensen, Clifford, Gadia, Segev, Snodgrass, 1992, p.41.)[2]

This is the same concept as my concept of an atomic clock tick. The first sentence of Jensen and Clifford's definition tells us how the concept is implemented. The second sentence tells us the semantics of the concept − what it means. So "atomic clock tick" and "chronon" are synonymous terms.

However, there is another important nondecomposable unit of time, one that is relative to a specific business requirement. For example, throughout this book, I use nondecomposable calendar months to represent the begin and end points of intervals of state time and intervals of assertion time. These intervals of time are nondecomposable in the sense that software, either within a DBMS or external to it, will not permit operations on them which distinguish smaller intervals of time within them. These intervals are nondecomposable relative to a defined *granularity* of time.

This is an important distinction, and we will need a terminology to keep track of it. Units of time which are nondecomposable by a DBMS I call "atomic clock ticks". Those units which are nondecomposable relative to a defined granularity I will call "granular clock ticks". Granular clock ticks are the ones that are most important for managing bitemporal time, and often atomic clock ticks will be used as granular clock ticks. For the most part, I will use the term "clock tick" by itself, and will be referring to granular clock ticks, whether or not they are also atomic.

Chronons, Time Periods, and Other Dependent Concepts

Based on chronons, Jensen and Clifford go on to define events, intervals and durations.

They say that "an *event* is an isolated instant in time. An event is said to occur at time *t* if it occurs at any time during the chronon represented by *t*." (p.42.)

This is a little puzzling. If an event can occur "at any time during (a) chronon" then presumably it can occur during, for example, the second half of a chronon. But in that case, the chronon is not "a nondecomposable unit of time", because we are able to locate an "isolated instant in time" at the mid-point of the temporal extent of the chronon.

Jensen and Clifford go on to define an *interval* as "the time between two events. It may be represented by a set of contiguous chronons." (p.42.) Jensen and Clifford add that an alternative term is "time period".

They say that "a duration is an amount of time with known length, but no specific starting or ending chronons." (p.43.) So a duration lasts for one or more chronons. But it has no location along a timeline. For example, one month is a duration.

Event is another important concept in Jensen and Clifford's glossary, but they seem to have two different definitions of it. One is that an event is "an isolated instant in time". (p.42.) The other is that an event is something that "is said to occur at (a) time *t*".[3] (p.42.) I will venture to

---

[2]Subsequent references to this article, in this chapter, will use page numbers only. Subsequent reference to the authors will, for short, refer to "Jensen and Clifford".

[3]This second definition of "event", as something that occurs at a specified time, is consistent with my definition of "event". What it is that occurs during an event, on my account, is that one or more objects change state.

rephrase this second definition: an event *is* something that "occurs at (a) time *t*". Something's *being* an event doesn't depend on our *saying* that it is an event, and nothing else that Jensen and Clifford say suggests that it does. So on their first definition, an event is a specific time; and on their second definition, an event is something that happens at a specific time.

As I am about to show, pointing out this distinction is not making a mountain out of a molehill. This distinction matters to what they say.

In defining "interval", Jensen and Clifford say that an interval is "the time between two events". (p.42.) So let's analyze their concept of an interval on the assumption that it is based on their second definition of "event", the definition of an event as something that happens at some time.

What about "from when Hank Aaron swung the bat for his 755th home run, until the fan ran out onto the field as Hank rounded third base"? Does this refer to an interval of time, i.e. to "the time between two events"? Clearly, it does. The interval it refers to is an interval of known extent. We know how many clock ticks are in that interval. We also know *when* Hank swung his bat for his 755th home run, and so we know both the location and the extent of that interval of time.

What about "from when you sign the contract until revenues for the product reach one million dollars"? Two delimiting events are referred to, but until revenues reach one million dollars, the terminating event hasn't occurred, and we don't know if or when it will occur. That isn't a problem, however, if our concept of an interval covers intervals of unknown extent as well as intervals of known extent. And in fact, it does.

What about "the first six months of 2009"? The referred-to time is entirely in the past, so reference to the future isn't an issue. But where are the events? This phrase doesn't refer to anything that occurred or may occur "at (a) time *t*". So using Jensen and Clifford's second definition of "event", this phrase does not denote an interval of time.

On the other hand, "the first six months of 2009", clearly does refer to a *time period*, and Jensen and Clifford have already said that "time period" is an alternative term for "interval". So if the first six months of 2009 is to be an interval, then we must use Jensen and Clifford's first definition of "event", an event as "an isolated instant in time", rather than their second definition.

With respect to their first definition of "event", I don't know what "isolated" means. I don't know what would distinguish an isolated from a non-isolated instant in time, and what difference it would make for the concepts Jensen and Clifford are defining. So on neither definition of "event" can I make sense of what they understand an interval to be.

To clarify these issues, and to establish some terminology that will be needed in the rest of this book, let a *length of time* refer to a group of one or more contiguous clock ticks situated on a timeline. The two parameters of lengths of time are *location* and *extent*. The location of a length of time is where it is on a timeline. The extent of a length of time is the number of clock ticks it contains.

A length of time may or may not have a known location on a timeline, and may or may not have a known extent. A length of time has a known location on a timeline when at least one of its component clock ticks can be paired with a known point on that timeline. A length of time has a known extent when the number of clock ticks in the length of time is known.

A *duration*, then, is a length of time with an unknown location but a known extent. An *interval* is a length of time with a known location. A *closed interval* is a length of time with a known location and a known extent. An *open interval* is a length of time with a known location and an unknown extent.

The last kind of length of time, then, is one which has an unknown location and an unknown extent. A remark like "It was a long, drawn-out process, and it happened a long time ago" seems to refer to a length of time of unknown location and unknown duration. "I'll get to it sometime soon, but I don't know how long it will take to finish it" is another such example. However, in the rest of this book, I will not consider this fourth kind of length of time.

TIME PERIODS

So clock ticks are important. They are important because time periods are important. *Time periods* are an unbroken series of one or more clock ticks, with a known location on a timeline. Time periods are temporal intervals.

As we will see, positional relationships among time periods on a common timeline are the foundation on which we define the constraints which give temporal data its semantics. Those are the constraints of temporal entity integrity and temporal referential integrity. So it would clearly be useful if we had a list of all possible positional relationships among time periods. And we do have such a list. It is known as the *Allen relationships*, and those relationships will be examined in Chapter 7.

Another question is how to represent time periods by means of a first and a last clock tick. The basic issue is whether either or both of those clock ticks are to be understood as included within the time period they delimit, or as lying "outside and next to" that time period. This gives us four possibilities. With "closed" and "open" designating, respectively, the inclusion of the clock tick in the time period, and its being outside but next to a clock tick that is within the time period, those four possibilities are these:

- closed/closed;
- closed/open;
- open/closed; and
- open/open.

Four Conventions for Time Period Representation With Delimiters

To illustrate, let's suppose that our clock ticks once a month, and consider the time period [Mar16 — Apr16]. If we are using the closed/closed convention, then this time period consists of two clock ticks. If we are using the closed/open convention, then this time period consists of the one clock tick of March 2016. If we are using the open/closed convention, then this time period consists of the one clock tick of April 2016. And if we are using the open/open convention, then this time period is empty, containing no clock ticks, since there is no month between March and April.

ASIDE

Jensen and Clifford's definitions do not allow for empty time periods, i.e. empty temporal intervals. And by "empty" here, I do not mean "nothing happening then". I mean "taking up no time at all". An empty temporal interval would be one that contains no clock ticks.

It is interesting to note that a pair of delimiter points in time can indicate an empty time period, but can do so only on the open/open convention. For example, on that convention, [Mar16-Apr16] is empty. On that convention, also,

[Mar16-Mar16] is undefined (because self-contradictory if defined). On either the open/closed or the closed/open convention, [Mar16-Apr16] is a one-month time period, and [Mar16-Mar16] is undefined. On the closed/closed convention, [Mar16-Apr16] is a two-month time period, [Mar16-Mar16] is a one-month time period, and there are no undefined time periods.

So a choice among these four conventions is not a choice among expressively equivalent conventions. It is a choice with consequences for bitemporal theory. Since the closed/open convention has been included as part of both SQL standards, and is implemented in such DBMSs as DB2 and Teradata, we are well along a path on which empty time periods cannot be represented.[4]

These conventions are equivalent in the sense that any non-empty time period can be expressed in any of them. But the closed/open and open/closed conventions have a very important advantage. With them, but not with the other two conventions, we can know when two time periods are adjacent, i.e. when they have no clock ticks between them, and we can know that without knowing the granularity of the clock ticks.

For example, using a closed/open or an open/closed convention, two time periods, t_1 and t_2, will have no clock ticks between them if and only if the clock tick marking the beginning of one of the time periods is the same as the clock tick marking the end of the other time period. A simple equality test is all that is needed to make this determination.

Let t_1 be the calendar year of 2014, and t_2 the calendar year of 2015. With the closed-open convention, t_1 is [Jan14-Jan15] and t_2 is [Jan15-Jan16]. With the open-closed convention, t_1 is [Dec13-Dec14] and t_2 is [Dec14-Dec15]. Using closed-closed, they are, respectively, [Jan14-Dec14] and [Jan15-Dec15], and using open-open, they are [Dec13-Jan15] and [Dec14-Jan16].

Notice that with either the closed-closed or open-open notations, we can't tell whether or not t_1 and t_2 have any clock ticks between them. To tell that, we must also know the granularity of the clock ticks that measure those time periods. But with the closed-open or open-closed conventions, we can immediately tell that there are no clock ticks between them, regardless of granularity, because the last clock tick of one is equal to the first clock tick of the other.

The closed/open notation, rather than the open/closed, has become a de facto standard. I suspect this is because we always begin counting a series with 1, and that is always the first element in the series – not the first element prior to the series.[5] The closed/open convention is also the de jure standard in both ISO 9075:2011 and TSQL2.

A time period is made up of one or more consecutive clock ticks of a known granularity, and I will assume in the rest of this book that either the first or the last clock tick in every time period has a known position on a timeline. If we simple knew that some amount of time was made up of, say 25 clock ticks, we would have a duration, but not a time period, i.e. not an interval. A time period is a set of consecutive clock ticks that has both a duration and a location on a timeline.

---

[4]The value of being able to designate zero-extent time periods is that they could be used to mark Dirichlet boundaries between time periods that have no clock ticks between them. This would have made it possible to represent both moments and instants. A time period whose begin and end delimiters are identical, on the open/open convention, would represent a durationless *instant* in time. All other time periods would represent contiguous series of one or more *moments* in time.

[5]Further discussion of why closed/open is, and should be, the preferred convention, can be found on pp. 56–59 of *MTRD*.

In commercial databases, we often deal with time periods whose first clock tick is known and whose extent into the future will last for an unknown amount of time. But we seldom deal with time periods whose last clock tick is known and whose extent back into the past has lasted for an unknown amount of time. For that reason, I will ignore such time periods in the rest of this book and therefore all time periods discussed in this book will begin at a known point in time.

Representing Open Time Periods

With this restriction, an open time period is a time period which starts at a specific clock tick, but whose extent (and therefore last clock tick) is unknown. Most of the time when we insert or update data, we do not know for how long that data will remain valid. When customer C123's name changed to "Smith" on March 2014, we had no idea how long that would remain her name. So we pretend that we do know these things. We pretend that they extend to the end of time, which we represent by the latest clock tick the DBMS can recognize and manage. For SQL Server, for example, that is December 9999. If our granularity were that of the Date datatype, that last representable clock tick would be 12/31/9999.

So a query asking what C123's name will be on May 2615 will return the answer "Smith". This, of course, is wrong. Well before then, there will no longer be a customer C123. At least, there will no longer be *that* customer C123.

By representing the last clock tick of an open time period with 9999, we are able to represent these open time periods with the same begin/end structure that works for other time periods. And because we implicitly understand that anything we say about the contingent future may turn out to be wrong, we are unlikely to misinterpret query results which ask about the future.

I will use the phrase *until further notice* for open time periods to suggest how we should think about them. A state-time period of [Jun11 − 9999] on a row of data for customer C123 says "This is the current state of C123, starting on June 2011, and you may assume that, as long as this row exists in the database, it will continue to describe the current state of that customer." It will be, in other words, the current state of that customer, "until further notice".

TEMPORAL TERMINOLOGY

We will need some standard terminology in order to discuss bitemporal data clearly. Unfortunately, several different sets of terms are currently in use in discussions of bitemporal data. Regrettably, I am responsible for some of this terminological proliferation.

The terminology with the longest pedigree is the terminology that is used in the computer science community, and that has been standardized in a glossary published by Jensen and Clifford (1992), and later in a consensus glossary published by Jensen and Dyreson (1998). A second set of terms are those which I introduced in the book I co-authored with Randy Weis in 2010, *Managing Time in Relational Databases*. A third set of terms are those which IBM began using at about the same time, and which are very similar to the official terminology of the ISO 9075:2011 SQL standard. As for the terminology of the TSQL2 standard, Snodgrass says, of a document presenting the proposed TSQL2 standard, that it "adheres to the terminology defined in the consensus database glossary". (Snodgrass et al., 1994, p.65.)[6]

TEMPORAL DIMENSIONS

Bitemporal data, as the adjective suggests, is data that is associated with two kinds of time. In databases, bitemporal data appears as rows of tables which include two time periods in any non-surrogate unique identifier for those tables and their rows. These two kinds of time are referred to as *temporal dimensions*. We need a standard terminology for these two temporal dimensions, and their time periods.

The TSQL2 and Computer Science Terminology

The computer science terms for the two temporal dimensions of bitemporal data are *valid time* and *transaction time*.[7]

Jensen and Clifford say that valid time of a fact is "the time when the fact is true in the modeled reality." (p.37) They define transaction time as "the time when the fact is stored in the database." (p.37)

However, in spite of the central role of the term "fact" in these definitions, Jensen and Clifford do not define that term itself. And because these two concepts are central to any discussion of bitemporal data, I think we should try to clarify them by saying something about what a fact is.

To begin with, I suggest that we think of a fact as the *state of affairs* in the world that is described by a statement − in this context, by the statement made by a row of data.

For example, the fact corresponding to the second S2 row in the Supplier table in Figure 1.2 is that there is a supplier S2, who has the name "Superior", the category SC3, and the type T22. This is what logicians call an *existentially quantified statement* in predicate logic. It says that some particular thing exists, and it attributes at least one characteristic to it, the characteristics in this case being name, category and type. These characteristics are the *predicates* of predicate logic.

The non-temporal Supplier table in Figure 1.2 does not tell us *when* there was this fact, of a supplier S2 with the indicated name, category and type. But with tables like these, tables that do not explicitly say when things were as their rows describe them to be, we all understand that these rows say what things exist *right now*, at the present moment, and what these things are like *right now*, at the present moment. We all understand that rows in non-temporal tables describe *current* facts.

There may have been a time when S2 did not exist, or when S2 did exist but with a different name and/or category and/or type. For example, the fact corresponding to the second S2 row in the Supplier-S table in Figure 1.3 is that, from March 2013 up to November 2013, there was a supplier S2 who had the name "Superior", the category SC3, and the type T15. This row describes no fact located outside of that temporal interval.

---

[6]Since this TSQL2 document was published in 1994, it cannot be referring to (Jensen and Dyreson, 1998). For that reason, I will discuss the definitions of key temporal terms as they appear in (Jensen and Clifford, 1992), not as they appear in the 1998 glossary. Nonetheless, I find no substantial difference in the definitions of the key terms between these two documents, although the commentary surrounding the terminology is somewhat different.

[7]The usual convention, when referring to a word or phrase, is to include it within quotation marks. However, I also use the convention of italicizing at least the first appearance of a word or phrase that will appear in the Glossary. So when this latter convention is used, I won't bother to also use quotation marks.

How can we describe what time this is? We can say that the time period of that row in the Supplier-S table is:

- when that supplier, possessing those specific characteristics, existed;
- when that state of affairs was in effect;
- when that supplier was in that state;
- when it was a fact that that supplier was in that state; and
- when the world was like that.

These ways of saying what this kind of time period is are equivalent. That time period is what computer scientists call a valid-time period.

As for transaction time, I think Jensen and Clifford's definition will be a little clearer if we substitute "row" for "fact", in which case their definition reads "The transaction time of a row is the time when the row is current in the database". Facts exist in the world, not in databases. What exist in databases are statements, each such statement being physically instantiated as a row in a table in a database. Facts are the states of affairs corresponding to statements.

This paraphrase associates transaction time with rows in database tables. The transaction time period, for every row, begins when the row is inserted, and ends when the row is deleted. As we shall see, however, rows which have transaction time periods are not physically deleted. Instead, each such row is deleted by setting the end date of its transaction time period to the point in time at which the delete transaction for that row physically took place.

We add a statement to a database by inserting a row into a table in that database. With a table that has a transaction-time period, a row's transaction begin time is when we add that row to that table. In the standard theory of bitemporal time, by adding a row to a table we are also adding the statement made by that row to the totality of statements made in that database. So, on the standard theory, transaction begin time indicates both a physical and a semantic event: when a row was created, and when a statement was added to a database.

ASIDE

Jensen and Clifford, the computer science community in general, the standards committees, and the DBMS vendors, do not distinguish between the physical event of adding a row to a table, and the semantic event of making a statement with that row. This would be little more than a pedagogical matter if the two were always co-extensive. But they are not.

The insertion of a row into a table is a physical event, and transaction begin time marks when that event took place. But making a statement is a semantic event, and there is no reason why it cannot begin sometime after the row representing it is physically created. In that case, however, one time period cannot represent both events.

The Asserted Versioning theory of bitemporal data supports the management of rows which will not begin to make statements until some future point in time. Details may be found in Chapter 12 of *MTRD* and in Chapter 14 of this book. But until that chapter, I will be describing the standard theory of bitemporality, in which that physical event and that semantic event are co-extensive.

With a table that has a transaction-time period, we change a statement by updating the row which makes the statement, but the update is not an overwrite. Instead, the original row is preserved, and the update is applied to a copy of the original row. The transaction end time of the original row is set to the point in time when the update took place, and the transaction begin time of the new row is set to the same point in time. In the standard theory, this moment in time is both the moment at which the original row is no longer asserted to be a true statement, and at which the new row begins to be asserted in its place. The original row remains physically present in the database. But that row no longer represents any current assertion. Instead, it is the record of a row which was asserted during its no-longer current transaction-time period.

With a table that has a transaction-time period, we *withdraw* the assertion of a statement by setting the transaction end point of the row which makes the assertion to the point in time when the delete transaction takes place. The row which up to that point had represented an assertion remains physically present in the database. But that row no longer asserts anything. Instead, it is the record of a row which did make an assertion once upon a time, during its no-longer current transaction-time period.

So from the start of a row's transaction-time period, up to either the present moment or to the end of the time period, whichever is earlier, that row represents an assertion. During that time, it makes a statement that those responsible for that data believe to be true. But if the row is logically deleted, then although the physical *inscription* of the statement made by that row continues to exist, the *assertion* of that statement does not. In the standard theory, the physical action of ending a transaction-time period is also the semantic action of withdrawing a statement. In the Asserted Versioning theory, it is not.

The ISO and IBM Terminology

IBM's preferred terminology, corresponding to my terminology of state time and assertion time, and Jensen and Clifford's terminology of valid time and transaction time, is *application time* and *system time*. As Jensen and Clifford did, IBM defines their concepts in primarily physical terms.

Here are IBM's definitions:

- *"system period* A pair of columns with system-maintained values that indicate the period of time when a row is valid, which can also be referred to as SYSTEM_TIME period.
- *application period* A pair of columns with application-maintained values that indicate the period of time when a row is valid, which can also be referred to as BUSINESS_TIME period." (DB210 for z/OS, 2010, Technical Overview. p.205)

Note that "the period of time when a row is valid" is used in both definitions. Since "valid" cannot mean the same thing in both cases, it is clearly a homonym. What, then, does IBM mean by "valid"? We do know what the computer science community means by that term; or, at least, we know that for them, the term is not a homonym. For them, the term refers only to what IBM here calls an application time period.

The current SQL standard — ISO 9075:2011 — uses the same terminology that IBM does, and their definitions are also purely physical definitions.

Here are the ISO 9075:2011 definitions:

- "A period whose period name is SYSTEM_TIME is also known as a system-time period and the corresponding period descriptor is also known as a system-time period descriptor. . . . .
- "A period whose period name is not SYSTEM_TIME is also known as an application-time period and the corresponding period descriptor is also known as an application-time period descriptor." (ISO/IEC 9075-2, 2011, p.56)

The Asserted Versioning Terminology

In our book *Managing Time in Relational Databases*, my co-author and I introduced the concepts of effective time and assertion time.

Asserted Versioning's effective time is equivalent to Jensen and Clifford's valid time and to the SQL standard's application time. It is what I now call "state time".

State-time periods are represented in the same way that valid-time periods and application-time periods are represented. That is as a begin and end point in time, using the closed/open convention. Next, under identical insert, update and delete transactions, state-time periods take on the same values as do valid-time periods in a computer-science-compliant database (such as Teradata's) and in an ISO-compliant database (such as IBM's).

Asserted Versioning's assertion time is an extension to transaction time and system time. More formally stated, assertion time is a proper superset of transaction time and system time. With computer science's transaction time and the SQL standard's system time, tables may contain rows that assert statements and rows that *no longer* assert statements. Asserted Versioning's assertion time makes it possible for tables to also contain rows that do *not yet* assert statements.

Asserted Versioning's assertion time extension, which is the subject of Chapter 14, introduces the concept of future time periods along this temporal dimension. Of course, the term "future transaction time" is an oxymoron. Rows are created and modified by means of transactions, and since future transactions haven't taken place yet, there can be no rows resulting from them.

It would seem to follow that rows with future transaction-time periods are an impossibility. As we will see later, however, they are far from an impossibility. They are, indeed, a very useful extension of bitemporal capabilities beyond what has been discussed in the computer science literature up to this time.

But except for that extension, Asserted Versioning's assertion time is equivalent to Jensen and Clifford's transaction time and to the SQL standard's system time in the same way that Asserted Versioning's effective time is equivalent to state time and application time.

TYPES OF TABLES

The Computer Science Terminology

Jensen and Clifford define four kinds of relations. For purposes of comparison, we may take these to be definitions of tables in a relational database.

"Relations of a conventional relational database system incorporating neither valid-time nor transaction-time timestamps are *snapshot relations*." (p.38)

These are what most IT professionals would call "non-temporal tables". I will stick with the IT terminology, and will also use the term "conventional table". However, Jensen and Clifford's term brings out an important fact, namely that all data is temporal, even non-temporal data!

The rows in non-temporal tables do not give us information about non-temporal states of affairs. There is no such thing as a non-temporal state of affairs. Rather, they give us information about the *current* state of each object represented in those tables. As soon as the current moment has passed, the information about that moment in the life history of those objects is lost from non-temporal tables. Even if the data in a row does not change from one moment to the next, what that data stands for does change with each passing moment. A second ago, a row in a Customer table stood for what that customer was like a second ago. A second later, and even though the row remains unchanged, that row will stand for what that customer will be like then, and not for what the customer was like a moment ago, or at any other moment in time.

"A *valid-time relation* is a relation with exactly one system supported valid time." (p.38)

Given Jensen and Clifford's own definition of "valid time", I don't know what a relation with two valid times would look like. If there can be multiple kinds of valid time, is any one of those multiple kinds privileged in any way? Are there any important semantic relationships among those different kinds of valid time, or are they all orthogonal to one another?

"A *transaction-time relation* is a relation with exactly one system supported transaction time." (p.38)

The same comment I made about Jensen and Clifford's definition of "valid-time relation" applies here also.

"A *bitemporal relation* is a relation with exactly one system supported valid time and exactly one system-supported transaction time." (p.38)

The same comment I made about Jensen and Clifford's two previous definitions applies here also.

The Asserted Versioning Terminology

Assertion time is the time during which a row represents the assertion that the statement made by that row is true. In conventional tables, that corresponds to the time when the row is physically present in the table. However, if some kind of logical delete flag is used, then a row can physically remain in a conventional table after it has been deleted. In that case, it will remain in the table as a row which, beginning when the delete flag is set, expresses a statement that is no longer asserted to be true. Physically deleting a row removes it from its table, and therefore removes both the assertion and the statement itself from that table. Logically deleting a row leaves the row present in its table, and so also leaves the statement made by that row present in its table. But it semantically withdraws the assertion of the statement made by that row.[8]

Now suppose that a row has a physical row create date, and that instead of a logical delete flag, it has a row delete date. When that row is created, its delete date is either null or some special value which indicates that the row has not yet been deleted. It remains that way unless or until the user issues a delete for that row, at which time the row is updated to set its row delete date to the date the delete transaction is applied. These pair of dates, then, delimit a time period. What time period is that?

It is assertion time, the time during which the statement made by a row is claimed to be true. In a conventional table, after a row is physically deleted, it is no longer there to make a statement and no longer there to be asserted to be true. That is, semantically, what physical deletion does. It removes a statement from the set of statements that a business currently stands behind. That is also what any kind of logical deletion does, whether done with a flag or with a deletion date. It leaves the row physically in the table, and relies on queries to exclude the logically deleted row. An

---

[8]This distinction between rows as physical inscriptions, rows as expressing statements, and rows as representing assertions about statements, will be explained in Chapter 6. Later on, in Chapter 19, it will be the basis on which I develop a *tritemporal* theory of data, one which I believe should be the objective towards which today's bitemporal standards and their implementations should evolve.

alternative strategy is to move logically deleted rows to a separate table, which is what IBM does. In that case, the table the row was originally in is a table of rows all of which make assertions. By moving a logically deleted row to a separate table, IBM is withdrawing that row, thereby changing the status of that row to the status of representing a no-longer asserted statement.

A CHOICE OF TERMINOLOGIES

There are five sets of terminologies used to talk about bitemporal data, as shown in Table 2.1. The terminology I will use in this book is shown in the right-most column.

Table 2.1 Bitemporal Terminology

TSQL2 SQL Standard	ISO SQL Standard	IBM	MTRD	This Book
chronon	—	—	clock tick	clock tick
valid time	application time	business time	effective time	state time
transaction time	system time	system time	assertion time	assertion time
snapshot relation	—	—	conventional table	conventional table
valid-time relation	—	application-period temporal table	effective-time table	state-time table
transaction-time relation	system-period temporal table	system-period temporal table	assertion-time table	assertion-time table
bitemporal relation	bitemporal table	bitemporal table	bitemporal table	bitemporal table

With respect to the first row in this table, I referred to clock ticks rather than chronons in *MTRD*, and will continue to do so in this book. One reason is that the concept of logical clocks which tick at different rates is more comprehensive than that of chronons. The different sized clock ticks are the various granularities that can be used to define different domains for time periods of either temporal dimension. Chronons are just a special kind of clock tick, one whose granularity is defined as the smallest granularity a given DBMS can recognize and manage. They are atomic clock ticks.

Another reason for using the terminology of clock ticks is that it provides a clear mental image. We record when anything happens relative to a clock we have available. And we can't record when anything happened with more precision than the ticks of that clock make available to us. Those ticks are the best realization we have of the concept of points in time. They are points because they are indivisible. They are indivisible because they are the ticks of the timepiece we use to measure time with, and we have no means to distinguish an "earlier" or "later" within any tick of that timepiece.

With respect to the second row in this table, in the course of several decades of consulting work in the IT industry, I have found that the term "effective time" is the most widely-used term for what computer scientists and DBMS vendors call "valid time". But although the influence of vendors has made "valid time" a de facto standard, and the standards committees have made it a de jure standard, I will instead use the term "state time". My reasons for introducing this new term will become clearer in Chapter 6.

With respect to the third row in this table, I will again differ with the other terminological sources. The term "transaction time" emphasizes the physical interpretation of this temporal dimension. The transaction-time period of any row begins when the row is physical created, and ends when an update or a delete is applied to that row. My own term "assertion time", by contrast, emphasizes the semantic interpretation of this temporal dimension. The assertion-time period of a row begins when we are willing to assert that what the row tells us is in fact the case. It ends when the statement made by the row is withdrawn, which is what we do when we are no longer willing to assert that it is true. Normally, the times associated with these physical and semantic actions coincide. But sometimes they do not. That will be the topic of Chapter 14.

GLOSSARY LIST

assert	fact	state time
assertion time	granularity	statement
assertion-time table	inscribe	state-time table
atomic clock tick	inscription	temporal dimension
bitemporal table	instant	thing
clock tick	interval	time period
closed/open	length of time	transaction time
conventional table	location	tritemporal
duration	moment	valid time
empty time period	open time period	withdraw
event	point in time	
extent	predicate	

THE RELATIONAL PARADIGM: MATHEMATICS

3

The mathematics of the Relational Paradigm have been described many times. However, there are few mathematically informed presentations which are intended for an audience of IT professionals, an audience who may not be familiar with set theory, functions and relations. Among these few mathematically informed presentations, the first and probably still the best is C. J. Date's seminal book *Introduction to Database Systems*. I myself learned most of how this mathematics is used in relational theory from studying the chapter "*Advanced Normalization*" in the third edition of that book (Date, 1983).

So as brief as my discussion of this mathematics will be, it may have value as a different approach to explaining what Date has already explained so well. But another reason for its inclusion here is that this mathematics constitutes the abstract framework for which the ontology described in the next chapter provides an interpretation. That interpretation is what makes it possible to use those mathematical structures to persist information about the world around us.

The mathematics of the Relational Paradigm is based on sets, functions, Cartesian Products, relations and tuples. This mathematical structure is the framework on which a relational database is defined. As we will see:

- Cartesian Products are the mathematical objects which give database tables their structure.
- Each relation on those Cartesian Products determines a set of rows which may be present in a database table at any given time.
- The sets on which those relations are defined are the mathematical objects which give the columns of those database tables their structure. And
- The ordered set of those sets is the mathematical object which gives the rows of those database tables their structure.

Each table defines the syntax of a statement — an *existentially-quantified statement* in logic — and its columns define the *domains* of values for each variable in the statement. Each row provides an ordered set of values which, when used to bind the variables of those statements, results in a statement that something exists, and a description of that something. For instance, in the Customer table example used in this chapter, one statement is that customer C1 exists, and the associated description is that C1 belongs in demographic group B and has a customer status of Gold.

TABLES AND COLUMNS

A *relational table* is an ordered set of columns. Because these columns are sequentially ordered, we can identify each one, and distinguish it from all the other columns of that table.

In a database, we use column names to identify each column. But as mathematical structures, as the sets on which a Cartesian Product is defined, which is itself the mathematical object on which relations are defined, these columns have no names.

One way to define a set is to list its members, separated by commas, and then delimit that list. To indicate a sequentially ordered set, I will delimit the list with brackets ([. . ..]), and otherwise with braces ({. . ..}). Using these conventions, Figure 3.1 shows an ordered set of three sets.

$$S_X = \left(\begin{array}{ccc} \overset{S_1}{\boxed{}}, & \overset{S_2}{\boxed{}}, & \overset{S_3}{\boxed{}} \end{array}\right)$$

FIGURE 3.1

An Ordered Set of Three Sets: a Minimalist View.

In Figure 3.1, the ordered set is S_X. The brackets indicate that the sets on which S_X is defined — S_1, S_2 and S_3 — occur in a specific sequence. S_1, S_2 and S_3 are represented as empty rectangles because as yet we know nothing about them, and nothing about their members.

S_X is the mathematical structure on which, when interpreted, one or more database tables may be defined. I will consider only one such table, and will call it T_X. The sets S_1, S_2 and S_3 on which S_X is defined are the mathematical structures on which, when interpreted, the columns of T_X — call them $T_X.C_1$, $T_X.C_2$ and $T_X.C_3$ — will be defined.[1]

COLUMNS AND DOMAINS

Each *column of a relational table* is defined on a domain. A *domain* is a set of values. A *datatype*, which is also defined for each column, consists of a domain of values and a set of operations on those values. The sets S_1, S_2, and S_3 are sets of values.[2] In the context of a database, they are domains of columns.

When assigned to a column of a table, a domain defines the set of the only values, and only the values, which are valid in row-level instances of that column. For example, the domain of a customer status column is the set of all valid customer status codes.

Sometimes domains include all the values permitted by the datatype of the column they are assigned to. At other times, domains contain only some of those values.

---

[1]Although there are no strict rules governing mathematical notation, it is common to use script/subscript combinations to indicate types and their instances. Thus, in "S_x", "S" represents a type, and "x" an instance of that type. In this example, "S" stands for "set", and "x" for a specific set. And similarly for "T_x", "C_1", etc. This keeps, front and center, the important point that S_x is a particular *set*, T_x is a particular *table*, C_1 is a particular *column*, and so on.

[2]In first normal form databases, these sets are sets of atomic values. This means that they are sets whose members are not sets. In this book, I will not consider non-first normal form databases, in which the contents of columns may be sets composed of lists, or even of other tables.

Figure 3.2 shows three domains, D_1, D_2 and D_3. The first two domains are not ordered, shown by using braces; the third one is ordered, shown by using brackets. These domains are the sets S_1, S_2, and S_3, but understood as functioning as domains for the columns of database tables. Later on, we will assign them to $T_X.C_1$, $T_X.C_2$, and $T_X.C_3$, the columns of table T_X.

```
D₁ = {C1,C2,C3}
D₂ = {A,B,C}
D₃ = [Platinum,Gold,Silver]
```

FIGURE 3.2

Three Domains.

Domain D_1 appears to be ordered, since it would seem that we can sort the members of that set. For similar reasons, domain D_2 appears to be ordered. But in fact, these domains are not ordered. The character strings "C1", "C2" and "C3", and "A", "B" and "C" each have an obvious ordering. But these character strings aren't the members of these two sets. They are the symbols used to represent those members. The ordering of a set is an ordering of its members, not of the symbols which represent those members.

D_3 isn't as obviously ordered, and it might not have been ordered at all. To say that it is ordered is to say that the position of any of its members in the set is known, which is to say that each one can be paired with one of the first three positive integers. Given that there is an order to the members of D_3, and that the order is Platinum first, Gold second, and Silver third, we recognize that order as intuitively right because we understand that platinum is more valuable than gold and gold is more valuable than silver. But we could have called the three customer statuses Mike, Susan, and Frank, and we would still have had the same set and the same ordering in terms of relative rank or value. What the set consists of is three customer statuses, one of which is most highly ranked, another of which is least highly ranked, and the third of which is ranked between those two.

If we combine Figures 3.1 and 3.2, we have a description of S_X which shows the members of the sets on which it is defined, and also shows that the third of those sets is itself an ordered set. This is shown as Figure 3.3.

```
Sₓ = [{C1,C2,C3},{A,B,C},[Platinum,Gold,Silver]]
```

FIGURE 3.3

An Ordered Set of Three Sets.

CARTESIAN PRODUCTS

A Cartesian Product is defined on an ordered set of sets. It is the set of all possible ordered combinations consisting of one member from each of those sets. The Cartesian Product of S_X is shown in Figure 3.4.

```
CP(Sx) =
{
[C1,A,Platinum],
[C1,A,Gold],
[C1,A,Silver],
[C1,B,Platinum],
[C1,B,Gold],
[C1,B,Silver],
[C1,C,Platinum],
[C1,C,Gold],
[C1,C,Silver],
[C2,A,Platinum],
[C2,A,Gold],
[C2,A,Silver]
[C2,B,Platinum],
[C2,B,Gold],
[C2,B,Silver],
[C2,C,Platinum],
[C2,C,Gold],
[C2,C,Silver],
[C3,A,Platinum],
[C3,A,Gold],
[C3,A,Silver],
[C3,B,Platinum],
[C3,B,Gold],
[C3,B,Silver],
[C3,C,Platinum],
[C3,C,Gold],
[C3,C,Silver]
}
```

FIGURE 3.4

The Cartesian Product of S_X.

Each member of $CP(S_X)$ is called a *tuple*. Each tuple is itself an ordered set, and all the tuples defined on a given Cartesian Product have the same number of members. In this example, the tuples have three members, so we can also say that each member of $CP(S_X)$ is a *3-tuple*, also called a *triple*.

When S_X appears in a database as (the mathematical structure of) table T_X, and S_1, S_2, and S_3 are assigned as the domains of columns $T_X.C_1$, $T_X.C_2$, and $T_X.C_3$, then each member of $CP(S_X)$ is a possible row of T_X, and $CP(S_X)$ itself is the set of all possible rows of T_X. At every point in time in the life history of T_X, the rows that T_X contains will be a subset of the tuples of $CP(S_X)$. That subset of tuples is a *relation* on $CP(S_X)$.

FUNCTIONS AND PRIMARY KEYS

A *function* is a mapping from one value to another value. For each first value that is mapped, there is one and only one second value. The set of all first values is called the *domain* of the function, while the set of all second values is called the *range* of the function. But if we think of the function as an executable piece of code, then we can think of the domain as the set of all *input values* to the function, and the range as the set of all *output values* from the function.

A relational table has a primary key. For any given row, its primary key value is an input value to a function, and an ordered set of non-primary key values is the output value from that function. I call that function the *defining function* of the table.

A relational table also has a *natural key*. A primary key is the unique identifier of a row of data. A natural key is the unique identifier of what that row stands for. I will call the natural key of a table its *referent identifier* or, for short, its *RefId*.

Sometimes natural keys are used as primary keys. Although I advocate keeping them separate, I will assume, in order to simplify this discussion, that they are not separate, that the primary key of the table used as an example is also the natural key.

The fact that one column (or columns) of a relational table is a primary key is a restriction on which subsets of the Cartesian Product of all its columns may appear in the table at any given time. In our example, it means that at no time may T_X contain two or more tuples of $CP(S_X)$ which have the same first value.

With this restriction, any valid set of rows in T_X, i.e. any relation on $CP(S_X)$, can include, at any one time, no more than one of the first nine members of $CP(S_X)$, no more than one of the second nine members, and no more than one of the third nine members, and can include no other members. It follows that T_X can never have more than three rows at any given time.

Figure 3.5 shows the defining function for T_X at the level of sets, and below that, the defining function for T_X at the level of set members.

$$T_X \ (\text{def}): \ t_1(fT_X\{T_X.C_1\} \ = \ CP\{T_X.C_2, T_X.C_3\})$$

$$T_X \ (\text{def}): \ t_1(fT_x\{C1, C2, C3\} \ =$$
$$\{$$
$$[A, \text{Platinum}], [A, \text{Gold}], [A, \text{Silver}],$$
$$[B, \text{Platinum}], [B, \text{Gold}], [B, \text{Silver}],$$
$$[C, \text{Platinum}], [C, \text{Gold}], [C, \text{Silver}]$$
$$\})$$

FIGURE 3.5

The Defining Function of Table T_X.

Figure 3.5 shows fT_X, the defining function for T_X, as a *time-varying function* from $T_X.C_1$, the primary key of T_X, to the Cartesian Product of $T_X.C_2$ and $T_X.C_3$, the non-primary key columns of T_X. At any time t_1, fT_X will pair one and only one output value with an input value. How it does this is, of course, application specific, and will be different from table to table.

But this is not the same thing as pairing one and only one input value with an output value. Functions that do that are called *one-to-one* functions (because they are one-to-one "both ways").

The defining functions of relational tables are not necessarily, or even usually, one-to-one functions. To illustrate, suppose that T_X is a Customer table, $T_X.C_1$ its primary key, $T_X.C_2$ a demographic code, and $T_X.C_3$ a status code. It's hard to imagine any reason why two or even all three customers in T_X could not have both the same demographic code and the same status code. So the defining function of this table is not a one-to-one function.

Some functions are *onto* functions. This means that all possible output values can be generated by the function. One output value of T_X is one member of $CP\{[T_X.C_2,T_X.C_3]\}$, which is the Cartesian Product of the ordered set of the non-primary key columns of T_X. So a table whose defining function is an onto function is one in which each possible combination of non-primary key values is represented in the table.

The defining functions of relational tables are not necessarily, or even usually, onto functions. Suppose again that T_X is the same Customer table mentioned above. It's hard to imagine a business which would have the requirement that there be at least one customer for every demographic group and customer status code combination. So the defining function of this Customer table is not an onto function.

In fact, the defining function of most tables in most relational databases is neither one-to-one nor onto. But for an example of a table whose defining function is both one-to-one and onto, consider a code table in which the code (which is the natural key) is also the primary key, in which each code has a category, and in which each code has a name. No code will have more than one category/name combination, so this is a function. No category/name combination will belong to more than one code, so this function is one-to-one. And every category/name combination will have an associated code, so this function is onto.

Tables like this are one-to-one and onto because the complete set of both input values and output values is known in advance, and the association of one input value (a code) with one output value (a category/name combination) has already taken place before the table is introduced into the database. In other words, a specific subset of the Cartesian Product of code, category and name has already been fully determined.

Primary keys are how functions get us to first normal form. Each $T_X.C_1$ value of T_X is a primary key value. For each $T_X.C_1$ value, there is a $T_X.C_2$ value and also a $T_X.C_3$ value, and they are both jointly and individually *functionally dependent* on the $T_X.C_1$ value. And so every row in a first normal form relational table is a function from a specific primary key value to a specific member of the Cartesian Product of its non-primary key columns.

ASIDE

Cartesian Products of real tables can get quite large. For example, suppose we add a third non-primary key column to T_X which is a CHAR(30) column, and which represents customer names. To simplify, assume that the character set used is restricted to the upper and lower cases of the alphabet, plus the space character. This is a total of 53 characters, and so this column is defined on a set consisting of 53^{30} thirty-character strings, which is 53 million trillion trillion possible names.[3] Every name of thirty or fewer characters that can be written with those 53 characters will be found somewhere in this very large set. And to get the Cartesian Product of this extended T_X, we still have to multiply that number by 9!

So Cartesian Products on real database tables can be very large. This may be one reason why few IT professionals think of the rows in a database table as selections from the tuples of that table's Cartesian Product. But mathematically, that's what those rows are.

---

[3] "Trillion trillion" is not a mistake. Since 10^6 is a million, and 10^9 is a billion, 10^{12} is a trillion; and so 10^{30} is a million trillion trillion.

Compared to the astronomical number of tuples of the Cartesian Product of most real tables, the number of tuples actually instantiated in those tables at any one time is miniscule. To switch metaphors, it is a light sprinkling of colored grains of sand on a white sand beach along the ocean. Those grains of sand were selected by someone based on a rule which was used by that person and understood by the people who are interested in what those colored grains of sand can tell them. It is by conforming to mutually-understood rules that physical things like strings of characters can represent semantic things like statements. No rules, and strings of characters are just marks on a page, inscriptions full of sound and fury, signifying nothing.

RELATIONS

A *relation* is a set which is a subset of a Cartesian Product. T_X is a time-varying relation on the Cartesian Product of its three columns. That means that at any one point in time, call it t_1, the set of all the rows in T_X is a collection of one or more of the ordered sets which are the members of $CP(T_X)$. After a row has been inserted, updated or deleted, time has passed to, let's say, t_2. Assuming the update was not a "do nothing" update, i.e. assuming that it did add a row, delete a row, or change one or more of the values on a row, the result is that, at t_2, T_X is now a different relation, a different subset of $CP(T_X)$.

This completes my brief survey of the mathematics of the Relational Paradigm. These are the mathematics on which the *structures* of relational databases are defined. There is also a mathematics of the *processes* which access and manipulate instances of these structures. That mathematics, of how these structures are populated and queried, is a matter of logic, and I discuss that topic in the next chapter.

GLOSSARY LIST

defining function	instance	type
existentially-quantified	natural key	
statement	referent identifier	

THE RELATIONAL PARADIGM: LOGIC

4

Logic is a set of rules for deriving true statements from true statements. In one form of logic, these statements are atomic units; they can't be split apart. This is propositional logic. In another form of logic, these statements can be split apart into components. These components are subjects, predicates, and quantifiers, and this form of logic is predicate logic.

Both propositional and predicate logic are part of the Relational Paradigm. We use them to tell the DBMS what data we are looking for.

PROPOSITIONAL LOGIC

Propositional logic is the logic of *declarative sentences*, sentences that can be true or false. The truth tables of propositional logic determine the truth value of a combination of sentences from the truth value of each component sentence. In propositional logic, these sentences are called *statements*. The component statements that cannot be broken down into further components are *atomic statements*, and all other statements are *compound statements*.

For example, "Some people are allergic to rosewood" is either true or false. So too is "Ethane is the simplest hydrocarbon". The first happens to be true, and the second false. But "Some people" isn't true or false; and "allergic to rosewood" isn't either. Neither are "ethane" and "the simplest hydrocarbon". The distinction is that the first two quoted strings in this paragraph are statements, while the latter four are not.

So statements are the components that propositional logic works with, and their combinations are *compound statements*. Compound statements are created by putting component statements together with statement connectives.

CONNECTIVES

The usual set of *statement connectives* used in propositional logic are formal equivalents of what is expressed in ordinary language by "and", "or", "not", "if…then" and "if and only if". The usual symbols for these connectives are, respectively, "∧", "∨", "∼", "→" and "↔". Equivalent symbols for these connectives are, respectively, "AND", "OR", "NOT", "IF/THEN" and "IFF".

In standard SQL, only the first three connectives are used. The other two can easily be defined in terms of the first three. In fact, based on either AND and NOT, or on OR and NOT, all three other connectives can be defined.[1,2]

AND

The logical AND operator applies between two statements, and forms a compound statement called a *conjunction*. It says that if either or both of a pair of component statements is false, then their conjunction is false, and otherwise is true. To put it another way, the conjunction $(X \wedge Y)$ is true is when both its components are true, and otherwise is false.

A truth table contains one row for every assignment of true (T) and false (F) to the component statements of a compound statement, and then shows the truth-value assignment to the compound statement, given those component assignments.

The truth table for conjunction — the formalization of "and" — is this:

AND

X	Y		$X \wedge Y$
T	T		T
T	F		F
F	T		F
F	F		F

FIGURE 4.1

The Truth Table for AND.

OR

The logical OR operator applies between two statements, and forms a compound statement called a *disjunction*. It says that if either or both of two component statements is true, then their disjunction is true, and otherwise is false. To put it another way, the disjunction $(X \vee Y)$ is false when both its components are false, and otherwise is true.

The truth table for disjunction — the formalization of "or" — is this:

OR

X	Y		$X \vee Y$
T	T		T
T	F		T
F	T		T
F	F		F

FIGURE 4.2

The Truth Table for OR.

---

[1]"AND" designates the formalization of the "and" of ordinary English, and so too for "OR" and "or", and "NOT" and "not". Thus, these three strings of capital letters are not English words; they are equivalent strings for, respectively, "$\wedge$", "$\vee$" and "$\sim$".

[2]There is even a single operator in terms of which all the others may be defined. It is called the Sheffer stroke. But it is so terse and non-intuitive a connective that it is almost never used in solving problems in logic.

The components of compound statements can themselves be compound statements. For example:

$$(X \lor (Y \land {\sim} Z)) \land ({\sim} Y \land (Z \lor X))$$

is false if either $(X \lor (Y \land {\sim} Z))$ or $({\sim} Y \land (Z \lor X))$ is false. This is because this statement is a conjunction, both of whose components happen to be compound statements, and a conjunction is false if either (or both) of its conjuncts is false.

The complete statement of the truth conditions of this compound statement is its truth table, shown in Figure 4.3.

X	Y	Z	$(X \lor (Y \land {\sim} Z)$	$({\sim} Y \land (Z \lor X)$	$(X \lor (Y \land {\sim} Z) \land ({\sim} Y \land (Z \lor X))$
T	T	T	T	F	F
T	T	F	T	F	F
T	F	T	T	T	T
T	F	F	T	T	T
F	T	T	F	F	F
F	T	F	T	F	F
F	F	T	F	T	F
F	F	F	F	F	F

FIGURE 4.3

The Truth Table for a Compound Statement.

Figure 4.3 shows three atomic statements, X, Y and Z. The first three columns list all possible truth-value combinations for these three statements. The next two columns show the truth value of each of the two conjuncts.[3] These truth values are computed using the truth tables for AND, OR and NOT. Finally, the last column uses the truth table for AND.

The two highlighted rows are the only ones for which the conjunction turns out to be true. They show that if X is true and Y is false, then the conjunction is true, and otherwise is false. The truth value of Z doesn't matter.[4] Sometimes truth tables tell us useful things like that.

NOT

The logical NOT operator applies to a single statement, and forms a new statement called the *negation* of the original statement. It says that if a statement is true, then its negation is false, and vice versa.

The truth table for negation − the formalization of "not" − is this:

---

[3]Each of those two conjuncts could be shown with its own truth table. In this case, they are each simple enough that we can compute their truth values "on the fly".

[4]And knowing this, we could replace the WHERE clause in a SQL query based on the original statement with a WHERE clause based on the statement $(X \land {\sim} Y)$, in which case query evaluation performance would be greatly improved.

NOT

X		~X
T		F
F		T

FIGURE 4.4

The Truth Table for NOT.

IF/THEN

The material implication operator applies between two statements, and forms a compound state-ment called a *material implication*, an *implication*, an *if/then*, or a *hypothetical* statement. Its sym-bol is "→". The statement coming before the connective is the *antecedent*, and the statement coming after the connective is the *consequent*.

Material implication is meant to capture the truth-functionally minimal sense of any statement of the form "If X then Y". In this minimal sense, $(X \rightarrow Y)$ is true whenever X is false, or Y is true, or both. This can be stated as follows:

$$(X \rightarrow Y)\,[=]\,(\sim X \vee Y)$$

"[=]" is the symbol I will use for the metalinguistic statement that two strings of symbols are equivalent.[5] This means that wherever either string occurs, the other one may be substituted for it without altering the truth value of the compound statement of which it is a part.

However, this does seem to be somewhat counter-intuitive. For example, consider the statement "If cocobolo is a tropical wood, then the Higgs boson was discovered in 2013." Since the Higgs boson was indeed discovered in 2013, this is a true statement, and it is a true statement whether or not cocobolo is a tropical wood. In any if/then statement, if the consequent is true, the statement itself is true whether or not its antecedent is also true. That's well enough; except, what does coco-bolo have to do with the Higgs boson discovery?

Or consider the statement "If maple is a tropical wood, then the Higgs boson was discovered in 2010." Since maple is not a tropical wood, this is also a true statement, and it is a true statement even though the Higgs boson was not discovered in 2010. In any if/then statement, if the antecedent is false, the statement itself is true whether or not its consequent is also true. Once again, that's well enough; except, once again, what does maple not being a tropical wood have to do with the Higgs boson discovery?

To take another example, when I was a child, disbelief was often expressed with the phrase "monkey's uncle", as in "If you really swam the hundred meters in under a minute at the last swim meet, then I'm a monkey's uncle." And without saying anything more, we all understand that I'm

---

[5]Anything we say *about* a system of logic, such as descriptions of the operands of the system, of the rules for formulas being well-formed, of transformation rules, rules of inference, the process of deriving conclusions from premises — all such statements take place in the *metalanguage* used to talk about that system of logic. By contrast, anything we say *within* that system of logic, such as writing down premises of an argument, and then a series of wffs (well-formed formulas) derived from the premises by means of transformation and/or inference rules — all such statements take place in the *object language* employed in using that system of logic. The distinction between an object language and a meta-language is due to Alfred Tarski.

saying that I don't believe that you swam the hundred meters in under a minute. In other words, since the consequent (I'm a monkey's uncle) is false, then by uttering that if/then statement, I am claiming that the antecedent cannot be true.

So there are instances, in ordinary conversation, where we do use if/then statements whose antecedents and consequents have nothing to do with one another. And the way we use them — using a blatantly false consequent as an indirect way of claiming that a totally unrelated antecedent is false — illustrates this material implication sense of if/then.

So if X (materially) implies Y, then if Y is false, X must be false also. Conversely, if X (materially) implies Y, then if X is true, Y must be true also. If this is all we want to capture of the ordinary language use of "implies", then "X implies Y" will be considered true except when X is true and Y is false. This minimum sense of "implies" — minimal in that it doesn't require that the antecedent and consequent have anything to do with one another — is expressed in the truth table for material implication.

IF/THEN

X	Y		X→Y
T	T		T
T	F		F
F	T		T
F	F		T

FIGURE 4.5

The Truth Table for Material Implication.

Often, however, we clearly do mean more than this minimal sense when we use an if/then statement. And the attempt to formalize more of what we mean by if/then is what led logicians to develop systems of *modal logic*. But that is a story which takes us well beyond the logic which is part of the Relational Paradigm.

So these are the *operators* of propositional logic. Their *operands* are statements. Statements are either atomic statements or compound statements. *Atomic statements* are statements that are assigned a truth value. They get their truth value from *outside* the system of logic. *Compound statements* are statements whose truth value is computed, by means of the rules stated as truth tables for the operators of the system, from the truth value of their component statements. They get their truth value from *within* the system of logic.

WELL-FORMED FORMULAS

Like ordinary language, systems of logic need rules to eliminate nonsensical, i.e. ungrammatical, sentences.[6] In systems of logic, this is done by means of the rules which define *well-formed*

---

[6]Note the syntax/semantics parallel here (not that the parallelism doesn't occur throughout any account of ends and means, or whats and hows). "Nonsensical" is a semantic judgment; "ungrammatical" is a syntactical one.

formulas (wffs). A *formula* is a string of symbols which, if grammatically well-formed, expresses the schema for a statement. So these rules would eliminate nonsensical strings, like

$$XY \lor \land \sim \lor ()Z$$

Once we can be sure that we will be working only with wffs, the next issue is how to derive new wffs from one or more wffs that we start with. The wffs that we start with may be the *axioms* of a formal system, in which case the wffs that are derived are called *theorems* of the system. Alternatively, the wffs that we start with may be the *premises* of an argument. In that case, we are usually also given a wff that we think *deductively follows* from the premises, that wff being called the *conclusion* of the argument. The construction of the argument is then a process of deriving new wffs from the premises until either the conclusion or its negation is derived. If the premises happen to be self-contradictory, then it will be possible to derive both the conclusion and its negation.

In both cases, the derivation of new wffs is a process that uses either transformation rules, or rules of inference, or both.

TRANSFORMATION RULES

Transformation rules allow us to simplify formulas. One of the places where IT professionals most frequently encounter an opportunity to simplify a formula of propositional logic is in the WHERE clauses of SQL statements. We'll consider an example of simplifying a WHERE clause later in this section.

Logical NOT is not just an operand of propositional logic. It is also a transformation rule. It says that if we have X, then we can write down $\sim \sim$ X, and that if we have $\sim \sim$ X, then we can write down X. This rule is based on the fact (in English, but not in all languages) that we can add a double negative to a statement, or remove a double negative from a statement, without changing truth values, i.e. without making a true statement false or a false statement true.[7] So if we had $\sim \sim \sim$ X, that entitles us to write down $\sim$ X. It also entitles us to write down $\sim \sim \sim \sim \sim$ X. And if we had X, that entitles us to write down $\sim \sim$ X, or $\sim \sim \sim \sim$ X, or $\sim \sim \sim \sim \sim \sim$ X, and so on, and vice versa.

Two more transformation rules are the *deMorgan's equivalences.* One of those two rules is that if two things are both true, then neither of them is false. Again using "[=]" as the metalanguage symbol indicating that two formulas are equivalent, this first deMorgan's rule is:

$$(X \land Y)[=] \sim (\sim X \lor \sim Y)$$

The second deMorgan's rule is that if either of two things is true, then they aren't both false.

$$(X \lor Y)[=] \sim (\sim X \land \sim Y)$$

Propositional logic also has two transformation rules which eliminate superfluous components in compound statements. The two rules of simplification in propositional logic are these:

$$(X \land X)[=]X$$
$$(X \lor X)[=]X$$

These are often called rules of *idempotence.*

---

[7] In classical Greek, for example, in a string of two or more negations, the first negates the statement, and the subsequent ones intensify the force of the negation.

Many of these transformation rules may seem trivial, especially the deMorgan's and idempotence rules. But it may be helpful to think of these rules in terms of their use by software. From that point of view, compound statements are wffs — properly-formed character strings — and these transformation rules are recursive rules by which strings may be transformed into other strings. A program to solve problems in propositional logic, then, would include a set of functions, one for each transformation rule. Solving a problem would be deriving a desired string of symbols from a given string of symbols, using those string manipulation rules.

Two additional transformation rules allow us to rearrange conjuncts, and to rearrange disjuncts. These are called *commutative* rules, and they are:

$$(X \wedge Y) [=] (Y \wedge X)$$
$$(X \vee Y) [=] (Y \vee X)$$

Propositional logic also has two *distribution* rules. They are:

$$X \wedge (Y \vee Z) [=] (X \wedge Y) \vee (X \wedge Z)$$
$$X \vee (Y \wedge Z) [=] (X \vee Y) \wedge (X \vee Z)$$

In summary, these are the transformation rules for the set of logical operators that is used in standard SQL.

	Rule	From (To)	To (From)
1	Idempotent	$X \wedge X$	X
2	Idempotent	$X \vee X$	X
3	Commutative	$X \wedge Y$	$Y \wedge X$
4	Commutative	$X \vee Y$	$Y \vee X$
5	Associative	$X \wedge (Y \wedge Z)$	$(X \wedge Y) \wedge Z$
6	Associative	$X \vee (Y \vee Z)$	$(X \vee Y) \vee Z$
7	Double negation	$\sim\sim X$	X
8	demorgan's equivalence	$\sim(X \wedge Y)$	$\sim X \vee \sim Y$
9	demorgan's equivalence	$\sim(X \vee Y)$	$\sim X \wedge \sim Y$
10	Distributive	$X \vee (Y \wedge Z)$	$(X \vee Y) \wedge (X \vee Z)$
11	Distributive	$X \wedge (Y \vee Z)$	$(X \wedge Y) \vee (X \wedge Z)$

FIGURE 4.6

Propositional Logic Transformation Rules.

One of the most important reasons for IT professionals to be familiar with these rules is that they can be used to simplify SQL WHERE clauses. For example, suppose we had the clause:

```
WHERE dcode = A OR
(dcode = Y AND status = Gold) OR
(NOT-dcode = A AND status = Silver)
```

Written against a Customer table, this clause tells the DBMS to select all and only those customers who meet at least one of three conditions: a demographic code of A; a demographic code of Y together with a customer status of Gold; or any demographic code other than A together with a customer status of Silver.

By Rules 4 and 6, we can transform that WHERE clause into this one:

```
WHERE ((dcode = A) OR
(NOT-dcode = A AND status = Silver))
OR (dcode = Y AND status = Gold)
```

Here I've rearranged the disjuncts of the WHERE clause and used Rule 6 to put the first two of them in parentheses. The interesting thing is that in those first two disjuncts, we have both dcode = A and the negation of that predicate, and also that we have a statement of the type shown on the left-hand side of Rule 10. So using Rule 10, we can transform this intermediate form of the original WHERE clause into the following:

```
WHERE ((dcode = A OR NOT-dcode = A) AND
(dcode = A OR status = Silver))
OR (dcode = Y AND status = Gold)
```

Notice the component (dcode = A OR NOT-dcode = A). No one would write that as part of a WHERE clause, because it wouldn't filter out anything. Every row in the Customer table (barring nulls) would meet that condition. And yet implicit in the original WHERE clause was just that component.

So since (dcode = A OR NOT-dcode = A) is always true (is a tautology), and is part of a conjunction, the truth value of the conjunction depends on the other conjunct, and only on the other conjunct. Therefore, we can simply drop out the tautology because the truth of the conjunction will then be determined by the truth of the other conjunct. So we get:

```
WHERE (dcode = A OR status = Silver)
OR (dcode = Y AND status = Gold)
```

Of course, some SQL optimizers will be clever enough to do this translation for us, before the DBMS begins to use the clause to search the database. But I suspect that not all optimizers will be that clever. And with arbitrarily more complex clauses, we could certainly come up with simplifications on our own that would not be derived by any given optimizer.

Another reason for doing this propositional logic ourselves is that the simplified results are often surprising, and therefore provide insight into what is really being requested. If the clause was supplied to us by someone else, we can then use its simplification as feedback, asking whether it means the same thing as the original clause. If it doesn't, something's wrong — specifically, that the person supplying the clause didn't state what he really meant.

For example, if we look at the original form of the WHERE clause, we see that we have (dcode = A) as one disjunct, and (NOT-dcode = A AND status = Silver) as another disjunct. But in the final simplification, we have:

```
WHERE (dcode = A OR status = Silver)
OR (dcode = Y AND status = Gold)
```

And we can prove that this simplification is valid with the following truth table. We can ignore (dcode = Y AND status = Gold) because it is the same disjunct in the original and final form of the WHERE clause. So what we need to prove is that (dcode = A OR (NOT-dcode = A AND status = Silver)) has the same truth conditions as (dcode = A OR status = Silver). So let X be dcode = A, and Y be status = Silver.

X	Y	X∨(~X∧Y)	(X∨Y)
T	T	T	T
T	F	T	T
F	T	T	T
F	F	F	F

FIGURE 4.7

Validating a Transformation.

Any system of logic has two main "manipulation" components (the same sense of "manipulation" used in "Data Manipulation Language"). One component are the valid transformations on wffs. With propositional logic, those wffs are statements, the linguistic objects to which truth values may be applied. Figure 4.6 lists the transformation rules of propositional logic.

RULES OF INFERENCE

The other component are the deductively valid arguments that can be constructed in the logic. An *argument* is the derivation of a statement from one or more other statements – equivalently, the derivation of one wff from one or more other wffs. The derived statement/wff is the conclusion of the argument; the statements/wffs it is derived from are the premises of that argument.

The supreme responsibility which any system of deductive logic has is to never permit a false conclusion to be derived from true premises. This means that from a set of statements that are true, all other statements derived by means of transformation rules or inference rules will also be true.

The following are some *rules of inference* used in many systems of propositional logic. All of them fulfill this responsibility, as do the transformation rules listed in Figure 4.6. These inference rules permit us to add a statement to the set of statements consisting of the premises of the argument and any previously derived statements.[8]

$$X∧Y$$
$$\# X$$

FIGURE 4.8

Rule of Simplification.

The semantics of this rule is that if we know that both X and Y are true, then we can be sure that X is true. The syntax of this rule (expressed as a function in a string manipulation program, for example) is that if we have (X ∧ Y) as one line of an argument, then we can write down X as a new line.

---

[8]I use the pound sign (#) as the metalinguistic symbol indicating a statement derived by a rule of inference. The statements which do not have a pound sign are the premises of the argument, and the pound-signed statement is the conclusion. These inference rules are really argument schemas, not arguments, because the Xs, Ys, and Zs can stand for any atomic statement or for any arbitrarily complex compound statement.

$$
\begin{array}{l}
\text{X} \\
\text{Y} \\
\text{\# X} \wedge \text{Y}
\end{array}
$$

FIGURE 4.9

Rule of Conjunction.

The rule of conjunction says that from X and Y, we can derive $(X \wedge Y)$.[9] So if a string manipulation program that includes this rule finds two lines, one X and the other Y, it can generate a new line $(X \wedge Y)$. Since this rule could be applied by a program to any conjunction, no matter how complex the conjunction and how complex any of its conjuncts, then although the rule itself may seem trivially obvious, it can still be a very useful rule.

$$
\begin{array}{l}
\text{X} \\
\text{\# X} \vee \text{Y}
\end{array}
$$

FIGURE 4.10

Rule of Addition.

The rule of addition says that from X, we can derive $(X \vee Y)$. For example, if it's true that water only flows downhill, then it's also true that either water only flows downhill or the sun is 10 million miles from the earth. (There is no requirement that an added disjunct be a true statement.)[10]

$$
\begin{array}{l}
\text{X} \rightarrow \text{Y} \\
\text{X} \\
\text{\# Y}
\end{array}
$$

FIGURE 4.11

Rule of Modus Ponens.

The rule of modus ponens says that from $(X \rightarrow Y)$, and also X, we can derive Y. This is the most widely-used rule of inference in propositional logic. From the truth table for $(X \rightarrow Y)$, we know that the one and only case in which $(X \rightarrow Y)$ is false is the case where X is true and Y is false. Since our premises are that $(X \rightarrow Y)$ is true, and that X is also true, we know that Y cannot be false.

$$
\begin{array}{l}
\text{X} \rightarrow \text{Y} \\
\sim \text{Y} \\
\text{\# } \sim \text{X}
\end{array}
$$

FIGURE 4.12

Rule of Modus Tollens.

---

[9]Here I use "can derive" as a way of condensing a statement of the semantics and a separate statement of the syntax of a rule of inference. "From .... can derive" is part of the metalanguage used to define the rules. In addition, "and" and "or" are also part of the metalanguage although, of course, "∧" and "∨" are not. They are part of the object language, the symbolic system we are defining.

[10]Some mathematicians, especially those known as intuitionists, deny that this is a valid inference rule. It seems to them a way to introduce arbitrary statements that clearly do not "follow from", and are not "inferable from", the original set of statements. But since Y cannot validly be derived from $(X \vee Y)$, we can never get Y on a line by itself. This is semantically equivalent to never being able to assert that Y is true, so the intuitionists' worries are (from this point of view) groundless.

The rule of modus tollens says that from $(X \rightarrow Y)$ and $\sim Y$, we can derive $\sim X$. It is the corollary of modus ponens. From the truth table for $(X \rightarrow Y)$, we know that the one and only case in which $(X \rightarrow Y)$ is false is the case where X is true and Y is false. Since our premises are that $(X \rightarrow Y)$ and $\sim Y$ are both true, we know that X cannot be true.

$$X \rightarrow Y$$
$$Y \rightarrow Z$$
$$\# X \rightarrow Z$$

FIGURE 4.13

Rule of Chain Deduction.

The rule of chain deduction expresses the transitivity of material implication. It says that from $(X \rightarrow Y)$ and $(Y \rightarrow Z)$, we can derive $(X \rightarrow Z)$.

$$X \vee Y$$
$$\sim X$$
$$\# Y$$

FIGURE 4.14

Rule of Disjunctive Simplification.

The rule of disjunctive simplification says that from $(X \vee Y)$, and $\sim X$, we can derive Y. For example, if it's true that either Mike or Steve went to Harvard, and also that Mike went to Stanford (in other words, that Mike didn't go to Harvard), then it follows that it's Steve who went to Harvard.

Usually, systems of propositional logic use only a few rules of inference. It is interesting to note that none of the rules of inference for material implication are necessary. Since $(X \rightarrow Y)$ is equivalent to $(\sim X \vee Y)$, we can transform any statement containing $(X \rightarrow Y)$ into a statement containing $(\sim X \vee Y)$. In particular, the full functionality of propositional logic is possible in a system in which only conjunction, disjunction and negation are used to form statements — a system such as SQL, for example. In such a system, the only rules of inference that would apply are those that warrant the derivation of a statement from one or more other statements when all compound statements are expressed with the connectives "$\wedge$", "$\vee$" and "$\sim$", and with no other connectives.

PREDICATE LOGIC

Logic is a set of rules for deriving true statements from true statements. In one form of logic, those statements are atomic units that can't be split apart. That is propositional logic. But another form of logic operates on components of those statements. Those components are the subjects and predicates of those statements, and that form of logic is predicate logic.

Predicate logic begins with the insight that a statement picks something out, and then says something about it. What is picked out is the *subject* of the statement, and what is said about it is the *predicate*.

To return to an earlier example, "Some people are allergic to rosewood" is a statement; it is either true or false. In that statement, we can distinguish three components. One is what is picked out — "people". The second is what is said about people — that they "are allergic to rosewood". So people are the subject, and "are allergic to rosewood" is the predicate.

The third component is the *quantifier*. It's the "some" component of the statement. It's an essential part of the statement because if all we say is "People are allergic to rosewood", it won't be clear if we are talking about all people, or only about some people. If we are talking about all people, the statement is false. But if we are talking about only some people, the statement is true. And so predicate logic uses two quantifiers, "some" and "all". The standard symbols for these quantifiers are, respectively, "∃" and "∀".

Quantifiers *govern* variables. They specify, for each variable in a statement, whether the statement is true for *all* possible values of the variable, or only for *some* of those values. When all variables in a statement are governed by quantifiers, the statement is a *fully quantified statement*. When a specific value is assigned to each of the variables in a fully quantified statement, those variables are *bound* to those values, and the result is a *fully instantiated statement*.

The statements expressed by rows in a relational table result from binding the ordered set of variables in the header row with the ordered set of values in the non-header rows. So to simplify the terminology, instead of referring to header rows as quantified statements, I will call them *statement schemas*; and instead of referring to the results of binding the variables in statement schemas to specific values as instantiated statements, I will call them *statements*.

Returning to our rosewood example, suppose that we are talking about some people, not about all people. In that case, we can paraphrase our statement as follows: "Some things are people and are allergic to rosewood". And now we can use a variable to represent *things*, in the widest sense of the word: people, dogs, cliffs, ideas, suppositions, photon pairs, vacations, bank deposits, etc. All that's required to be a thing is to be distinguishable from other things of the same kind. I'll use the traditional "x", "y", etc. to represent these variables.

Next, we have two predicates: "is a person", and "is allergic to rosewood". I'll use the traditional way of representing predicates, as capital letters. Let "P" stand for "is a person" and "R" stand for "is allergic to rosewood". Then we can express "Some people are allergic to rosewood" in predicate logic notation as:

$$(\exists x)(Px \wedge Rx)$$

(Pronounced "For some x, Px and Rx", or "There exists an x such that x is P and x is R".)

This is an *existentially quantified statement*. In standard systems of predicate logic, the "some" quantifier is taken as the claim that at least one such thing as is described in the statement exists — hence the name "existential quantification".

If our statement had been "All people are allergic to rosewood", its symbolic representation would have been:

$$(\forall x)(Px \rightarrow Rx)$$

(Pronounced "For all x, Px implies Rx", or "For all x, if x is P, then x is R".)

Here, material implication is used. So this statement could also be read back into English as "If anything is a person, then it is allergic to rosewood", or more tendentiously as "For every thing, if it is a person, then it is allergic to rosewood". It is this reading which gives this form of quantification its name: *universal quantification*. With universal quantification, there is no assumption that anything having the first predicate (Px, called the *antecedent*) really exists, only that *if* anything exists that has that predicate, then that thing also has the other predicate (Rx, called the *consequent*).[11]

In the Relational Paradigm, universal quantification is not used. But there is an equivalence — a pair of transformation rules — that allow us to say the same thing without using universal quantification. It is analogous to the deMorgan's rules for propositional logic.

The first transformation rule is that if a statement isn't true of everything, then there's something it isn't true of. The second is that if there is nothing a statement is true of, then it's not true of anything.

$$\sim(\forall x)Px \; [=] \; (\exists x)\sim Px$$
$$\sim(\exists x)Px \; [=] \; (\forall x)\sim Px$$

FIGURE 4.15

Universal/Existential Quantification Transformation Rules.

These four formulae (two on each side of the metalinguistic "[=]") are pronounced:

- It is not the case that, for all x, x is P.
- There is an x such that it is not the case that x is P.
- It is not the case that there is an x such that x is P. And
- For all x, it is not the case that x is P.

The metalinguistic operator says that the first two formulae are equivalent, and that the last two formulae are also equivalent. Equivalent formulas can be substituted one for the other, in any formula or string of formulas, *salve veritate* (preserving truth values).[12] Strictly speaking, however, we can use the first equivalence to derive the existentially-quantified statement only given the assumption that at least one x does exist.

More colloquially yet: if not everything is P, then something isn't P; and if there isn't anything that is P, then nothing is P.

As with propositional logic, predicate logic consists of both transformation rules and of rules of inference. And while the Relational Paradigm makes heavy use of the transformation rules of propositional logic, it uses neither the transformation rules nor inference rules of predicate logic. Instead, it uses predicate logic to formulate queries as *partially instantiated existentially quantified statements*.

STATEMENTS AND STATEMENT SCHEMAS

A statement schema contains quantified variables. When a value is bound to each of those variables, the result is a statement. But instead of being a statement about some things, or about all

---

[11] An excellent discussion of the logical assumption that "some" has existential import while "all" does not, can be found in (Paul Vincent Spade, 1996, pp. 15–18).

[12] Although not necessarily preserving truth values in such special contexts as propositional attitudes or beliefs. For example, it may be true that John believes that the morning star is the planet Venus, and also true that John believes that the evening star is not the planet Venus, thinking that the morning star and the evening star are different astronomical objects.

things, it is a statement about a particular thing. These are the kind of statements that populate relational databases.

For example, consider the Part table of Chapter 1, reproduced here as Figure 4.16. Each row in this table is an ordered set of values which, when substituted for the ordered set of variables in the statement schema of the table, makes a true statement. For example, the statement corresponding to the second row of the Part table is: "there exists a part such that its part id is P2, its part number is A02, its part name is 'axle' and its unit price is $4.50".

```
Part
p-id p-nbr p-nm    p-upr
P1   W45   wheel   $3.25
P2   A02   axle    $4.50
P3   C01   chassis $13.25
```

FIGURE 4.16

A Part Table.

Expressed in predicate logic, the statement schema for this table is:

$$(\exists x)(Px \wedge Qx \wedge Rx \wedge Sx)$$

where P, Q, R and S are the respective column headings of the four columns of the Part table.

But this is something of a fudge because the columns of a relational table are not predicates. They are sets of predicates, and the members of those sets are values from the domains of those columns. So we should use a distinct variable for each of those columns. In that case, the statement schema for the Part table is:

$$(\exists x)(\exists y)(\exists z)(\exists w)(Px \wedge Qy \wedge Rz \wedge Sw)$$

With the predicates representing the columns of the table, this schema is pronounced "There exists an x, y, z, and w such that x is a part identifier, y is a part number, z is a part name and w is a part unit price". Each row of the Part table, then, is an ordered set of values for, respectively, x, y, z and w. When those values are bound to those variables, the result is a true statement about an instance of a type — in this case, about a specific part.

This shows how the relational Select operator works. With that operator, a *partially instantiated statement schema* is presented to the DBMS, and the job of the DBMS is to return a set of zero or more rows whose values match the values in that partial instantiation (according to whatever comparison operator is used). With the other values of those rows bound to the other variables in the statement schema, the result in each case is a true statement in which one or more predicates are ascribed to an instance of the type represented by the table. For example:

$$(\exists x)(\exists y)(\exists z)(\exists w)(Px \wedge Qy \wedge Rz \wedge Sw = \$4.50)$$

will return all rows in the Part table whose unit price is $4.50. Each row will bind the remaining variables, resulting in a true statement.

However, we can describe a still more expressive formalism. So far, the variables we have used in our sketch of a predicate logic range over things, i.e. over the universe of whatever can be picked out and counted. Those variables range over the *universal domain*.

But in the Part table, x ranges over the domain of part identifiers, not the universal domain. y ranges over the domain of part numbers, not over a domain that includes the names of Cleopatra's lovers, or the birthdates of all Nobel laureates born in the U.S. in the twentieth century (both being members of the universal domain) — and not of part identifiers or part names or part unit prices, either. And similarly for z and w. None of the variables in the statement schema for a relational table range over the universal domain. Instead, those variables are what are called *typed variables*. Their type is their domain, and the instances of each type are the members of the domain of the corresponding column.

A predicate logic which incorporates types is called, naturally enough, *typed predicate logic*. And it is typed predicate logic that is used to formulate (in SQL, of course) the statement schemas of tables, and the statement schemas based on projections of tables and joins with other tables. A SQL query which searches for all parts with a unit price of $4.50 is not searching a domain which includes female koala bears, or prime numbers between ten and twenty trillion, or customers who have purchased parts with a unit price of $4.50. It is searching a domain of parts, and only of parts.

But unless and until we are ready to formalize relationships among these types, the most straightforward way to represent types in predicate logic is simply to make predicates of them. So in the statement schema for the Part table, which is:

$$(\exists x)(\exists y)(\exists z)(\exists w)(Px \land Qy \land Rz \land Sw)$$

P, Q, R and S represent the types, respectively, Part Identifier, Part Number, Part Name and Part Unit Price.[13] And the table definition for the Part table, in the database catalog, represents the type Part, and associates that statement schema with that type.

LOGIC AND THE RELATIONAL PARADIGM

Both propositional and predicate logic are part of the Relational Paradigm. We use them to tell the DBMS what data we are looking for.

The Relational Paradigm uses typed predicate logic to express its statement schemas. Partially instantiated statement schemas are directions to a DBMS to pick out all rows (either rows of a single table, or instantiations of a set of columns produced by the relational Project and Join operators) that match the pattern expressed by the partially-instantiated schema.

The predicates of WHERE clauses are value assignments to the variables of the statement schemas specified by the SQL statements they occur in. They provide the instantiations of some of the variables in those schemas.

The propositional logic operators AND, OR and NOT allow us to combine these value assignments. An OR between two sets of predicates in a WHERE clause distinguishes two partial instantiations of the same statement schema. It is part of a SQL statement that is a "two-for-one offer" — one SQL statement which will qualify rows which satisfy either of two partial instantiations of a common statement schema.

---

[13]As I will explain in the next chapter, I will capitalize the names of types but leave the names of their instances un-capitalized.

But what of extensions to the Relational Paradigm? In what sense does the incorporation of bitemporality into the Relational Paradigm amount to an extension of that paradigm?

In one sense, a vast amount of the work on computer databases, within computer science, is work done to extend the Relational Paradigm. That sense is that nearly all work presumes that the basic structures for data in databases are sets, that tables are sets whose members constitute a time-varying relation on the Cartesian Product of properties or relationships expressed as columns and typed by means of column domains.

In a stronger sense, we can distinguish extensions from elaborations. Elaborations are less central; extensions are part of the "core" of the paradigm. My view is that adding bitemporality to the Relational Paradigm affects the core of the paradigm. One reflection of that is that adding bitemporality breaks down the one object to one row correlation which has been central to the Relational Paradigm since its inception. We will see more of this later.

GLOSSARY LIST

assertion	instance	subject
atomic statement	predicate	thing
existentially-quantified statement	statement schema statement	type

THE RELATIONAL PARADIGM: ONTOLOGY

5

In Philosophy, *ontology* is the study of being. Historically, ontologies have turned out to be lists of a small number of closely related categories such that everything that is said to exist can be found in one or more of those categories. Democritus, for example, said that the world is made up of indivisible particles called atoms (*atomos*), and that everything we see around us is a combination of those atoms. Plato said that the things we see around us are less real than the Ideas or Forms (*eidos*) which they exemplify; for example, that there is an abstract Idea or Form of triangularity which is more real, and certainly more perfect, than any triangle anyone could draw, no matter how carefully. For example, if I say "I drew a better triangle than you did", that seems to imply that there is something that our two drawings are drawings of; that is, that there *is* something that our two drawings are drawings of, that something being the *real* triangle. How else could we tell whose drawing was better unless there was a standard to compare them to?

Within the last few decades, what are also called ontologies have become a topic for discussion within the computer science community. Although there is little agreement, except in very general terms, about what these kinds of ontologies are, most researchers working in this field would agree with Tim Gruber's definition of an ontology as "... a formal, explicit specification of a shared conceptualisation." (Gruber, 1993).

The difference between the classical ontologies that philosophers study and the ontologies of computer scientists lies in the "formal" part of Gruber's definition. So I will distinguish them by calling the latter *formal ontologies*. What makes an ontology formal is that it can be expressed in a system of logic as a set of axioms and the theorems that can be derived from them. As a result, every statement within the ontology can be formally proved to be consistent with all the other statements also in that ontology.[1] When software carries out these proofs, the process is called *automated inferencing*, and the software is called an *inference engine*. The set of formalized statements is called a *knowledge base*, and the expression of statements in this way is called *knowledge representation*.

The Relational Paradigm Ontology is a set of categories which interpret the mathematical structures of sets and relations, as they are used in relational databases. It is a very modest ontology, far smaller than most ontologies under development today.

The mapping between the ontology and the mathematics of a relational database is the assignment of a category in the ontology to each of the structures described by the mathematics.

---

[1]To avoid complications whose discussion would be outside the scope of this book, the reader may assume that the sets of statements I am discussing are monotonic.

Assigned these categories, these structures become the tables, rows, columns, domains, primary keys, foreign keys and non-keys of a relational database.

Of course, the ontology of every database will be different. The ontology of a Product database will be different from the ontology of a Customer database, for example. However, at a high level, these and all other databases share a common ontology.

Ontologies at such high levels are called *upper-level ontologies*. Many upper-level ontologies have been proposed, and many are currently under active development. But the upper-level ontology I will describe in the remainder of this chapter is not a *prescriptive* ontology. It is a *descriptive* one. It is an upper-level ontology which has been implicitly used and also intensively studied since well before the advent of relational databases and is, in fact, in almost all important respects Aristotelian.

This ontology is common to all relational databases, and so I refer to it as the Relational Paradigm Ontology. But its roots go deep — back to Aristotle for its first explicit expression; and its scope is wide constituting, in fact, a *folk ontology* shared by nearly all human cultures and expressed in nearly all human languages.

The concepts developed in this ontology will help us understand what we are doing when we deploy such relational constructs as tables, rows and columns. And conversely, our familiarity with these database constructs will help us understand what the key concepts in this ontology mean.

I should more properly say that the Relational Paradigm Ontology is a *fragment* of an upper-level folk ontology. Although it is a core fragment, it is far from complete. Some areas in which it is incomplete include:

- *Space*. Spatial concepts, such as region, dimensionality, location, distance, relative position, containment, and surfaces and interiors, are not included.
- *Mind*. Mental concepts, such as mind itself, perception, belief, other propositional attitudes, knowledge, and plans and goals, are not included.
- *Thematic Roles*. Roles such as agent, patient, instrument, donor and recipient, and cause and effect, are not included.

The reason these concepts are not included is not that I have overlooked them. It is that the Relational Paradigm does not employ them. If these concepts are to be included in a particular database, doing so is a matter for the developers designing and implementing the database.

Also, the Relational Paradigm Ontology's inclusion of the concept of time is not extensively developed. It assumes that time is what is measured by the clock ticks of a computer, thus finessing many important issues about the nature of time. It develops this basic notion into the concept of time periods which are continuous located sequences of clock ticks which have a stated semantics in which they exist as part of the same temporal dimension. It employs this notion by associating time periods from two temporal dimensions with rows of data, and by extending entity and referential integrity to apply to the data thus bitemporalized. It completes its account of time by including a taxonomy of the Allen relationships that obtain between pairs of time periods on the same timeline.

I begin by discussing two of the most basic concepts of the Relational Paradigm Ontology — types and instances.

TYPES AND INSTANCES

I will discuss *types* and *instances* from four different perspectives.[2] They are:

- data modeling;
- Philosophy;
- set theory; and
- logic and language.

A DATA MODELING PERSPECTIVE

The concepts of type and instance are often used in data modeling, and in object-oriented programming as well. Consider the well-known data modeling construct of a Party entity and its two immediate subtypes, Person and Organization. Each of these entities is the realization, in a data model, of one of three types: Party and its two subtypes Person and Organization.[3] Every instance of these three entities is . . . . . well, an instance. Every row of the three tables which realize these modeling constructs in an actual database, is an instance of the type represented by its table. In object orientation, the distinction between types and instances is the distinction between classes and objects.

There are many parties but only one Party, many persons but only one Person, many organizations but only one Organization. In the Relational Paradigm, this distinction, within a data model, between types and their instances is the distinction between *entities* and *entity instances*. Within a database, of course, it is the distinction between tables and rows.

A PHILOSOPHICAL PERSPECTIVE

A second way to understand types and instances is based on two concepts borrowed from Philosophy. Types are *universals*, subtypes are types of types, and instances of types are *particulars*. Each universal is what there can be many of. Each particular is what there can be only one of.

Supplier is a universal. Superior, Inc. is a particular which is an instance of that universal. Thus tables represent universals, and rows represent particulars. There are many suppliers, and Superior, Inc. is one of them. As a type of company with which another company does business, Supplier is one of those types. There is only one such type.

It might seem, then, that T22 is a particular which is an instance of the universal Supplier Type. If that were true, then columns, like tables, would represent universals, and column values, like rows, would represent particulars. But things aren't so straightforward.

T22 is not a particular. It is a universal, and there is only one such universal. It is, in fact, a universal which is a *subtype* of Supplier Type. There are many universals which are subtypes of Supplier Type, T22 being just one of them. But there can be multiple instances (instantiations) of that specific type, the T22 type of each T22 supplier being one of those instances. Each of those instances is a particular of the universal T22. On the other hand, there aren't multiple instances of Superior, Inc.

---

[2]In much of the philosophical and logical literature, the distinction between types and instances is called the distinction between *types* and *tokens*.

[3]Names of types, from now on will, in general, be capitalized. By the same token, names of universals will be capitalized.

Superior is one thing, one company, and so there is only one instance of it. Superior is not a subtype of the universal Supplier. It is an instance of the type Supplier, a particular of that universal.[4]

Here is a perhaps simpler example. There are many colors. Color is a universal. Let's say that one of those colors is a specific shade of green, for example the color RGB-82-213-29. I'll just call this specific color "green".

I am holding a leaf in my hand. It is an instance of the universal Leaf. Its color is green. This specific leaf I am holding in my hand can be found nowhere else in the world. But the color green can be found in lots of places in the world — in other leaves, as a color on 2014 Toyota Prius automobiles, and so on.

So a specific leaf is a particular of the universal Leaf. There can be only one of each specific leaf. But a specific color is not a particular, although ordinary usage may call it a particular color. It is not a particular because there can be many instances of that specific color. So Green is a universal, and the greenness of every green leaf is a particular.

Universals and particulars are concepts at the heart of classical ontology. For nearly a thousand years, during the medieval period of European history, the central debate in ontology was about whether only particulars exist, or whether universals exist as well and, if universals do exist, in what sense they exist. For example, *is there* a color green? Does that specific color *exist*? Or is it just that we have observed a similarity in color among different things that do exist, and used the term "green" to designate that similarity?

Suppose we say that there is such a color, that such a color really exists. If it really exists out there in the world, it's a strange kind of existent, one that exists as a myriad of spatially-temporally unconnected pieces found all around the world — in leaves, other growing things, cars, and other man-made products, and so on. If that color really exists out in the world, then it's a strange kind of existent in another sense, too, because it exists only *as* a color that something else *has*. That shade of green is the color of something, say a green car. But that car isn't a car *of* something. A car isn't something that something else *has*. It's just a car.

Suppose that, in spite of these difficulties, we decide to say that the color green does exist. But since it doesn't exist in the straightforward sense that ordinary things exist, what can we say about the sense in which it does exist? For example, does it exist in the mind and only in the mind? That is, is green an idea? If so, there must be as many instances of green as there are people who have ideas of it. Or does green have some kind of non-physical extra-mental existence? Perhaps, as some medieval philosophers argued, it exists in the mind of God, who uses it as a pattern when He (She) creates and sustains the existence of individual things.

A SET THEORETIC PERSPECTIVE

A third way to understand types and instances is based on set theory. A type of anything is a collection of like things, and those like things are the instances of that type. The collection is the set of all things which are similar in a relevant respect. A subtype is a set all of whose members are also members of the type it is a subtype of. An instance is something, some *thing*, that is a member of a set.

---

[4]Supplier Type should not be confused with the type Supplier. The type Supplier has, in this discussion at least, no subtypes. Instead, it has instances, such as Superior, Inc. and Acme, Inc. Supplier Type has, in this discussion, subtypes such as T15 and T22. T15 and T22 are types which do have instances. Thus, some universals have particulars only indirectly, by means of intermediate universals. Other universals (the leaf nodes of a hierarchy, for example), have particulars directly.

What all the customers in demographic region B have in common is that they are customers in demographic region B. The collection of all and only the customers in demographic region B is a set. The collection of all and only the customers in demographic region B who also have a customer status of Silver is a subset of that set.

A LOGIC AND LANGUAGE PERSPECTIVE

A fourth way to understand types and instances is based on language. Types are the predicates of sentences which are instantiations of existentially-quantified statement schemas, and instances are the subjects of those sentences. Particulars (instances) are what those sentences are about; they are the subjects of those sentences. Universals (types) are what those sentences say about them, i.e. what features those sentences ascribe to them. They are the predicates of those sentences.

It used to be thought that, prior to Frege, formal logic was limited to the forms of the Aristotelian syllogism. But the last several decades have revealed that the work on logic done by medieval philosophers was extremely sophisticated, (see Spade, 1996) as was earlier work done by the Stoic philosophers. (See Mates, 1953).

More will be said about this linguistic perspective on the Relational Paradigm in the next chapter.

AN ANALOGY

Filing cabinets were used and sometimes still are used by businesses to contain different kinds of forms. Purchase orders were kept in one filing cabinet, and invoices in a different one. The filing cabinet corresponds to a type, and each filled-out form in that filing cabinet is an instance of that type. Later on, when computers began to be used to manage data, this same distinction was physically realized in terms of files and their records. That appears to be the etymology of the terms "file" and "record", as in "computer files and the records they contain".

SUMMARY

We have now distinguished types and instances in four ways. In data modeling terms, types are entities and instances are entity instances. In philosophical terms, types are universals and instances are particulars. In set-theoretic terms, types are sets and instances are members of those sets. In grammatical terms, types are predicates and instances are subjects. We have also noted that, in database terms, types are tables and instances are rows. This is summarized in Table 5.1.

Table 5.1 Types and Instances	
Types	**Instances**
Entities	Entity instances
Universals	Particulars
Sets	Members
Predicates	Subjects
Tables	Rows

INSTANCES AND IDENTITY

From set theory, we know that every member of a set is distinct from every other member. In set theory, there must be something about every member of a set that distinguishes it from every other member. I will call that distinguishing something the *identity* of the set member.

Identities may be strong or weak. A *strong identity* is one which "sticks with" the thing it identifies. Something that has a strong identity can, if encountered on multiple occasions, be identified each time as the same thing that was encountered on those other occasions. Serial numbers on manufactured items, for example, provide a strong identity. Strong identity supports re-identification.

A *weak identity* is an identity which does not support re-identification. Weak identities often rely on distinguishing characteristics that are specific to the occasion on which something is encountered.[5] "The man with the red tie across the street from us" will usually pick out one particular person each time that phrase is used. But it's not likely to identify the same person every time it's used; and as soon as that person crosses the street, or shows up again wearing a different tie, it won't identify him any longer.

THE RELATIONAL PARADIGM ONTOLOGY: ARISTOTELIAN ROOTS

A statement does two things. It picks something out, and it says something about it. In the statement "Superior, Inc. is a type 22 supplier", what is picked out is the Superior corporation, and what is said about it is that it is a type 22 supplier.

In terms of syntax, the part of a statement that picks something out is the subject, and the part of a statement that says something about it is the predicate. But what is the ontological difference that corresponds to this grammatical distinction?

ARISTOTLE ON SUBSTANCE

In classical ontology, there is a distinction between two kinds of things. One kind are things that exist on their own. Aristotle called something that exists on its own a *substance (ousia)*, and it is what there is in the world that corresponds to the subject of a statement. *Primary substances* are individual things, like specific customers, or parts, or invoices. But there are also *secondary substances*, which are types of things. Customer is a type; it is the type of all and only those specific things that are customers.

This distinction between primary and secondary substances exists in the Relational Paradigm as the distinction between relational tables and their rows. The secondary substance Customer is represented as a table. The primary substances which are individual customers are represented as rows in that table. And so we have yet one more way to distinguish types from instances, a way based on the *categories* of Aristotle's logic and ontology.

---

[5]Although the terms "strong identity" and "weak identity" are my own, anyone wishing to investigate the distinction should google on the terms "indexicals" and "open sentences". Strong identity tolerates no unbound variables; weak identity does. Strong identity does not rely on indexicals; weak identity does.

Every primary substance can be distinguished from all other instances of the same secondary substance. So every customer can be distinguished from every other customer, from every other instance of the secondary substance Customer. Otherwise, if not all customers could be distinguished from one another, a Customer table would not be a relation because that collection of customers would not be a set.

In ordinary language, *names* and *definite descriptions* are the means of distinguishing one thing from another. In the Relational Paradigm, primary keys and candidate keys play these roles. Primary keys are the names of rows. Single-column candidate keys are the names of referents. Multi-column candidate keys provide definite descriptions of referents.

A secondary substance can be distinguished from other secondary substances by means of what Aristotle called "genus and specific difference". Each secondary substance is a *genus*. Similar secondary substances are those that fall under the same next-level-up genus, and this distinguishes all of them from all the secondary substances that don't fall under that common genus. Among those secondary substances that do fall under that common genus, there is a *specific difference* (i.e. a difference in species) that distinguishes each of them from the others. For example, both octagons and triangles are polygons; the specific difference that distinguishes them is the number of sides each has. To use an example Aristotle used, both men and dogs are animals; the specific difference that distinguishes men from dogs (and from all other animals) is rationality.

In the Relational Paradigm, every relational table is a set. As a set, it has a set membership criterion. This criterion is satisfied by every primary substance which is a member of that set, and by no primary substance which is not a member of that set. That is, this criterion is true of everything that is a member of that set, and is false of everything else.

This criterion is the specific difference that distinguishes the secondary substance which is the set from all other secondary substances which have the same parent secondary substance. That parent secondary substance is the genus under which all those secondary substances are grouped. So secondary substances have an identity, just as primary substances do. The identity of a secondary substance is its genus and its specific difference.

All of the primary substances which satisfy the set membership criterion of the genus constitute the *universe of discourse* from which potential members of a secondary substance are chosen. For example, if Supplier and Customer are subtypes of Party, then all the individual instances of Party constitute the universe of discourse for Suppliers and Customers, and every instance (primary substance) of Supplier or Customer (secondary substances) is also an instance of Party.

ARISTOTLE ON ACCIDENTS

Accidents are the features that things have. Some accidents are properties of things, like size, weight, or location. Other accidents are relationships among things, like cause and effect, being larger or smaller than, or being the giver or receiver of something. In the Relational Paradigm, this distinction between properties and relationships is as far as the categorization of accidents goes. Aristotle, however, distinguished nine categories of accidents. They are features of substances, the things which primarily exist. This makes a total of ten categories, which are:

- Substance
- Quantity
- Property

- Relationship
- Possession
- Location in space
- Location in time
- The arrangement of the constituent parts of a whole
- Being an actor
- Being acted on

In the Relational Paradigm, in terms of semantics, secondary substances are entities, primary substances are entity instances, and accidents are attributes. In terms of syntax, secondary substances are tables, primary substances are rows, and accidents are columns.

The row-level instances of some columns represent property instances of the primary substance that the row represents. The row-level instances of other columns represent instances of relationship types between that row's secondary substance and another secondary substance. Those columns are property and relationship types, and those row-level instances of those columns are property and relationship instances.

Most medieval philosophers concluded that Aristotle's list needed to be simplified. William of Ockham, in particular, simplified the list to substances, properties and relationships. And so it would be more accurate to say that the Relational Paradigm Ontology being presented here is an Ockhamist ontology, derived from the Aristotelian one.

In these terms, relationships are accidents which are implemented in the Relational Paradigm by means of foreign keys. Properties are accidents which are implemented in that paradigm by means of non-key columns. Primary substances can be uniquely identified, and are represented in that paradigm by means of rows. Secondary substances can also be uniquely identified, and are represented by means of tables.

In fact, this arrangement is not an unfamiliar one. In ordinary language, as I said earlier, primary substances are picked out by means of either names or definite descriptions. For example, "Jack Nicklaus" is a name, and it picks out one specific person. "The golfer who (as of 2014) had won more major championships than anyone else" is a definite description, and it picks out that same person. This definite description describes a property of Jack Nicklaus or, looking at it another way, a relationship between Jack and all other golfers to date.

The work of Aristotle just described constitutes his account of the *structure* of things, and is contained in his early works *Categories* and *De Interpretatione*. Later work, in particular *Metaphysics*, focuses on the *dynamics* of things, in particular on change such as coming into existence, going out of existence, and continuing to exist over time and through various kinds of changes to properties and/or relationships.

I think that this account of the structural elements of Aristotle's ontology — of primary and secondary substances, and of different kinds of accidents — is pretty easy to understand. I think that many of us could have developed many of the same concepts, and made many of the same distinctions, although we would have used the more modern terminology of either the semantics of the Relational Paradigm or of the syntax of that paradigm.

But this does not detract from the significance of what Aristotle did in *Categories*. As obvious as these concepts and distinctions may seem to us today, Aristotle was the first one to articulate them, and his development of these concepts has hardly been improved on since. Many of these concepts seem obvious to us today in large part because these insights of Aristotle have been incorporated as part of the conceptual inheritance of Western thought.

These concepts may seem particularly straightforward to we IT professionals whose specialty is data management. But as I have indicated above, that is at least in part because the conceptual structure of the Relational Paradigm, with which we are all familiar, is strongly based on Aristotelian concepts. (It is not, as far as I know, because Dr. Codd was familiar with the metaphysical and logical works of Aristotle. Rather, it is because Dr. Codd was familiar with set theory, and the resemblances between the axioms of set theory and Aristotle's ontology are particularly strong.)

Here are some examples. A customer is an object, and thus also a referent. Aristotle would call it a primary substance. The status code of a customer is a property of that customer. Aristotle would call it an accident of that primary substance. Customers exist "on their own", but customer status codes do not. We can have a customer without a status code, but not vice versa. Those status codes exist only as the status codes of objects, which do exist on their own, in this case, of customers.

The assignment of a salesperson to a customer is another kind of Aristotelian accident. It is a relationship which that salesperson has with that customer. It is also a relationship which that customer has with that salesperson. While both the customer and the salesperson exist "on their own", the assignment of each to the other does not. Without that customer and that salesperson, that assignment would not exist. But remove that assignment, and the customer and the salesperson continue to exist.

Everything that exists on its own is an instance of a type. Every referent, then, is an instance of the type Referent. Every object is an instance of the type Object. So a customer is an object, and Customer is an indirect subtype of Referent, being (more directly) a subtype of Object. I will call this kind of existence *strong existence* because it is the existence of those kind of things that exist on their own.

Things that do not exist on their own are also instances of types. Called accidents of substances by Aristotle, I will call those things *attributes* of referents. The different types of attributes are different subtypes of the type *Attribute*. So a specific customer's name is an attribute of the Customer-name subtype of Attribute. I will call this kind of existence *weak existence* because it is the existence of things that do not exist on their own.

In summary: types are either Referents or Attributes. The two types of Referents are Objects or Events. The two types of Attributes are Properties and Relationships. Instances are either instances of Referents or instances of Attributes. Instances of Referents are specific things that are referents. Instances of Attributes are either properties of referents, or relationships between referents.

BEYOND THE ARISTOTELIAN ROOTS

There one important way in which the ontology of the Relational Paradigm goes beyond its Aristotelian roots. It is in the distinction between objects and events. Aristotle's primary substances are objects, in the ordinary sense of "object". In fact, Aristotle's technical term is *ousia*, whose pre-technical meaning, in the 4th century BCE, was simply "something that belongs to you".[6]

---

[6]"that which is one's own, one's substance, property". (Liddell and Scott, 1994, p. 579)

In Chapter 1, I introduced the distinction between objects and events. But in a traditional Aristotelian ontology, and also in folk ontology, events are not given the same ontological status as objects. Objects, for Aristotle and for common sense, are ontologically fundamental. They are what is most real. The world is made up of objects.

But I give equal ontological billing to events, and I do so for three reasons. One is personal, based on my long familiarity with Whitehead's ontology, in which events are in fact *more* ontologically basic than objects. This reason, of course, is not really important, but the second and third reasons are.

The second reason is that events, like objects, can have properties and relationships, i.e. can have attributes. Their attributes can't exist without them, just as the attributes of objects can't exist without those objects. So given the most fundamental ontological distinction of all — that between what exists on its own and is the bearer of properties and relationships, and those properties and relationships themselves — and given that both objects and events are the bearers of properties and relationships, I give equal ontological weight to them. For this reason, I need a category which includes both of them and which includes nothing else. That is the category, already introduced, of Referent.

The final reason is that in relational databases, tables are used to represent both Objects and Events, i.e. both types of objects and types of events. In both cases, the columns of those tables represent Attributes of those Objects and Events. The rows of those tables represent instances of those Objects and Events. And the column values of those rows represent instances of those Attributes of those Objects and Events, i.e. attributes of those objects and events. So in the Relational Paradigm Ontology, objects and events are given equal ontological weight.

In summary: where Aristotle has objects as the fundamental ontological category, the Relational Paradigm Ontology has both objects and events. Where Aristotle has nine types of accident, the Relational Paradigm Ontology, with William of Ockham, has two types of attributes — properties and relationships.

THE RELATIONAL PARADIGM ONTOLOGY

Referents, which I will more informally call *things*, are either objects or events. Objects are things that can change over time, like molecules, or customers, or minds. *Events* are things that can't change over time. Events happen, and then they are over.

Every thing is a particular, an instance of some subtype of Referent. As an instance of a type, i.e. as a member of a set, every thing has an identity. So every object is an instance of some subtype of Object and every event is an instance of some subtype of Event, and both objects and events can be distinguished from other objects and events of the same type.

Every thing may also have one or more *attributes*. The attributes which characterize a thing at any point in time constitute the *state* of that thing at that point in time. So whenever one or more attributes of an object change, that object enters a new state. It is recognizably the same object because of its strong identity.

Objects exist *through* time. They come into existence at some point in time, prior to which they do not exist. While they exist, they may change; but throughout these changes, each object retains its identity. Because of this, we can encounter the same object over and over again, at different times. If this were not the case, then every time an object changed, there would be a new object, not a new state of the same object.

Events exist *at* a time. They happen at some point in time, prior to which they do not exist. But once they happen, they are over with. No matter how much time goes by, events never change. Because of this, we can encounter an event only once, that being the one time when it happens. Nonetheless, because they are referents, events have an identity, and also have attributes.

Figure 5.1 shows these ontological categories, and their relationships.

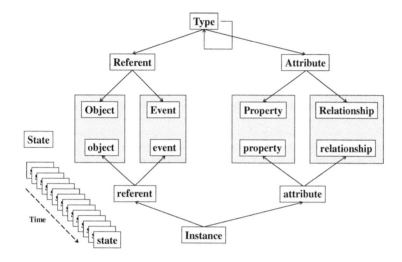

FIGURE 5.1

The Relational Paradigm Ontology.

Here is how to read this diagram. All types are subtypes of Type. There are two immediate subtypes of Type. One them is Referent. Referent has Object and Event as its immediate subtypes. The other immediate subtype of Type is Attribute. Attribute has Property and Relationship as its immediate subtypes. The recursion symbol shown on Type is there to emphasize that any of these types may be subtyped. This will be illustrated in the next section.

Turning now to the lower half of the diagram, instances are either instances of Referents or instances of Attributes. Instances of Referents are referents, specifically either instances of Objects or instances of Events. Instances of Attributes are attributes, specifically either instances of Properties or instances of Relationships. Both referents and attributes are set members. Their sets are the subtypes of Referent and Attribute that they belong to.

Every statement consists of a subject and a predicate. The subject is a referent. The predicate is an attribute. The subject is either a specific object or a specific event. The attribute is either a specific property or a specific relationship.

In the lower-left quadrant of the diagram, States and Time are shown. These components of the ontology will be discussed later in this chapter. Suffice it to say, at this point, that every referent exists in a state, which is the set of its attributes. Objects can exist in a succession of states, but in only one state at a time. Events can exist in only one state.

A MIDDLE LEVEL EXTENSION TO THE RELATIONAL PARADIGM ONTOLOGY

In Figure 5.2, Party, Person and Organization are three subtypes of Object. They extend the Relational Paradigm Ontology into middle-level categories, and the result is a fragment of a *middle-level ontology*. If different types of Persons such as Employees and Consultants were distinguished, and different types of Organizations such as Suppliers and Customers were distinguished, this would extend this ontology fragment into very specific categories, and the result would be a fragment of a *lower-level ontology*.

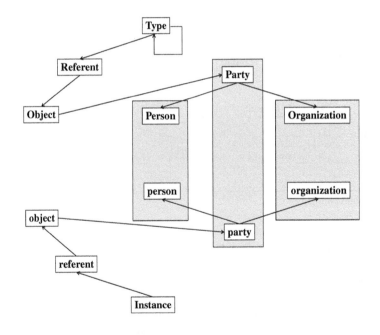

FIGURE 5.2

A Middle-Level Extension to the Relational Paradigm Ontology.

STATES AND CHANGE

Change occurs during events. Events are periods of time in which objects change. In events, only the *current states* of objects are involved. *Change* is a process in which the current states of one or more objects alter the current states of one or more other objects. So a *process* is temporally co-extensive with an event. A nested set of events contains a nested set of processes.

There are also States of course, i.e. types of states. The state of a contract negotiation is a different kind of state than a state of mind. The state of a grain mash as its sugars are converted into alcohol is another kind of state. Correlatively, the processes by which these states succeed one another are different kinds of processes.

So states are the states *of* things. This seems to make *things* more ontologically fundamental than states. Things are what *have* states. No things, no states. On the other hand, things are always *in* a state. This seems to make *states* more ontologically fundamental than things. States are what "contain" things. So no states, no things. I say: let's call it a draw. Things are important. So are the states of those things.

Two states are similar if they are the same set of properties and relationships for the same referent. Another way of saying this is to say that that those similar *temporal states* are *temporal instances* of a single *atemporal state*.

An atemporal state is a specific set of properties and relationships of a specific referent. A temporal state is an atemporal state located in a continuous series of one or more clock ticks along a state-time timeline. For example, `[C1|B|Platinum]` is a tuple of a Cartesian Product which describes an atemporal state of customer C1. If this tuple is instantiated in a row which also has a state-time period, e.g. the row `[Mar14|Dec14|C1|B|Platinum]`, then this row describes a temporal state which is the intersection of that atemporal state with that period of state time.

We have distinguished atemporal states of referents from temporal states by abstracting time from the notion of a series of temporal states. If object X is in state Y in ten non-overlapping sets of one or more series of continuous clock ticks, each pair of adjacent sets having at least one clock tick between them, then there are ten temporal states Y of object X, but only one atemporal state Y.

In the Relational Paradigm, all referents are always in a temporal state − even those represented in nontemporal tables. The rows of nontemporal tables describe the current temporal states of their referents. So the Relational Paradigm Ontology is incomplete without temporal states.

The initial temporal state of an object begins when the object is created, and successive temporal states begin every time a change happens to the object. The last temporal state of an object ends when the object is destroyed, and all other temporal states end every time a change happens to the object. So adjacent temporal states of the same object are distinguished by being temporally located instantiations of different atemporal states. Those atemporal states are states which differ in one or more properties or relationships, but are not themselves located in time.

Like objects, temporal states of objects have *strong identity*. The strong identity of objects is what allows the same object to be identified as the same object throughout a continuous series of clock ticks. It is also what allows the same object to be re-identified as the same object when it appears again after an absence.

The strong identity of temporal states is what allows the same atemporal state of an object to be identified as the same atemporal state whenever it pops up in the *life history* of the object. So one object, with one set of properties and relationships, is one atemporal state of that object. Whenever that object gets like that, it's a temporal instance of that atemporal state. Since no object can be in two states at the same time, the strong identity of a temporal state of a referent is its RefId plus a state-time period. I will call this the *state identifier* of that temporal state, its *StId*.

PRIMARY KEYS NATURAL KEYS, FOREIGN KEYS

Referents have an identity, and so do the rows which represent those referents. Primary keys are the identity of rows. Natural keys are the identity of the things those rows represent. A natural key is a referent identifier. So rows must include both primary keys and RefIds, both of which consist of one or more columns. Sometimes, the same column or columns are used for both the primary key and the RefId of a table.

Foreign keys are references to other tables. So at the level of types, they are subtypes of Relationship. For example, an Owns relationship is a subtype of Relationship or, as we would more naturally say, a kind of relationship. At the level of instances, a foreign key implementing one specific Owns relationship — one instance of Owns — refers to a specific row in a specific table.

OBJECTS, EVENTS AND CHANGE

One way to understand how objects and events weave a basic framework for thinking about the world is this: events are the occasions on which objects change and are changed by other objects. This point, made previously but expanded on here, is illustrated in Figure 5.3.

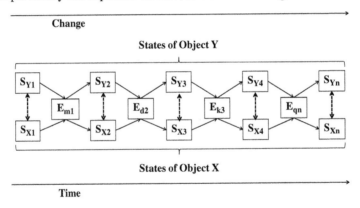

FIGURE 5.3

Objects and the Events in Which They Change.

In Figure 5.3, two objects, X and Y, are shown. The boxes labeled "S" are states of those objects. The boxes labeled "E" are the events in which those objects participate. The subscript numbers (1, 2, 3, n) on all three sets of boxes indicate sequence. The Y subscripts in the top row of state boxes indicate that those states are all states of object Y; and similarly for the bottom row showing object X and its states. The alphabetic subscripts on the event boxes indicate different types of events. An object can participate in different types of events.

The solid arrows show each state of an object being superceded by a new state as the result of that object *participating in* an event. The double-headed dashed-line arrows indicate states of objects that can affect and be affected by other states of objects. Of course, some objects can take part in events without being changed. For instance, they may be objects which, in those events, cause other objects to change but are not themselves changed. Or they may be objects which are instruments by which other objects are changed, without themselves being changed.

The illustration shows that only current states of objects can affect and be affected by other states. Past states of objects don't affect anything, except through their effect, directly or indirectly, on current states. Future states of objects don't affect anything because future states don't yet exist, and what doesn't exist can't affect anything (although, of course, the present anticipation of future states by sentient beings may affect current states of those sentient beings, and through them, the current states of other objects).

Change is what results from a process. It is what goes on "inside" an event. This process is a process of *state transition*. Before an object changes, it is in a given temporal state. It remains in that temporal state until it changes. After it changes, it is in a new temporal state – which may or may not also be an atemporal state that it has been in before. These changes are what go on in the events that happen to the object. This process of state / change / new state occurs over and over again, from when the object begins to exist to when it no longer exists.

Change is the heart of the matter; it is why we need temporal data. If objects aren't like what they used to be like, it's because they have changed. If they aren't like what they will be like, it's because they are going to change. If what they used to be like, and what they are going to be like, is important to us, then it's not enough to keep track just of what they are like right now.

Temporal data is about keeping track of changes to the referents that interest us enough that we represent them in our databases.

ON USING ONTOLOGIES

As I mentioned earlier, much of the ontology developed thus far may seem straightforward to many data management professionals. Most of the value of this ontology may seem to have already been incorporated into the Relational Paradigm, and more specifically into the discipline of logical data modeling.

From that perspective, the lengthy discussion of Aristotle's categories seems to be of historical interest only. But from the dual perspective of data architect and modeler, and also of someone with a background in ontology and logic, I believe that this account of the Relational Paradigm Ontology is of more direct, practical value than that.

The reason is that this account, I believe, can serve as a prolegomenon to a formal ontology. Recursive relationships, for example, can easily be formalized in logic. Formalized in predicate logic, upper-level ontological categories can therefore be extended down the recursion to middle-level and lower-level types and instances, with no loss of logical rigor.

At each level, concepts specific to that level can be incorporated into the formal ontology as new types. As definitions of these types are formalized in terms of primitive concepts and other already-defined concepts, a rich network of semantic relationships is developed and is expressed in predicate logic. In that formalization, inferences can be proposed, and formally proven to be either valid or invalid. In that formalization, this network of concepts is an instance of knowledge representation, called a *knowledge base*; and the software that proves or disproves proposed inferences on this knowledge base – those inferences being, in effect, queries about types – is an *inference engine*.

With respect to the most important concepts for an enterprise, which are the concepts on which run-the-company databases are built, these knowledge bases are formalized *data dictionaries* for each such database. The formal integration of these data dictionaries is a knowledge base for the enterprise. The formalization of those portions of enterprise knowledge bases which are necessary to support the semantic interoperability of data sharing among similar enterprises, is an industry-level knowledge base. And semantic interoperability among industry-level knowledge bases is the benefit provided by upper-level ontologies such as the one I have described here.

The bottom-line value of such ontologies should already be understood by those who have influenced their companies to purchase and use ontology management tools. But here is one simple but ubiquitous example to illustrate the point.

In the nearly twenty companies for which I have worked either as an employee or a contractor, I have not found any company whose business experts could clearly say what a customer was. But the objective these companies all failed to meet was not the objective of producing a definition which those business experts could agree on. Those kinds of definitions were never very hard to come by.

But there are more important kinds of definitions to capture. They are ones that define the criteria which determine whether a given referent, from a given universe of discourse, is or is not an instance of a given type of referent. If a company did produce this "instance of a type" kind of definition of what a customer of theirs is, for example, then they would be able to say, for every person or company who could possibly become a customer, what would have to be true for them to actually become customers, and once they did become customers, what would have to be true for them to remain customers, and what would cause them to be removed as customers.

With definitions like these, our concepts could become measurable and manageable. For example, suppose that we and one of our suppliers wanted to see who has the most customers. We run a SQL COUNT statement on our respective Customer table or tables. Suppose our supplier has 25,367 customers, and we have 18,449 customers. Does our supplier have more customers than we do?

It depends. Suppose our supplier had the rule "Once a customer, always a customer", while we had the rule "A customer who hasn't made an invoiced purchase in five years stops being a customer". Suppose we had the rule "Anyone who responds to a marketing communication of ours counts as a customer", while our supplier had the rule "No one is a customer until they make an invoiced purchase".

So who has the most customers? It depends on what definition of customer we use. But by "definition" here, I do not mean a sentence or two that business experts are comfortable with. I mean the criteria which jointly determine when someone or some organization becomes a customer, and when they stop being a customer. If these criteria are to be found anywhere, they are to be found in the data entry policy manuals of a company — in this case, the policies that govern the process of adding and removing rows in the company's production Customer table.

We can imagine business experts from both companies sitting down and eventually figuring out that they mean different things when they talk about customers. But if both sets of criteria were expressed in a predicate-logic formulated knowledge base, then *software* could discover these incompatibilities, in real time, each time a query about customers in both databases was submitted. When these incompatibilities were later brought to our attention, we could work together to develop a common definition which would say, for purposes of comparing our two databases, what we agree a customer is. And this common definition would not be just a matter of two sets of business experts agreeing to accept the definition. It would be a definition that cross-enterprise query software could use. It would be a definition that *mattered*. Without such definitions, such cross-enterprise queries would be counting apples and oranges. And in the world of today's databases, that is often what they do.

The ability for databases and software to cooperate so that cross-enterprise queries are run against equivalent universes of discourse, so that "customer" means the same thing when a customer query is run against both enterprises' databases, is the *semantic interoperability* of those databases. It is what, in Chapter 15 where I discuss Inmon's definition of a data warehouse, I call the "semantic integration" of those databases.

INTEGRATING THE MATHEMATICS AND ONTOLOGY OF THE RELATIONAL PARADIGM

The mathematics of the Relational Paradigm provides a set of structures, foundational among them sets and set members. The ontology of the Relational Paradigm provides a set of categories, foundational among them types and instances. By mapping these types onto these structures, relational DBMSs can be used to insert, update, delete and retrieve members of those sets / instances of those types.

The highest-level distinction in the Relational Paradigm's ontology is the distinction between referents and their attributes. This distinction is embedded in our folk ontology as the distinction between things and their attributes. It was first formalized by medieval nominalists such as William of Ockham as the distinction between substances (*ousia*), properties of substances, and relationships among substances.[7]

As the upper-two heavy arrows in Figure 5.4 show, Referent is a type which is realized in a relational database by a table, and is defined by the schema row of that table. In fact, Referent is the supertype of all tables in all relational databases. As we saw earlier, every *thing*, i.e. every referent, is an object or an event, and thus every table is an object table or an event table. And so the set represented by any table is a set of things, either objects of a specific type or events of a specific type.

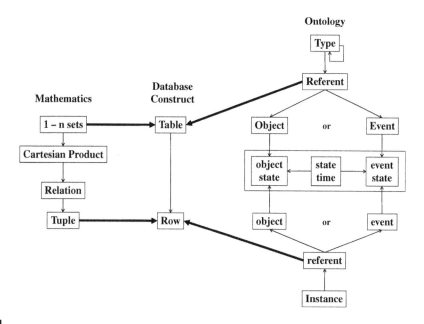

FIGURE 5.4

Mathematics, Ontologies and Databases: Referents.

[7]This is probably more in the way of ontological commitment than Ockham, as a philosopher, was comfortable with. Many scholars think he would have preferred to say that only Aristotle's primary substances exist, and that it was only because, as a Catholic theologian, he believed in the doctrine of transubstantiation, that he needed properties, in particular, to make sense of that doctrine.

The members of those sets are individual things, instances of the type Referent (or Thing). They are what Aristotle called primary substances (*ousia*). For every type of property of a thing, or every type of relationship between one thing and another, there is a set whose members are instances of that type. Thus, if a property of customers is that they have a name, then there is a set whose members are the names of customers.

A Referent, e.g. the set Customer, is associated, via functional dependencies, with one or more Properties and/or Relationships, e.g. with the set of customer names, addresses, status codes, demographic groups, and so on. We can define the Cartesian Product of the members of all these functional-dependency-related sets, and the set of rows making up the corresponding relational table, at any point in time, expresses a subset of that Cartesian Product. That time-varying set of rows is a mathematical relation on that Cartesian Product. Each row in the set is a tuple, and each represents an instance of the Referent represented by the table itself.

There is no need to further recapitulate the material developed earlier in this chapter, and in earlier chapters. The point of Figure 5.4 is to graphically illustrate this beautiful association of a structured ontology with a structured set of mathematical objects. This association, as shown in Figure 5.4, is physically realized in the tables, columns and rows of a relational database to which the mathematics gives a structure that can be managed by propositional and predicate logic, and to which the ontology gives an interpretation which can be expressed as a formalism that can be managed by propositional and predicate logic.

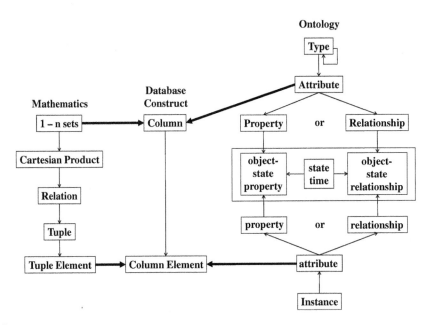

FIGURE 5.5

Mathematics, Ontologies and Databases: Attributes.

Figure 5.5 is a companion illustration to that in Figure 5.4. While relational tables represent sets of *things*, non-surrogate columns in those tables represent sets of *properties* and *relationships* of those things. In a fully normalized database, the non-surrogate columns of a table represent all the attribute types that belong to the referent type represented by the table. Because these are the properties and relationships of the things with which they are associated – things whose types are referent types and whose types are implemented as relational database tables – there is a functional dependency from a set of things of a specific type to each of those sets of properties of a specific type and relationships of a specific type.

The functional dependencies aren't what is fundamental; it is what they represent that is fundamental. A functional dependency is a mathematical relationship which we define to represent the *existence dependency* of properties and relationships on the things they are properties of and relationships of.

As these figures illustrate, the Relational Paradigm's upper-level ontology is a structured ontology, not merely a list of terms used in one another's definitions. That ontology is the framework for a more extensive set of types, ones which at the lower level of the type hierarchies are instantiated as tables.

Instantiation at higher levels of these type hierarchies provides flexible and powerful structures, but ones which have less information about their instances than do instantiations at lower levels of these hierarchies. For example, if the organizational structure of an enterprise is implemented in an Organizational Unit table with a recursive hierarchy, then additional levels of organizational unit can easily be added to the table, and entire subtrees of the organizational hierarchy can easily be *cut* from one node of the tree structure and *grafted* onto another node. But the price paid for this flexibility is that another way must be found to indicate what type each of the organizational units is, and to represent the properties and relationships unique to each type.

On the other hand, a hierarchy of tables might be defined as a set of supertype/subtype related tables, with each level in the hierarchy corresponding to one type of organizational unit, e.g. corporate HQ, division, major department, minor department, etc. This is an implementation of types which occur farther down the type hierarchy whose root node is Referent. It is clearly less flexible, but just as clearly carries more information about organizational units in a more straightforward way.

As a practicing data modeler for several decades, I have made design trade-offs like this throughout my career. This is nothing new to the experienced data modeler. But until recently, I only imperfectly understood what I was doing in making those trade-offs. I now understand those design decisions as choices of where best to link specific ontological types to specific database tables, and I invite the reader to understand them that way as well.

From that perspective, we can see the ordinary everyday work of the data modeler as part of a larger effort to clarify the ontology of our relational databases. That larger effort will eventually lead to formalized ontological structures for specific databases that permit software called *inference engines* to carry out *theorem-proving* on these database-associated ontologies, and thus to finally begin to realize the promise of software-mediated semantic interoperability among databases.

GLOSSARY LIST

assertion time
atemporal state
Attribute
attribute
bitemporal
change
clock tick
current state
Event
event
existence dependency
formal ontology
identity
indexical
instance
life history

natural key
Object
object
ontology
participate in
predicate
Property
property
referent identifier
Referent
referent
Relationship
relationship
semantic
   interoperability
State

state
state identifier
statement
state time
subject
temporal data
temporal dimension
temporal instance
temporal state
thing
Thing
time period
Type
type
universe of discourse

THE RELATIONAL PARADIGM: SEMANTICS

Linguists almost universally regard spoken language as primary, and written language as merely a means of recording spoken language. The Internet may shift that balance, but whether or not it does, written language has importance in its own right. One value of the written word as a substitute for the spoken word is that what we write down can remain available long after the acoustical disturbances of the original utterance have faded away. A second value of the written word as a substitute for the spoken word is that what we write down can be copied, and those copies can be distributed as widely as we like.[1]

Since the time of Thomas Edison, of course, we have had the technology to record spoken language, and later to copy those recordings. But this has not diminished reliance on the written word. I think there are two main reasons for this. One is that we can read faster than we can speak, so we can absorb more information in less time when we read. The second is that we can scan text faster than we can listen to speech, so we can find what we're looking for in less time when we read.

Because this book is about data in databases, it is about written language, not spoken language. In particular, it is about language written down in the restricted syntax of rows in relational tables.

Syntax is about the structures within which pieces of language are assembled. The syntax used in relational databases is very simple. As we saw in Chapter 4, it is the syntax of existentially-quantified statements in typed predicate logic.

Semantics is about how physical things, like strings of characters, tell us about something else, for example how the thirty-five character string "The unit price of part P03 is $5.25" tells us that the unit price of part P03 is $5.25.[2]

These physical things are *signs*. The things beyond themselves that they tell us about are the *things signified*. When the signs can be anything at all, the subject is *semiotics*. When the signs are units of language, the subject is semantics.

Pragmatics is about how language is used. It is about, as the philosopher J. L. Austin said, how to do things with words. (Austin, 1961b) One thing we do with words is to say that something is or is not the case. Other things we do with words are to ask questions, issue commands, make recommendations, make promises, terminate contracts, tell lies, encourage someone else, comfort someone else, and so on.

---

[1]For a beginner's survey of the field of linguistics, see (Burton, Dechaine, Vatikiotis-Bateson, 2012).

[2]This point is perhaps clearer with a font change. Semantics is about how a string of characters like "Τηε υνιτ πριχε οφ παρτ Π03 ισ Ǝ5.25" can tell us that the unit price of part P03 is $5.25.

ROWS, STATEMENTS, ASSERTIONS AND KINDRED NOTIONS

It will be useful, in this chapter, to begin with our conclusions. They are as follows:

1. Every *row* in a relational table is an *inscription*.
2. That inscription is a *declarative sentence*.
3. That declarative sentence can be used to make a *statement*.
4. That statement expresses a *proposition*.
5. Someone may *assert* that a statement is true.
6. Someone may later *withdraw that assertion*.
7. Someone may *assent* to an assertion that a statement is true.
8. Someone may later *withdraw that assent*.
9. Someone may *dissent* from an assertion that a statement is true.
10. Someone may later *withdraw that dissent*.
11. Someone may *take notice* of a statement.

Most of the work in this chapter is to establish the first eight of these conclusions. Dissenting and taking notice are things we do with words that I will not discuss until the penultimate chapter of this book.

A row is an inscription in a relational table. That inscription is a declarative sentence whose syntax is expressed by the schema of that table. If the sentence is free of ambiguities, it expresses a statement. In a conventional table, the presence of that sentence as a row of that table is also taken to represent the assertion, by the party responsible for the statement, that what the statement says is, in fact, true.

Statements may or may not be made with the intent of saying something true. Statements that are made with that intention are *asserted* to be true; they are assertions. Assertions may be withdrawn. But if they are, they are still statements, just ones no longer asserted to be true.

If several statements tell us the same thing, those statements express the same proposition. A *proposition* is the information content of a statement. For example, "John loves Mary" and "Mary is loved by John" are different statements expressing the same proposition. It is an ideal that a database would express, at all times, a consistent set of propositions. But it is beyond the capability of any DBMS to prevent inconsistencies at the level of propositions. It is even beyond the capability of present-day DBMSs to manage statements. The best that today's DBMSs can do is to manage inscriptions, whose interpretation, by us, as statements, is no concern of theirs.

A statement is a specific way of expressing a specific proposition. If several inscriptions are orthographically identical, they express the same statement. For example, "John loves Mary" and "John loves Mary" are two inscriptions that express the same statement. A DBMS can keep orthographically identical inscriptions out of a table. It does so by requiring a substring of those inscriptions, at the same location within the overall string, to be unique across all the rows of that table. So a DBMS can prevent inconsistencies at the level of inscriptions of statements.

A DBMS can also prevent inconsistencies at the level of statements themselves *within a normalized database*. That is because a statement is always about some thing, and all statements about the same type of thing, within a normalized database, are contained in the same table. By enforcing primary key uniqueness, a DBMS can prevent two inscriptions of the same statement from concurrently appearing in a table. And therefore the one inscription of that statement, in that database, is the one and only representation of the statement itself, within that database.

A statement may or may not be asserted. Asserting a statement is making the statement with the intention of saying something that is true, in a context in which it would be unreasonable to interpret you as doing anything else. For example, "A man walks into a bar" is a statement. But in the contexts in which that statement is usually made, it is not an assertion. It's the opening line of a joke.

An assertion of a statement may be withdrawn. If I assert that Johnny Unitas won two Super Bowls and later learn that I was wrong, I will withdraw that assertion.

Let us examine all this now, in more detail.

ROWS, INSCRIPTIONS AND SENTENCES

In the beginning — before syntactic, semantic, or pragmatic analysis is brought to bear — the basic unit of verbal exchange is an *utterance*. At the same level, there is a basic unit of written exchange. It is an *inscription*.

An *utterance* is an acoustical waveform. Components of those waveforms are phonemes of the language. An *inscription* is a set of marks used to write down utterances. In a language based on an alphabet, those marks are letters of the alphabet.

Figure 6.1 shows an inscription. This inscription is a string of twenty characters, which we may assume is stored somewhere on a computer storage device.

```
2375R5-C3857150Smith
```

FIGURE 6.1

A Row as an Inscription.

Inscriptions and utterances are physical objects created with the basic physical units of languages — letters and phonemes. An inscription is a physical object consisting of one or more letters.[3] It has physical properties, such as the physical length of the string of symbols used in the inscription. It also has alphabetical properties, such as the number of letters used in the inscription. But it has no properties beyond physical and alphabetical. For example, in the inscription in Figure 6.1, it looks like the last five characters represent a person's name. But as an inscription, we know nothing about that. As part of that inscription, that five-letter substring is just the last five letters in that inscription, nothing more.

In Figures 6.3, 6.5 and 6.7 below, the strings labeled "Inscription" all look like the string in Figure 6.1. But they are not the same strings, and they are not the same inscriptions. They, and the string in Figure 6.1, are all *orthographically identical*. But they are different physical objects; they are located in different places. Changing one string doesn't change all of them. Removing one string doesn't remove all of them.

---

[3]The units of an alphabet are letters, which represent sounds in which vowels and consonants are distinguished. The units of syllabaries are syllables, which are units in which vowels and consonants are combined; Japanese Katakana is an example. The basic inscriptional units of other languages are units of meaning rather than units of sound, or else are units which are based on both principles; Mandarin Chinese is an example.

So if a row of data is copied from an enterprise data warehouse table to a department-level data warehouse table, and the two rows are character-for-character the same, then we don't have two copies of the same inscription. We have two inscriptions of the same statement.

The header row of a relational table defines the grammatical structure of a sentence, and all rows in a table conform to that grammatical structure. Thus, a row of data is a grammatically well-formed declarative sentence. It is grammatically well-formed because DBMSs don't permit ungrammatical sentences in their databases. It is a well-formed declarative sentence because declarative sentences are the only kind of sentences expressed in the rows of tables in relational databases.

STATEMENTS

A row is the inscription of a sentence, specifically of a declarative sentence. But that alone doesn't make a row a statement. Statements are declarative sentences which are meaningful, and which are not ambiguous. The reason we are interested only in statements is that, with an ambiguous declarative sentence, we don't know what the sentence says. Perhaps, taken in one sense, what the sentence says is true, but taken in another sense it is not.[4]

As for *ambiguity*, some of the disambiguation of sentences is provided by context. For example, the states of things described by rows in conventional tables are always their current states. Those rows have no explicit state-time period, but they don't need one. Their status as rows in a nontemporal table makes it clear what their state time is.

This, however, is ambiguity at the level of instances. Type-level ambiguity is a different matter. For a table to unambiguously represent the type Customer, for example, it must be clear what the universe of discourse is from which customers are drawn (anyone who can validly enter into a financial agreement, for example), and it must also be clear what the criteria are for distinguishing, among those people, customers from non-customers – the criteria satisfied by the ones who are customers and not satisfied by the ones who are not.

This is no easy matter. As a matter of fact, in working or consulting for a dozen and a half companies over the course of my career, I have never found a company whose business experts could define what a customer of their company was, at this level of explicitness.

In a language, information is asked for and given, encoded in and decoded from, statements. I focus on the inscriptions which express statements because, although there are many different things we can do with words, saying what there is and what it is like can only be done with statements. And that is what rows in relational tables do. They say what things there are, and what each of those things is like. Each row, as we saw in Chapter 5, picks out an instance of a type, and describes the state that thing is (or was, or will be) in.

At the level of *syntax*, distinctions among the different things we can do with sentences are distinctions of *mood*. Sentences which are in the declarative, or realis, mood are the only ones that can be used to make statements. Sentences which ask for information are in the interrogative mood.

---

[4]There might be a temptation, at this point, to say that an ambiguous declarative sentence expresses two different statements, and that disambiguating it is a matter of figuring out which statement is intended. Terminology might be worked out that way, but that's not the way I am doing it. In my terminology, an ambiguous sentence expresses no statement at all.

Sentences which tell someone to do something are in the imperative mood. Sentences which express what might have been or what might be are in the subjunctive mood.

Things, i.e. referents (which are either objects or events), are what the statements expressed by rows in relational tables are about. In terms of our ontology, such statements identify things, and then describe the states of those things. This is shown in Figure 6.2. The primary key component identifies the statement.[5] The RefId component identifies the "thing", i.e. the referent, that the statement is about. The State component describes what the thing is like.

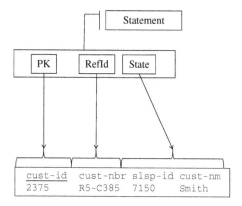

FIGURE 6.2

A Row as a Statement.

I said earlier that a statement identifies something and says something about it. The grammatical subject of a statement does the identifying. The grammatical predicates of a statement say something about what the subject identifies, by ascribing one or more properties and/or relationships to it.

The primary key, RefId and *state description* are the grammatical components of a statement. They identify different roles played by different pieces of the statement. Customer id is the primary key; as such, it is the *identity element* of the row which inscribes the statement. Customer number is the RefId; as such, it is the identity element of the thing referred to by the statement.[6]

---

[5] It would be more accurate to say that the primary key identifies the row that represents the statement. But since rows and statements are not distinct managed objects, either in computer science discussions or in the real-world of application databases, that refinement isn't necessary at this point. (However, see Chapter 19 for the sketch of a world of databases in which rows/inscriptions and statements *are* distinct managed objects, and of the progress in information management that will be possible when this distinction makes it way into practice.)

[6] To return to the point made in the previous footnote, there is a possibly deep issue here, which I will not allude to again until the last two chapters. It is this: is a primary key the identity element of a statement or of an inscription? In other words, is it the unique identifier of a row considered as a statement, or of a row considered as an inscription (or of a row considered as both)? Until those last two chapters, I will treat a primary key as the unique identifier of both a statement and its inscription in a database. This is, in effect, what the standard theory, the standards bodies, and DBMS vendors have done.

They have done this by default, as it were, by not distinguishing between statements and their inscriptions. Perhaps this is because it isn't obvious how one can represent statements made by rows in tables except by means of those rows themselves. But it is both important and possible to make this distinction, to make it in a relational database, and to make it in a way that is accessible to the DBMS and to the SQL that maintains and queries the distinction.

The primary key is what the DBMS is concerned with. The RefId is what the database user is concerned with. The primary key identifies a piece of data. The RefId identifies what that piece of data is about.

The foreign key salesperson id is the grammatical component by which a relationship with a specific salesperson is ascribed to the customer. Customer name is the grammatical component by which a specific property is ascribed to the customer, the property of having the name "Smith". Salesperson id and customer name are the predicates of the statement.

The rows of a conventional table are about things, and the statements those rows make describe those things. This means that to manage statements about things, there must be a one-to-one correspondence between a statement and its referent. This correspondence is established by associating a primary key with a RefId, as shown in Figure 6.2. When this one-to-one correspondence breaks down, we have semantic anomalies such as *synonyms* (multiple signs for the same thing signified, i.e. multiple rows representing the same referent) and *homonyms* (multiple things signified by the same sign, i.e. multiple referents represented by the same row).

Sometimes relational tables are designed so that the same piece of an inscription is used as both primary key and RefId. For example, if the inscription didn't include "2375", and the syntactic analysis of the inscription designated "R5-C385" as both the primary key and the RefId, the row would still be a valid sentence.

So a row in a database table is an inscription which is a declarative sentence. If it is unambiguous, it expresses a statement. This is shown in Figure 6.3.

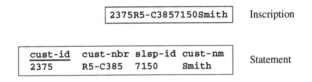

FIGURE 6.3

Inscriptions and Statements.

I said earlier that if two rows are character-for-character the same, then we don't have two copies of the same inscription. We have two inscriptions that are orthographically identical. These two orthographically identical rows express the same statement. So while rows to inscriptions of sentences are one-to-one, inscriptions of sentences to statements are many-to-one. And, as we will see later in this chapter, statements to propositions are many-to-one. But none of this is a matter of deep insight. It is just a matter of drawing important distinctions, and assigning terminology to those distinctions.

DISAMBIGUATING STATEMENTS

In ordinary written or spoken language, many declarative sentences are not fully explicit. For example, the sentence "He's the one who was in possession of it" will be true under some assignments of values to the variables "he" and "it", and false under other assignments. It doesn't become a statement until all its explicit and implicit variables are bound to values.

The *explicit variables* I am referring to here are the pronouns "he" and "it". Pronouns are variables which, when properly used, are assigned a value by the context in which the sentences containing them appear. "He" refers to a specific person, and "it" to a specific object. But if we can't be sure who that person is and what object is being referred to, then the sentence is, although grammatically correct, not a statement. It is ambiguous.

Implicit variables are whatever else can affect the truth value of a declarative sentence. They are sometimes called *indexicals*. For example, on being told "He's the one who was in possession of it", we might already know who "he" and "it" are, but we might reasonably want to know *when* he was in possession of it. The past tense tells us that it was sometime in the past, but we don't know when in the past that was. If we did know when that was, then, provided that there are no other ambiguities, the sentence would be a statement.[7] If things were, during that period of time, as the statement says they were, then it would be a true statement, and otherwise a false one.[8]

So a declarative sentence is a statement provided that it is fully *semantically determinate*. To be fully semantically determinate is for a declarative sentence to say one thing and one thing only. There are no two ways about a semantically determinate sentence. In terms of the mechanics of implementing statements as rows of relational tables, these rows are statements because all variables in them have been bound to values, and all relevant indexicals have been resolved.

Two of the indexicals relevant to a statement are temporal. One of them is about when the referent of the statement was/is/will be like what the statement says it was/is/will be like. The second is about when the statement was/is/will be asserted to be true (since, by Gricean convention, no statement is entered into a database which its authors believe to be false).[9]

The former indexical is what the SQL standard, and everyone else, calls *valid time*. One reason I prefer "state time" to "valid time" is that the kind of time being referred to *is* the time during which the referent of a row was/is/will be in the state described by the row. The term "valid time" doesn't make that clear. Indeed, it seems to me that the term "valid", on the face of it, would more likely be about being well-formed, e.g. that a valid sentence would be one that is grammatically well-formed.

I don't deny that those of us who are more than beginners in discussions about bitemporal data have no problem with the term "valid time". But even for us, the term does not bring to mind the fact that "valid", as used in "valid time", means "correct description", and that consequently "valid time" means "the time during which a description is correct", i.e. the time during which the referent was/is/will be in the state corresponding to the description.

---

[7]Of course, if the author of that sentence wasn't trying to tell us when that person was in possession of it, and if it also wasn't part of what the audience for that sentence could reasonably expect him to be telling them, then that temporal indexical isn't relevant, and the sentence is a statement even though it lacks that indexical.

[8]For a look at indexicals from the point of view of formal semantics, see (Chierchia and McConnell-Ginet, 1990), Chapter 6.

[9]See the sections "Speech Acts" and "Statements and Assertions", later in this chapter.

So for a sentence to be fully explicit, it must be clear when its referent was/is/will be in the state it describes. For example, in order for the sentence "Customer C123 had customer status = Gold" to be fully explicit, it must be clear *when* C123 had/has/will have that status. It must be clear when that *fact* was/is/will be true in the world.

In conventional tables, no such time is explicitly stated. However, no such time needs to be explicitly stated because all rows in conventional tables are associated with a known time by the fact that they exist in a conventional table. That time is an interval which always begins with the current moment on which a row is retrieved. And that interval always ends with the last moment of recorded time, i.e. the latest moment in time which the DBMS can recognize, qualified with the Gricean promise to update or delete the data as soon as the need for an update or delete is recognized.

This kind of time, an interval which tells us when something was/is/will be in the state ascribed to it by a statement, is what I call a *state-time period*. It is also the time period which everyone else calls a *valid-time period*.

For conventional tables, the value for this time period, stated in terms of its implementation, is a time period value which I call *Henceforth*, because its semantics is that it refers to a time period that always begins with the current moment in time, and that extends to the last moment in time, and is always accompanied by the implicit promise that whenever the state of the referent changes, the assertion that that statement is true will be withdrawn, and will be replaced with (a) the assertion that the statement was true from its state-time beginning up to the moment of the update, and (b) the assertion of a new statement describing the new current state of the referent.

When a state-time period is added to a conventional table, the table becomes a state-time table, and its rows become *temporally-explicit statements*. This is shown in Figure 6.4.

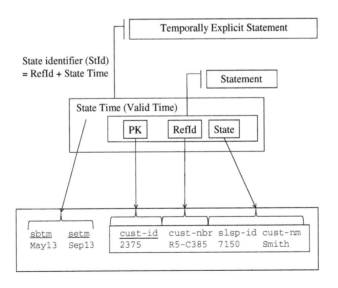

FIGURE 6.4

A Row as a Temporally-Explicit Statement.

Figure 6.4 graphically depicts a temporally-explicit statement as a statement contained in a state-time "envelope". By containing the statement in this *envelope*, we create a statement about a statement. More precisely, we create a statement about when the world was such as to make the contained statement true. It is a statement about when the world included the fact described by the contained statement.

A statement which does not have a temporally-explicit state-time period may still be temporally unambiguous, provided that it is about something that isn't temporal to begin with, or that it has a *temporally-implicit* state-time period.

In the first case, consider statements in logic and mathematics. For example, consider the statement that the square of the hypotenuse of a triangle is equal to the sum of the squares of the other two sides. That statement always was, is now, and always will be true. And so it makes no sense to ask *when* that statement was/is/will be true. The statement has nothing to do with time. Triangularity, as Plato pointed out, is, like other Forms, perfect, unchanging, and timeless.

In the second case, we have statements about what things are currently like. If I write down the statement "Customer C123 has a customer status of Gold" as a row in a conventional table, I have written it down in a list of statements that I implicitly assert are true, and that I implicitly agree to maintain as a list of true statements. And in that case, as soon as C123 ceases to exist, I am under an obligation to remove that row from that list. If C123 takes on a different customer status, I am under an obligation to replace that statement with one which correctly describes the new state of that customer. These obligations are part of the application of Gricean rules of *conversational implicature* to relational databases.

So now we have a clearer idea of what rows in relational tables are. As we saw in Chapter 4, they are instantiations of existentially-quantified statements in a typed predicate logic. If no state-time period is attached to those statements, they are represented by rows in conventional tables, and are implicitly assigned the Henceforth time period. Otherwise, they are temporally explicit statements, represented by rows in tables that do have an explicit state-time period.

The analysis, to this point, is summarized in Figure 6.5.

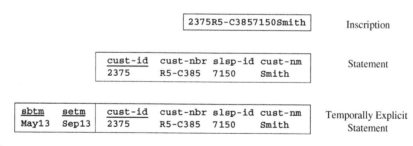

FIGURE 6.5

Inscriptions, Statements and Temporally-Explicit Statements.

For as long as a row physically exists, it is an inscription, a grammatically-correct declarative sentence; and it is a meaningful and unambiguous statement. Rows whose state-time period is not implicitly clear are given an explicit state-time period to disambiguate them. Those rows are temporally explicit statements.

STATEMENTS AND STATEMENT SCHEMAS

In Chapter 4, I distinguished between existentially-quantified statements and instantiations of existentially-quantified statements. I prefer to call the existentially-quantified statement corresponding to a table in a relational database a *statement schema*, reserving the term *statement* for a sentence which contains no variables. That statement schema is described by the *schema row* of that table and, more fully, by the CREATE TABLE metalinguistic statement which defines that table to a DBMS.

From a mathematical and logical point of view, a row in a database table is an ordered set of values that instantiate the ordered set of variables in that table's statement schema, resulting in a statement which conforms to the schema of that table.

The statements made by rows in database tables are not *universal statements*, like "All suppliers are organizations". They are *existential statements*, saying that a specific instance of a specific type exists. The type is represented by the table whose schema defines the syntax of all the statements in the table. Each row in a Customer table, for example, states that a specific customer exists, and tells us something about that customer. All rows in the Customer table have the same grammatical form, the same statement schema.

So: a row in a relational table is the inscription of a statement which says that an instance of a type exists, and which also describes the state of that referent, doing all this by being an ordered set of values which are instantiations of typed variables. In short, a row in a relational table, used to instantiate the statement schema of that table, is the inscription of a statement about a referent. That statement identifies a referent, and describes its state.

SPEECH ACTS

All of the things we do with words are what Austin calls *speech acts*. Each speech act is a little bit like a brief, informal performance — a performance in which I tell you to do something, a performance in which I enter into a legal contract with you, a performance in which I ask you for information, a performance in which I provide information, and so on. Austin says that each of these speech acts has its own distinct *performative force* (Austin, 1961b).

One of those speech acts is the speech act of *making a statement*. Statements are made by means of uttering or writing down unambiguous declarative sentences, in the context of the appropriate *felicity conditions*.[10] The principal felicity condition for making a statement is that the sentence uttered or inscribed be unambiguous. There must be just one thing its author means, and one thing its audience understands its author to mean, and they must be the same thing.

---

[10]The topic of felicity conditions for speech acts was taken up and extensively developed by H. P. Grice. He called the conditions which make a speech act legitimate the "rules of conversational implicature" for that speech act. For example, if a Sergeant in the Army says to a General "Give all the troops a day off today", he has uttered a sentence in the imperative mood. But he has not performed the speech act of giving a command to the General, because Sergeants can't give commands to Generals. See (Grandy, Warner, 2009), (Pagin, 2012).

Two more speech acts I will be discussing are the acts of *making an assertion* and *withdrawing an assertion*. The speech act of making a statement, as I said above, is the act of creating an utterance or an inscription of an unambiguous declarative sentence. But it is a separate speech act to *assert* that statement. It is the speech act of claiming, explicitly or implicitly, that what that statement says is true. A statement, accompanied by that speech act, is an assertion. So an *assertion* is a statement. It is an unambiguous declarative sentence, uttered or inscribed with the intention of saying something true, and understood to have been uttered or inscribed with that intention.

Correlatively, we can indicate that we are no longer willing to assert that a statement is true. This is like cancelling a contract. The contract is no longer in force, but it is still there, and can still be consulted by anyone interested in it, as a record of a contract that once was in force. This is the speech act of cancelling an assertion. I call it the act of *withdrawing* that assertion.[11]

So a declarative sentence is not, by itself, a statement. It must be unambiguous to be a statement. And a statement is not, by itself, an assertion. In order to be an assertion, a statement must be made with the intention of saying something true, and also be made in a context in which it is understood as having been made with that intention.

However, as a matter of fact, most statements are made as assertions. This is as true of statements made in ordinary conversations as it is of statements made in academic papers or legal contracts. It is just as true of statements made by adding rows to database tables. Indeed, the standard theory of bitemporal data *requires* that all statements added to a database be added as assertions — a requirement which I do not accept.

I reject that requirement because it clearly isn't *always* the case that when we make a statement, we also make an assertion. Sometimes, for example, we make a statement in talking about what we think *might* be true. Sometimes we make a statement in the act of telling a joke. Later on, I will show that we can design database management systems so that rows of data can be added to a database that are statements, but are not assertions. Since language is flexible enough to allow us to make statements other than ones we claim to be true, databases should also be flexible enough to manage statements like that.

STATEMENTS AND ASSERTIONS

Statements are the units of language that can be true or false. Rows in relational tables express statements. When a written statement is inscribed by an author who intends, by inscribing it, to state something he believes is true, and when he is or can reasonably be expected by those who read the statement to have been doing that, then the statement is asserted to be true, and thus is an assertion. Asserting that what a statement says is true (to the best of the author's knowledge), is a speech act. A complementary speech act is the speech act of *withdrawing* an assertion. As withdrawn, that statement is an inscription which once was an assertion, but which no longer is.

---

[11]With the help of his most famous student, John Searle, Austin's perspective on language was later developed into *speech act theory*. See (Searle, 1969). An important topic in recent work in pragmatics is integrating speech act theory with Grice's rules of conversational implicature.

ASIDE

Neither the standard theory of bitemporal data, nor my own Asserted Versioning theory, manage the distinction between a statement and an inscription. Neither, that is, can keep track of multiple inscriptions of the same statement.

However it is clear that the same statement may be expressed by more than one inscription. And, as we shall see, an assertion is withdrawn by setting the end point of its assertion-time period to a non-9999 value, i.e. to a real point in time. But since this physical activity is applied to a row as a physical object, it means that it is possible to leave a set of databases in an inconsistent state. If the same statement is expressed by one row in an enterprise data warehouse, and by another row in an operational database, for example, then when it is the user's intention to withdraw a statement, both inscriptions – the one in the enterprise warehouse and the one in the department-level warehouse – should be withdrawn as part of the same atomic unit of work.[12]

This might suggest that we re-interpret assertion time (which everyone else calls "transaction time") as being the assertion of one inscription of a statement, of which there may be other inscriptions. Indeed, since database transactions manage individual inscriptions, the use of transaction time (assertion time) in fact amounts to this. Bitemporal DBMSs, like all DBMSs, create and manage physical rows of data. They manage *inscriptions*, and don't attempt to help us keep track of which inscriptions are inscriptions of which statements.

But from the semantic point of view, what a user is doing when he creates a row of data is not asserting a physical inscription. Physical objects aren't the kind of thing that can be asserted. Rather, the user is asserting the statement expressed by that inscription.

This issue could actually be raised to yet another level, because it obviously applies to sets of statements which express the same proposition. When a statement is asserted, what is being asserted is that what the statement says is what is indeed the case. What a statement says is the proposition it expresses. So that statement and all other statements that say the same thing should, to maintain semantic consistency in the database, be asserted during exactly the same temporal intervals, which means that if they are withdrawn, they should be withdrawn at the same point in time.

But until the next-to-last chapter, this book will continue to treat a statement and its inscription as one managed object, just as the standard theory, the standards committees, and DBMS vendors do. In the meantime, let us turn to the question of under what conditions a statement can be asserted. This is the question of what the felicity conditions for asserting a statement are.

Consider, again, the statement "John loves Mary". The statement "John loves Mary" contains no variables (pronouns), and the present tense makes its temporal indexical determinate. The statement is true if it is a present fact that John loves Mary, and is otherwise false.

But suppose some kind of party game is being played, in which the prize goes to the person who can create the most made-up statements. Each made-up statement is created by choosing two entries from one list, and one entry from a second list. "John" and "Mary" are two entries in the first list; "loves" is one entry in the second list. The only constraint is that the first letters of each of the three words must be in alphabetical sequence.

That would be a pretty boring game, of course; but that's not the point. The point is that if the statement "John loves Mary" is written down as part of that game, it doesn't make sense to ask

---

[12]A metadata model that describes how this relationship between a statement and its multiple inscriptions could be managed, is presented in the penultimate chapter of this book. This model also interprets asserting and withdrawing an assertion as speech acts made by a specific person or group of persons, and extends this set of speech acts to also include assenting to an assertion and dissenting from an assertion. With this extension, "assertion time" becomes a poor choice of words for the name of the time periods associated with these speech acts. "Speech act" time would be better. But that terminology will not be introduced until Chapter 19.

whether or not the person who created it believes that it is true. Written down as part of that game, that statement is not and cannot be asserted. By writing down that statement, as part of that game, we are not writing down anything that we are asserting is true, or false. Truth and falsity don't enter into it.

Rows in conventional tables and in state tables are implicitly asserted. By putting them in these tables, it is understood that we are not playing a party game. It is understood that we believe that what those rows say is true, and that we assert that what those rows say is true.

PROPOSITIONS

Consider the following two statements:

John loves Mary.

Mary is loved by John.

These statements are clearly different inscriptions. But are they also different statements, or are they two inscriptions of the same statement?

On the one hand, it seems that they are different statements. One sentence uses an active verb and the other a passive verb. The order in which the two proper names occur is different; and in English, word order helps to determine grammatical role, which helps to determine meaning.

On the other hand, both, in some sense, say the same thing. Doesn't that make them inscriptions of the same statement? If I say that John loves Mary, I have said the *same thing* as I would have said by saying that Mary is loved by John.

But in my terminology, that does not mean that the two inscriptions express the same statement. It means that the two statements have something in common, which we may say is their *information content*. They say the same thing in the sense that they provide the same information.

Logicians usually express this distinction by saying that the two statements express the same *proposition*. And that is how I will make this distinction. Thus, a proposition is a purely semantic object. It is what two statements that mean the same thing have in common. A proposition is the information content of a statement.

Inscriptions, as I have said, are purely physical objects. Consider the following two inscriptions:

John loves Mary.

John loves Mary.

These inscriptions are orthographically identical. Are they two statements, or two inscriptions of the same statement? Well, although I have said that "John loves Mary" and "Mary is loved by John" are different statements, I will now say that "John loves Mary" and "John loves Mary" are different inscriptions of the same statement. So multiple inscriptions can express the same statement, and multiple statements can express the same proposition. If we could manage all that, we would be doing information management indeed!

It follows, then, that statements are *mediating* objects between physical inscriptions and semantic propositions. On the one hand, a proposition is what semantically identical statements have in common. On the other hand, a statement is what orthographically identical inscriptions have in common.

EXPRESSING ASSERTIONS EXPLICITLY

In a conventional table, just as the state time of the rows in the table is implicit, so is the assertion time of those rows. And just as the implicit state time of those rows is Henceforth, so is the implicit assertion time of those rows.

It works like this. Rows in conventional tables are implicitly about what things are like right now. They are also implicitly about what we right now assert to be true. These rows come with an implicit promise to alter the data if and when that is called for. If whatever it is that a row refers to changes its state, we will keep that promise by updating that row to describe the new current state of that thing. If a referent of the type represented by the table comes into existence or goes out of existence, we will keep that promise by inserting a row for that referent into the table or deleting the row for that referent from the table. This is the Gricean promise which guarantees that the implicit state-time periods of those rows are correctly maintained.

But sometimes we make a mistake with our data. Sometimes we insert a row that we shouldn't have inserted, or delete a row that we shouldn't have deleted. In these cases, a correcting deletion or insertion will fulfill our promise. As for updates, sometimes we update a row, not because the referent has changed state, but because we made a mistake when we originally entered the data, and are now correcting that mistake.

But the semantics of those acts have nothing to do with state changes to the things represented by those rows. The semantics of those acts are about correcting mistakes in the data itself. Insertions and deletions, in those cases, take place without there being any corresponding coming-into-existence or going-out-of-existence of referents. Updates, in those cases, take place without any changes to the states of the things represented.

With conventional and state-time tables, however, the results of these transactions are the same in both cases. An insertion is an insertion, an update is an update, a deletion is a deletion. We can't tell, by looking at a conventional or a state-time table, which rows resulted from recording state-time changes and which rows resulted from correcting mistakes in data.

With conventional tables, the issue is moot. All there is in conventional tables is one row for each referent, and it describes the current state of that referent.

But with state-time tables, the issue is not moot. The reason is that if we use state time to record when corrections are made, then we have used state time to do two things — to say when things were/are/will be in a given state, and to say when incorrect data was replaced with correct data.

In the first case, the start of a row's state-time period tells us when the referent of the row began to be in that state. We know that, the moment prior to that time, the referent either was in a different state, or did not exist (as far as our database is concerned).[13] In the second case, the start of a row's state-time period tells us when we became aware of an error in the row and corrected it. In the first case, the thing represented by the row changed. In the second case, it did not.

In this situation in which state time is used for two purposes, state time becomes a homonym. We no longer know what the time periods of rows in the state-time table really mean. Any row

---

[13]This presupposes, however, that the rows in the table are coalesced. Two rows in a state-time table can be coalesced if and only if they are for the same referent and for periods of state time that have no clock ticks between them, and also designate the same atemporal state, i.e. the same set of property and relationship values. A coalesced table contains no such pairs of rows.

could be telling us when its referent entered the state described by the row. Any row could be telling us when we fixed a mistake in that row's data.

If a catcher uses three fingers down to signal either a fast ball or a slider, then when he uses that sign, the pitcher doesn't know which pitch to throw, and the catcher doesn't know which pitch he will be catching. That's what making corrections in state-time tables is like.

To avoid this homonymous treatment of time periods, the standard theory of bitemporal data associates a second time period with relational tables — a period which I call assertion time. But to make the following discussion clearer — a discussion in which I criticize the standard theory — I will temporarily revert to the standard theory's terminology of "transaction time" and "valid time".

Computer scientists, standards organizations, and DBMS vendors, all agree that the transaction-time period of a row begins when the row is physically created. Indeed, they all agree that the transaction-time period of every row in a transaction-time table or a bitemporal table starts life with the value Henceforth.

But why is that so? Why does the standard theory allow a row to be created with a valid-time period that begins in the past or in the future, but require the row to be created with a transaction-time period that begins at the then-current moment in time? Those *are* the data manipulation rules governing transaction time as described in the computer science literature, as standardized in the ISO and TSQL2 standards, and as implemented in DB2, Teradata and other bitemporal data management systems.

To understand *why* those are the rules that implement the standard theory's account of transaction time is to understand the semantics expressed by those rules. So what is it about the semantics of transaction time that restricts initial transaction-time values to Henceforth?

The answer is *not* that a row must begin life in Henceforth transaction time because that marks the moment when a transaction creates it. That answer just repeats the question, re-stating what the implementation rules for transaction time are. What we need to know is *why* we have those rules. What we need to know is the semantics which those rules implement.

I propose that the answer is that transaction time marks the moment (or so computer scientists have assumed) when a row is first asserted to make a true statement. That would explain why a row cannot be created with a transaction time that begins in the past. A statement can't be asserted before it exists to be asserted, and in databases that means that a statement can't be asserted before it exists as a row in a table.

So the simple fact is that a statement doesn't exist to be asserted until it is physically embodied in an utterance or an inscription, and this simple fact provides the semantics which explains why a row can't be created with a transaction-time period that begins in the past.

There's nothing here to take issue with. I am not about to argue that a statement can be asserted before it exists. But "everyone else", i.e. the advocates and implementers of the standard theory, also requires that a row cannot have a transaction-time period that begins in the future. And so they must have a reason for that rule, too. What could that reason be?

It seems to me that instead of having a reason, they have an assumption. It is the assumption that just as a statement can't be asserted before it exists, a statement must be asserted as soon as it exists.

But as we have seen earlier in this chapter, we don't always assert the statements we make. Assertion presupposes a statement to assert; but asserting a statement is a speech act we may or may not choose to make. We may make a statement in the process of telling a joke, or describing a hypothetical situation, or describing a purported fact that we don't agree is a fact at all. In all these cases, we make those statements but we don't assert them.

Transaction time does mark the moment when a row is physically created. I have no quarrel with that. It marks the moment when the statement made by that row first exists. I have no quarrel with that, either. But I do take issue with the assumption that it also marks the moment when the statement made by that row is first asserted to be true.

In tables that do not have explicit transaction time, this issue doesn't arise. When inserting and deleting rows in nontemporal tables, the only way to make an assertion is to add a row, and the only way to withdraw an assertion is to delete a row. So *in these tables*, when a row is added and when the statement made by that row is asserted, are the same point in time. When a row is deleted and when that assertion is withdrawn, are the same point in time.

This could lead one to believe that the same should be true of bitemporal tables. Perhaps it is this assumption that led computer scientists, standards bodies and database implementers to believe that that is so. But in fact, it is not so. And the fact that it is also not true in ordinary language indicates that the distinction between a statement and an assertion is part of ordinary language.

In ordinary language, we can make statements about what we think might possibly be true, but which we are not yet ready to assert are definitely true. So why shouldn't this useful ability of ordinary language be carried over to relational databases?

Here is another argument against the standard theory's assumption that statements in bitemporal tables must exist as assertions from the moment they are added to their tables to the moment they are logically deleted. Statements in bitemporal tables are logically deleted by setting the transaction end time of their rows to the time of the transactions that did the deletions. But after they are logically deleted, those rows remain physically present in their tables (or, in DB2's implementation, physically present in the database, but moved from their original tables to associated history tables). They are all rows which have a transaction-time period that ends in the past.

What is the information content of these rows? They must have some information value, or else we are being foolish to go to the trouble and expense of keeping them in our databases.

Bitemporal rows in current transaction time are statements that we currently assert to be true. If anyone asks us about them, we will say that they are true. We will say that what they describe about the past, present or future states of things is correct (to the best of our current knowledge). We will be willing to base our actions and other decisions on what those rows tell us. But we will not be willing to base our actions and other decisions on statements made by rows in past transaction time. And why not? The reason is that rows in past transaction time represent statements that are no longer asserted or believed to be true.[14]

Rows in past transaction time cannot be modified by any temporal transaction. Rows in past transaction time are excluded from consideration by normal temporal queries, ones which specify either no time or only valid time. They aren't excluded because they have been logically deleted. They have been logically deleted because they no longer belong to the set of statements which represent what we currently assert to be true. So, even in implementations of the standard theory,

---

[14]Note that statements no longer asserted to be true are one thing, but statements asserted to be no longer true are another thing. No longer asserting that a statement is true is a matter of ending its assertion (transaction) time. Asserting that a statement is no longer true is a matter of ending its state (valid) time.

bitemporal tables contain two kinds of statements: those which are assertions, and those which are not assertions although they used to be assertions.[15]

So if bitemporal tables can contain both statements which are assertions and statements which are no longer assertions, why can't they also contain statements which are not yet assertions? My answer is that there is no valid reason for that restriction. And so, in Chapter 14, I will show how to extend the standard theory of bitemporal data to include future assertions as well as past and present ones.

In Figure 6.6, assertion time is shown as an envelope containing state time which is, in turn, shown as an envelope containing a statement. State time makes it clear what time period that statement is about. Assertion time makes it clear within what time period that temporally-explicit statement was and perhaps still is an assertion.

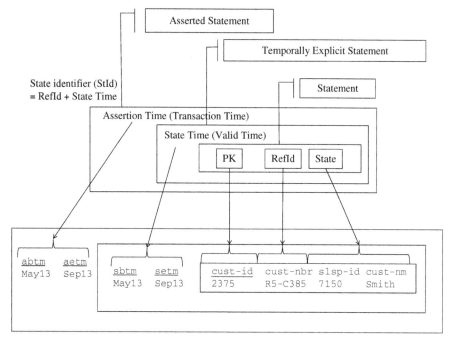

FIGURE 6.6

The Structure of an Assertion.

Figure 6.7 summarizes the stages in which an inscription becomes an assertion. The inscriptions we deal with in relational databases are those that can be parsed into declarative sentences.

[15]Nor does the ISO's specification that rows in past transaction time be moved from their tables of origin to associated history tables, affect this point. That's a purely technical feature included, I believe, to make it easier to physically partition these two groups of rows. For I can just as well say that the standard theory of bitemporal data retains, in a database, both statements that are assertions, and statements that are no longer assertions, and this applies equally to IBM's history table implementation and to implementations which retain rows in past transaction time in their original tables.

Sentence to statement is the transition point at which semantics are introduced. "Time flies like an arrow" and "The doctor recommends that we postpone the elective surgery" are both grammatical sentences. But only the latter is a statement (and it is a statement only on the assumption that we know who the doctor is, who the "we" in the sentence refers to, and what elective surgery is being recommended).

Sometimes, a sentence needs a little help in crossing the sentence/statement boundary. Specifically, the sentence must be unambiguous. If it isn't, then there isn't one thing that it says, and so there isn't one statement. The constraints imposed by a DBMS on rows in tables eliminate most sources of ambiguity. But there is one source of ambiguity which manifests itself as soon as we attempt to use data to keep a history of changes that happen to things we are interested in. That is the ambiguity that is removed by adding a valid-time period (to use the standard theory's terminology), turning the statement into a temporally-explicit statement.

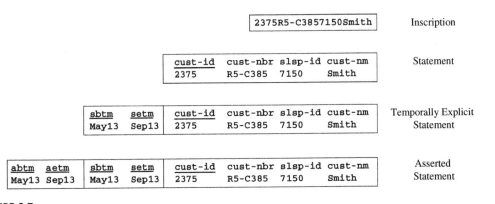

FIGURE 6.7

The Many Roles of a Bitemporal Row.

We have now arrived at a multi-perspectival understanding of the structures and contents of relational databases.

- The *mathematics* of the Relational Paradigm, described in Chapter 3, provide a template for the structures in which data is stored.
- The *logic* of the Relational Paradigm, described in Chapter 4, defines transformations on instances of those structures, and derivations of new instances from other ones.
- The *ontology* of the Relational Paradigm, described in Chapter 5, provides an interpretation of the structures as representing types of things, types of properties and types of relationships, and an interpretation of the instances of those structures as representing instances of those types of things, properties and relationships.
- The *semantics* of the Relational Paradigm, described here in Chapter 6, explain how the rows of relational tables are used to make statements and assertions about the past, present and future of what those statements are about.

Time periods are now becoming very important. Relationships among time periods will be particularly important. To analyze these time periods and their relationships, the most important tool we have is the Allen relationships. That is the topic of the next chapter.

GLOSSARY LIST

assent
assert
assertion
assertion-time period
bitemporal table
conventional table
event
existentially-quantified
    statement
fact
future assertion
homonym
indexical
information content
inscription

instance
object
predicate
property
proposition
referent
relationship
schema row
speech act
state description
state time
state
State
statement schema
statement

state-time period
state-time table
subject
synonym
temporal interval
thing
time period
transaction time
transaction-time period
type
universe of discourse
valid time
withdraw

THE ALLEN RELATIONSHIPS

Any given time period may be longer or shorter than another time period, or the same duration as that other time period. It may begin or end before or after that other time period, or at the same time that that other time period begins or ends. Two *adjacent time periods* — time periods with no other time periods between them — may or may not have a temporal gap between them, a *temporal gap* being a series of one or more *clock ticks* which aren't in either time period.

It will prove essential to have a complete list of all possible positional relationships between two time periods, of equal or unequal durations, along a common timeline. That list is known as the Allen relationships. (Allen, 1983).

WHY THE ALLEN RELATIONSHIPS ARE IMPORTANT

Clearly, these relationships among time periods matter. For example, consider the following two rows in the Supplier-S table:

[Aug10|Mar11|S2|Superior|*SC3*|T22]
[Mar11|Nov12|S2|Superior|*SC3*|T15]

Nothing seems to be wrong here. These rows indicate that supplier S2 was a Type 22 from August 2010 up to March 2011, and a Type 15 from March 2011 up to November 2012. These two time periods — [Aug10-Mar11] and [Mar11-Nov12] — are contiguous and they do not overlap. Because they are contiguous, they also indicate that S2's name was "Superior" from August 2010 up to November 2012, and that S2's supplier category was SC3 during that same period of time.

But suppose the two rows are as follows:

[Aug10|Mar11|S2|Superior|*SC3*|T22]
[Feb11|Nov12|S2|Superior|*SC3*|T15]

Now there is a problem. The problem is that these two rows make contradictory statements. The first row says that S2 was a Type 22 in February 2011, but the second row says that S2 was a Type 15 in that same month. These two time periods — [Aug10-Mar11] and [Feb11-Nov12] — overlap. There is one clock tick that is found in both time periods, the clock tick of February 2011.

Just as conventional entity integrity prevents two rows in a table from representing the same thing, *temporal entity integrity* prevents two rows in a table from representing the same state of the same thing at the same time. In fact, conventional entity integrity is just a special case of temporal entity integrity, the case in which the time periods are implicit, not explicit.

This shows that the positional relationship between two time periods is important. That importance motivates our examination of the Allen relationships. We need to know all the positional relationships between two time periods, and understand the significance of each.

I will discuss two time periods, which may or may not be the same length (duration). They are situated on the same timeline, which we will assume is the state-time timeline. They have various positional relationships with respect to one another, depending on where on the timeline each is located, and their relative lengths. Combining these two factors of duration and location, we can see that their positional relationships depend on which clock ticks each time period includes.

The two time periods I will use as examples are t_1 and t_2. Allen's analysis shows that there are exactly thirteen positional relationships possible between t_1 and t_2. But Allen provided us with more than a list. He provided us with a list whose entries are a partitioning. A partitioning is a list which is complete, and whose entries are mutually exclusive.

Because the Allen relationships are a partitioning, they are useful as a checklist. If we are developing or testing software to compare two time periods, no matter how they are situated with respect to one another, we can use the checklist to make sure that we have considered all the possibilities.

A TAXONOMY OF THE ALLEN RELATIONSHIPS

In Chapter 3 of *MTRD*, I provided a taxonomy of the Allen relationships. That taxonomy is a binary partitioning.

A *taxonomy* is a *hierarchical partitioning*. This taxonomy of the Allen Relationships is also a *binary partitioning* because each parent node in the hierarchy has exactly two child nodes. The Allen relationships themselves are leaf nodes in this hierarchy, nodes which have no child nodes.

This hierarchy also identifies sets of multiple Allen relationships, those sets being all and only the child nodes for each non-leaf node in the hierarchy, recursively. The root node is the concept being partitioned. In this case, it is the set of all the Allen relationships.

A binary taxonomy consists of two child nodes under each parent node, recursively, until child nodes are reached which have no child nodes of their own. Since every instance of a parent node is an instance of one of its child nodes, and no instance of a child node is also an instance of a sibling node, the taxonomy is a partitioning. We can be sure that all the cases are covered, and that none are covered more than once.

THE BASIC ALLEN RELATIONSHIPS

I will indicate Allen relationships, and also the nodes in this taxonomy, by enclosing their names in brackets. The Allen relationships themselves are these:[1]

[starts]
[finishes]

---

[1]Some of these terms — especially "overlaps' — have proven to be confusing. I keep these terms because they are Allen's own terms, and thus the official ones. I will clarify any terminological issues caused by Allen's choice of terms, whenever it seems necessary. In addition, I note that Allen did not enclose his terms in brackets. That is my own convention.

[equals]
[during]
[overlaps]
[before]
[meets]

There are actually thirteen Allen relationships. We get thirteen from this list because for the six relationships other than [equals], there is a reciprocal relationship. The standard way of indicating a reciprocal Allen relationship is with a " $-$ 1" superscript, for example "[starts^{-1}]".

In the following discussion, I will show a graphic of each Allen relationship, as well as an example and the predicate expression that defines the relationship.

In the graphics, each dash represents one clock tick. Time period 1 (t_1) is represented as a string of "1"s, and time period 2 (t_2) as a string of "2"s. Each "1" represents a clock tick in t_1, and each "2" represents a clock tick in t_2.

In the examples, I will continue to use month-granularity time periods with the *closed/open* convention.

In the predicates, I will use "b_1" and "e_1" to represent the beginning and ending clock tick of one time period, and "b_2" and "e_2" to represent the beginning and ending clock tick of a second time period.

[Starts]

We can graphically represent [starts] like this:

```
111
22222
-----------
```

FIGURE 7.1

t_1 [starts] t_2.

Both time periods start on the same clock tick, but they do not end on the same clock tick. Thus, a [starts] relationship is only possible between time periods of unequal duration.

Here is an example of a [starts] relationship:

```
[Nov14|Jan15|S2|Superior|SC3|T22]
[Nov14|Mar15|S2|Superior|SC3|T15]
```

In this example, t_1 begins on the same clock tick as t_2, but ends two clock ticks before t_2 ends. This is a relationship that, for the same referent, will not be allowed to occur in a database, because the two rows make contradictory statements about their referent from November 2014 through December 2014.

The predicate for the [starts] relationship is this:

$$(b_1 = b_2) \wedge (e_1 < e_2)$$

This predicate says that t_1 and t_2 begin on the same clock tick, and that t_1 ends on a clock tick that is earlier than the clock tick that t_2 ends on.

The predicate for the $[\text{starts}^{-1}]$ relationship is this:

$$(b_2 = b_1) \wedge (e_2 < e_1)$$

This predicate says that t_1 and t_2 begin on the same clock tick, and that t_2 ends on a clock tick that is earlier than the clock tick that t_1 ends on.

In many cases, it may not be important to distinguish between an Allen relationship and its reciprocal. In this case, for example, it may not be important which of the two time periods ends first (or, equivalently, is shorter than the other one). When it is not important to distinguish a relationship from its reciprocal, I will use a *reciprocally neutral* form of the relationship, which I will designate with a capital letter. In this case, the reciprocally neutral form is [Starts], and its formula is:

$$[(b_1 = b_2) \wedge (e_1 < e_2)] \vee [(b_2 = b_1) \wedge (e_2 < e_1)]$$

By the distributive rule (Rule 11, Figure 4.6), and the fact that equals is a commutative relationship, this simplifies to:

$$[(b_1 = b_2)] \wedge [(e_1 < e_2) \vee (e_2 < e_1)]$$

And since $[(e_1 < e_2) \vee (e_2 < e_1)]$ is equivalent to $\sim(e_1 = e_2)$, [Starts] simplifies to:

$$(b_1 = b_2) \wedge \sim(e_1 = e_2)$$

This predicate says that a [Starts] relationship exists between two time periods if and only if they begin on the same clock tick but do not end on the same clock tick.

[Finishes]

We can graphically represent [finishes] like this:

```
          1111
          222
        -----------
```

t_1 [finishes] t_2.

Neither time period starts on the same clock tick, but they both end on the same clock tick. Thus, a [finishes] relationship is only possible between time periods of unequal duration.

Here is an example of a [finishes] relationship:

```
[Nov14|Mar15|S2|Superior|SC3|T22]
[Sep14|Mar15|S2|Superior|SC3|T15]
```

In this example, t_1 begins two clock ticks after t_2 begins, but ends on the same clock tick as t_2. Again, this is a relationship that will not be allowed to occur in a database, since the two rows make contradictory statements about supplier S2 from November 2014 through February 2015.

The predicate for the [finishes] relationship is this:

$$(b_1 < b_2) \wedge (e_1 = e_2)$$

This predicate says that t_1 begins on a clock tick that is earlier than the clock tick that t_2 begins on, and that t_1 and t_2 end on the same clock tick.

The predicate for the [finishes^{-1}] relationship is this:

$$(b_2 < b_1) \wedge (e_2 = e_1)$$

This predicate says that t_1 begins on a clock tick that is later than the clock tick that t_2 begins on, and that t_1 and t_2 end on the same clock tick.

In many cases, it may not be important which of the two time periods began first. In that case, there is a [Finishes] relationship which is the disjunction of [finishes] and [finishes^{-1}]:

$$[(b_1 < b_2) \wedge (e_1 = e_2)] \vee [(b_2 < b_1) \wedge (e_2 = e_1)]$$

By the same set of rules that simplified [Starts], [Finishes] simplifies to:

$$\sim (b_1 = b_2) \wedge (e_1 = e_2)$$

This predicate says that a [Finishes] relationship exists between two time periods if and only if they end on the same clock tick but do not begin on the same clock tick.

[During]

We can graphically represent [during] like this:

```
            11
       2222222
       -------------
```

FIGURE 7.3

t_1 [during] t_2.

[during] is another relationship that is only possible between time periods of unequal lengths. Here is an example of a [during] relationship:

```
[Nov14|Jan15|S2|Superior|SC3|T15]
[Aug14|Mar15|S2|Superior|SC3|T22]
```

In this example, three months at the start of t_2 are not in t_1, two months at the end of t_2 are not in t_1, and the two months of November and December 2014 are clock ticks in both time periods. Again, this is a relationship (between states of the same referent) that will not be allowed to occur in a database, since the two rows make contradictory statements about supplier S2 in November and December of 2014.

The predicate for the [during] relationship is this:

$$(b_1 > b_2) \wedge (e_1 < e_2)$$

This predicate says that t_1 begins on a later clock tick than t_2 begins on, and that t_1 ends on an earlier clock tick than t_2 ends on. In the ordinary English sense of the word "during", then, this is the relationship in which t_1 occurs during t_2.

The predicate for the [during^{-1}] relationship is this:

$$(b_2 > b_1) \wedge (e_2 < e_1)$$

In this case, t_2 occurs "during" t_1. And if it is not important which of the two time periods occurs during the other, the reciprocally neutral [During] is defined as:

$$[(b_1 > b_2) \wedge (e_1 < e_2)] \vee [(b_2 > b_1) \wedge (e_2 < e_1)]$$

This formula says that a [During] relationship exists between two time periods if and only if one of them begins after the other one begins and ends before the other one ends.

[Equals]

We can graphically represent [Equals] like this:

```
            1111111
            2222222
         -------------
```

FIGURE 7.4

t_1 [Equals] t_2.

Both time periods start on the same clock tick, and both end on the same clock tick. Since there are no gaps within time periods, it follows that an [Equals] relationship is possible only between time periods that have the same number of clock ticks.

Here is an example of an [Equals] relationship.

```
[Aug14|Mar15|S2|Superior|SC3|T22]
[Aug14|Mar15|S2|Superior|SC3|T15]
```

In this example, all the clock ticks in one time period are also in the other time period. These two rows, both for supplier S2, thus contradict one another in every one of their clock ticks. Again, this is a relationship that will not be allowed to occur in a database, since the two rows make contradictory statements about supplier S2 throughout their time periods.

The predicate for the [Equals] relationship is this:

$$(b_1 = b_2) \wedge (e_1 = e_2)$$

This predicate says that t_1 and t_2 begin on the same clock tick and end on the same clock tick. [Equals] is its own reciprocal relationship.

[Overlaps]

We can graphically represent [overlaps] like this:

```
            1111111
              222222222
         ---------------------
```

FIGURE 7.5

t_1 [overlaps] t_2.

In an [overlaps] relationship, each of the two time periods includes some clock ticks that the other does not, and also some clock ticks that the other does include.

I gave an example of an [overlaps] relationship at the start of this section. To repeat:

$$[\text{Aug14}\,|\,\text{Mar15}\,|\,\text{S2}\,|\,\text{Superior}\,|\,SC3\,|\,\text{T22}]$$
$$[\underline{\text{Feb15}}\,|\,\underline{\text{Nov15}}\,|\,\text{S2}\,|\,\text{Superior}\,|\,SC3\,|\,\text{T15}]$$

In this example, the months of August 2014 through January 2015 are clock ticks in t_1 that are not also in t_2. The months of March 2015 through October 2015 are clock ticks in t_2 that are not also in t_1. And the month of February 2015 is a clock tick that is in both t_1 and t_2. Again, this is a relationship that will not be allowed to occur in a database, since the two rows make contradictory statements about supplier S2 in February 2015.

The predicate for the [overlaps] relationship is this:

$$(b_1 < b_2) \wedge [(e_1 > b_2) \wedge (e_1 < e_2)]$$

In this relationship, t_1 overlaps t_2. This predicate says that t_1 begins before t_2 begins and ends after t_2 begins and before t_2 ends. In other words, t_1 begins before t_2 begins, and ends "while t_2 is going on". In the formula above, the brackets are unnecessary; but I have included them because they pick out the "while t_2 is going on" part.

The predicate for the [overlaps^{-1}] relationship is this:

$$(b_2 < b_1) \wedge [(b_2 > e_1) \wedge (e_2 < e_1)]$$

In this case, t_2 overlaps t_1. This predicate says that t_2 begins before t_1 begins and ends after t_1 begins and before t_1 ends. In other words, t_2 begins before t_1 begins, and ends "while t_2 is going on".

If it is not important which of the two overlapping time periods is earlier, the [Overlaps] relationship is the disjunction of [overlaps] and [overlaps^{-1}]:

$$[(b_1 < b_2) \wedge (e_1 > b_2) \wedge (e_1 < e_2)] \vee [(b_1 > b_2) \wedge (b_1 < e_2) \wedge (e_1 > e_2)]$$

So note that while [overlaps] and the ordinary language "overlaps" do not mean the same thing, [Overlaps] and "overlaps" do mean the same thing.

[Before]

We can graphically represent [before] like this:

```
1111111 22222222222
-----------------------
```

FIGURE 7.6

t_1 [before] t_2.

In a [before] relationship, the two time periods do not share even a single clock tick. In addition, there is a gap between them, the gap consisting of one or more clock ticks that are in neither time period.

Here is an example of a [before] relationship.

[Aug14|Mar15|S2|Superior|*SC3*|T22]

[Apr15|Mar16|S2|Superior|*SC3*|T15]

In this example, the month of March 2015 occurs after the end of t_1 (remember that we are using the closed-open notation), and before the start of t_2. Thus there is a gap of one clock tick between the two time periods. These two rows say nothing about supplier S2 during the month of March 2015. This is a relationship that would be allowed to occur in a database, because there is no clock tick that the two time periods have in common, and thus no possibility of the two rows contradicting one another.

The predicate for the [before] relationship is this:

$$(e_1 < b_2)$$

This predicate says (given the closed/open convention) that the last clock tick in t_1 is earlier than the clock tick immediately prior to the clock tick on which t_2 begins. That is, there is at least one clock tick between the two time periods.

The predicate for the [before^{-1}] relationship is this:

$$(e_2 < b_1)$$

And the predicate for the reciprocally neutral [Before] relationship is this:

$$(e_1 < b_2) \vee (e_2 < b_1)$$

[Meets]

We can graphically represent [meets] like this:

```
1111111222222222222
-------------------------
```

FIGURE 7.7

t_1 [meets] t_2.

In a [meets] relationship, the two time periods do not share even a single clock tick. In addition, there is no gap between them; there is no clock tick between the last clock tick of one time period and the first clock tick of the other time period. Because of the closed/open convention, this means that the representation of the adjacent clock ticks will use the same value.

Here is an example of a [meets] relationship:

[Aug14|Mar15|S2|Superior|*SC3*|T22]

[Mar15|Mar16|S2|Superior|*SC3*|T15]

In this example, the last clock tick in t_1 is February 2015, and the first clock tick in t_2 is March 2015. Since our level of granularity is a calendar month, there are no clock ticks between the end of t_1 and the start of t_2. This is also a relationship that would be allowed to occur in a database, because once again there is no clock tick that the two time periods have in common, and thus no possibility of the two rows contradicting one another.

The predicate for the [meets] relationship is this:

$$(e_1 = b_2)$$

This predicate (given the closed/open convention) says that t_1 ends one clock tick before t_2 begins. That is, there are no clock ticks between the two time periods.

In the reciprocal relationship, t_2 is an earlier time period than t_1, and so the predicate for [meets^{-1}] is:

$$(e_2 = b_1)$$

And the reciprocally neutral [Meets] is:

$$(e_1 = b_2) \vee (e_2 = b_1)$$

As we saw earlier, the ordinary English "overlaps" does not mean the same thing as the Allen relationship [overlaps]. It does mean the same thing as [Overlaps], which is the disjunction of the [overlaps] and [overlaps^{-1}] relationships. Allen, however, defines no [Overlaps] relationship.

The terms used for [before] and [meets] are doubly infelicitous. They are closely related Allen relationships in that they are the only two relationships in which the two time periods do not share any clock ticks. And yet the ordinary sense of "before" is clearly a reciprocal-distinguishing sense, while the ordinary sense of "meets" is not. If A is before B, then B can't be before A. But if A meets B, then B must meet A. So "before" is the meaning of [before], but "meets" is not the meaning of [meets]; it is the meaning of [Meets], a relationship Allen never defined.

I and others have found that the names provided by Allen are sometimes confusing. Nonetheless, Allen defined these relationships over a quarter of a century ago, and it is his terminology which has been used since then. So I will continue to use his terminology, in spite of its difficulties.

COMBINATIONS OF THE ALLEN RELATIONSHIPS

We would like some assurance that the Allen relationships are a complete list of all the positional relationships, along a common timeline, of two time periods which may be of any duration and which do not have to be of the same duration. This means that every pair of time periods will be an instance of an Allen relationship. We would also like some assurance that there is no duplication of coverage, i.e. that no pair of time periods are an instance of more than one Allen relationship. The way we will do this is to construct a binary taxonomy, working from the top-down.

A BINARY PARTITIONING OF THE ALLEN RELATIONSHIPS TAXONOMY

In the following discussion, leaf nodes in the taxonomy are individual Allen relationships. I will also use the reciprocally neutral form of each Allen relationship.

COMMON TIMELINE TIME PERIODS: [INCLUDES] OR [EXCLUDES]

Clearly, two time periods positioned on a common timeline will either have at least one clock tick in common, or else they won't. I will call the set of Allen relationships in which two time periods have at least one clock tick in common [Includes], and the set of all the other Allen relationships [Excludes].

So here is the top level of the taxonomy.

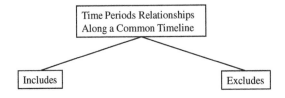

FIGURE 7.8

A Binary Partitioning of the Allen Relationships −1.

At this level, we clearly account for all relationships between two time periods. Just as clearly, there is no overlap. Any two time periods will either [Include] one another, or [Exclude] one another. Since one of these nodes is defined as the negation of the other, no pair of time periods will fall under both nodes.

Among the Allen relationships, only two of them are relationships in which there is no clock tick in common between the two time periods. These are the [Before] and [Meets] relationships. Since we know that [Includes] is the negation of [Excludes], we know that all the other Allen relationships are [Includes] relationships.

[INCLUDES]: [CONTAINS] OR [OVERLAPS]

If two time periods [Include] one another, they have at least one clock tick in common. Among these time periods, we can distinguish two cases. Either each time period will also have at least one clock tick that the other does not have, or this won't be true. If each does have at least one clock tick that the other does not have, then the two time periods [Overlap]. Otherwise, all of the clock ticks in one or both of the two time periods will be included in the other time period. In that case, I will say that there is a [Contains] relationship between them.

[Contains] and [Overlaps] are clearly exhaustive; no pairs of [Including] time periods fail to fall into one or the other of these categories. The two time periods must have at least one clock tick in common, because they are [Includes] relationships. And either both time periods have at least one clock tick that the other does not have, or that is not the case. So clearly, these two categories are mutually exclusive; no pairs of time periods fall into both of them. Thus, by definition of "partition", our taxonomy remains a partition when these categories are added to it.

The predicate for [Includes] is the disjunction of the predicates of its components:

$$[[[[(b_1 = b_2) \wedge \sim (e_1 = e_2)] \vee$$
$$[\sim (b_1 = b_2) \wedge (e_1 = e^2)]] \vee$$
$$[(b_1 > b_2) \wedge (e_1 < e_2)] \vee [(b_2 > b_1) \wedge (e_2 < e_1)]] \vee$$
$$[(b_1 = b_2) \wedge (e_1 = e_2)]] \vee$$
$$[(b_1 < b_2) \wedge (e_1 > b_2) \wedge (e_1 < e_2)] \vee [(b_1 > b_2) \wedge (b_1 < e_2) \wedge (e_1 > e_2)]$$

Here is the taxonomy so far:

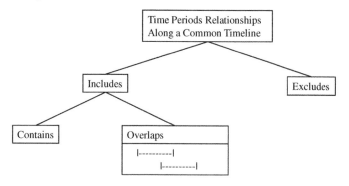

FIGURE 7.9

A Binary Partitioning of the Allen Relationships -2.

As we noted before, when two rows in a temporal table have the same referent, and there are any clock ticks which their time periods have in common, then both rows make statements about that referent as it was/is/will be in those one or more clock ticks. If those rows differ in any of their other columns, then they make contradictory statements. Since keeping contradictory statements out of a database is essential, software which manages temporal data must prevent this from happening.

[CONTAINS]: [EQUALS] OR [ENCLOSES]

[Contains] is the relationship in which every clock tick in one time period is also found in the other time period. To be clear, I should add "but not necessarily vice-versa". So if one time period consists of clock ticks [3, 4, 5, 6], and the other time period consists of clock ticks [2, 3, 4, 5, 6, 7, 8, 9], that is a [Contains] relationship. The latter time period [Contains] the former time period, and so the former is [Contained In] the latter.

[Contains] can be partitioned into [Equals] and [Encloses]. [Equals] is the [Contains] relationship in which every clock tick in one time period is also found in the other time period, and vice-versa. In other words, the two time periods have exactly the same clock ticks. [Encloses], then, is the [Contains] relationship in which every clock tick in one time period is also found in the other time period, but *not* vice-versa. The other time period, then, has at least one clock tick that is not part of the first time period.

Again, this is clearly a partitioning. Every [Contains] relationship is either an [Equals] or an [Encloses] relationship, and no [Contains] relationship is both.

The predicate for [Contains] is the disjunction of the predicates of its components:

$$[[[(b_1 = b_2) \wedge \sim (e_1 = e_2)] \vee$$
$$[\sim (b_1 = b_2) \wedge (e_1 = e_2)]] \vee$$
$$[(b_1 > b_2) \wedge (e_1 < e_2)] \vee [(b_2 > b_1) \wedge (e_2 < e_1)]] \vee$$
$$[(b_1 = b_2) \wedge (e_1 = e_2)]$$

Here is the taxonomy so far:

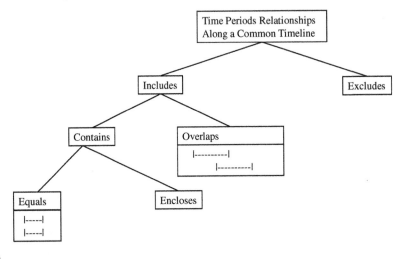

FIGURE 7.10

A Binary Partitioning of the Allen Relationships −3.

[ENCLOSES]: [ALIGNS WITH] OR [DURING]

Because [Encloses] is an [Includes] relationship, there must be at least one clock tick shared by the two time periods that it relates. Because it is a [Contains] relationship, all the clock ticks in one time period (let it be t_1) must also be in the other time period (let it be t_2). Since it is not the [Equals] relationship, there must also be at least one clock tick in t_2 which is not in t_1.

Since t_1 and t_2 are not [Equal], and yet t_1 is [Contained In] t_2, it follows that t_2 is longer than t_1, including at least one clock tick than t_1 does not include. This clock tick may be earlier than the first clock tick in t_1 or later than the last clock tick in t_1. If t_2 includes at least two clock ticks that t_1 does not, then both clock ticks may be earlier than the first clock tick in t_1, or both clock ticks may be later than the last clock tick in t_1, or one may be earlier and the other later.

The binary distinction for [Encloses] is this. If t_1 has at least one clock tick earlier than t_2's first clock tick, and also at least one clock tick later than t_2's last clock tick, it is the [During] relationship. In the two other cases, either t_1 and t_2 begin on the same clock tick, or they end on the same clock tick. In those cases, I will call it the [Aligns With] relationship.

Again, this is clearly a partitioning. Every [Encloses] relationship will be either a [During] or an [AlignsWith] relationship, and no [Encloses] relationship will be both.

The predicate for [Encloses] is the disjunction of the predicates of its components:

$$[[(b_1 = b_2) \wedge \sim(e_1 = e_2)] \vee$$
$$[\sim(b_1 = b_2) \wedge (e_1 = e_2)]] \vee$$
$$[(b_1 > b_2) \wedge (e_1 < e_2)] \vee [(b_2 > b_1) \wedge (e_2 < e_1)]]$$

Here is the taxonomy so far:

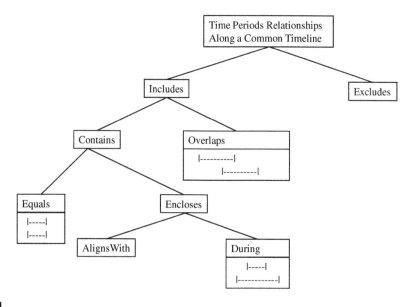

FIGURE 7.11

A Binary Partitioning of the Allen Relationships −4.

[ALIGNS WITH]: [STARTS] OR [FINISHES]

Since [Aligns With] is an [Includes] relationship, there must be at least one clock tick shared by two [Aligned] time periods. Since it is also a [Contains] relationship, every clock tick in one of the [Aligned] time periods must also be in the other time period. Since it is an [Encloses] relationship, i.e. a not-[Equals] relationship, one of the time periods must be longer than the other so that there is at least one clock tick in one of the time periods (the longer one) that is not also in the other time period. Since it is not a [During] relationship, then all the clock ticks that make the longer period longer are at "one end" of the smaller time period, not at both ends.

It follows that at that "other end", the two time periods do have the same clock tick. That is, they either start on the same clock tick, or they end on the same clock tick. (They couldn't do both, because that would make them [Equal]).

The predicate for [Aligns With] is the disjunction of the predicates of its components:

$$[(b_1 = b_2)] \wedge \sim(e_1 = e_2) \vee$$
$$[\sim(b_1 = b_2) \wedge (e_1 = e_2)]$$

Here is the taxonomy so far:

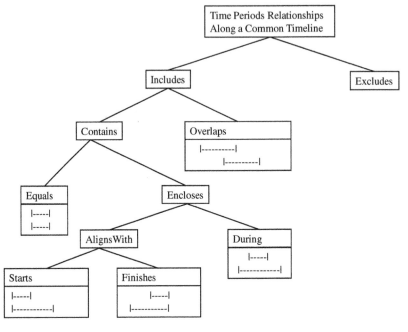

FIGURE 7.12

A Binary Partitioning of the Allen Relationships −5.

If two time periods start on the same clock tick, they have a [Starts] relationship. If they end on the same clock tick, they have a [Finishes] relationship. Once again, this is clearly a partitioning.

[Starts] and [Finishes] are both leaf node Allen relationships.

This completes our partitioning of the [Includes] relationship. [Includes] is a particularly important node in this taxonomy because all cases in which two time periods share at least one clock tick are [Includes] relationships. If those time periods occur on rows representing the same referent, the result will be that the pair of rows make contradictory statements about that referent, during all of those shared clock ticks. So simply by excluding rows for the same referent whose time periods have an [Includes] relationship, we can avoid contradictory statements in our database.

[EXCLUDES]: [BEFORE] OR [MEETS]

If there is an [Excludes] relationship between t_1 and t_2, then the two time periods have no clock ticks in common. But there may or may not be one or more clock ticks between them. If there is at least one clock tick between two time periods, one is [Before] the other. Otherwise, the two time periods [Meet].

Again, this is clearly a partitioning. Every pair of time periods with an [Excludes] relationship has either a [Before] or a [Meets] relationship.

The predicate for [Excludes] is the disjunction of the predicates of its components:

$$[(e_1 < b_2) \vee (e_2 < b_1)] \vee$$
$$[(e_1 = b_2) \vee (e_2 = b_1)]$$

An interesting point is that, since [Includes] and [Excludes] are a binary partitioning, the predicate for either of them is the negation of the predicate for the other. A logical proof is provided in *MTRD*, pp.326–332.

Here is the taxonomy so far:

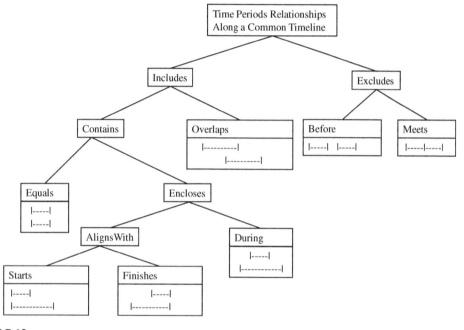

FIGURE 7.13

A Binary Partitioning of the Allen Relationships −6.

In addition, all the Allen relationships except [Equals] have two forms, one the reciprocal of the other. This allows us to distinguish the two time periods in those relationships. For example, if t_1 is [before] t_2, then t_2 is [before^{-1}] t_1. I indicate the disjunction of a relationship and its reciprocal by capitalizing the name of the relationship, for example [Before].

One of the benefits of this taxonomy is that it makes it clear that the Allen relationships are a partitioning. It makes it clear that there are no other positional relationships, along a common timeline, of two time periods. It also makes it clear that no pair of time periods traces more than one path from an Allen relationship (a leaf node of this hierarchy) to the root node. In other words, the taxonomy shows us that the Allen relationships are jointly exhaustive and mutually exclusive. They are, indeed, a partitioning of positional temporal relationships.

This completes this binary taxonomy of the Allen Relationships. The complete taxonomy is shown in Figure 7.13.

AN ALLEN RELATIONSHIP THOUGHT EXPERIMENT

There is another way to understand how the Allen relationships provide complete and non-overlapping coverage of all possible positional relationships between two time periods located on a common timeline. If the two time periods are positioned so there is at least one clock tick between them, and then one starts to move towards the other one, it will eventually reach the other one and pass by it. After it has passed by the other one, their sequence on the timeline will be reversed. Clearly, after this process is completed, all possible positional relationships between them will have been traversed.

We begin by assuming that t_1 and t_2 are the same length, i.e. that they have the same number of clock ticks. They are positioned on a timeline such that t_1 [before] t_2.

Now imagine that t_1 starts moving to the right, one clock tick at a time. At some point, t_1 will "catch up" to t_2. The *leading edge* of t_1 (e_1) will be immediately next to the *trailing edge* of t_2 (b_2), i.e. the two edges will be on adjacent clock ticks. At that point, $e_1 = b_2$, and t_1 [meets] t_2.

With just one more clock tick to the right, t_1 [overlaps] t_2.[2] How long the overlaps condition lasts, as t_1 moves to the right, depends on how long the time periods are. But eventually, the leading edges of the two time periods will rest on the same clock tick: $e_1 = e_2$. And because the time periods are the same length, it will also be true, at that point, that $b_1 = b_2$, which means that t_1 [Equals] t_2.

With one more clock tick, the sequence begins to reverse itself. First, t_1 [overlaps^{-1}] t_2. Then it [meets^{-1}] t_2, and at the next clock tick, it is [before^{-1}] t_2. The two time periods have now reversed positions. The one that was in front is now in back.

With these equal length time periods, it is clear that they cannot have a [During] relationship. It is also clear that they cannot have a [Starts] or [Finishes] relationship because if either their leading or training edges line up on the same clock tick, the other pair of edges will line up on their own same clock tick. And in that case, the two time periods will have the [Equals] relationship.

On the other hand, if the two time periods are of unequal lengths, then clearly they can never be [Equal]. Also, they can [Start] or [Finish] one another because when either their leading or trailing edges line up, the other one will not.

So we continue by supposing that t_1 is shorter than t_2, i.e. that it has fewer clock ticks than t_2 has. If t_1 and t_2 start out as before, then as t_1 moves to the right, the first three relationships between them will be the same as when the two time periods were of equal length. But after unequal time periods overlap, new Allen relationships come into play as t_1 continues to move to the right.

The first thing that happens is that the trailing edge of t_1 catches up to the trailing edge of t_2: $b_1 = b_2$. At that point, the leading edge of t_1 has still not caught up to the leading edge of t_2, so $e_1 < e_2$, in which case t_1 [starts] t_2.

On the next clock tick, one of two things happens, depending on how much longer t_2 is than t_1. If t_2 is just one clock tick longer than t_1, then on the clock tick after t_1 [starts] t_2, the leading edges of the two time periods align, and then t_1 [finishes] t_2. Otherwise, if t_2 is two or more clock ticks

---

[2]Of course, if t_1 and t_2 are both single clock ticks, then they cannot overlap. In that case, what immediately follows [meets], as t_1 moves another clock tick to the right, is [equals].

longer than t_1, then on the clock tick after t_1 [starts] t_2, t_1 [during] t_2. Nonetheless, in this case, t_1 eventually moves far enough to the right that $b_1 > b_2$ and $e_1 = e_2$. At that point, t_1 [finishes] t_2.

At this point, the differences between equal and unequal length time periods become irrelevant. With the next clock tick, t_1 [overlaps^{-1}] t_2. Later on, the trailing edge of t_1 passes just beyond the leading edge of t_2; they are on adjacent clock ticks. At this point, t_1 [meets^{-1}] t_2, and one clock tick after that, t_1 [before^{-1}] t_2.

The only three Allen relationships not encountered in these two thought experiments are [starts^{-1}], [during^{-1}] and [finishes^{-1}]. The reader who works through this exercise, using the assumption that t_1 is longer than t_2, will find that [starts^{-1}] is encountered where [starts] was encountered on the assumption that t_1 is shorter than t_2, and similarly for [during^{-1}] and [during], and for [finishes^{-1}] and [finishes].

It is clear that if two time periods are positioned on a timeline, one before the other and with a gap between them, and then one or both time periods move so that they end up with their positions reversed, all possible positional relationships among those time periods will be passed through. In this way, we have independent proof that the set of Allen relationships is complete.[3]

GLOSSARY LIST

closed/open	statement	time period
granularity	temporal entity	
predicate	integrity	
referent	temporal gap	

---

[3]It would be an interesting, instructive, and useful exercise to list the Allen relationships that are possible between (a) two time periods each a single clock tick in length; (b) two time periods only one of which is a single clock tick in length; (c) two time periods each two clock ticks in length; (d) two time periods only one of which is two clock ticks in length; and (e) two time periods each three or more clock ticks in length.

TEMPORAL INTEGRITY CONCEPTS AND NOTATIONS

8

Two of the principal constraints on relational tables are entity integrity and referential integrity. Primary key declarations set up the mechanisms by which a DBMS enforces entity integrity. Foreign key declarations set up the mechanisms by which a DBMS enforces referential integrity.

As we will see, these two constraints apply to bitemporal and unitemporal tables as well as to conventional tables. With all types of tables, entity integrity is enforced in order to prevent a relational database from including contradictory statements. Enforced on both conventional and temporal tables, these two constraints are the same constraints; that is, their semantics are the same. With all types of tables, referential integrity is enforced in order to prevent a relational database from including a reference to something that is existence-dependent on something else, unless a reference to that something else also exists in the database. Enforced on both conventional and temporal tables, these two constraints are the same constraints; that is, their semantics are the same.

CUBES, SLICES AND CELLS: DATA IN THREE-DIMENSIONAL TEMPORAL SPACE

It will be helpful to visualize a multidimensional space associated with every relational table. This space is a cube, and each referent represented in that table corresponds to one slice through that cube. The cube is three-dimensional, and so each slice is two-dimensional.

In Figure 8.1, the type cube represents a Part table and each slice of the cube represents one part. If that Part table is a conventional table, then each slice of that cube contains exactly one row of that table. If the Part table is a temporal table, then, as we will see, a slice may contain any number of rows, as long as all the rows represent the same part.

In Figure 8.2, X and Y axes are drawn on each slice. The X axis represents state time, and the Y axis represents assertion time. A "master" X/Y axis is drawn behind the cube to indicate that the X/Y axes on each slice represent the same set of clock ticks. That is, any (x,y) coordinate pair on one slice identifies the same two-dimensional temporal location as the same coordinate pair on any other slice.

This is important. It means that the time periods for any two rows are commensurable, i.e. able to be compared in measurements. If time periods were not commensurable within a type cube, then it would be impossible to know when temporal entity integrity constraints were satisfied and when they were not. That will be discussed in Chapter 9. As we will see in Chapter 10, if time periods

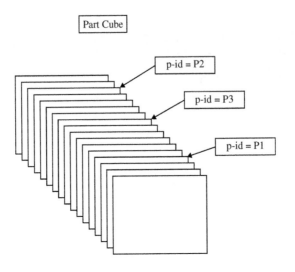

FIGURE 8.1

Type Cubes and Referent Slices.

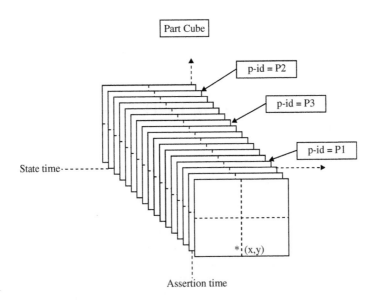

FIGURE 8.2

Metrics for Temporal Space.

were not also commensurable across type cubes, then it would be impossible to know when temporal referential integrity constraints were satisfied and when they were not.

The smallest bitemporal unit that can be defined with these temporal (x,y) coordinates is a *bitemporal cell* that is one clock tick wide and one clock tick high. This cell is an important unit in bitemporal data. It is the basis on which bitemporal entity integrity and bitemporal referential integrity are defined.

A bitemporal cell of a referent, to use a metaphor, is a "Planck area" of that thing in bitemporal space. It is bitemporally atomic. Temporal distinctions within a bitemporal cell have no meaning.

Figure 8.3 shows a slice through a cube, on which a bitemporal cell is shown. The (x,y) coordinates of the cell are its assertion-time period (designated "A") and its state-time period (designated "S"). I will refer to the lower-left corner of any bitemporal area as its "origin", the origin being the earliest bitemporal cell in the area.

Let the first depicted clock tick in both assertion time and state time be January 2014. In that case, the axes on these graphs extend out through July 2016. The cell shown in Figure 8.3 represents the assertion of a statement, an assertion made in May 2014, but withdrawn the following month. The statement is about the state of a referent during the month of January 2015. In this example, the slice is for part P2, in a cube for the bitemporal Part table.

The bitemporal cell which contains this row is shown in Figure 8.3.

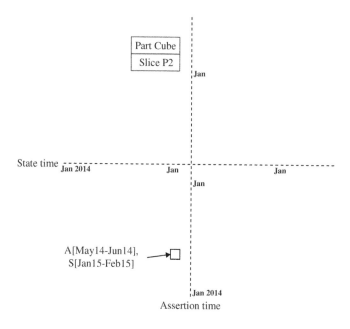

FIGURE 8.3

A Minimum Bitemporal Unit.

So this bitemporal cell contains the following row:

[May14 | Jun14 | Jan15 | Feb15 | P2 | A02 | axle | $5.50]

From a semantic point of view, the first four columns are the bitemporal coordinates of the cell, and the cell contains the statement represented by the last four columns of the row.

In May 2014, the statement made by this row was asserted to be true. Prior to that time, it was not asserted to be true. Since a row cannot be added to a bitemporal table with a transaction begin point in time earlier than the moment in which the row was physically created, we know that prior to May 2014, the row itself did not exist.

Beginning in June 2014, the statement ceased to be asserted. At that point in time, those responsible for that data were no longer willing to claim that what the statement said is true. But the statement itself remains in the table (or, in some methods of supporting bitemporal data, in some other table) as a record of a statement that, for that one month, was asserted by its authors to be true.

If bitemporal data were represented this way, with each row representing only one bitemporal cell, then bitemporal entity integrity could be enforced with the same mechanism that is used to enforce conventional entity integrity – primary key uniqueness. This is because the semantics of bitemporal entity integrity is the same as the semantics of conventional entity integrity. In both cases, those semantics are that no database may ever contain conflicting assertions. Assertions conflict when they are asserted at the same time and are about the same state of the same referent. In a referent slice through a bitemporal table, this means that no bitemporal cell in that slice may contain (be contained in) more than one row.

But most bitemporal areas are not single cells. For example, in May 2014, we knew that A02 was going to have the name "axle" and a unit price of $5.50 in January 2015 and also in the following month. This could be represented, so as to preserve a one-to-one correlation between rows and cells, as follows:

```
[ May14 | Jun14 | Jan15 | Feb15 | P2 | A02 | axle | $5.50]
[ May14 | Jun14 | Feb15 | Mar15 | P2 | A02 | axle | $5.50]
```

But bitemporal data is not usually persisted in tables in this manner, because there is a more efficient way of recording the same information. It is to coalesce the representation of cells that bitemporally [Meet] into a single row.[1] The rules for coalescing cells are these:

- The cells must be in the same cube. They must be for the same type of referent.
- The cells must be in the same slice. They must be for the same referent, i.e. for the same instance of the same type.
- The state descriptions in the two cells must be the same. They must describe the same atemporal state of the same referent.
- The assertion-time clock ticks of the two cells must [Meet] one another. There can be no assertion-time clock ticks between them.
- The state-time clock ticks of the two cells must [Meet] one another. There can be no state-time clock ticks between them.

---

[1] Of course, efficiency is relative to some standard. In this case, "more efficient" means "taking up less storage space". But as the cost of storage for character-set data becomes increasingly insignificant, we might eventually want to consider restricting the bitemporal areas of rows to single bitemporal cells. This would simplify the DBMS code that manages bitemporal data because the DBMS code that today manages nontemporal data actually manages data which has an implicit bitemporal area which is a single bitemporal cell – that cell being the current clock tick in both assertion time and state time. This point is taken up again in Chapter 19.

The result of coalescing the two single-cell rows for P2 is the following single row:

[May14 | Jun14 | Jan15 | Mar15 | P2 | A02 | axle | $5.50]

This is graphically shown in Figure 8.4.

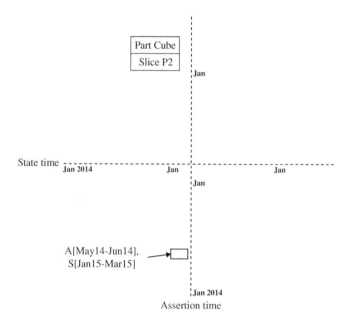

FIGURE 8.4

Coalesced Bitemporal Cells.

Figure 8.4 shows the two bitemporally-adjacent cells whose rows were listed just below Figure 8.3. Note that the line between the two cells is not shown. This illustrates a graphic convention I will use with these diagrams, that any series of adjacent cells that are represented by one row in a relational table will not be shown as a group of cells, but instead will be shown as a rectangle. These rectangles depict the bitemporal areas for rows in a relational table. In the next chapter, after the concept of an episode is introduced, I will use a rectangle to represent the bitemporal area of the group of rows I will call an episode.

The horizontal sides of an area represent the assertion-time period of a row, the time during which the statement made by the row was or is asserted to be a true statement. The vertical sides of an area represent the state-time period of a row, the time during which the thing represented by the slice was/is/will be in the state ascribed to it by the row.

A good metaphor for these cubes, slices, cells and areas is the structure of Microsoft Excel data. Think of each table as corresponding to an Excel workbook. Then each worksheet in a workbook corresponds to one referent of the type represented by the table. If the table represented by a cube is a Supplier table, for example, then each worksheet in the workbook represents one supplier.

On each worksheet, the horizontal and vertical axes represent the two temporal dimensions of bitemporal time. An area on the worksheet corresponds to a block of adjacent cells, a rectangle with no "holes" in it. In other words, if a boundary is drawn around an area, then every cell inside that boundary is part of that area.

Finally, in each cell in an area, there is a state description of a state of the corresponding referent. It is the state description provided by the one row for that referent whose assertion-time period contains the assertion-time clock tick of the cell, and whose state-time period contains the state-time clock tick of the cell.

With these concepts, and these graphics, we can analyze both temporal entity integrity and temporal referential integrity. Those will be the topics of the next two chapters. But before I proceed to those topics, I need to clear up an issue about primary keys and natural keys or, equivalently, about rows and referents.

SEMANTICALLY ANOMALOUS RELATIONAL TABLES

I noted before that the primary key and the RefId of a table do not have to be the same columns of data, the same substrings in the inscriptions which are the rows of that table. When they are the same, the primary key/RefId is functionally a homonym, one physical object playing two different roles. Primary key/RefIds, as I argued in (Johnston, 2000a; 2000b), are the source of the most costly form of inflexibility in databases that I have come across while consulting for companies in nearly a dozen different industries.

On the other hand, when primary keys are also RefIds, entity integrity is complete. That is, entity integrity guarantees not only the mathematical requirement that each row is unique, but also the semantic requirement that each row represents one and only one thing. So when RefIds are not the exact same columns as primary keys, entity integrity alone cannot enforce this semantic requirement.

To illustrate: as far as the DBMS is concerned, the transaction in Figure 8.5 is valid.

```
INSERT INTO Part
VALUES (P2, W45, axle, $5.50)
```

FIGURE 8.5

An Invalid Insert.

And the result would be as shown in Figure 8.6 (with the strike-through indicating that there is something wrong with the resulting row).

```
Part
p-id p-nbr p-nm  p-upr
P1   W45  wheel  $3.25
P2   W45  axle   $5.50
```

FIGURE 8.6

An Error in the Part Table.

The DBMS will allow this transaction, because the result satisfies primary key uniqueness. But in spite of primary key uniqueness, the table now contains two rows representing the same referent, the referent with part number W45. Part number is the referent identifier of the table; it identifies the referent that the row refers to. Part-id is the primary key of the table; it identifies the row itself. DBMS-enforced entity integrity will permit this semantic mistake to be entered into the database.[2]

This is important. Part-id does not identify parts; it identifies rows in a Part table. Part number does not identify rows in a Part table; it identifies parts.

If part number were also the primary key of the Part table, of course, then it would uniquely identify both a row and the part the row stands for. In that case, entity integrity would prevent the semantic anomaly I am describing here. But that would create the situation in which the same column or columns of a row are both a primary key and a RefId. That is the situation I called functional homonymy, and the articles I referred to (Johnston, 2000a-c) explain why I think that functional homonymy should be avoided in relational databases.

The entity integrity enforced by DBMSs, therefore, would be less misleadingly called *row integrity*. Since part number is indeed the RefId of this table, then the designers and developers of this database must insure that no two rows have the same part number. And the usual way to do this, of course, would be to define a unique index on part number. This additional work, that developers have to do, enforces the semantic mirror-image of row integrity, which I will call *referent integrity* (the "semantic side" of entity integrity, having nothing to do with referential integrity.)

The Part table, as shown in Figure 8.6, has row integrity. But it does not have referent integrity. It supports the syntax of row uniqueness, but not the semantics of referent uniqueness. For this reason, I will call such tables *semantically anomalous relational tables*.

More generally, entity integrity should insure both that primary keys are unique and that RefIds are also unique − both the candidate referent identifier chosen as the RefId, and any other candidate referent identifiers. Indeed, because of the importance of this distinction, I would like to see an addition to SQL DDL which identifies the RefId for every relational table, as well as all instances of candidate referent identifiers. If a RefId is used as all or part of a primary key, its status as a RefId should still be defined in the DDL.

The reason I would like to see this new DDL declaration isn't that it is difficult for developers to define unique indexes. It is that, lacking a RefId DDL declaration, relational table definitions fail to reflect the fact that these tables have a semantics and not just a syntax, that the purpose of rows of conventional relational tables is to designate referents, instances of the types represented by those tables.

I note, however, that in commercial databases, there is often a need to record information about things that we can't always distinguish from one another. For example, in an acquisition of Company X by Company Y, customer tables from the two companies will need to be combined. But if the customer referent identifiers used by the two companies differ, then there will be no way to discover the pairs of rows, one from each company's Customer table, which may in fact be for

---

[2]To point out that well-written application code would prevent this, is to miss the point. Insuring that, in a conventional table, only one row represents each thing, is not the job of application code. It is too important a job for that. It is, rather, the job of the DBMS. But since the current SQL DDL language does not allow us to specify referent identifiers, but instead only row identifiers, there is no way for the DBMS to prevent multiple rows in the same conventional table from representing the same thing. There is no way for the DBMS to prevent logically inconsistent statements from populating the database.

the same customer. Match logic may resolve many such cases; but often match logic cannot resolve all of them. In that case, the combined Customer table will still be a relational table, assuming that some kind of unique surrogate primary key is used. But it will be a semantically anomalous relational table because there will be no RefId which uniquely identifies the customers represented by those rows, no way to guarantee that there are not multiple rows for the same referent, rows which are logically inconsistent with one another.

In the days before relational databases, entity integrity and referential integrity were enforced on the "master files" which contained a company's data. The terms "entity integrity" and "referential integrity" were not used, but those requirements were enforced nonetheless. They were enforced by application program code, written over and over again for each new set of files.

Just as the enforcement of those constraints has been taken over by DBMSs, I believe that much of the work of managing semantically anomalous relational tables could also be taken over by DBMSs. This process of moving application logic into a DBMS always involves finding the right level of abstraction at which to implement that logic in that DBMS. Application-specific details must be abstracted away, leaving the logical core of the techniques to be implemented in the DBMS. Application-specific details are then added back by means of declaratively specified metadata.

Some of the techniques for managing semantically anomalous database tables, and for which a level of abstraction could be found at which they could be implemented in DBMSs, include:

- parameter-driven match logic engines;
- merging rows found to represent the same thing;
- splitting rows found to represent different things;
- cascading merges and splits along foreign key chains;
- gathering and applying user-specified merge and split decisions;
- logically partitioning a table into rows known to possess semantic entity integrity as well as physical (row-based) entity integrity, and rows possessing physical entity integrity only; and
- logically partitioning tables into rows against which merge transactions are valid from rows against which they are not valid.

As a final point, just as rows in conventional tables may have unreliable referent identifiers, rows in temporal tables may have unreliable time periods. For example, perhaps we are reconstructing some Part table data from 2005, and are using damaged archival data. We can tell from the data that part W45 was assigned a unit price of $1.75 sometime in June of that year. But all our recent Part table data defines state time for Part data to the level of a calendar day, and we don't know which day that $1.75 price became effective for part W45.

This suggests an analogy. Rows with unreliable referent identifiers are *referent multisets*, even if they are sets at the level of physical inscriptions. Rows with unreliable state-time periods are *state-time multisets*.

IMPLICIT BITEMPORAL TIME

For a conventional table, entity integrity prevents two or more rows for the same referent existing in the table at the same time. This is because, in conventional tables (but *not* in bitemporal tables), the presence of a row in a table *is* the assertion of the statement it makes. We insert a row when we wish to assert a statement that we believe to be true, and delete a row (or overwrite it) when we no longer wish to assert the truth of that statement. Since rows in conventional tables have no assertion-time periods, they are always currently asserted rows.

And here we see how unfortunate the choice of "transaction" as the name of this kind of time is. For on the next clock tick after a row is added to a conventional table, its implicit assertion-time period does not tell us when the row was physically added to the table. But it does tell us when we claim that the row makes a true statement. We make that claim right now, at the present moment, and we make it with the Gricean promise that, being data in a database that contains reliable information, that row will be physically removed from that database as soon as we are no longer willing to claim that what it says is true.

But perhaps the moral of this story is not that computer scientists have made an unfortunate terminological choice. Perhaps the moral is: so much the worse for my semantic interpretation of assertion time. So much the worse for my suggestion that "transaction time" is the name given to the physical implementation of an only partial understanding of the semantics of assertion time.

If I am wrong, however, then computer scientists should be able to say what the semantics of their concept of transaction time are.[3] Those semantics are not that a transaction-time period records when a row was added to a table, and may later record when a delete was issued against that row, because that's not any kind of semantics. That's a pair of physical actions taken with physical data. What do we *mean* by taking those actions? What are we understood to mean by those who look at our databases? What change in the information content of a database is effected by those actions?

I claim that there is no other interpretation than the one I have given. In a bitemporal table, the way we set values for transaction-time periods guarantees that when the transaction-time period of a row is current, that row is a row we present to database users as a row which makes a true statement. When we end a row's transaction-time period, then that row remains in the database; it is, we say, logically deleted but not physically deleted. As a logically deleted row, it represents a past period of time when we did present that row as a true statement. It tells us that, during that past period of time, that row was a "normal row", one which made a statement that we believed was true.

The following thought experiment demonstrates this point. Suppose that a bitemporal table is maintained with exactly the same set of transactions used to maintain a corresponding conventional table. In that case, all the transactions against the bitemporal table use the (default) Henceforth-based time periods. After any set of transactions are applied to both tables, it will always be the case that if a view selects from the bitemporal table all and only those rows which are current in both transaction time and valid time, then that view and the corresponding conventional table will have identical contents. Both will have the same number of rows. Corresponding rows in the two tables will make the same statements about the same things.

In a conventional table, although no time periods are explicitly expressed, there must also be a period of time during which we are ready to present the row to database users as making a true statement. And there is. That implicit period of time is co-extensive with the time during which the row is physically present in the table.

---

[3]As a minor point of grammar, the word "semantics" is one of those words that some authors treat as singular and others as plural, of which some will say "Semantics is ...." and others will say "Semantics are ...". And there are arguments supporting each position. Throughout this book, I have intentionally used both forms, since I find the arguments for each form equally persuasive. Eventually, one or the other usage will dominate. But that time has not yet arrived.

If two rows were statements about different state-time clock ticks, of course, then there would be no conflict. But with conventional tables, state time is not explicit; there is no state-time period on a row in a conventional table. So a row in a conventional table is always about the current state of the referent it represents.

What this description makes clear is that rows in conventional tables exist in bitemporal time. They are about assertions made right now, and about the promise to remove a row when it is no longer asserted. They are about the states of referents right now, and about the promise to remove the row when the referent is deleted and update the row when its referent changes state.

Conventional tables, therefore, are not nontemporal tables. They are *implicitly bitemporal* tables. They are bitemporal tables for which the user cannot specify valid or transaction time, i.e. state or assertion time, on transactions. They are bitemporal tables all of whose rows are current in transaction (assertion) time and in valid (state) time. They are bitemporal tables which record no history and anticipate no future.

But there is no reason why the system could not physically persist state-time periods and assertion-time periods on rows in conventional tables, keeping those columns of data hidden from the user. If that were done, then a full bitemporal history of data in those tables could automatically be preserved, without the need for the user to do anything. That full bitemporal history would be available for querying. And a later request to convert those conventional tables to explicitly bitemporal tables could be implemented by making those time period columns visible, and by removing the restriction on specifying time periods on transactions and queries.

GLOSSARY LIST

assertion time
assertion
assertion-time period
atemporal state
bitemporal area
bitemporal cell
bitemporal table
clock tick
coalesce
conventional table
episode
existence-dependent
information content

inscription
instance
referent identifier
referent integrity
referent slice
referent
row integrity
semantic anomaly
state description
state time
state
statement
state-time multiset

state-time period
temporal entity
   integrity
temporal referential
   integrity
temporal table
thing
transaction time
transaction-time period
type
unitemporal table
valid time

TEMPORAL ENTITY INTEGRITY

9

The previous chapter provided us with several useful concepts. First of all, it distinguished the implementation mechanics from the semantics of entity integrity, calling the former *row integrity* and the latter *referent integrity*. This distinction, as we will see in the next chapter, also applies to referential integrity (not to be confused with referent integrity). The previous chapter also introduced concepts useful for analyzing the temporal dimensions of both integrity constraints. These concepts are:

- type cubes;
- referent slices through type cubes;
- bitemporal cells within referent slices; and
- temporal areas as groupings of adjacent bitemporal cells.

The implementation mechanics of entity integrity are well-understood by most data management professionals. But the ontology and the semantics of this constraint are, in general, not well understood.

Conventional tables represent types. Rows of conventional tables represent the current states of instances of those types, and can represent no other states. This is a restriction on conventional tables. State-time tables lift that restriction.

From an ontological point of view, entity integrity is a constraint that applies to rows in the same table because instances of the same type are distinct referents and because no referent can be in two states at the same time. From a semantic point of view, entity integrity is a constraint that applies to rows in the same table because a database must be prevented from containing contradictory statements about the same states of the same things.

ENTITY INTEGRITY

Each row in a conventional table is a statement about a referent, specifically about the current state of that referent. The semantics of conventional entity integrity are that only one statement about anything may exist in a database at any point in time.

The DBMS sees to it that no two rows with the same primary key exist in a relational table at the same time. This data constraint is usually carried out by requiring that the primary key of each row in a relational table be unique within that table. Since rows and referents (i.e. current states of referents) are in one-to-one correspondence in conventional tables, this data constraint enforces the semantic constraint that a database cannot concurrently contain two statements about the same referent or referent state.

What is done with data is done to some purpose. It is done to manage information about things in the world. These things are distinct (or else they wouldn't be things). Things can never be in two states at the same time, and so states of things can be distinguished by the clock ticks they occur in.

Temporal entity integrity may appear to be an extension of conventional entity integrity. However, as we have already seen, it is perhaps more accurate to say that conventional entity integrity is a restriction on temporal entity integrity, a restriction in which it is applied to tables about only the current states of things.

BITEMPORAL ENTITY INTEGRITY

I will start by defining a bitemporal form of temporal entity integrity. *Bitemporal entity integrity* is implemented as the requirement that no bitemporal table may ever be in a state in which two or more rows in that table, with the same RefId, occupy the same bitemporal cell. That is, there can be no combination of an assertion-time clock tick and a state-time clock tick that is included in the time periods of multiple rows for the same referent.

Here is another way of stating what bitemporal entity integrity is. Two bitemporal cells in the same referent slice may (and often will) contain the same state description. But no bitemporal cell in a referent slice may contain more than one state description.

SOME BITEMPORAL TRANSACTIONS

To illustrate, consider an empty Part-B table. Assume it is Now() May 2015, and the transaction shown in Figure 9.1 is submitted to the DBMS:[1]

```
INSERT INTO Part-B
VALUES (P1, W45, wheel, $3.25)
```

FIGURE 9.1

A Bitemporal Insert - 1.

No state time is specified on this transaction, and so the DBMS assigns Henceforth as the assertion-time period value and the state-time period value associated with the transaction.[2]

---

[1]"Now()" is my implementation-agnostic notation for a variable which, whenever queried, returns the current point in time.

[2]The temporal transactions that I think a temporally-enabled DBMS should support are not identical to the temporal transactions specified in the ISO 9075:2011 or the TSQL2 SQL standards. In this and the following chapter, I introduce some of my preferred temporal transactions informally, by showing examples of them and commenting on them. I will discuss all of my recommended transactions in greater depth in Chapter 12. It is my hope that if other data management professionals agree that they represent important functionality, we can persuade the SQL standards committees to include them in future releases of the SQL standards.

Since no other rows for P1 exist in the table at this time, there is no possibility of a temporal entity integrity conflict, and so the transaction is applied to the Part-B table. The result is as shown in Figure 9.2.

```
Part-B
abtm   aetm   sbtm   setm   p-id  p-nbr p-nm   p-upr
May15  9999   May15  9999   P1    W45   wheel  $3.25
```

FIGURE 9.2

The Bitemporal Part Table - 1.

Each statement in a bitemporal table is a temporally-explicit statement about one bitemporal timeslice in the life histories of the thing that statement is about, and that statement itself. Throughout the assertion-time interval associated with the row that makes the statement — and at no other time — the statement is asserted to be true.

A bitemporal area is the Cartesian Product of the assertion-time period and state-time period of a row. So it represents the assertion, in every clock tick in that assertion-time period, that the statement is true of the thing represented by the row, in every clock tick in that state-time period.

A bitemporal DBMS guarantees that the assertion-time period for a row created by a bitemporal transaction will always be assigned a Henceforth-based value. It will always be an open time period that begins when the transaction commits. The current SQL standards, and the DBMS vendors, guarantee this by not providing a way for a user to designate an assertion-time period on a bitemporal transaction. The assertion-time Henceforth value is assigned by the DBMS itself.

The semantics enforced by this restriction is that a statement cannot exist prior to its being uttered or inscribed. If a row were created with an assertion time that began in the past, then that row would indicate that the statement it represents was asserted to be true, by an assertion associated with that inscription, before that inscription existed. Propositions, as we have already seen, are timeless abstract objects whose existence does not depend on any physical object. But statements exist only as the semantic content of utterances or inscriptions.

The bitemporal area for this row is shown in Figure 9.3. As in the previous chapter, the arrows on the top and on the right-hand side of the area indicate that the corresponding time periods are open periods.

So where in bitemporal time could additional rows for P1 be added? The origin of the bitemporal area — the cell which occupies the lower left-hand corner — conveniently divides bitemporal space into four quadrants. First of all, any attempt to insert a row for P1 anywhere in the upper-right quadrant will be rejected, because such a row would constitute a temporal entity integrity violation. Both time periods being open, the bitemporal area occupies all the space above and to the right of its origin.

No row can be inserted into the lower-right or lower-left quadrant because it is Now() later than May 2015. The lower-left and lower-right quadrants are the area of past assertion time, and data cannot be entered into the database at any point in past assertion time.

This leaves us with the upper-left quadrant, since nothing presently in the table says anything about P1 as it existed prior to May 2015. So let's assume that it is Now() July 2015, and we are about to enter a new row for part P1.

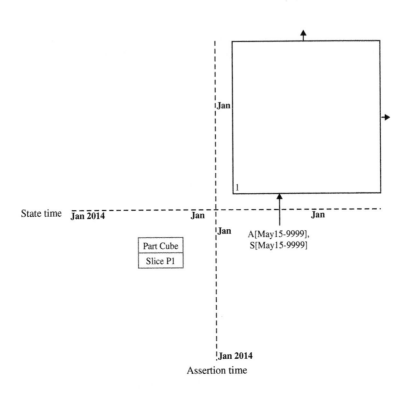

State time   Jan 2014 - - - - - - - - - - - - - Jan   Jan

Jan

Jan

| Part Cube |
| Slice P1 |

A[May15-9999],
S[May15-9999]

Jan 2014
Assertion time

FIGURE 9.3

Bitemporal Area for Row 1 of the Part Table.

Here are some options for the Insert transaction. The assertion time associated with the transaction is shown as the first time period, and the state time is shown as the second time period. Since we are not considering future assertions until Chapter 14, the assertion-time value, in all cases, must be [Jul15-9999]. For each option, the Allen relationship of its state-time period to the state-time period of the row for P1 already in the table, is indicated.

- [Jul15-9999], [Jul15-9999] [Finishes]
- [Jul15-9999], [Jul16-9999] [Finishes]
- [Jul15-9999], [Jul15-Jul15] [During]
- [Jul15-9999], [Feb 13-9999] [Finishes]
- [Jul15-9999], [Feb14-Jul15] [Overlaps]
- [Jul15-9999], [Feb14-Feb14] [Before]
- [Jul15-9999], [Feb14-May15] [Meets]
- [Jul15-9999], [Feb14-Apr15] [Before]

The row already in the table has an assertion-time interval of [May15-9999]. That interval [Contains] the transaction's assertion-time interval [July15-9999]. Since that row, and all the above-listed possible bitemporal areas for a new row for P1, [Contain] that same assertion-time interval, we can compare each of them to the row already in the table along their state-time intervals only.

The first five relationships are all [Includes] relationships. Therefore, adding a row for P1 with a Henceforth assertion-time period of [July15-9999] and any of these state-time periods would result in a temporal entity integrity violation.

But the last three relationships are [Excludes] relationships, and so they are not [Includes] relationships. Therefore, adding a row for P1 with a Henceforth assertion-time period of [July15-9999] and any of these state-time periods would not result in a temporal entity integrity violation.

For example, Figure 9.4 shows the addition of a P1 row using the time periods in the last of the eight options listed above. Figure 9.5 shows the transaction which uses these time periods, and Figure 9.6 shows the result of adding that row to the table.

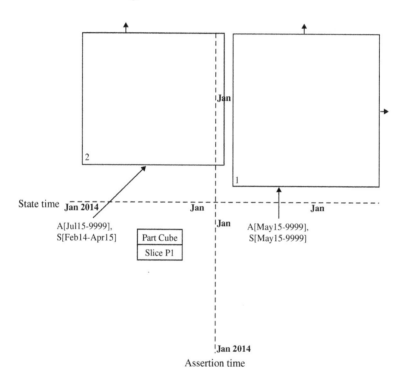

FIGURE 9.4

Bitemporal Areas for Rows 1 & 2 of the Part Table.

In Figure 9.4, we can see that no matter how far bitemporal area 1 extends up and to the right, as time goes by, and no matter how far bitemporal area 2 extends up, these bitemporal areas will never have even a single bitemporal cell in common. They will always [Exclude] one another.

And so we can indeed add that row to bitemporal area 2 without violating temporal entity integrity.

```
INSERT INTO Part-B
IN STATE INTERVAL (Feb14, Apr15)
VALUES (P1, W45, wheel, $2.75)
```

FIGURE 9.5

A Bitemporal Insert - 2.

Assertion time cannot be specified on a temporal transaction, and so for the transaction in Figure 9.5, the DBMS assigns a Henceforth value to the assertion-time period. The state-time period of [Feb14-Apr15] is specified on the transaction by its author. The result of applying the transaction is shown in Figure 9.6.

```
Part-B
abtm   aetm   sbtm    setm   p-id  p-nbr  p-nm   p-upr
May15  9999   May15   9999   P1    W45    wheel  $3.25
Jul15  9999   Feb14   Apr15  P1    W45    wheel  $2.75
```

FIGURE 9.6

The Bitemporal Part Table - 2.

Next, assume that it is Now() October 2015. We submit the Update transaction against the Part-B table, shown in Figure 9.7, to the DBMS:

```
UPDATE IN Part-B
SET p-nm = wheel-A, p-upr = $4.50
WHERE p-id = P1
```

FIGURE 9.7

A Bitemporal Update.

Since no assertion time is, or can be, specified, abtm = Oct15 and aetm = 9999. Since no state time is specified, sbtm = Oct15 and setm = 9999. The result of this transaction is as follows:

```
Part-B
abtm   aetm   sbtm    setm   p-id  p-nbr  p-nm     p-upr
May15  Oct15  May15   9999   P1    W45    wheel    $3.25
Jul15  9999   Feb14   Apr15  P1    W45    wheel    $2.75
Oct15  9999   May15   Oct15  P1    W45    wheel    $3.25
Oct15  9999   Oct15   9999   P1    W45    wheel-A  $4.50
```

FIGURE 9.8

The Bitemporal Part Table - 3.

The result of applying this transaction is that the first row in Figure 9.6 is *withdrawn* as of October 2015. It is withdrawn because after the transaction is applied, that row will no longer make a true statement. It will state, for example, that the unit price of P1 is $3.25 from October 2015 going forward. But the whole point of the Update transaction is to change that unit price (and part name) for precisely that state-time period. But since the Update transaction says nothing about any state-time period for P1 prior to October 2015, then everything said by that row about that earlier state time is not affected by the transaction, and must be preserved in current assertion time.

The third row in Figure 9.8 preserves that statement about the state of P1 prior to October 2015. The fourth row is about the state of P1 from October 2015 going forward.

It is the state description of P1 going forward from October 2015 that the transaction is about. The transaction reflects a business user wanting to enter into the database the fact that from October 2015, and for as long as nothing else happens to part P1, the part's name is and will remain "wheel-A", and its unit price is and will remain $4.50.

Figure 9.9 shows the states of P1 after the Update transaction is applied.

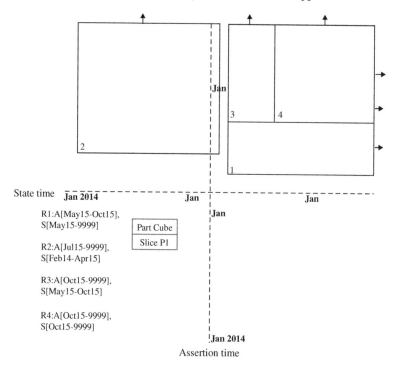

FIGURE 9.9

Bitemporal Areas for Rows 1 - 4 of the Part Table.

Note, in Figure 9.8, that the third row's state-time period is not open. This is shown in Figure 9.9 by the absence of a right-pointing arrow on bitemporal area 3.

Now let's suppose that it is February 2016, and we realize that we had a sale on P1 in December of 2015 that we failed to record. To fix this, we issue the retroactive update shown in Figure 9.10.

```
UPDATE IN Part-B
IN STATE INTERVAL (Dec15, Jan16)
VALUES (P1, W45, wheel-A, $3.60)
```

FIGURE 9.10

A Bitemporal Insert - 3.

The bitemporal area specified by this transaction is (A[Feb16-9999], S[Dec15-Jan16]). The fourth row in Figure 9.8 includes the same assertion time, and its state time begins on October 2015. In Figure 9.9, this is shown as bitemporal area 4.

After the transaction, the Part-B table looks like this:

```
Part-B
abtm   aetm   sbtm   setm  p-id  p-nbr  p-nm    p-upr
May15  Oct15  May15  9999  P1    W45    wheel   $3.25
Jul15  9999   Feb14  Apr15 P1    W45    wheel   $2.75
Oct15  9999   May15  Oct15 P1    W45    wheel   $3.25
Oct15  Feb16  Oct15  9999  P1    W45    wheel-A $4.50
Feb16  9999   Oct15  Dec15 P1    W45    wheel-A $4.50
Feb16  9999   Dec15  Jan16 P1    W45    wheel-A $3.60
Feb16  9999   Jan16  9999  P1    W45    wheel-A $4.50
```

FIGURE 9.11

The Bitemporal Part Table - 4.

The current snapshot of bitemporal slice P1 now is as shown in Figure 9.12.

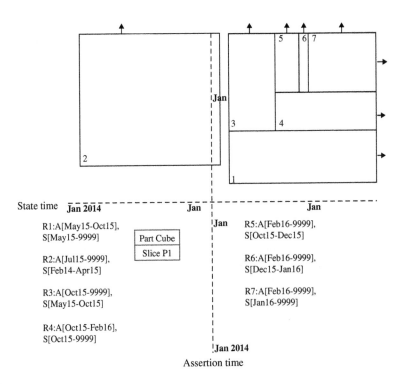

FIGURE 9.12

Bitemporal Areas for Rows 1 - 7 in the Part-B Table.

Clearly, bitemporal entity integrity does not prevent two rows for the same thing from having some or all of their state-time clock ticks in common. The semantics of this constraint, then, does not prevent the database from containing multiple statements about the same temporal interval in the life history of the same thing. It just prevents the database from containing multiple *assertions*, at any point in assertion time, about the same temporal interval in the life history of the same thing.

Nor does bitemporal entity integrity prevent two rows for the same thing from having overlapping assertion-time clock ticks. In Figure 9.11, for example, all the rows in current assertion time have all their future assertion-time clock ticks in common, and always will. The second row's assertion time completely contains that of the third row. The semantics of bitemporal entity integrity, then, does not prevent the database from concurrently asserting statements about different temporal intervals in the life history of a thing. It just prevents the database from concurrently asserting statements about the *same* (or overlapping) temporal intervals in the life history of the same thing. For example, all the rows with current assertion-time periods together represent two intervals in the life history of P1. The first interval started on February 2014 and lasted until May 2015. Then, after a month's absence, the second interval started on May 2015, and is ongoing as of the current moment.

What the implementation *mechanics* of bitemporal entity integrity does is keep out of the database multiple rows with the same RefId that have [Including]-related assertion-time periods and also [Including]-related state-time periods. Otherwise put, it prevents multiple bitemporal areas for the same thing having even a single bitemporal cell in common. The *semantics* of bitemporal entity integrity, which the implementation enforces and which the graphics illustrate, is that no two statements in a database for the same temporal interval in the life history of a thing may be asserted at the same time.

STATE-TIME ENTITY INTEGRITY

State-time tables are unitemporal tables which have explicit state-time periods but which do not have explicit assertion-time periods. The user can specify state time on her Insert, Update and Delete transactions. But just as with nontemporal and bitemporal tables, she cannot specify assertion time.

Assertion-time tables, of course, are also unitemporal tables. They are unitemporal tables which have explicit assertion-time periods but which do not have explicit state-time periods. However, the user cannot issue transactions against assertion-time tables. They play the role of system-maintained table-specific logfiles.

In terms of implementation, assertion-time tables contain before images of updated data, and also contain deleted data. In terms of semantics, they contain statements once but no longer asserted to be true. Their contents are both necessary and sufficient to produce *as-was-asserted* responses to queries. Without a record of past assertions, we could not recreate a report that was run at some time in the past, if anytime between then and now, a retroactive insert, update or delete was issued against data in the state-time interval of the original report.

Because the user cannot write transactions against assertion-time tables, I will not discuss temporal entity integrity as it applies to assertion-time tables. However, once state-time entity integrity is understood, it should be apparent how assertion-time entity integrity works.

To begin with, we may consider a *state-time unit* as a bitemporal cell with the assertion time dimension ignored. It follows that a state-time unit is the same thing as a state-time clock tick. The mechanics of state-time temporal entity integrity are that, for the same referent, a state-time unit is included in the state-time period of at most one row in a state-time table.

To illustrate, consider the following Part-S table. All the rows shown in the table are for one part, because the implementation of temporal entity integrity is as a constraint among rows representing the same thing.

```
Part-S
sbtm   setm  p-id p-nbr p-nm   p-upr
Jan15  Mar15 P1   W45   wheel  $3.25
Jul15  Sep15 P1   W45   wheel  $3.50
Aug15  9999  P1   W45   wheel  $3.75
```

FIGURE 9.13

A State-Time Part Table - 1.

The strike-throughs in Figure 9.13 indicate that the database cannot contain both the second and the third rows. Figure 9.14 graphically illustrates why. It is because there are two months — August and September 2015 — that are contained in the state-time periods of both rows. One row says that P1's unit price was $3.50 during those two months. The other row says that P1's unit price was $3.75 during those same two months. Both rows can't be right.

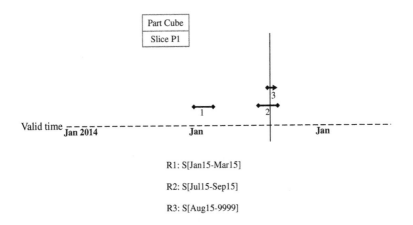

R1: S[Jan15-Mar15]

R2: S[Jul15-Sep15]

R3: S[Aug15-9999]

FIGURE 9.14

A Violation of State-Time Temporal Entity Integrity.

State-time periods are shown here as lines, not areas. State-time units are single state-time clock ticks. State-time intervals are sets of one or more contiguous state-time units.

The lines in this Figure representing state-time periods are marked with a diamond for their start time. If the time periods are open, then there is an arrowhead on the right. Otherwise, there is another diamond to mark their known end point in time.

In a state-time table, no history of when an insert took place is retained. Often, the state-time begin point in time is also the time the transaction took place. But rows can be inserted with state-time periods that begin in the past, or that begin in the future, in which cases the begin point in time is not the time the transaction took place.

In a state-time table, no history of updates is retained, and only the cumulative result of all the updates, for each row, is shown. Most of those updates were likely made because the referent represented by the row changed state, and so a new state description was needed. Others of those updates may have been made, however, to correct mistakes in the original data entered. Without assertion time, however, we can't tell which is which.

In a state-time table, a history of deletes can be retained, by setting the state end time to the time of the Delete transaction. But this kind of delete might better be called a *state-time termination*, since what it indicates is that from that point in time on, the row is no longer a description of the state of the thing it represents.

If there is a next row which begins on the very next state-time clock tick, we don't know whether that next row was inserted later on, after some amount of time had passed, or was created by an Update transaction. In the former case, the row just before it was state-time terminated by a Delete transaction. In the latter case, the row before it was state-time terminated by an Update transaction, and in that case there never was a period of time in which that row appeared to mark when a thing ceased to be represented in the table. We can't tell the one case from the other.

Without assertion time, state-time tables contain these unknowns. Sometimes, these unknowns may matter. Every time a report has to be rerun and must produce exactly the same results as when it was originally run, they will matter.

In fact, and although the 9075:2011 SQL standard permits them, retroactive transactions in a state-time table are semantically invalid. For example, if we realize, on the fifteenth of the month, that we changed a part's unit price to the wrong price beginning on the first of that month, then we have only two choices. On the one hand, we can set the end time on that row to the fifteenth, leaving the erroneous impression that the price change, as originally recorded, really did take place, and then insert a new row, with the correct price, starting on the fifteenth. On the other hand, we can overwrite the incorrect price, leaving the erroneous impression that the correct price had been in effect all along. Either introduces a falsehood into the database, which is why retroactive transactions against a state-time table are always semantically invalid.

Further examples of state-time temporal entity integrity are not necessary. Just as bitemporal temporal entity integrity prevents two statements about the same referent from sharing the same bitemporal cell, state-time temporal entity integrity prevents two statements about the same referent from sharing the same state-time clock tick.

CONVENTIONAL ENTITY INTEGRITY

When entity integrity is enforced on a conventional table, the DBMS guarantees that at no time may the table contain more than one row with the same primary key. So much is straightforward. But that is just a description of how entity integrity is implemented.

The mathematics of that implementation are based on the requirement that, in any table, the table is a set and the rows are the members of that set. Each set member must appear in its set only once, and each set member must be distinguishable from all other members of that same set. The DBMS recognizes the primary keys of rows as the row identity element of those rows, the components of those rows which distinguish them from one another.

But the semantics which those mechanics implement are something else again. Those semantics are based on the requirement that, in a conventional table, each row represents one state of one thing, that state being the current state of that thing. A row's RefId is the identity element for the thing the row represents. So if a conventional table contained two rows with the same RefId, then unless those rows were column-for-column identical, they would contradict one another. They would be different statements about the current state of the same thing. Since nothing can be in two states at the same time (quantum phenomena aside), at most one of those statements can be true, in which case one or both of those statements must be false.

Entity integrity also prevents any row in a relational table from having a null primary key. In terms of the mathematics of the Relational Paradigm, the reason is that a relational table is a set of rows, and every member of a set must have an identity which picks it out from every other member of that set. Primary keys are row identity elements, and (as far as the DBMS is concerned) they are the only identity elements of rows in relational tables. So if a primary key is null or partially null, it cannot fulfill its role as a row identity element.

In terms of the semantics of the Relational Paradigm, the issue is again with referent identifiers, not with primary keys. RefIds are referent identity elements, and the only referent identity elements, of the referents represented by rows in relational tables. So if a RefId is null or partially null, it cannot fulfill its role as a referent identity element.

Just as the graph of a state-time table is the same as the graph of a bitemporal table, but with the assertion-time axis removed, so too the graph of a conventional table is the same as the graph of a state-time table, but with the state-time axis removed. That leaves us with a referent slice on which no temporal axes appear. What interpretation can we give to that referent slice?

In fact, we all tacitly recognize the temporal aspect of rows in conventional tables. Speaking about production tables only — tables where an enterprise keeps the data that it relies on and asserts to be true — we all understand that those rows are about what we believe right now that things are like right now. We also all understand a set of implicit promises made by those responsible for the data.[3]

There are, in fact, four such promises. One promise is that if those responsible for the data acquire, or recognize, a new instance of a type for which there is a table in the database, they will promptly insert a row representing that new instance into that table. As a result, those custodians of that data support the *Closed World Assumption*, that the only instances of that type that there are, are represented in the database.

For example, all of the customers of a company are represented in its Customer table. If they weren't, they wouldn't be that company's customers. They might be former customers, or prospective customers, or something of the sort — but not current customers, not customers right now.

A second promise is related to the first one. It is that if those responsible for the data no longer have, or no longer recognize, an existing instance of a type for which there is a table in the database, they will promptly delete the row representing that instance in that table.

---

[3]These promises are an extension of H. P. Grice's rules of conversational implicature to databases. These rules, and these promises, are part of the pragmatics of language. See (Grandy and Warner, 2009).

A third promise is that if a mistake in the data is discovered, the custodians of that data will promptly fix it. One fix is to belatedly make an insertion or a deletion that should have been done some time ago. Another fix is to belatedly replace a row containing incorrect data with a new row containing the correct data. Other actions taken in accordance with this Gricean promise are to "improve" the data, wherever and whenever possible. This would include adding late-arriving data to a row, or replacing an initial estimate of some value with a later, more accurate, one.

A fourth promise is that if the current state of the thing represented by a row changes, the custodians of that data will promptly update the state description of that thing in the database.

The mechanics of entity integrity, at this point, need no further commentary. Row integrity is enforced by the DBMS as primary key non-nullity and primary key uniqueness. Referent integrity (not to be confused with referential integrity) is enforced by application developers as the requirement that all relational tables have a non-nullable referent identifier (sometimes called a *natural key*) which, for each thing represented in the table, is unique.

This works, but it comes up short. Vendors, and the SQL standards committees, have committed DBMSs only to enforcing row integrity, and claimed that by doing so they are enforcing entity integrity. But they are not. In doing that, they have enforced the *mechanics* of entity integrity, by managing *rows of data*; but they have ignored the *semantics* of entity integrity by failing to manage *statements about things*.

GLOSSARY LIST

assertion
assertion-time interval
assertion-time period
assertion-time table
bitemporal area
bitemporal cell
bitemporal table
clock tick
conventional table
inscription

life history
proposition
referent identifier
referent integrity
referent slice
referent
retroactive transaction
row identifier
row integrity
state description

state
statement
state-time interval
state-time period
state-time table
temporal entity
  integrity
temporal interval
thing
time period

TEMPORAL REFERENTIAL INTEGRITY

10

Referential integrity is a well-understood relational constraint. It applies to conventional tables. Temporal referential integrity is an extension of conventional referential integrity. However, as we will see later, it is really the case that all referential integrity is temporal, and that conventional referential integrity is temporal referential integrity restricted to tables which permit only one row, at any time, to represent one referent.[1]

Two key concepts are required in order to discuss temporal referential integrity. They are temporal foreign keys, and episodes.

TEMPORAL FOREIGN KEYS

Foreign keys are a mechanism well-known to the data management professional. They are declared in the DDL which defines a table. They designate one or more columns in a *child table* as pointers to a *parent table*. The foreign key column or columns are the same datatype and length as the column or columns which make up the primary key of the parent table. In each row in a table with a (non-null) foreign key, the value or values in its foreign key column or columns match the value or values in the primary key column or columns of some row in the parent table.

In the Supplier-Part table shown below in Figure 10.1, *sp-sfk* and *sp-pfk* are conventional foreign keys to, respectively, the Supplier and Part tables. Foreign keys between conventional tables link one row in the referring (child) table to one row in the referenced (parent) table. In the first Supplier-Part row, for example, the value "S1" in *sp-sfk* matches the value of the primary key of the first row in the Supplier table, and the value "P3" in *sp-pfk* matches the value of the primary key of the third row in the Part table.

Temporal foreign keys are both like and unlike conventional foreign keys. For example, consider the Supplier-S, Part-S, and Supplier-Part-S tables, in Figure 10.2. In that figure, the column *esbt* has been added. "esbt" stands for "episode state begin time", and will be discussed in a later section of this chapter.

In the Supplier-Part-S table of Figure 10.2, *sp-sfk* and *sp-pfk* are temporal foreign keys to, respectively, the Supplier-S and Part-S tables. Temporal foreign keys between temporal tables link one row in the referring (child) table to *one or more rows* in the referenced (parent) table.

---

[1]Another extensive treatment of temporal referential integrity can be found in *MTRD*, pp. 108-111 and Chapter 11. That chapter, in particular, provides a more extensive example-driven explanation of cascade delete operations on temporal tables than is to be found in this chapter.

```
Supplier
s-id s-nm       s-scfk s-type
S1   Acme       SC1    T4
S2   Superior   SC3    T22

Part
p-id p-nbr p-nm     p-upr
P1   W45   wheel    $3.25
P2   A02   axle     $5.50
P3   C01   chassis  $13.25

Supplier-Part
sp-id sp-sfk sp-pfk
SP1   S1     P3
SP2   S2     P1
SP3   S2     P2
```

FIGURE 10.1

Conventional Foreign Keys.

```
Supplier-S
sbtm   setm   s-id esbt   s-nm       s-scfk s-type
Feb14  9999   S1   Feb14  Acme       SC1    T4
Aug14  Mar15  S2   Aug14  Superior   SC3    T22
Mar15  Nov15  S2   Aug14  Superior   SC3    T15

Part-S
sbtm   setm   p-id esbt   p-nbr p-nm     p-upr
May14  9999   P1   May14  W45   wheel    $3.25
Jul14  Mar16  P2   Jul14  A02   axle     $5.50
Mar16  9999   P2   Jul14  A02   axle     $6.25
Jun15  9999   P3   Jun15  C01   chassis  $13.25

Supplier-Part-S
sbtm   setm   sp-id esbt   sp-sfk sp-pfk
Sep15  9999   SP1   Sep15  S1     P3
Oct14  Jan15  SP2   Oct14  S2     P1
Jan15  9999   SP3   Jan15  S1     P2
```

FIGURE 10.2

Temporal Foreign Keys.

The *sp-sfk* temporal foreign key in the SP2 Supplier-Part relationship, for example, contains the value "S2". But this value does not pick out a unique row in the Supplier-S table. It does not match any primary key in that table. Instead, it matches the supplier RefId of the Superior company. Similarly, Supplier-Part SP3 is referentially dependent on part P2, but there are two rows in the Part-S table for that referent.

Conventional and temporal referential integrity, then, differ in that the former is a one-to-one relationship between rows, while the latter is a one-to-many relationship. But they are alike in their ontology, in what they represent about the world.

The ontology of referential integrity has to do with the fact that some things cannot exist unless other things exist, and at the same time. Let's say that the former things are *existence-dependent* on the latter things. For example, there can't be an insurance policy without an issuing company and an insured party. A Supplier-Part relationship cannot exist unless both the supplier and the part that it relates also exist. There can't be an invoice without a customer to send it to.

The difference between foreign keys and temporal foreign keys, expressed in terms of syntax, might be said to be this: foreign keys point to primary keys; temporal foreign keys point to RefIds. But in fact, this is a distinction without a difference because both temporal foreign keys *and* foreign keys point to referents. A temporal foreign key does so directly, by means of the RefId of its referent. A conventional foreign key does so indirectly, by means of the primary key of the single row that designates that referent.

In the case of conventional (nontemporal) tables, there can be only one row representing each referent. Therefore, there can be only one row with a given RefId value. This is why a conventional foreign key relationship always links one row to one row.

In the case of temporal tables, however, there can be any number of rows representing the same referent. Every time that referent changes from one state to another, another row for that referent is added to its table in the database. The new row and the previously current row will be *temporally contiguous*, representing the unbroken continuous existence of the referent they represent.

And this temporally continuous existence is all that matters to an existence dependency relationship. The fact, as shown in Figure 10.2, that S2 changed its supplier type, matters not at all to the SP2 Supplier-Part relationship. All that matters, as far as SP2 is concerned, is that supplier S2 exists throughout the time that SP2 refers to it. How many rows are required to express that continued existence throughout that time, is not important to SP2.

EPISODES

In terms of its implementation mechanics, temporal referential integrity is a relationship between a row and a collection of one or more rows. The one row contains a temporal foreign key, and is the child managed object in the relationship. The collection of rows is the parent managed object in the relationship. I call these collections *episodes* of the referents they represent.

In terms of ontology, an episode is a temporal interval in the life history of a referent X on which another referent Y is existence-dependent.

The term "temporal interval" applies to both state time and bitemporal time. As a state-time concept, it refers to state-time intervals. In this case, temporal referential integrity means that the state-time interval of X begins no later and ends no earlier than the state-time interval of Y.

As a bitemporal concept, it refers to bitemporal areas. In this case, temporal referential integrity means that there is no bitemporal cell in the bitemporal area of Y that is not also in the bitemporal area of X. This means that the state-time interval of X begins no later and ends no earlier than the state-time interval of Y, and also that the assertion-time interval of X begins no later and ends no earlier than the assertion-time interval of Y. X's bitemporal area [contains] (but does not [Contain]) the bitemporal area of Y.

In terms of its implementation, an episode in a bitemporal table is:

1. a set of rows which have (a) the same RefId, (b) a shared period of assertion time, and (c) state-time periods which, in state-time chronological sequence, [Meet] the rows adjacent to them; and

2. for which there is no other row which has (a) the same RefId, (b) an assertion-time period which has even a single clock tick in common with the assertion-time period common to all the

rows in the set, and (c) a state-time period which [Meets] the state-time period of either the state-time earliest or latest row in the set or which shares even a single state-time clock tick with that set of rows.[2]

Clause (1a) tells us that all the rows in an episode represent the same referent. An episode is not a collection whose components represent different referents (as, for example, a relational table is). So episodes always exist on single referent slices. No episode "reaches through" a cube to touch multiple referent slices.

Clause (1b) tells us that the assertion time of the episode is the intersection of the assertion times of the rows in the episode. Since assertion times begin when rows are added, this means that the assertion time of an episode is the same as the assertion time of the row in the episode which was the last row to be physically added to the table.[3] This row is usually but not necessarily the row which is the chronologically latest state-time row in the episode. I call this assertion time the *shared assertion time* of the rows in the episode.

Clause (1c) tells us two things. It tells us, first of all, that the state time of the episode is the union of the state times of the rows in the episode. This means that the begin time of an episode is the begin time of the state-time earliest row in the episode, and that the end time of an episode is the end time of the state-time latest row in the episode.

We also know that within shared assertion time, no two rows in any set of rows with the same RefId have state-time periods either of which [Includes] the other. This is guaranteed by the constraint of temporal entity integrity. It follows that every pair of state-time adjacent rows in an episode [Meet] one another.

There are no state-time gaps between state-time adjacent rows in an episode because that's how episodes are defined. If a temporal gap appears in an episode, because of a Delete transaction, then the episode has split into two episodes. If a gap is eliminated between two episodes, because of an Insert transaction, then the two episodes have merged into one episode.

So within shared assertion time, and among rows with the same RefId, there may be temporal gaps between any two state-time adjacent pairs of those rows. But each such gap defines the end of one episode of the referent represented by that RefId, and the beginning of another episode of the referent represented by that RefId. Thus, episodes in state-time tables are bounded by unoccupied state-time clock ticks, and episodes in bitemporal tables are bounded by *unoccupied bitemporal cells*.

In terms of semantics, episodes — *not* rows — are the parent managed objects in temporal referential integrity relationships. Every child row in a temporal referential integrity relationship is related to a parent episode. That episode may consist of one row, but it will often consist of more than one row.

Figures 10.2 and 10.3 provide several examples. Supplier-Part SP1, as shown in the associative table Supplier-Part-S, is the relationship in which the Acme company is authorized to supply chassis to our company. Supplier-Part SP2, as shown in the associative table Supplier-Part-S, is the

---

[2]Keep in mind that names of Allen relationships, when capitalized, indicate the reciprocal form of the relationship. When in lower case, they indicate a non-reciprocal form of the relationship. Thus, [Meets] and [meets] are not the same thing.

[3]This is true, however, only if rows with future assertion time are not considered. Future assertion time, which is an extension of the standard theory of transaction time, is discussed in Chapter 14.

relationship in which the Superior company is authorized to supply wheels to our company. Note that, during the time that Superior is authorized to supply wheels, the company changed from a supplier type 22 to a supplier type 15.

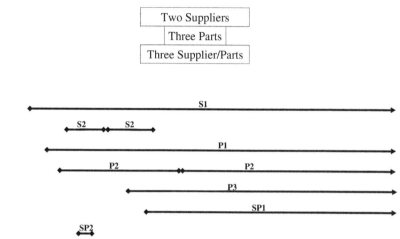

FIGURE 10.3

Comparing Referent Slices.

Supplier-Part SP3, as shown in the associative table Supplier-Part-S, is the relationship in which the Acme company is authorized to supply axles to our company. The Part episode that satisfies temporal referential integrity for SP3 is a two-row episode. The Supplier episode is a one-row episode.

In Figure 10.2 (and graphically, in Figure 10.3), the two supplier rows for S2 make up a *closed episode* of that supplier, and the two part rows for P2 make up an *open episode* of that part. In both episodes, there is no temporal interval which [Meets] the first or last temporal intervals in the episode, and which is occupied by the same referent.

The state-time latest row in any episode is the only row that, without reference to any other rows, can tell us the complete state-time interval of the episode. The episode state begin time, on all rows, indicates when the episode that contains the row began. So the episode state begin time, on the last row in the episode, together with that row's own state end time, are the delimiters of the state time period of that episode.

This means that no matter how many rows there are in an episode, each row indicates a state-time subset of the state time of the episode. That subset is the state-time period that extends from the start of the episode up to the state end time of that row. If that row is the state-time latest row in the episode, then the state-time period that extends from the start of the episode up to the state end time of that row is the state-time period of the episode itself.

Figure 10.3 is a graphical representation of the rows shown in Figure 10.2. In order to accommodate the range of time expressed in this example, I have altered the scale of the axes from the scale used in earlier chapters. In this chapter, instead of each dash on an axis representing one month, each dash represents two months.

Figure 10.3 is a new type of diagram because it is not a referent slice diagram. There is a referent slice corresponding to each of the eight rows in the diagram shown in Figure 10.3. This diagram stacks referent slices to make a composite referent slice diagram. This is necessary in order to show the dependency relationships among referents, and the temporal referential integrity relationships between parent episodes and child rows.

The two foreign keys in the Supplier-Part-S table, as well as the one foreign key in the Supplier-S table, are temporal foreign keys. This means, first of all, that the tables they reference are temporal tables, in this case state-time tables. It also means that, unlike conventional foreign keys, these foreign keys do not pick out a unique row in the parent table they reference. That is because the value they contain is not a primary key value in the referenced table. It is the RefId component of the primary key, and in temporal tables, RefIds are not unique identifiers.

Although episodes are an important concept, it isn't *necessary* to add an episode state begin time, or any other representation of an episode, to temporal tables. Because an episode is as defined above, it is always possible to determine the episodes of any referent. In a state-time table, all that is required, for any RefId and any point in state time, is to find the row with that RefId which contains that point, and then to look, recursively, backwards and forwards in shared asssertion time, for state-time contiguous rows with the same RefId, until a state-time clock tick not occupied by that RefId is encountered. That clock tick marks the boundary (beginning or end) of the episode that contains the row we started with.

Note, however, that temporal referential integrity parents can include any number of rows, in particular any large number of rows. Therefore, to confirm temporal referential integrity, without using episodes, would require, in many cases, that a large number of rows in the parent table be retrieved and assembled, "on the fly", into an episode of the referenced RefId. That can be quite costly in terms of performance, and by repeating the state begin time of the earliest row in an episode on all other rows in that episode, that performance cost can be avoided.[4]

We now have the necessary concepts to begin discussing temporal referential integrity. I will begin with the state-time form of temporal referential integrity.

STATE-TIME REFERENTIAL INTEGRITY

We begin with some Delete transactions. If a delete is issued against a table which is a parent table in a referential integrity relationship, the delete is governed by either a block, set null or cascade option. In all three cases, the objective is to avoid a database state in which a dependent child row in a referential integrity relationship is left with a *dangling reference* foreign key.

With conventional tables, the concept of a dangling reference is easy to understand. It means that a foreign key value is not matched by a primary key value in the parent table in the

---

[4]See *MTRD*, pp. 98-100, 142-143, and Chapter 11. However, episodes as managed objects, and in particular their use to enhance the performance of temporal referential integrity checks, are protected by U.S. patents 8,219,522 and 8,713,073. A license for the use of episodes may be secured from Asserted Versioning LLC.

relationship. In state-time tables, the concept is a temporally circumscribed one. It means that a RefId value is not matched, at every clock tick in the state-time period of the child row, by a row in the parent table with a matching RefId value.

The first of the three Delete options blocks the delete that would create a dangling reference. The second option nullifies the temporal foreign key that links the child row to the one or more parent rows. The third option deletes all child rows that reference each parent row being deleted, and does this recursively until no dangling reference temporal foreign keys are left, and does this as part of an all-or-nothing atomic transaction.

A STATE-TIME DELETE: BLOCK MODE

The referential integrity relationship between the Supplier-S and Supplier-Part-S tables is a temporal referential relationship. This requires that every clock tick in the state-time interval of any child row in the relationship is also occupied by a parent row in the relationship, the parent row being a row whose primary key includes a RefId whose value matches the RefId value in the temporal foreign key. Preventing a dangling reference, in other words, is something now done within the scope of the state-time interval associated with the transaction. This state-time interval is either an interval specified on the transaction, or is the interval specified by a Henceforth-based open-time period associated, as a default, with the transaction.

The intent of a state-time Delete transaction, i.e. its semantics, is to remove a state-time interval from a referent slice. It designates a group of one or more contiguous state-time clock ticks, and specifies that the referent being deleted should be removed from those clock ticks.

We submit the following Delete transaction against the Supplier-S table in Figure 10.2.

```
DELETE FROM Supplier-S
IN STATE INTERVAL (Nov14, Jun15)
WHERE s-id = S2
```

FIGURE 10.4

A State-Time Delete.

This transaction tells the DBMS to remove S2 as a supplier for the seven months beginning on November 2014. If this transaction were allowed to complete, the Supplier-S table would look like this:

```
Supplier-S
sbtm   setm   s-id  esbt   s-nm       s-scfk  s-type
Feb14  9999   S1    Feb14  Acme        SC1     T4
Aug14  Nov14  S2    Aug14  Superior    SC3     T22
Nov14  Mar15  S2    Aug14  Superior    SC3     T22
Mar15  Jun15  S2    Aug14  Superior    SC3     T15
Jun15  Nov15  S2    Aug14  Superior    SC3     T15
```

FIGURE 10.5

A Temporal Referential Integrity Error.

The two struck-through rows in Figure 10.5 are the ones that would be physically deleted by the transaction, if that transaction were allowed to complete. But this transaction is invalid, and cannot be allowed to complete, because it violates a temporal referential integrity relationship with this row from the Supplier-Part-S table:

[Oct14 | Jan15 | SP2 | Oct14 | *S2* | *P1*]

This row for Supplier-Part relationship SP2 exists in the last three months of 2014. But if the Delete transaction in Figure 10.4 were allowed to complete, then supplier S2 would no longer exist in the last two months of 2014. This would violate the existence dependency of Supplier-Part SP2 on supplier S2 in those two months.

A STATE-TIME DELETE: CASCADE MODE

If the state-time Delete transaction shown in Figure 10.4 were carried out in cascade mode, the Supplier-S and Supplier-Part-S tables would be as shown in Figure 10.6.

```
Supplier-S
sbtm   setm   s-id  esbt   s-nm       s-scfk  s-type
Feb14  9999   S1    Feb14  Acme       SC1     T4
Aug14  Nov14  S2    Aug14  Superior   SC3     T22
Jun15  Nov15  S2    Jun15  Superior   SC3     T15

Supplier-Part-S
sbtm   setm   sp-id  esbt   sp-sfk  sp-pfk
Sep15  9999   SP1    Sep15  S1      P3
Oct14  Nov14  SP2    Oct14  S2      P1
Jan15  9999   SP3    Jan15  S1      P2
```

FIGURE 10.6

The Result of a Temporal Cascade Delete.

Now there is no temporal referential integrity violation. The Supplier-Part relationship SP2 has been removed from the state-time interval specified on the Delete transaction. It's as if the state-time interval of the Delete transaction were laid over the referent slices of the referent designated in the transaction and, recursively, all of its temporal referential integrity-dependent referents, and then the database were updated so that none of those referents were represented anywhere within that temporal interval.

Figures 10.7 and 10.8 graphically represent the effect of this transaction. Figure 10.7 shows the rows which will be affected by this cascade Delete, before the Delete takes place. Figure 10.8 shows those rows after the delete has taken place. In both figures, the gray area is the seven-month state-time interval specified on the Delete transaction.

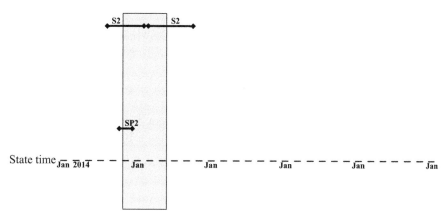

FIGURE 10.7

Before a Cascade Delete Transaction.

The gray area is the temporal interval that the Delete transaction says that S2 should be removed from. But SP2 is a child row in a temporal referential integrity relationship with S2, and so if the S2 row were deleted, the SP2 row would have a dangling reference during November and December. So the cascade option on a temporal Delete transaction results in every row in a referential integrity chain of dependent rows being removed from the temporal interval specified by the transaction. Semantically, it means that when a referent is said to no longer exist during a period of time, or to stop existing at a specified point, then all referents which are existence-dependent on that referent, recursively, must be said to no longer exist during that period of time, or to stop existing at that specified point.

Figure 10.8 shows the results of the Delete transaction. Supplier S2 is the target of the Delete transaction, and Supplier-Part SP2 is existence-dependent on that supplier. This existence

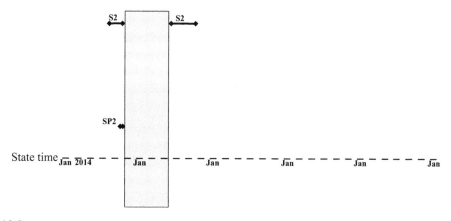

FIGURE 10.8

After a Cascade Delete Transaction.

dependency is expressed by a temporal foreign key in SP2, whose value matches the RefId in the two supplier rows for S2. After the Delete transaction completes, neither S2 nor SP2 are represented anywhere within the temporal interval specified on the transaction.

A STATE-TIME DELETE: SET NULL MODE

If the state-time Delete transaction shown in Figure 10.4 were carried out in set null mode, the Supplier-S and Supplier-Part-S tables would be as shown in Figure 10.9.

```
Supplier-S
sbtm   setm   s-id  esbt   s-nm       s-scfk  s-type
Feb14  9999   S1    Feb14  Acme       SC1     T4
Aug14  Nov14  S2    Aug14  Superior   SC3     T22
Jun15  Nov15  S2    Jun15  Superior   SC3     T15


Supplier-Part-S
sbtm   setm   sp-id  esbt   sp-sfk  sp-pfk
Sep15  9999   SP1    Sep15  S1      P3
Oct14  Nov14  SP2    Oct14  S2      P1
Nov14  Jan15  SP2    Oct14  --      P1
Jan15  9999   SP3    Jan15  S1      P2
```

FIGURE 10.9

The Result of a Temporal Set Null Delete.

In this case, SP2 is not removed from any state-time clock ticks. Instead, for the two months from which S2 was removed by the Delete transaction, and in which SP2 also existed, the temporal foreign key from SP2 to S2 is nullified.

This required that an SP2 row be isolated from the before-delete SP2 row and split into a pair of information-equivalent rows such that one of those rows is entirely outside the transaction's temporal interval and the other one is entirely inside the transaction's temporal interval. This is exactly the reverse of a coalesce transformation. I will call it a *decoalesce* transformation. As we will see in Part 2, when temporal transactions are applied to a relational database, decoalesce transformations are often required to get rows about to be updated temporally aligned with the implicit or explicit time periods on the transactions. Coalesce transformations are never required, and neither kind of transaction changes the semantics of the database. Before and after any coalesce or decoalesce transformations, a database contains exactly the same information.

BITEMPORAL REFERENTIAL INTEGRITY

Bitemporal transactions are transactions whose targets are bitemporal tables. State-time periods may or may not be specified on bitemporal transactions. But assertion-time periods are never specified on transactions. If a bitemporal table is being updated, the system assigns a Henceforth value to the assertion-time periods of all rows added to that table.

A *bitemporal referential integrity* relationship from a child row X is satisfied if and only if the bitemporal area of X is [contained] in the bitemporal area of a set of one or more rows representing the referent on which the referent represented by X is existence dependent.

Mixing terminology, we can say that every bitemporal cell occupied by a temporal referential integrity child row must also be occupied by a temporal referential integrity parent row, although for multiple cells in a temporal referential integrity child row, there may be different temporal referential integrity parent rows.

Figure 10.10 shows the set of tables I will use to illustrate bitemporal referential integrity.

```
Supplier-B
abtm   aetm   sbtm   setm   s-id  esbt   s-nm       s-scfk  s-type
Feb14  9999   Feb14  9999   S1    Feb14  Acme       SC1     T4
Aug14  9999   Aug14  Mar15  S2    Aug14  Superior   SC3     T22
Mar15  9999   Mar15  Nov15  S2    Aug14  Superior   SC3     T15


Part-B
abtm   aetm   sbtm   setm   p-id  esbt   p-nbr  p-nm     p-upr
May14  9999   May14  9999   P1    May14  W45    wheel    $3.25
Jul14  9999   Jul14  Mar16  P2    Jul14  A02    axle     $5.50
Mar16  9999   Mar16  9999   P2    Jul14  A02    axle     $6.25
Jun15  9999   Jun15  9999   P3    Jun15  C01    chassis  $13.25


Supplier-Part-B
abtm   aetm   sbtm   setm   sp-id  esbt   sp-sfk  sp-pfk
Sep15  9999   Sep15  9999   SP1    Sep15  S1      P3
Oct14  9999   Oct14  Jan15  SP2    Oct14  S2      P1
Jan15  9999   Jan15  9999   SP3    Jan15  S1      P2
```

FIGURE 10.10

A Set of Bitemporal Tables.

It is Now() July 2014. Figure 10.11 is a graphical representation of the row for Supplier-Part SP2, and of the two rows whose RefIds are specified by its temporal foreign key *sp-sfk* — rows for supplier S2. Figure 10.12 is a graphical representation of the row for supplier-part SP2, and for the row whose RefId is specified by its temporal foreign key *sp-pfk* — the row for part P1. In these two diagrams, the notations XX-Rn, for example SP-R2, or S-R1, indicate the row in the corresponding table in Figure 10.10 that corresponds to the rectangle so labeled.

We can see from Figures 10.11 and 10.12 that bitemporal temporal referential integrity is currently satisfied. The bitemporal area of the child row SP2 is [contained] in the bitemporal areas of its two parent episodes.

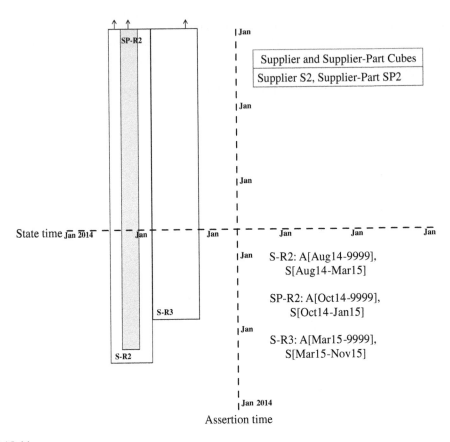

FIGURE 10.11

Supplier and Supplier-Part Bitemporal Areas.

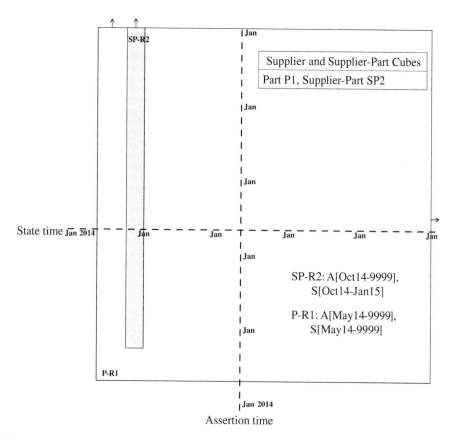

FIGURE 10.12

Part and Supplier-Part Bitemporal Areas.

Let's assume that we want to retroactively extend Supplier-Part relationship SP2 back to June 2014. Since SP2 already is represented as far back as October 2014, this means that we want to insert a row for SP2 whose state-time period is [Jun14-Oct14]. This transaction is shown in Figure 10.13.

```
INSERT INTO Supplier-Part-B
IN STATE INTERVAL (Jun14, Oct14)
VALUES (SP2, S2, P1)
```

FIGURE 10.13

A Bitemporal Insert.

The intent of a bitemporal Insert transaction, i.e. its semantics, is to add a bitemporal area to a referent slice. It designates a group of one or more contiguous state-time clock ticks, and specifies that the referent being inserted should be added to the bitemporal area whose state-time boundary is determined by those clock ticks.

For this Insert, there are two referential integrity relationships to check. One is with part P1. Since P1 was asserted, on May 2014, to have been a part since May 2014, and is still asserted, until further notice, to still be a part, until further notice, the proposed insert satisfies this temporal referential integrity constraint.

As for supplier S2, the state-time interval for that supplier extends only back to August 2014. Therefore, there are no bitemporal cells for S2 for June or July 2014. In this case, the proposed insert would fail this referential integrity constraint.

CONVENTIONAL REFERENTIAL INTEGRITY

There is always a current bitemporal cell in the bitemporal area of any bitemporal row that hasn't been deleted, and that has an open state-time period.[5] As time goes by, Now() moves from one moment to the next, moving one clock tick upwards and also one clock tick to the right on these bitemporal diagrams. With each clock tick, we continue to assert that the statement made by the row is true. With each clock tick, the statement continues to be about the *current state* of the referent represented.

With bitemporal rows whose time periods are open (end in 9999), their intervals grow as time goes by. Their assertions, and what they assert, remain current "until further notice".

In this passage of time, the origins of these rows remain visible for all to see. But with conventional tables, this is not the case. The reason is not that conventional tables are nontemporal. They are indeed the tables that most data management professionals would say are nontemporal, and they are indeed tables which include neither assertion-time nor state-time period columns. But in reality, conventional tables are bitemporal. They are bitemporal tables whose time periods are not persisted as columns of data, and whose rows are always currently asserted statements about what the referents they describe are currently like.

It is Now() January 2015. Figure 10.14 shows the bitemporal area of part P1, in the conventional Part table. This is, in fact, the bitemporal area of every row in that "nontemporal" table. For every row, the assertion-time period and the state-time period begin with Now(), i.e. every row in a nontemporal table is always the assertion of a statement. For every row, the assertion-time period and the state-time period end with 9999, i.e. every row in a nontemporal table is always a current assertion about the current state of a referent, and will remain so until further notice.

Let's jump six months ahead, and assume that it is Now() June 2015. In this case, the bitemporal diagram for P1, as well as for every other row in the Part table, as of June 2015, is the diagram shown in Figure 10.15.

---

[5]In the diagramming conventions used in this and the two previous chapters, the bitemporal areas of rows are not shown. Instead, the bitemporal areas shown are the areas of episodes of the referents represented. But to help make the comparison with conventional tables, in which there is only one row for each referent, we can assume, in this section, that with bitemporal tables, we are talking about one-row episodes.

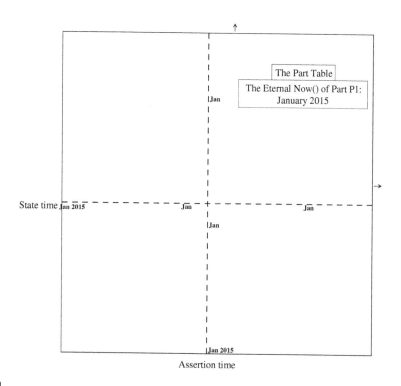

FIGURE 10.14

The Eternal Now() of all Rows in the Part Table — January, 2015.

Figure 10.15 provides no information about any time prior to June 2015. That is indicated by the shaded area on the diagram, which represents the now missing information about the previous six months. So in this passage of time, history has been lost. Back in January, the one row for P1 represented the then-current assertion about the then-current state of P1. Now, on June 2015, this one row represents the now-current assertion about the now-current state of P1.

The bitemporal area for every row in a conventional table is a single bitemporal cell whose coordinates are [Now()-9999] in assertion time, and [Now()-9999] in state time. Notice that these coordinates are *not* [Now(!)-9999]. "Now(!)" represents a constant, a particular moment in time. When a new row is assigned an assertion time of Henceforth, the begin time of that value is the moment in time when the transaction takes place. This serves as a place-marker, telling us when this row first appeared. Semantically, it tells us when this row was first asserted to make a true statement. If the row is also assigned a state time of Henceforth, the begin time of that value is the moment in time when the referent represented by the row entered that state.

But [Now()-9999] is not Henceforth because Now() is a variable. Since we always know what time it is now, we don't need to store the begin time of a conventional row's assertion-time period or its state-time period. And since 9999 is a constant, we don't need to store the end time of a

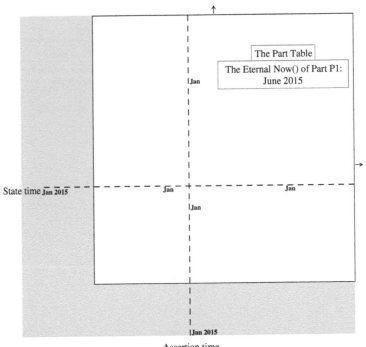

FIGURE 10.15

The Eternal Now() of all Rows in the Part Table — June, 2015.

conventional row's assertion-time period or its state-time period. And so, in a conventional table, these two time periods are implicit. There is no need to express them as columns of persisted data.

A row in current assertion time is currently asserted. So a row in a conventional table is currently asserted. When a row in a conventional table is deleted, it is no longer present to make an assertion. That is the only way to withdraw an assertion in a conventional table. But a row in a bitemporal table can remain physically present even though it has been deleted. In its case, the transaction end time is set to the time specified on its Delete transaction, or to the time when the system internally *withdraws* the row.[6] In both cases, though, the semantics of the deletion is the same. It is that the statement made by the row is no longer asserted to be true.

When a row in a conventional table is updated (by means of an overwrite), it no longer describes the same state of the referent. It describes a new state. For example, a supplier may be updated because of a supplier-type change; or the unit-price of a part may have changed. In describing this new state, the row makes a new statement. An update in a nontemporal table replaces one statement with another one.

---

[6]Internally withdrawing a row, and other details of how temporal transactions work, are discussed in the next chapter.

But a row in a bitemporal table can remain physically present even though the state it describes is no longer current. In its case, the state end time is set to whatever state end time is associated with the Update transaction. In both cases, though, the semantics of the update is the same. It is that the referent described by the row is no longer in the state which the row ascribes to it.

So in terms of its semantics, a row in a conventional table *is* a bitemporal row. It represents a current assertion about the current state of a referent. The conventional table retains no history, and anticipates no future. In terms of its syntax, a row in a conventional table is a bitemporal row with implicit time periods. Its bitemporal area is always one bitemporal cell in extent, and the bitemporal coordinates of that one cell are always [Now()-9999].

It might seem that if the *implicit temporality* of rows in conventional tables are as I have described them to be, the *implicit time periods* of those rows should actually be [Now()-Now()] and not, as I have said they are, [Now()-9999].

But that isn't so. As I described earlier, two of the *implicit promises* that accompany production databases are that those responsible for the data will make their best effort both to correct mistakes and amend incompletions in a timely manner, and to keep up with changes to what the data is about, also in a timely manner. These promises are part of the extension of Grice's rules of conversational implicature to databases. The first promise is the promise to tell the truth, the whole truth, and nothing but the truth. The second promise is the promise that, when anything happens to the things we are keeping track of, we will record those changes in the database as quickly as possible.

Without these promises, the implicit time periods of rows in conventional tables would indeed be [Now()-Now()]. But with these promises, we can truthfully claim an "until further notice" status for both temporal dimensions. With these promises, the implicit time periods of rows in conventional tables are [Now()-9999].

I think that these facts about conventional tables and rows are very significant. For let's suppose that a DBMS is extended to manage bitemporal data. Let's call those extensions its *bitemporal code*. I contend that bitemporal code is all that a DBMS needs, that its bitemporal code can manage conventional tables as well as bitemporal tables, including referential integrity relationships between bitemporal and conventional tables.

The key to this codebase integration and simplification is that the DBMS can associate a [Now (!)-9999] assertion-time and state-time period with all conventional rows retrieved from persistent storage, at the moment those rows are retrieved and under the management of an atomic unit of work. As for transactions, there are no time periods involved because there is no physical persistence of time periods on conventional table rows.

Once that is done, these *bitemporally materialized rows* will be just like rows which are persisted in explicit bitemporal form. By enforcing temporal entity integrity on these transactions and these rows, conventional entity integrity will be enforced. By enforcing temporal referential integrity on these transactions and these rows, conventional referential integrity will be enforced.

And this leads to a natural next step, which is to physically persist conventional tables as bitemporal structures. All transactions against these tables, in that case, would be temporal transactions on which time periods could not be specified. They would be temporal transactions to which the system assigned a Henceforth value to both time periods. All queries against these tables, in that case, would be temporal queries with a system-supplied restriction to rows in current assertion time and current state time. From this perspective, the restriction of conventional data to an eternally current single bitemporal cell can be seen for what it is: a self-imposed temporal amnesia and a self-imposed temporal myopia which, because of the advent of bitemporal data management capabilities, is no longer necessary.

We don't have to lose our past. We don't have to ignore our future. With no disruption to application code, transactions, or queries, we can make conventional tables fully bitemporal. And by managing all tables as bitemporal tables "under the covers" of transactions using Henceforth default values, and under the covers of views and queries which make tables appear to be conventional nontemporal tables, or unitemporal state-time tables, we make it possible to keep a full bitemporal history of changes to all tables in a database, and to enforce entity and referential integrity on all these types of tables with a single implementation in code.

GLOSSARY LIST

assertion-time interval
assertion-time period
bitemporal area
bitemporal cell
bitemporal table
clock tick
coalesce
contiguous clock ticks
conventional table
current assertion
current state

decoalesce
episode
existence dependent
future assertion time
implicit temporality
life history
open time period
referent slice
referent
statement
state-time interval

state-time period
state-time table
temporal foreign key
temporal gap
temporal interval
temporal referential
  integrity
temporal table
withdraw

PRACTICE

2

We now have a rich set of concepts with which to understand temporal data and what we are doing when we design, create, populate and query temporal tables in relational databases. Understanding these things, we are less likely to make mistakes with the new temporal capabilities that DBMS vendors are making available, and more likely to minimize the impact of their shortcomings and to maximize the value they provide.

For example, the concept of a referent explains in what way foreign keys and temporal foreign keys are similar. They are similar in that both point to referents. Foreign keys point to referents in tables which are restricted to having only one row for each referent because rows in those tables record only the current states of their referents. Temporal foreign keys point to referents in tables in which multiple rows can have the same referent, each of those rows describing a different temporal state of its referent. Thus foreign keys pointing to single rows is just a special case of temporal foreign keys pointing to any number of rows.

We know that referents are instances of types. We know that they are either objects or events. And the concepts of referents and referent states are but one component of the conceptual apparatus we have developed by examining the ontology and the semantics of the Relational Paradigm, as well as its mathematics and logic.

With this set of concepts, we turn now from theory to practice. This is "practice", of course, not in the sense of doing the same thing over and over again, but in the sense of applying the bitemporal theory we developed in Part 1 to real issues in data management. It is "practice" in the sense that doctors practice medicine and lawyers practice law. It is the practice of IT professionals managing data so as to preserve information and make it available to those who need it.

The first four chapters in Part 2 are about transactions and queries. As I mentioned before, the syntax I use for temporal transactions and queries is not the syntax defined in the standards documents or implemented by major DBMS vendors. I prefer my own syntax primarily because it doesn't intermingle references to columns which implement temporal or bitemporal features with references to columns of business data. Columns of business data are the predicates of their tables. In the rows of those tables, business data values describe properties and relationships of the referents of those rows. That is not what state-time periods or assertion-time periods do.

State-time and assertion-time columns are not predicates. In the rows of their tables, state time describes when the referents of those rows were/are/will be as those rows' business columns describe them to be.[1] In the rows of their tables, assertion time distinguishes statements asserted in the past, from statements currently asserted and, as Chapter 14 will describe, also from statements that may be asserted in the future.

I recommend that readers develop their own sample tables corresponding to the ones that appear in these chapters, and write transactions and queries that correspond to the ones that appear in these chapters. To achieve a greater degree of real-world verisimilutude, I recommend that timestamps be substituted for the ersatz month-year datatype I am using. Readers that have access to bitemporally-capable DBMSs should use the bitemporal features of those DBMSs. Readers that do not can still define bitemporal tables to their DBMSs, and can still code bitemporal transactions and queries in pre-bitemporal SQL. Two good sources of pre-bitemporal SQL examples are (Snodgrass, 1999) and *MTRD*.

The last of these first four chapters − Chapter 14 − presents the theory of *future assertions*, an extension to the standard theory of bitemporal data that I and my *MTRD* co-author call the *Asserted Versioning* theory of bitemporal data. Future assertion time is not defined in the temporal SQL standards, and is not implemented in today's bitemporal DBMSs. But those readers using pre-bitemporal DBMSs will be able to write transactions that create and maintain future assertions, and queries that retrieve future assertions. Those readers will find that the Asserted Versioning extension to the standard theory is fully upward compatible with that standard theory.

Chapter 15 is written for business analysts, data modelers and others whose job is to gather requirements from business users, clarify those requirements, and express those requirements in a form from which developers can begin to build and later to maintain the databases and database extensions that implement those requirements.

To support my contention that there is important business afoot in that chapter, let me state the need for clarification in the expression of temporal business requirements this way. Long-standing best practices for implementing temporal requirements have nearly always resulted in semantically invalid tables, specifically in tables in which it is impossible to always tell the truth. Moreover, these mistaken practices are supported by the ISO 9075:2011 SQL standard. Temporal

---

[1] State time would be, to logicians, a temporal modal operator on the statements made by rows. I have avoided this way of treating state time because I am neither interested in developing a temporal modal logic for bitemporal data, nor qualified to do so. Instead, I have treated state time as a disambiguation of a temporal indexical associated with statements about things, distinguishing one temporal state of something from other temporal states of that same thing as being that atemporal state of that thing which uniquely occupies that temporal interval.

implementations, in ISO temporally compliant databases, can result in tables in which it is impossible to always tell the truth. ISO should never have supported this mistake.

In Chapter 16, I turn to one of the two major data warehousing paradigms, Inmon's Corporate Information Factory and, since 2008, his Data Warehouse 2.0. The other paradigm, of course, is Kimball's star schema design pattern, and its supporting conformed dimensions architecture.

I have two points to make with respect to Inmon's architecture. The first is that the use of bitemporal tables in the Inmon enterprise data warehouse will preserve all the historical information that a series of snapshots of operational databases will preserve, and will usually do so using significantly less disk space.

My second point is that the use of snapshots, no matter how frequent, cannot capture a complete historical record. Nor can real-time data warehousing, no matter how real-time it is. Only bitemporal data can do that. Bitemporal tables are a complete record of the history of both changes to the things the data is about, as those changes are recorded in that data and, orthogonally, a history of changes to the data itself. The historical data in an Inmon data warehouse does not and cannot capture both of these orthogonal histories. And neither can the slowly-changing dimensions (hereafter, SCDs) of Kimball's star schemas. Without bitemporal data, any claim that an historical data warehouse supports both time-variance and nonvolatility is mistaken.

I have two similar points to make with respect to Kimball's data warehouse architecture and to his star schema design pattern. The first is that the use of any kind of SCD other than type 2 is unwarranted except in such nearly unimaginable circumstances as petabyte-sized dimension tables, with very large rows, which are updated very frequently. The second point is that even a full type 2 implementation, applied to every attribute of a dimension, will not capture a complete historical record.

What we need to do is to abandon SCDs, and replace them with bitemporal dimensions. Without bitemporal dimensions, any claim that a Kimball star schema supports a complete historical record of the data in a dimension, or that it fully supports as-was reporting, is a mistaken claim.

I note that in neither Inmon's 2008 book nor Kimball's 2013 book does the word "bitemporal" appear. More importantly, the concept doesn't appear either. We all know by now that bitemporal data preserves and provides information that unitemporal data cannot. We all know by now that much of the data that contains this information is important enough that we should make it as readily and easily available as current data is.

As I mentioned above, bitemporal tables will, in general, use less disk storage to preserve the same amount of information that Inmon snapshots and Kimball slowly changing dimensions preserve. I don't consider this very important, however, since we are talking only about the management of character-set, structured business data, which is an increasingly small proportion of the total data managed by an enterprise. But for those who still think that it's worth elaborate architect-level or DBA-level constructions to save as little as a few terabytes of storage, then this point should be reassuring.

In Chapter 17, I discuss an SOA (service-oriented architecture) approach to physically implementing an *enterprise data model* as a set of mapping rules in an SOA messaging layer. I will show that this provides the "integration", as Inmon calls it, that he claims is possible only by transforming data into a standard format and persisting that transformed data in an enterprise data warehouse.

Inmon has repeatedly deprecated the concept of a virtual data warehouse and its associated federated queries. But although an historical database which provides a standard representation of standard types and domain values is a useful component of an enterprise's total data asset, that component is unable to semantically integrate real-time data with non-real-time data. For real-time data, in operational databases, semantic integration means the ability to exchange data without loss of information. And to achieve that objective, what is needed is a set of mapping rules, applied to messages between those databases, which map messages into and out of an enterprise *canonical format* described by the enterprise's enterprise data model.

In Chapter 18, I discuss the second of the two major data warehousing paradigms, Kimball's conformed dimensions data warehouse architecture. Just as bitemporal tables preserve a complete historical record in less space than Inmon's historical warehouse tables preserve a partial historical record, they also preserve a complete historical record in less space than Kimball's slowly-changing dimensions preserve a partial historical record. Just as Inmon's historical record cannot express both a history of changes to the things represented by the data, and also a history of changes to the data itself, neither can Kimball's SCDs.

Here are two basic numbers that we should keep in mind when deciding when it is cost-effective to use any of Kimball's new hybrid SCD types. A conservative estimate for the cost of a loaded man-hour of an IT professional's time is $80 per hour.[2] The cost of a terabyte of disk storage, as I finish this manuscript, is under $40. So for any proposed use of any SCD, we should add up the total man-hours devoted to the design, coding, testing, implementation, use and maintenance of that SCD that exceed the total hours required to develop a bitemporal solution. To justify the expenditure of those man-hours, the use of any SCD type should result in a savings of at least two terabytes of disk space for each man-hour required to implement it.

I suggest that there are, in the real-world, *no* situations in which that incremental effort would save enough disk space to justify itself. Classical business data just isn't that big a consumer of the total disk space managed by an enterprise anymore. Kimball's new hybrid SCDs, defined in his 2013 toolkit book, were announced just in time to be irrelevant.

There is something else flawed about all of Kimball's SCD types, including type 2. It is that, regardless of their cost/benefit profile, SCDs do not and cannot capture a complete bitemporal history.

In the second half of this chapter, I illustrate this point by considering a set of transactions against a highly simplified star schema whose one dimension is a hierarchical structure. In this example, this dimension is a bitemporal table with a recursive hierarchy. I show how that structure can preserve a complete bitemporal history of changes to that table by means of SQL transactions no more difficult to write than transactions against nontemporal tables. I show how that complete history makes two kinds of as-was reporting possible, whereas SCDs support only one kind. I point out that SCDs, in contrast, are not only unable to support both kinds of as-was reporting, but also that their implementation as flattened hierarchies and associated structures such as bridge tables is awkward, difficult to query, and unintuitive.

As with Inmon's architecture, the solution to the temporal data problems of Kimball's architecture is simple. It is to use bitemporal tables. In Kimball's case, this means that SCDs should no longer be used and that, in all cases, when changes over time need to be captured in dimension tables,

---

[2]In fact, this number is unrealistically low. However, that only serves to make the point even more forcefully, that techniques such as SCDs which might reduce disk space usage by even many terabytes, are almost never worth the incremental cost of creating and supporting them.

those tables should be bitemporal. In fact, I see no reason why *all* dimension tables should not be bitemporal, by default.

In Chapter 19, I describe three ways in which I believe the expressive capabilities of relational databases should be extended. They are:

- to distinguish between statements and the inscriptions that express them;
- to link the database catalogs of relational databases to the Relational Paradigm Ontology; and
- to replace relational tables with binary tables representing single-predicate statements about referents.

Two things would implement the first of these three extensions. The first is to add a third temporal dimension, so that a different temporal dimension is associated with assertions, with statements, and with inscriptions. The second is to extend the notion of the assertion of a statement, or the withdrawal of that assertion, with the explicit recognition that it is people, individually or in groups, who take these "stances" with respect to statements.

The second of these three extensions would be implemented by linking each table definition in a database catalog with the subtype of Referent, in the Relational Paradigm Ontology, that represents the same type as does that table. For example, it would link the catalog's entry for a Customer table with the ontology's entry for the Customer type. As we know by now, that ontology entry would situate that type in one or more type hierarchies, and would provide a formal set-theoretic definition of the type. In addition, both universally and existentially-quantified statements would link the definition of that type into a rich semantic network, creating an ontologized knowledge base representation of a wealth of true statements about the types which are so interesting to an enterprise that they have created tables in relational databases to organize instances of them.

The third of these three extensions decomposes multi-predicate statement schemas into a set of single-predicate schemas all of which are associated with the same Referent type. These are atomic units of information in that they pick out one subject (a referent) and say one thing about it. They provide a state description which consists of a single attribute.

Chapter 20 is the concluding chapter of this book. The first part consists of a set of recommendations for implementing bitemporal technology. These recommendations are addressed to end-user organization IT professionals, including business analysts, data architects, data modelers, DBAs, and developers. The second part consists of a set of recommendations for improving bitemporal technology. These recommendations are addressed to the standards committees responsible for the ISO and TSQL2 temporal SQL standards and the DBMS vendors who implement those standards.

Finally, I present as an Afterword a reflection on connections between the Buddhist concept of *smirti*, and bitemporal data. This book began with T. S. Elliot's reflections on the Buddhist understanding of time. It ends with my own reflections on that Buddhist concept.

TEMPORAL TRANSACTIONS

11

The syntax used in this book for transactions is not that of the 2011 SQL standard or the TSQL2 standard. For one thing, the representation of month-granularity time periods is non-standard. In addition, time zone issues are ignored. In general, special formatting for specific datatypes is kept to a minimum. This is because I want to avoid cluttering up these examples with grammatical details that have nothing to do with the concepts being illustrated.

It will also be apparent that several of the specific types of temporal transactions presented in this chapter are not ISO or TSQL2 temporal transactions, or transactions supported by the major DBMS vendors. They are, instead, temporal transactions which I believe will be useful in the maintenance of temporal databases. Their value to the data management professional, then, is that they show what data maintenance capabilities are possible when dealing with state-time data and with bitemporal data. If others within the IT community also find these or similar types of temporal transactions to be useful, then if a sufficient consensus is developed, we may be able to persuade the SQL standards committees to consider including these types of temporal transactions in later releases of their standards, and to persuade the DBMS vendors to support them in their future product offerings.

Figure 11.1 lists the seven types of temporal transactions which I will discuss in this book.

AN OVERVIEW OF TEMPORAL TRANSACTIONS

The metaphor behind my proposed temporal transactions is this: a temporal transaction specifies, either implicitly or explicitly, a *temporal scope*. For transactions against state-time tables, this scope is one-dimensional. It is an interval in state time, composed of one or more state-time clock ticks. For transactions against bitemporal tables, this scope is two-dimensional. It is an area defined by an interval in state time and an interval in assertion time, and is composed of one or more *bitemporal cells*, each of which is a pair consisting of one clock tick in assertion time and one clock tick in state time.

The user cannot specify assertion time on a transaction (not until Chapter 14, that is), and so the assertion-time interval of that temporal scope is always the time period defined by binding Now() in the Henceforth variable to the current moment in time. As for state time, if a state begin time is not supplied, it defaults to Now(!). If a state end time is not supplied, it defaults to 9999. If neither

(i)   *Basic Temporal Insert*: similar to a conventional insert, but restricted to the temporal scope associated with the transaction. This insert takes place only if there is a no-match everywhere within the transaction's temporal scope.

(ii)   *Basic Temporal Update*: similar to a conventional update, but restricted to the temporal scope associated with the transaction. This update takes place only if there is a match everywhere within the transaction's temporal scope.

(iii) *Basic Temporal Delete*: similar to a conventional delete, but restricted to the temporal scope associated with the transaction. This delete takes place only if there is a match everywhere within the transaction's temporal scope.

(iv)   *Whenever Insert*: similar to a basic temporal insert, and takes place if there is a no-match anywhere within the transaction's temporal scope, i.e. in at least one temporal unit within that scope.

(v)   *Whenever Update*: similar to a basic temporal update, and takes place if there is a match anywhere within the transaction's temporal scope, i.e. in at least one temporal unit within that temporal scope.

(vi)   *Whenever Delete*: similar to a basic temporal delete, and takes place if there is a match anywhere within the transaction's temporal scope, i.e. in at least one temporal unit within that temporal scope.

(vii) *Temporal Merge*: similar to a conventional merge, but restricted to the temporal scope associated with the transaction. This transaction acts as a Whenever Insert wherever there is a no-match in the transaction's temporal scope, and acts as a Whenever Update everywhere else in the transaction's temporal scope.

FIGURE 11.1

Seven Types of Temporal Transactions.

is supplied, state time defaults to [Now(!)-9999]. If both are supplied, then end time must be later than begin time. If only an end time is supplied, it must be in the future, because otherwise begin time could not default to Now(!).[3]

So a temporal transaction is a conventional transaction that has a temporal scope. Any data outside the transaction's temporal scope is unaffected by the transaction. On updates and deletes, if there are rows of matching data which span one of the transaction's temporal scope boundaries, then those rows are *decoalesced* into equivalent pairs of rows such that one is entirely outside the

---

[3]In the standard theory, and in the ISO standard itself, transactions against state-time tables may specify a time period which begins and/or ends in the past, in which case if a state end time is specified on the transaction, a state begin time must also be specified. However, as I said earlier, and as I will demonstrate in Chapter 15, all such transactions should be avoided, because they introduce semantic anomalies into databases.

transaction's temporal scope and the other entirely inside it.[4] If there are rows of matching data that span both the begin and end state-time boundaries of a transaction's temporal scope, those rows are decoalesced into an equivalent set of three rows such that the middle one is inside the transaction's temporal scope and the other two are outside it. Once that is done, every matching row in a transaction's target table is either entirely within the transaction's temporal scope, or entirely outside it.

Each transaction applies to a *referent*. The transaction results in the addition of a statement about that referent to the temporal area specified by the transaction, the replacement of a statement about that referent in that temporal area, or the removal of a statement about that referent from that temporal area.

A referent is identified by a referent identifier, a RefId. Note that a RefId consists of the one or more columns in the *temporal unique identifier* of a state-time table which are not the state-time period, and the one or more columns in the temporal unique identifier of a bitemporal table which are not the state-time period or the assertion-time period.[5]

A conventional Insert transaction will fail if the target table already contains a matching row. Similarly, a temporal Insert transaction will fail if the target table already contains a matching row anywhere within the transaction's temporal scope. A conventional Update or Delete transaction will fail if the target table does not already contain a matching row. Similarly, a temporal Update or temporal Delete transaction will fail if the target table does not already contain one or more matching rows everywhere within the transaction's temporal scope.

BASIC TEMPORAL TRANSACTIONS ON STATE-TIME TABLES

I begin with a series of basic temporal transactions, and the empty state-time Part-S table shown in Figure 11.2.

```
Part-S
sbtm   setm   p-id esbt   p-nbr p-nm      p-upr
```

FIGURE 11.2

The State-Time Part Table - 1.

---

[4]The decoalesce transformation is called a "cut" or a "split" transformation in the literature. I have never seen the term "decoalesce" used in discussions of temporal data. I use the term because the transformation it refers to is, precisely, the inverse of the coalesce transformation. A decoalesce on any row, followed by a coalesce on the rows produced by that operation, will always result in the original row (and vice versa). The fact that both operations are important, and that one is the inverse of the other, is significant. The significance is this: together, these two operations overcome the impedance mismatch between the Relational Paradigm and the contextualization of relational constraints to temporal intervals.

[5]I assume here, in order to simplify the discussion, that the primary key of a state-time table consists of a state-time period and a RefId, and that the primary key of a bitemporal table consists of a state-time period, an assertion-time period, and a RefId. In fact, these two components, in the case of state-time tables, and these three components, in the case of bitemporal tables, are *semantic identifiers*, not physical ones. They are *temporal unique identifiers*, and they identify statements, not inscriptions. Temporal unique identifiers may also be used as primary keys, thus identifying inscriptions too, but that is neither necessary nor desirable. A primary key is a *row identifier*, and should normally not be all or any part of a RefId.

A STATE-TIME INSERT WITH DEFAULT TIME

It is Now() May 2014. The transaction shown in Figure 11.3 is submitted to the DBMS.

```
INSERT INTO Part-S
VALUES (P1, W45, wheel, $3.25)
```

FIGURE 11.3

A State-Time Insert.

A state-time period is not specified on this transaction, so the system uses Henceforth for state time. The result is shown in Figure 11.4.

```
Part-S
sbtm  setm  p-id esbt  p-nbr p-nm    p-upr
May14 9999  P1   May14 W45   wheel   $3.25
```

FIGURE 11.4

The State-Time Part Table - 2.

This is pretty straightforward. The row in Figure 11.4 is an existentially-quantified statement that, starting on May 2014 and continuing until further notice, there exists a part P1 whose part number is W45, whose name is "wheel" and whose unit price is $3.25.

An assertion is a claim, made within an assertion-time interval, that a statement is true. But being a row in a state-time table, the row in Figure 11.4 appears to have no assertion time associated with it.

Appearances, however, can be misleading. In this case, there is an assertion time associated with this row. It is the time period specified, at each moment in time, by Henceforth. Because this is a state-time table, no assertion-time history is kept; and so with each passing moment, the assertion-time past is lost. Therefore, if this row is retrieved, updated, or deleted at t_1, it is associated with the assertion-time period [t_1-9999]. If it is retrieved, updated, or deleted at a later time t_n, it is associated with the assertion-time period [t_n-9999].

All rows in state-time tables are current assertions. The only way to end an assertion in a state-time table is to overwrite it or delete it.

There is no Henceforth state-time period, because Henceforth is a variable, and commercial DBMSs do not manage stored variables. Rather, Henceforth is used to determine a time period when none is specified. [Now()-9999] becomes [Now(!)-9999], with Now(!) being a constant set to the moment in time current when the transaction completes.

A STATE-TIME UPDATE WITH DEFAULT TIME

It is Now() January 2015. The transaction shown in Figure 11.5 is submitted to the DBMS.

```
                    UPDATE IN Part-S
                    SET p-upr = $3.50
                    WHERE p-nm = wheel
```

FIGURE 11.5

A State-Time Update - 1.

The transaction's temporal scope is [Jan15-9999]. Every row which matches the selection criterion and which occupies every clock tick within that temporal scope will be updated by the transaction. If any of those rows also occupy clock ticks outside the transaction's temporal scope, then those rows are first decoalesced into two or three rows such that one of them has a state-time period that matches the transaction's temporal scope, and the others have state-time periods that share no clock ticks with that temporal scope.

This transaction is applied to the table shown in Figure 11.4. Again, the system uses Henceforth for state time. The result is shown in Figure 11.6.

```
        Part-S
        sbtm  setm  p-id esbt  p-nbr p-nm   p-upr
        May14 Jan15 P1   May14 W45   wheel  $3.25
        Jan15 9999  P1   May14 W45   wheel  $3.50
```

FIGURE 11.6

The State-Time Part Table - 3.

This update's temporal scope is [Jan15-9999]. That is the value of Henceforth on January 2015. As shown in Figure 11.4, there is a row which occupies every clock tick in [Jan15-9999], and whose part name is "wheel". But that row spans the transaction's temporal scope because it also occupies clock ticks outside that scope. And so that one row is decoalesced, replaced by two rows one wholly outside the temporal scope and one wholly inside the temporal scope of the transaction. Those two rows are:

```
        [May14|Jan15|P1|May14|W45|wheel|$3.25]
        [Jan15|9999 |P1|May14|W45|wheel|$3.25]
```

Note that these two rows have the identical information content as the one row in Figure 11.4. Decoalescing that row into two rows, on the boundary of the transaction's temporal scope, altered only the physical inscriptions in the Part-S table. It did not alter the statement that, from May 2014 until further notice, there exists a part P1, with part number W45, part name "wheel", and unit price $3.25.

Having carried out the decoalesce, the transaction is now applied to the second of these two rows, the one which occupies all the state-time clock ticks in the transaction's temporal scope, and no other clock ticks. The result is shown in Figure 11.6.

A STATE-TIME UPDATE WITH SPECIFIED STATE TIME

It is Now() June 2015. The transaction shown in Figure 11.7 is submitted to the DBMS.

```
UPDATE IN Part-S
IN STATE INTERVAL (Oct14, Mar15)
SET p-nm = wheel-A
WHERE p-id = P1
```

FIGURE 11.7

A State-Time Update - 2.

In this transaction, by using the *IN STATE INTERVAL* clause, the author of the transaction has specified a state-time period of [Oct14-Mar15]. When this transaction is applied to the table shown in Figure 11.6, the result is as shown in Figure 11.8.

```
Part-S
sbtm  setm  p-id esbt  p-nbr p-nm    p-upr
May14 Oct14 P1   May14 W45   wheel   $3.25
Oct14 Jan15 P1   May14 W45   wheel-A $3.25
Jan15 Mar15 P1   May14 W45   wheel-A $3.50
Mar15 9999  P1   May14 W45   wheel   $3.50
```

FIGURE 11.8

The State-Time Part Table - 4.

In this case, the two rows in Figure 11.6 combine to occupy the entire temporal scope of the transaction. In addition, both cross the temporal boundary specified on the transaction, so both have to be decoalesced. The result of doing that is as follows:

```
May14 Oct14 P1 May14 W45 wheel $3.25
Oct14 Jan15 P1 May14 W45 wheel $3.25
Jan15 Mar15 P1 May14 W45 wheel $3.50
Mar15 9999  P1 May14 W45 wheel $3.50
```

The first and the fourth of these rows are entirely outside the temporal scope of the transaction, and so they will not be affected by it. The second and third rows are entirely within the temporal scope of the transaction, and so they are the target rows of the transaction. The temporal update transaction is applied to those two rows, and the result is as shown in Figure 11.8.

Note, however, that information has been lost. If we ask what the database says the name of part P1 was in November 2014, for example, the answer will be "wheel-A". But this is what the database currently says. Suppose we want to know what the database said back, for example, on January 2015. In fact, from May 2014 up to June 2015, the database would have told us that the name of part P1, in November 2014, was "wheel", not "wheel-A".

This illustrates what it means to say that, in a state-time table, assertion-time history is lost to us. In a state-time table, we never know what the database said. We only know what it says right now. To preserve an assertion-time history of modifications to a state-time table, we need to add assertion time to that table, converting it into a bitemporal table.

A STATE-TIME DELETE WITH DEFAULT TIME

It is Now() December 2015. The transaction shown in Figure 11.9 is submitted to the DBMS.

```
DELETE FROM Part-S
WHERE p-id = P1
```

FIGURE 11.9

A State-Time Delete.

The system uses Henceforth to set the temporal scope for the transaction. Within that interval — [Dec15-9999] — the last row in Figure 11.8 occupies every clock tick in that interval. That row is decoalesced, resulting in the following two rows:

[Mar15|Dec15|P1|May14|W45|wheel|$3.50]
[Dec15|9999 |P1|May14|W45|wheel|$3.50]

The second of those two rows is then physically deleted, resulting in the table shown in Figure 11.10.

```
Part-S
sbtm    setm   p-id  esbt   p-nbr  p-nm     p-upr
May14   Oct14  P1    May14  W45    wheel    $3.25
Oct14   Jan15  P1    May14  W45    wheel-A  $3.25
Jan15   Mar15  P1    May14  W45    wheel-A  $3.50
Mar15   Dec15  P1    May14  W45    wheel    $3.50
```

FIGURE 11.10

The State-Time Part Table - 5.

BASIC TEMPORAL TRANSACTIONS ON BITEMPORAL TABLES

In this section, I will start with the empty bitemporal table shown in Figure 11.11, and apply the same transactions already discussed to that table.

```
Part-B
abtm    aetm    sbtm    setm    p-id  esbt   p-nbr  p-nm     p-upr
```

FIGURE 11.11

A Bitemporal Part Table -1.

A BITEMPORAL INSERT WITH DEFAULT TIME

It is Now() May 2014. The transaction shown in Figure 11.12 is submitted to the DBMS.

```
INSERT INTO Part-B
VALUES (P1, W45, wheel, $3.25)
```

FIGURE 11.12

A Bitemporal Insert.

Except for the table which is the target of the transaction, this is the same transaction that was written against the state-time Part-S table. As it does on all temporal transactions, the system uses Henceforth for assertion time. The result is as shown in Figure 11.13.

Part-B								
abtm	aetm	sbtm	setm	p-id	esbt	p-nbr	p-nm	p-upr
May14	9999	May14	9999	P1	May14	W45	wheel	$3.25

FIGURE 11.13

The Bitemporal Part Table - 2.

There is little complexity here. The row in Figure 11.13 is an assertion of an existentially-quantified statement that, starting on May 2014 and continuing until further notice, there exists a part P1 whose part number is W45, whose name is "wheel" and whose unit price is $3.25.

An assertion, of course, is a claim, made within an assertion-time interval, that a statement is true. Being a row in a bitemporal table, the row in Figure 11.13 has an explicit assertion time associated with it. This row explicitly asserts that, from May 2014 until further notice, the statement made by this row is true.

Now we have an assertion-time history. On the next clock tick, it is June 2014, but our database has kept the information about what was asserted on May 2014. With the otherwise identical state-time table, from June 2014 onwards, we no longer know what was asserted on May 2014.

A BITEMPORAL UPDATE WITH DEFAULT TIME

It is Now() January 2015. The transaction shown in Figure 11.14 is submitted to the DBMS.

```
UPDATE IN Part-B
SET p-upr = $3.50
WHERE p-nm = wheel
```

FIGURE 11.14

A Bitemporal Update.

This transaction is applied to the table shown in Figure 11.13. Again, the system uses Henceforth for both time periods. The result is shown in Figure 11.15.

```
Part-B
abtm    aetm    sbtm    setm    p-id  esbt    p-nbr  p-nm    p-upr
May14   Jan15   May14   9999    P1    May14   W45    wheel   $3.25
Jan15   9999    May14   Jan15   P1    May14   W45    wheel   $3.25
Jan15   9999    Jan15   9999    P1    May14   W45    wheel   $3.50
```

FIGURE 11.15

The Bitemporal Part Table - 3.

Let's try to understand both the semantics and the syntax of this transaction. Beginning with the semantics, the key point is that this transaction does not cause any information loss. Before the temporal update transaction, the database asserted, from May 2014 until further notice, that from May 2014 until further notice, there was a part P1, with part number W45, name "wheel" and unit price $3.25.

The first row in Figure 11.15 represents that no longer asserted statement. The second and third rows in Figure 11.15 represent the current assertions, first asserted on January 2015, that P1 had a unit price of $3.25 from May 2014 up to January 2015, and that P1 currently has a unit price of $3.50 which it acquired on January 2015.

However, it appears that there is still information loss after the transaction of Figure 11.14 is applied. Prior to that transaction, the database contained an assertion about P1 which began on May 2014 and continued until further notice. After that transaction, there is no such assertion.

But once again, appearances are deceiving. The first row in the Part-B table, as shown in Figure 11.13, began life with a 9999 assertion end time. All rows in bitemporal tables begin life with an assertion end time of 9999. The reason is that no one is going to add a statement to a database, asserting that it is true, but knowing that at some later time, they will stop asserting that it is true.[6]

There is another feature of how bitemporal data is maintained that is relevant here. Once a row's assertion-time period ends, that row no longer represents the assertion of a statement. It takes on a new role. It becomes a record of when in the past that statement was asserted. It becomes a piece of database history, and like database logfiles and other repositories of database history, it is illegitimate to alter it. The future is open to possibilities, but the past is not. The past has occurred, and there is only one way that it occurred.

Because of this, if a row's assertion end time is ever changed from 9999, it is changed to the moment in time on which the statement ceased to be asserted. That moment in time must be the Now() of the transaction that caused the assertion to end. Here's why.

That moment in time can't be a moment of past time, because that would result in a lie. For example, suppose we decided, on January 2015, that we should have stopped asserting the statement shown in Figure 11.13 three months ago — on October 2014. And so we retroactively end the

---

[6]This, at least, is current computer science theory, is part of both temporal SQL standards, and is implemented in all vendor DBMSs that support bitemporal data. However, later in this chapter, I will indicate why I think there may be exceptions it would be useful to be able to manage.

assertion time of that row, setting its assertion end time to October 2014, resulting in the row shown in Figure 11.13 looking like this:

[May14|Oct14|May14|9999|P1|May14|W45|wheel|$3.25]

Based on this state of the database, a query about whether P1 existed in the last three months of 2014 will return a negative response, because this state of the database indicates that there was no assertion, during that time, that P1 did exist, during that time. However, until January 2015, the row that was present in the database was:

[May14|9999|May14|9999|P1|May14|W45|wheel|$3.25]

And so, in fact, that negative response is incorrect. In fact, during those three months, the database did contain the assertion that P1 existed during that time. So setting an assertion end time to any past moment in time makes the database tell a lie.

Next, that moment in time can't be a moment of future time. Or, rather, there appears to be no good reason why it should be. For suppose that, on January 2015, we changed the row to

[May14|May15|May14|9999|P1|May14|W45|wheel|$3.25]

If this were done as part of a Delete transaction on January 2015 there would be no contradiction introduced into the database. But if we know, on January 2015, that a statement is no longer true, then as soon as we know that, we should stop claiming that the statement is true. There is no good reason to wait for four more months before ceasing to claim that a statement we now know is false, is true.

Of course, there may be *bad* reasons to wait. For example, perhaps we want to keep certain knowledge to ourselves long enough to profit from it. However, this violates an implicit promise about production databases, the promise that we will only add true statements to them, that we will never change a true statement to a false one, and that we will remove false statements as soon as we become aware of them — the promise, in short, to tell, at all times, the truth, the whole truth, and nothing but the truth. These, as described in Chapter 7, are the Gricean conventions of conversational implicature, extended to databases.

However, I think that there may also be some not quite so bad reasons for wanting to set an assertion end time to sometime in the future. Suppose that each month, we add to a database of ours the unemployment numbers issued by the Bureau of Labor Statistics. Two weeks later, the bureau will send out a revised set of numbers for that same month, i.e. for the same period of state time. In this case, it seems to me, we know the assertion end time for the initial set of numbers, at the time that we enter them into our database. We know that two weeks from now, we will no longer assert that those numbers are the correct numbers describing the month just past.

Clearly there are other situations that would appear to warrant inserting rows with non-9999 assertion end times. For example, suppose that, at the start of each year, a company prepares sales forecasts for each month of the following year. Then, each successive month, the company revises those sales forecasts, taking into consideration year-to-date sales as well as other factors that may influence next year's sales. At the end of the year, the company will have a dozen sales forecasts for December of the upcoming year, eleven for November of the upcoming year, and so on.

Whether this is or is not a good reason for allowing future assertion end times to be put into a database, depends on the semantics of what is going on. Computer scientists and vendors tell us only that transaction time is transaction time. And so it follows that transaction time begins when a row is physically created, and ends when the row would have been physically deleted if means for logically deleting it were not used instead.

But transactions aren't their own justification. Neither are rows in tables. They are physical mechanisms for implementing a desired semantics. I have argued that state time delimits a specific period in the life history of the referent of a row, and that assertion time (the standard theory's transaction time) delimits a specific period during which we asserted/assert/will assert that the statement made by a row is true.

If computer scientists and vendors wish to provide some other semantics for transactions and rows, then let them. But as far as I can see, the semantics I have described are the semantics which in fact are the reason we create and maintain and use databases. And if that is true, then I think the above considerations provide good reason for extending the mechanisms of bitemporal data management so that rows in bitemporal tables can be created with non-9999 assertion end times. And I recommend to the SQL standards committees, and to vendors, that they consider adding this extension to the SQL standard and to its various implementations.

In fact, however, current bitemporally-enabled DBMSs do not permit this. They require an assertion end time of 9999 on all rows when those rows are added to a bitemporal table. And they require that when a bitemporal row is logically deleted, its assertion end time is set to the Now() of the transaction causing that to happen.

And this, at last, shows us why, in Figure 11.15, information about the state of the database prior to January 2015 has not been lost, even though a physical overwrite, an update in place, changed the original assertion end time of the first row in that Figure. For we know that, prior to that new assertion end time, the assertion end time of that row was 9999. And we know that the original 9999 assertion end time was overwritten precisely on January 2015. Therefore, although the database no longer contains the inscription

$$[\underline{May14}|9999|\underline{May14}|9999|\underline{P1}|May14|W45|wheel|\$3.25]$$

but instead now contains the inscription

$$[\underline{May14}|Jan15|\underline{May14}|9999|\underline{P1}|May14|W45|wheel|\$3.25]$$

we know that the database did contain that former inscription from May 2014 up to January 2015. Again, this overwrite has not caused any information to be lost.

A BITEMPORAL UPDATE WITH SPECIFIED STATE TIME

It is Now() June 2015. The transaction shown in Figure 11.16 is submitted to the DBMS.

```
UPDATE IN Part-B
IN STATE INTERVAL (Oct14, Mar15)
SET p-nm = wheel-A
WHERE p-id = P1
```

FIGURE 11.16

A Bitemporal Update - 2.

In this transaction, the author of the transaction has specified a state-time period of [Oct14–Mar15]. When this transaction is applied to the table shown in Figure 11.15, the result is as shown in Figure 11.17.

```
Part-B
abtm   aetm   sbtm   setm   p-id  esbt   p-nbr  p-nm      p-upr
May14  Jan15  May14  9999   P1    May14  W45    wheel     $3.25
Jan15  Jun15  May14  Jan15  P1    May14  W45    wheel     $3.25
Jan15  9999   May14  Oct14  P1    May14  W45    wheel     $3.25
Jan15  9999   Oct14  Jan15  P1    May14  W45    wheel-A   $3.25
Jan15  Jun15  Jan15  9999   P1    May14  W45    wheel     $3.50
Jun15  9999   Jan15  Mar15  P1    May14  W45    wheel-A   $3.50
Jun15  9999   Mar15  9999   P1    May14  W45    wheel     $3.50
```

FIGURE 11.17

The Bitemporal Part Table - 4.

This transaction has changed the Part-B table from the three rows shown in Figure 11.15 to the seven rows shown in Figure 11.17. The first row in Figure 11.15 was not affected by the transaction, because it was already in past assertion time. So it appears unchanged as the first row in Figure 11.17.

The second and third rows in Figure 11.15 were affected by the transaction because they were in current assertion time, their state-time intervals fell within the transaction's temporal scope, and their RefIds matched the transaction's RefId. Because the temporal scope of each of these rows crossed the temporal boundary of the transaction's temporal scope, the first step was to split each of those rows into two information-equivalent rows, one entirely outside the temporal scope of the transaction and one entirely inside that temporal scope. Decoalescing row 2 resulted in rows 3 and 4 in Figure 11.17. Decoalescing row 5 resulted in rows 6 and 7. Having done this, the next step was to *withdraw* rows 2 and 5 into past assertion time. The result of these two steps is shown in Figure 11.17. Rows 2 and 5 have been withdrawn by setting their assertion end times to the value of Now() when the transaction was taking place.

What I have called withdrawing a row is, of course, the semantic act of ceasing to assert that the statement made by the row is true, and the physical act of closing its assertion-time period. After the transaction is complete, these rows exist in past assertion time, as inscriptions of statements once but no longer asserted to be true. They have been logically deleted, but their physical inscriptions remain as a record of what, until that point in time, were rows that were current assertions in the database.

A BITEMPORAL DELETE WITH DEFAULT TIME

It is Now() December 2015. The transaction shown in Figure 11.18 is submitted to the DBMS.

```
DELETE FROM Part-B
WHERE p-id = P1
```

FIGURE 11.18

A Bitemporal Delete.

In this transaction, the system uses Henceforth to set both assertion time and state time to [Dec15-9999]. That is the bitemporal area that is the scope of the transaction. The result is as shown in Figure 11.19.

```
Part-B
abtm   aetm   sbtm   setm   p-id  esbt   p-nbr  p-nm     p-upr
May14  Jan15  May14  9999   P1    May14  W45    wheel    $3.25
Jan15  Jun15  May14  Jan15  P1    May14  W45    wheel    $3.25
Jan15  Jun15  Jan15  9999   P1    May14  W45    wheel    $3.50
Jun15  9999   May14  Oct14  P1    May14  W45    wheel    $3.25
Jun15  9999   Oct14  Jan15  P1    May14  W45    wheel-A  $3.25
Jun15  9999   Jan15  Mar15  P1    May14  W45    wheel-A  $3.50
Jun15  Dec15  Mar15  9999   P1    May14  W45    wheel    $3.50
Dec15  9999   Mar15  Dec15  P1    May14  W45    wheel    $3.50
```

FIGURE 11.19

The Bitemporal Part Table - 5.

As a basic temporal Delete transaction, this transaction would fail unless there were one or more rows with a RefId of P1 such that those rows occupied every bitemporal cell in the transaction's temporal scope. And the last row in Figure 11.17 does this. Its assertion-time period is [Jun15-9999], which is an interval which [contains] the transaction's assertion-time period of [Dec15-9999]. Its state-time period is [Mar15-9999], which is an interval which [contains] the transaction's state-time period of [Dec15-9999].

The first step in applying this transaction is to decoalesce the last row in Figure 11.17 into the following two rows:

```
[Dec15|9999|Mar15|Dec15|P1|May14|W45|wheel|$3.50]
[Dec15|9999|Dec15|9999 |P1|May14|W45|wheel|$3.50]
```

The second step is to add the first of those two rows to the Part-B table. The second row is not added to the table because it is [contained] within the transaction's temporal scope, being, in fact, [Equal] to it.

WHENEVER TEMPORAL TRANSACTIONS

The purpose of the *Whenever* variation on temporal transactions is to be able to perform a basic temporal transaction whenever, within the transaction's temporal scope, it is valid to do so.

Whenever temporal transactions are useful in two situations. In one situation, the exact temporal location to be modified is not known, but a temporal scope within which it is contained is known. This would most commonly be encountered with update transactions. For example, perhaps all suppliers in supplier category SCC are to have their supplier type changed to T18 for the calendar year 2014. If any of those suppliers are represented in some but not all of the clock ticks in 2014, it would be useful to have an Update transaction which "skips" from one sub-interval in which each supplier is represented, to the next sub-interval, and applies the update in each of those sub-intervals. In this way, the author of the updates does not have to know each sub-interval of each supplier, and specify each one on a transaction.

In the second situation, the locations of a referent in several sub-intervals within a given state-time interval may be known. In that case, the value of a Whenever update or Whenever delete transaction is to update or delete all of the referent's episodes in that state-time interval with one transaction. As for Whenever Insert transactions, their use would be to fill in the gaps between sub-intervals, probably using default values for the state described by the to-be-inserted statement.

Filling in gaps is useful when it is important to indicate that a referent existed during certain times, even though we do not know what state it was/is/will be in. For example, perhaps we know that, from 2011 through 2014, part P3 existed in inventory, but that it was not continuously offered for sale throughout those four years. Until now, company policy has been that a part is represented in the Part table only when it is being offered for sale. But now the company has decided that it wants to represent parts whenever they exist in inventory, whether or not they are being offered for sale. This, of course, is a redefinition of what it means to be a part, since it changes the criteria for something being represented in the Part table.

As for Whenever Delete transactions, we can suppose the definitions to be reversed. In that case, the objective would be to remove a part from whatever periods of time during those four years that the part was not offered for sale.

I begin a series of examples with a state-time Part-S table containing seven episodes and eight rows for part P1, and six inter-episode gaps.

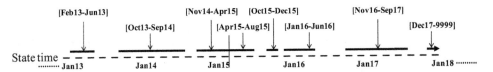

FIGURE 11.20

Seven Episodes for Part P1.

Figure 11.20 shows the rows and episodes for part P1. The vertical line appearing between November 2014 and August 2015 occurs at April 2015, and distinguishes the two rows which make up that episode. All other representations in the diagram are of single-row episodes.

Figure 11.21 shows the rows and episodes for part P1, as rows in the Part-S table.

```
Part-S
sbtm   setm   p-id   esbt    p-nbr  p-nm    p-upr
Feb13  Jun13  P1     Feb13   W45    wheel   $3.25
Oct13  Sep14  P1     Oct13   W45    wheel   $3.50
Nov14  Apr15  P1     Nov14   W45    wheel   $3.55
Apr15  Aug15  P1     Nov14   W45    wheel   $3.75
Oct15  Dec15  P1     Oct15   W45    wheel   $3.80
Jan16  Jun16  P1     Jan16   W45    wheel   $3.85
Nov16  Sep17  P1     Nov16   W45    wheel   $4.00
Dec17  9999   P1     Dec16   W45    wheel   $4.25
```

FIGURE 11.21

Episodes in State-Time Tables.

A WHENEVER INSERT TRANSACTION

Assume that it is now sometime in 2015. The business has decided to show part P1 existing throughout the year 2014 because it has been determined that P1 was present in inventory throughout that year. Realizing that, up to now, P1 was represented in the Part-S table only when it was actually offered for sale, the decision is to show P1 with a $0.00 unit price whenever during 2014 it was not offered for sale.

The transaction shown in Figure 11.22 is submitted to the DBMS.

```
INSERT INTO Part-S
WHENEVER IN STATE INTERVAL (Jan14, Jan15)
VALUES (P1, W45, wheel, $0.00)
```

FIGURE 11.22

A State-Time Whenever Insert.

In this transaction, with the *WHENEVER IN STATE INTERVAL* clause, the author of the transaction has specified a state-time interval of [Jan14–Jan15]. The upper timeline in the diagram in Figure 11.23 shows the representation of P1 before the transaction is applied. The shaded rectangle represents the state-time interval of the transaction's temporal scope.

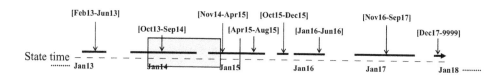

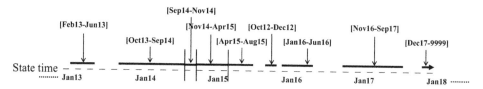

FIGURE 11.23

Before and After an Insert Whenever Transaction.

As a Whenever insert, this transaction "fills in the gap" between two episodes, that gap being the sub-interval [Sep14-Nov14]. When this transaction is applied to the table shown in Figure 11.21, the result is as shown in the lower timeline in Figure 11.23, and in the Part-S table in Figure 11.24.

Note that by filling in the two-month gap, this transaction merges two episodes into one episode. The result is a single episode, beginning in October 2013 and ending in August 2015. This has obvious temporal referential integrity implications for the Supplier-Part-S table. It means that, as far as a dependency on parts is concerned, it is now possible to add a row to the Supplier-Part-S table indicating which suppliers supplied part P1 during those two months.

```
Part-S
sbtm   setm   p-id esbt   p-nbr p-nm    p-upr
Feb13  Jun13  P1   Feb13  W45   wheel   $3.25
Oct13  Sep14  P1   Oct13  W45   wheel   $3.50
Sep14  Nov14  P1   Oct13  W45   wheel   $0.00
Nov14  Apr15  P1   Oct13  W45   wheel   $3.55
Apr15  Aug15  P1   Oct13  W45   wheel   $3.75
Oct15  Dec15  P1   Oct15  W45   wheel   $3.80
Jan16  Jun16  P1   Jan16  W45   wheel   $3.85
Nov16  Sep17  P1   Nov16  W45   wheel   $4.00
Dec17  9999   P1   Dec16  W45   wheel   $4.25
```

FIGURE 11.24

The State-Time Part Table - 5.

A WHENEVER UPDATE TRANSACTION

Suppose the part name for P1 is to be changed to "wheel-X", from 2015 on, whenever the unit-price on that part is $3.50 or above, but less than $4.00. With a whenever update, the business does not have to determine or specify the one or more exact time periods when P1 exists.

The transaction shown in Figure 11.25 is submitted to the DBMS.

```
UPDATE IN Part-S
WHENEVER IN STATE INTERVAL (Jan14, 9999)
SET p-nm = wheel-X
WHERE p-id = P1 AND p-upr ≥ $4.00
```

FIGURE 11.25

A State-Time Whenever Update.

In this transaction, the author of the transaction has specified an open state-time interval which begins on January 2014. When this transaction is applied to the table shown in Figure 11.24, the result is as shown in Figure 11.26.

```
Part-S
sbtm   setm   p-id esbt   p-nbr p-nm     p-upr
Feb13  Jun13  P1   Feb13  W45   wheel    $3.25
Oct13  Jan14  P1   Oct13  W45   wheel    $3.50
Jan14  Sep14  P1   Oct13  W45   wheel-X  $3.50
Sep14  Nov14  P1   Oct13  W45   wheel    $0.00
Nov14  Apr15  P1   Oct13  W45   wheel-X  $3.55
Apr15  Aug15  P1   Oct13  W45   wheel-X  $3.75
Oct15  Dec15  P1   Oct15  W45   wheel-X  $3.80
Jan16  Jun16  P1   Jan16  W45   wheel-X  $3.85
Nov16  Sep17  P1   Nov16  W45   wheel    $4.00
Dec17  9999   P1   Dec16  W45   wheel    $4.25
```

FIGURE 11.26

The State-Time Part Table - 6.

The referent slice for part P1 has not been altered by this transaction. The [Oct13-Sep14] row has been decoalesced into two rows, and the update applied to the decoalesced row that is within the transaction's temporal scope.

All temporal Update transactions leave the temporal scope of a referent unchanged. All temporal Insert transactions increase that temporal scope and, in the process, will either create new episodes, extend existing episodes, or merge existing episodes. All temporal Delete transactions reduce that temporal scope and, in the process, will either remove entire episodes, reduce the extent of existing episodes, or split existing episodes.[7]

A WHENEVER DELETE TRANSACTION

The transaction shown in Figure 11.27 is submitted to the DBMS.

```
DELETE FROM Part-S
WHENEVER IN STATE INTERVAL (Sep15, Feb17)
WHERE p-id = P1
```

FIGURE 11.27

A State-Time Whenever Delete.

In this transaction, the author of the transaction has specified a state-time interval of September 2015 up to February 2017. The upper timeline in the diagram in Figure 11.28 shows the representation of P1 before the transaction is applied. The shaded rectangle represents the state-time extent of the transaction's temporal scope.

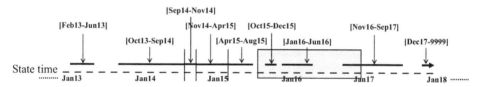

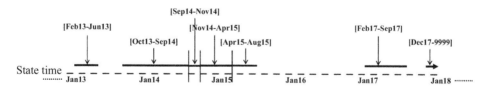

FIGURE 11.28

Before and After a Whenever Delete Transaction.

As a Whenever Delete transaction, this transaction removes the representation of P1 everywhere within the transaction's temporal scope. When this transaction is applied to the table shown in

---

[7]A full taxonomy of these temporal scope changes is presented and discussed in *MTRD*, Chapter 9.

Figure 11.26, the result is as shown in the lower timeline in Figure 11.28, and is shown as a table in Figure 11.29.

```
Part-S
sbtm   setm   p-id  esbt   p-nbr  p-nm     p-upr
Feb13  Jun13  P1    Feb13  W45    wheel    $3.25
Oct13  Jan14  P1    Oct13  W45    wheel    $3.50
Jan14  Sep14  P1    Oct13  W45    wheel-X  $3.50
Sep14  Nov14  P1    Oct13  W45    wheel    $0.00
Nov14  Apr15  P1    Oct13  W45    wheel-X  $3.55
Apr15  Aug15  P1    Oct13  W45    wheel-X  $3.75
Feb17  Sep17  P1    Nov16  W45    wheel    $4.00
Dec17  9999   P1    Dec16  W45    wheel    $4.25
```

FIGURE 11.29

The State-Time Part Table - 7.

This Whenever Delete transaction has removed two episodes of P1 and shortened a third episode. The episode which has been shortened is the [Nov16-Sep17] episode, which has been shortened "on the front end" to [Feb17-Sep17]. Because front-end shortening (or lengthening) alters the begin moment in time of the episode, the episode state begin time on all rows in the episode must be adjusted to show the new begin time. In this case, there happens to be only one row in the episode, but there might have been any number of rows.

TEMPORAL MERGE TRANSACTIONS

A conventional merge transaction is processed as an insert if no row in the target table matches it, and is processed as an update otherwise. A temporal merge is processed as a temporal insert wherever in the transaction's temporal scope it is not matched by a row in the target table, and is processed as a temporal update otherwise. It follows that if a temporal merge is applied to an empty temporal scope, it is equivalent to a temporal insert into that temporal scope, and that if a temporal merge is applied to a temporal scope with no unoccupied sub-intervals, it is equivalent to a temporal update on the entire temporal scope. It also follows that, after any temporal merge, the temporal scope specified on the transaction is fully occupied by the referent of that transaction. Any gaps that are filled in will merge the episodes on either side of those gaps, and the result will be that the entire temporal interval for the referent will belong to one episode.

The transaction shown in Figure 11.30 is submitted to the DBMS.

```
MERGE WITHIN Part-S
IN STATE INTERVAL [Apr13, Aug14]
SET p-nbr = W45, p-nm = wheel-Y, p-upr = $3.60
WHERE p-id = P1
```

FIGURE 11.30

A Temporal Merge.

In this transaction, the author of the transaction has specified a state-time interval of April 2013 up to August 2014. The upper timeline in the diagram in Figure 11.31 shows the representation of P1 before the transaction is applied. The shaded rectangle represents the state-time extent of the transaction's temporal scope.

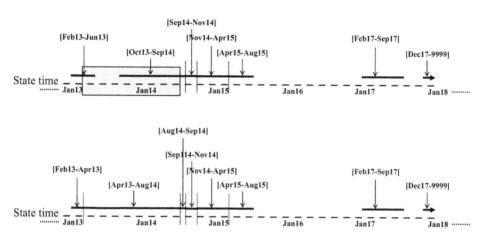

FIGURE 11.31

Before and After a Temporal Merge Transaction.

As an merge transaction, this transaction adds the representation of P1 to every clock tick within the transaction's temporal scope where it is not already present, and updates the representation of P1 in every clock tick where it is already present.

The first step in applying this transaction is to decoalesce the two rows that cross the state-time boundaries of the transaction's temporal scope. The result is shown in Figure 11.32.

```
Part-S
sbtm   setm   p-id  esbt   p-nbr  p-nm      p-upr
Feb13  Apr13  P1    Feb13  W45    wheel     $3.25
Apr13  Jun13  P1    Feb13  W45    wheel     $3.25
Oct13  Jan14  P1    Oct13  W45    wheel     $3.50
Jan14  Aug14  P1    Oct13  W45    wheel-X   $3.50
Aug14  Sep14  P1    Oct13  W45    wheel-X   $3.50
Sep14  Nov14  P1    Oct13  W45    wheel     $0.00
Nov14  Apr15  P1    Oct13  W45    wheel-X   $3.55
Apr15  Aug15  P1    Oct13  W45    wheel-X   $3.75
Feb17  Sep17  P1    Nov16  W45    wheel     $4.00
Dec17  9999   P1    Dec16  W45    wheel     $4.25
```

FIGURE 11.32

The State-Time Part Table - 8.

The second step in applying this transaction is to apply the transaction as a Whenever Update transaction. The result is shown in Figure 11.33.

```
Part-S
sbtm   setm   p-id  esbt   p-nbr  p-nm      p-upr
Feb13  Apr13  P1    Feb13  W45    wheel     $3.25
Apr13  Jun13  P1    Feb13  W45    wheel-Y   $3.60
Oct13  Jan14  P1    Oct13  W45    wheel-Y   $3.60
Jan14  Aug14  P1    Oct13  W45    wheel-Y   $3.60
Aug14  Sep14  P1    Oct13  W45    wheel-X   $3.50
Sep14  Nov14  P1    Oct13  W45    wheel     $0.00
Nov14  Apr15  P1    Oct13  W45    wheel-X   $3.55
Apr15  Aug15  P1    Oct13  W45    wheel-X   $3.75
Feb17  Sep17  P1    Nov16  W45    wheel     $4.00
Dec17  9999   P1    Dec16  W45    wheel     $4.25
```

FIGURE 11.33

The State-Time Part Table - 9.

The final step in applying this transaction is to apply the transaction as a Whenever Insert transaction. The result is shown in Figure 11.34.

```
Part-S
sbtm   setm   p-id  esbt   p-nbr  p-nm      p-upr
Feb13  Apr13  P1    Feb13  W45    wheel     $3.25
Apr13  Jun13  P1    Feb13  W45    wheel-Y   $3.60
Jun13  Oct13  P1    Feb13  W45    wheel-Y   $3.60
Oct13  Jan14  P1    Feb13  W45    wheel-Y   $3.60
Jan14  Aug14  P1    Feb13  W45    wheel-Y   $3.60
Aug14  Sep14  P1    Feb13  W45    wheel-X   $3.50
Sep14  Nov14  P1    Feb13  W45    wheel     $0.00
Nov14  Apr15  P1    Feb13  W45    wheel-X   $3.55
Apr15  Aug15  P1    Feb13  W45    wheel-X   $3.75
Feb17  Sep17  P1    Nov16  W45    wheel     $4.00
Dec17  9999   P1    Dec16  W45    wheel     $4.25
```

FIGURE 11.34

The State-Time Part Table - 10.

Several useful variations on a temporal merge are possible. One is to distinguish between column values which are to be used as insert values only, as update values only, or as either insert or update values.

Like all the temporal transactions described in this chapter, the temporal merge is not part of the ISO 9075:2011 or TSQL2 temporal SQL standards. But all of these transactions are temporal transactions that I consider useful.

GLOSSARY LIST

bitemporal area
bitemporal cell
clock tick
closed time period
decoalesce
episode

existentially-quantified
   statement
inscription
referent
row identifier
semantic identifier

statement
temporal area
temporal scope
temporal unique
   identifier
withdraw

BASIC TEMPORAL QUERIES

12

The queries discussed in this and the following chapter, like the transactions discussed in the previous chapter, are not based on either the ISO or the TSQL2 standards. These queries, like those transactions, use a syntax which I prefer, although the differences with the syntax defined in the standards is not great. But more important than differences in syntax are differences in functionality, and many of these queries, like many of those transactions, pbrovide functionality which is not found in either standard. In both cases, I think this added functionality will prove useful to those managing and querying bitemporal and state-time data.

Note that all intermediate results produced while processing a query exist in a working storage area that the DBMS sets aside for the query. None of the work is persisted to the database and, of course, none of the work, except the final result, is visible at the user interface.

TEMPORAL QUERY SYNTAX

In this section, I explain the syntax I use for temporal queries.

It is Now() March 2017. Here is a query.

```
SELECT
s-id, s-nm, s-scfk, s-type
FROM Supplier-B
WHERE s-id = S1
```

FIGURE 12.1

A Bitemporal Query With Two Default Times.

Because the target of this query is a bitemporal table, and seeing that no time period is specified on the query, the DBMS augments the query's WHERE clause with two additional predicates, one for state time and one for assertion time. Those predicates are:

```
(sbtm ≤ Mar17 AND Mar17 < setm) AND
(abtm ≤ Mar17 AND Mar17 < aetm)
```

In the syntax I use for queries, either or both of state time and assertion time can also be explicitly specified. State time is specified in an *IN STATE INTERVAL* clause. Assertion time is specified in an *IN ASSERTION INTERVAL* clause.[1] Thus, the above query, with March 2017 explicitly expressed as both the state time and assertion time, is written like this:

```
SELECT
IN STATE INTERVAL (Mar17, Mar17)
IN ASSERTION INTERVAL (Mar17, Mar17)
s-id, s-nm, s-scfk, s-type
FROM Supplier-B
WHERE s-id = S1
```

FIGURE 12.2

A Bitemporal Query With Two Explicit Times.

Because this query contains an **IN STATE INTERVAL** clause, there is no need to project state-time columns onto each row in the result set because the state time of all the rows in the result set will be the same. Because the query contains an **IN ASSERTION INTERVAL** clause, there is no need to project assertion-time columns because the assertion time of all the rows the result set will also be the same.

When a temporal interval applies to all the rows in a result set, an elegant way of conveying this information is to include that temporal interval in the header portion of the result set, instead of repeating it on every row.[2] I think it would also be useful to show temporal intervals in result set header information even when the rows in the result set have different temporal intervals. In that case, each temporal interval in the header clause would have the earliest begin point of all the rows as its begin point, and the latest end point of all the rows as its end point, this description applying to both assertion time and state time.[3]

In semantic terms, accepting the default value of March 2017 for assertion time tells the DBMS to carry out the query based on what the database currently says is the case. And accepting that default value for state time tells the DBMS to only retrieve data about the current state of the referents selected by the query, that being their current state as of March 2017.

The same query could also be written like this:

```
SELECT
IN STATE INTERVAL (Mar17, Mar17)
s-id, s-nm, s-scfk, s-type
FROM Supplier-B
WHERE s-id = S1
```

FIGURE 12.3

A Bitemporal Query With Explicit State Time.

---

[1]However, until we discuss future assertion time in Chapter 14, "assertion time" is an alternative term for the standard theory's term "transaction time". And in the standard theory, assertion/transaction time cannot be specified on temporal transactions, and always takes on a system-supplied Henceforth value.

[2]That is, this is an elegant way of displaying the information. Those temporal intervals, of course, are part of each row in the result set.

[3]Or perhaps the earliest and latest begin time, and the earliest and latest end time, for both state time and assertion time, could be displayed in result set headers. The specifics here aren't as important as the point that result sets are themselves managed objects, and have their own properties.

And, of course, the query could also be written like this, albeit only in the Asserted Versioning theory and not in the standard theory:

```
SELECT
IN ASSERTION INTERVAL (Mar17, Mar17)
s-id, s-nm, s-scfk, s-type
FROM Supplier-B
WHERE s-id = S1
```

FIGURE 12.4

A Bitemporal Query With Explicit Assertion Time.

But in all these forms, the DBMS begins by translating them into the following *query canonical form*:

```
SELECT
s-id, s-nm, s-scfk, s-type
FROM Supplier-B
WHERE s-id = S1
AND abtm ≤ Mar17 AND Mar17 < aetm
AND sbtm ≤ Mar17 AND Mar17 < setm
```

FIGURE 12.5

A Bitemporal Query in Query Canonical Form.

The IN STATE INTERVAL and IN ASSERTION INTERVAL clauses are what is sometimes called "syntactic sugar". They are clauses which the DBMS (or a query preprocessor) can easily translate into standard SQL. The point of providing these clauses isn't just that they are easier to write than the less-than-equal-to and less-than pairs in Figure 12.5. It is also that they separate the two temporal delimiters of a bitemporal query from the other WHERE clause predicates.

This separation emphasizes the point that these temporal delimiters, when translated into query canonical form, are not like other WHERE clause predicates. In a WHERE clause, a primary key (if specified) picks out a unique instance of the type represented by its table, and all other columns represent properties or relationships ascribed to that unique instance by the statement made by that row in that table.

But state time is not a referent, or a property or a relationship of a referent. It is a *temporal indexical*. It clarifies the declarative sentence it is appended to by delimiting the interval of time during which whatever it refers to was/is/will be in the state ascribed to it; in so doing, it does its part to make a statement out of that sentence. As for assertion time, it too is not a referent, a property or a relationship. It delimits the interval of time during which the statement made by that row was/is/will be asserted to be true, contributing its bit to disambiguating that declarative sentence.

So neither assertion-time periods nor state-time periods are referents, or properties or relationships of referents. It is for this reason that I do not treat them as ordinary predicates in a WHERE clause.[4]

---

[4]More specifically, both time periods are modal qualifiers of statements. State time is what logicians call a *de re* modality, and assertion time is what they call a *de dicto* modality.

BITEMPORAL TABLES AND VIEWS

In the remainder of this chapter, the queries I discuss will be queries issued against the following two tables.

```
S-Cat-B
abtm   aetm   sbtm   setm   sc-id  sc-abbr  sc-desc
Jan14  May15  Jan14  9999   SC1    SCA      tier 1
May15  9999   Jan14  Jan15  SC1    SCA      tier 1
May15  9999   Jan15  9999   SC1    SCA      tier 2
Dec14  9999   Dec14  9999   SC2    SCB      tier 2


Supplier-B
abtm   aetm   sbtm   setm   s-id  s-nm      s-scfk  s-type
Feb14  Aug14  Feb14  9999   S1    Acme      SC1     T4
Aug14  9999   Feb14  Oct14  S1    Acme      SC1     T4
Aug14  Feb15  Oct14  9999   S1    Acme      SC1     T3
Feb15  9999   Oct14  Jan16  S1    Acme      SC1     T3
Feb15  9999   Jan16  9999   S1    Acme      SC1     T5
Jan15  9999   Jan15  9999   S2    Superior  SC2     T3
```

FIGURE 12.6

The Bitemporal Supplier and Supplier-Category Tables.

I begin by describing various views which can be used to simplify queries written against this data.

THE CONVENTIONAL TABLE VIEW

The *conventional table view* presents as a *queryable* and *updatable object* what we currently say things are currently like. Neither assertion time nor state time appear in this view. Neither can be specified on queries or transactions against this view. For both queries and transactions, therefore, Henceforth is used to determine the state time and assertion time. As a result, a bitemporal history of data can be accumulated, but to those writing queries and/or transactions, they seem to be accessing a conventional, nontemporal table. This is the key to capturing bitemporal history while supporting full upward compatability of transactions and queries already written against a conventional table.

In *MTRD*, my co-author and I presented a way to convert conventional tables into bitemporal tables, without having to alter either existing queries or existing transactions against those tables. For queries, our recommendation is to give a view the name of the table to be converted into a bitemporal table, and to give the table itself a different name, perhaps its original name with a "-B" suffix added to it.

What would a view like this look like?

```
CREATE VIEW Supplier
SELECT s-id, s-nm, s-scfk, s-type
FROM Supplier-B
WHERE abtm ≤ Now() AND Now() < aetm
AND sbtm ≤ Now() AND Now() < setm
```

FIGURE 12.7

Conventional Table View Creation on a Bitemporal Table.

The query used in this view definition is, in one respect, the simplest kind of temporal query that can be issued against a bitemporal table because it specifies a single point in assertion time and a single point in state time. In the case of this view definition, that single point in time, in both cases, is Now().

A point in time assertion-time predicate specifies a past or present state of the database. Besides its use in a conventional table view definition, the principal use of this predicate is to rewind the database to a past point in time. The rest of the query then executes against that past state of the database.

A point in time state-time predicate specifies a past, present or future state in the life history of the referents that are selected by the nontemporal predicates in the query. Besides its use in a conventional table view definition, the principal use of this predicate is to select a moment in the life history of those referents. The rest of the query then executes against those states of those referents.

So when queries and reports have to be rerun with the condition that they will produce exactly the same results as they produced when they were originally run, we simply add an IN STATE INTERVAL and an IN ASSERTION INTERVAL clause to the original query. IN ASSERTION INTERVAL is set to select the point in assertion time at which the original query was directed. If no assertion-time predicate was included in the original query, that will be the point in time at which the query was run. IN STATE INTERVAL is set to select the point in state time at which the original query was directed. If no state-time predicate was included in the original query, that will also be the point in time at which the query was run.

It is still March 2017. As shown in the conventional table view, the data current in both assertion time and state time is:

```
IN ASSERTION INTERVAL: March 2017
IN STATE INTERVAL: March 2017
S-Cat
sc-id sc-abbr sc-desc
SC1   SCA     tier 2
SC2   SCB     tier 2


Supplier
s-id s-nm     s-scfk s-type
S1   Acme     SC1    T5
S2   Superior SC2    T3
```

FIGURE 12.8

A Conventional Table View on a Bitemporal Table.

Not surprisingly, there is only one row for each referent in each table. In terms of semantics, there is only one currently asserted row for any referent in any clock tick of state time because nothing, no referent, can be in more than one state at any one time. In terms of implementation mechanics, there is only one currently asserted row for any referent in any clock tick of state time because, for any given referent, no state-time clock tick can be included in more than one state-time period for the same referent.[5] Such correlations are how a given implementation supports a given semantics.

Existing transactions against the original nontemporal tables are supplemented with Henceforth-based values, in one implementation by means of Instead Of triggers. The triggers simply capture conventional insert, update and delete transactions, and use the Henceforth variable and the current moment in time to create [Now(!)-9999] values for both the assertion-time period and the state-time period of the row being inserted, updated or deleted.

Now here is a very important point. These Instead Of triggers provide *temporal upward compatibility* for inserts, updates and deletes against the original Supplier and S-Cat conventional tables. So clearly, we could run the following scenario.

Starting with empty conventional and bitemporal tables, we could submit a series of insert, update and delete transactions against both tables. For the bitemporal tables, Instead Of triggers would capture the transactions, and supplement them with Henceforth-based assertion-time periods and state-time periods. And clearly, the result, against these bitemporal tables, would be to accumulate a complete bitemporal history of all changes to those tables.

Is the data shown in Figure 12.8 a pair of conventional tables after transactions have been applied, or a view over a pair of bitemporal tables updated by the identical transactions? In fact, it is either or both.

It follows that, using this technique of renaming conventional tables and using their original names as the names of conventional data views, and of using Instead Of triggers for all inserts, updates and deletes against those original tables, a full bitemporal history of changes to those tables can be accumulated, without altering code, transactions, or queries in any way. That bitemporal history is then available to new queries which may want to look at what things used to be like or will be like, rather than what they are like right now, and/or what we used to say or may in the future say they were or will be like, rather than what we say right now they are like right now.

In addition, new transactions may now be written that make additional functionality possible that was not possible when only the original nontemporal tables were available. For example, it makes it possible to correct mistaken data while also preserving a record of the mistake and of the temporal interval during which it was not recognized as a mistake.

Another important additional functionality is the ability to describe the future before it happens. In other words, it is the ability to add rows to tables which describe then-future states of their referents. In terms of implementation mechanics, this means that it is possible to add rows to a table with future state-time periods.

THE LOGFILE VIEW

By a *logfile view*, I mean a view which provides a history of modifications to data about one or more specified referents. This is an assertion time history of that data.

---

[5]This "includes" is the ordinary language use of the word. It is neither [includes] nor [Includes] because they are Allen relationships which are relationships between pairs of time periods. This use of "includes" is talking about the inclusion of clock ticks in a single time period.

The most important logfile view, which I will call the *current logfile view*, is a view in which an assertion-time history is provided for those referents which exist in current state time. The following CREATE VIEW statement makes that history, for the Supplier-B table, available to queries.[6]

```
CREATE VIEW Supplier-Log
SELECT abtm, aetm, s-id, s-nm, s-scfk, s-type
FROM Supplier-B
WHERE sbtm ≤ Now() AND Now() < setm
```

FIGURE 12.9

Current Logfile View Creation on a Bitemporal Table.

Other views providing an assertion time history, of course, might differ from this one, for example by including state begin time and state end time on the qualifying rows. But what I mean by a "current logfile" view is a logfile of changes to data about any referent which was or is asserted to exist in now-current state time. It is a history of changes to things whose now current state we once kept track of, or are now currently keeping track of.

It is Now() March 2017. The view of Figure 12.9, on the Supplier-B table in Figure 12.6, makes the following rows from that table available for querying.

```
IN STATE INTERVAL: March 2017
Supplier-Log
abtm   aetm   s-id   s-nm       s-scfk  s-type
Feb14  Aug14  S1     Acme       SC1     T4
Aug14  Feb15  S1     Acme       SC1     T3
Feb15  9999   S1     Acme       SC1     T5
Jan15  9999   S2     Superior   SC2     T3
```

FIGURE 12.10

A Current Logfile View on a Bitemporal Table.

Figure 12.11 shows a query issued against the Supplier-Log view, in which an assertion-time history for supplier S1, between April 2014 and January 2017, is requested.

```
SELECT
IN ASSERTION INTERVAL (Apr14, Jan17)
s-id, s-nm, s-scfk, s-type
FROM Supplier-Log
WHERE s-id = S1
```

FIGURE 12.11

A Current Logfile Query - 1.

---

[6]abtm < 9999 is my way of specifying all of assertion time, since every assertion-time period will begin before the end of time. Similarly, sbtm < 9999 will specify all of state time.

The result of this query is shown in Figure 12.12.

```
IN STATE INTERVAL: March 2017
Supplier-Log
abtm    aetm    s-id  s-nm      s-scfk  s-type
Feb14   Aug14   S1    Acme      SC1     T4
Aug14   Feb15   S1    Acme      SC1     T3
Feb15   9999    S1    Acme      SC1     T5
```

FIGURE 12.12

A Current Logfile Query - 2.

This basic query result set contains all the data requested in the query. But it also contains data not requested in the query. This is the result set obtained when the IN ASSERTION INTERVAL clause is interpreted by the DBMS as simply syntactic sugar for, in the case of Figure 12.11, the following WHERE clause:

$$\text{WHERE abtm} \leq \text{Apr14 AND Jan17} < \text{aetm)}$$

But we can also interpret the IN ASSERTION INTERVAL clause as meaning what it says, i.e. that [Apr14-Jan17] is the assertion-time interval for the query and that, consequently, no data outside that query's temporal scope should be returned in the query. In that case, there is more for the DBMS to do to complete the work requested by the IN ASSERTION INTERVAL clause.

That work is the work of decoalescing rows which span a query's temporal scope boundary. In describing that work, the notation "SR1" – "SR7" in Figure 12.13 stand for "Supplier Row" 1-7, and is a convenient way to refer to those rows. Those rows are the struck-through rows in Figure 12.13. Here, and in the rest of the figures in this chapter, rows which the DBMS eliminates from its query working storage are first shown as struck-through and then, in the next and subsequent Figures, no longer appear.

```
      IN STATE INTERVAL: March 2017
        Supplier-Log
        abtm    aetm    s-id  s-nm      s-scfk  s-type
SR1     Feb14   Aug14   S1    Acme      SC1     T4
SR2     Aug14   Feb15   S1    Acme      SC1     T3
SR3     Feb15   9999    S1    Acme      SC1     T5
SR4     Feb14   Apr14   S1    Acme      SC1     T4
SR5     Apr14   Aug14   S1    Acme      SC1     T4
SR6     Feb15   Jan17   S1    Acme      SC1     T5
SR7     Jan17   9999    S1    Acme      SC1     T5
```

FIGURE 12.13

A Current Logfile Query - 3.

First, SR1 spans the query's temporal scope, and so is decoalesced into SR4 and SR5. SR1 is then dropped, because it is redundant with SR4 and SR5. SR4 is also dropped, because it is outside the query's temporal scope.

Next, SR3 also spans the query's temporal scope, and so it is decoalesced into SR6 and SR7. SR3 is then dropped, because it is redundant with SR6 and SR7. SR7 is also dropped, because it is outside the query's temporal scope.

```
IN STATE INTERVAL: March 2017
IN ASSERTION INTERVAL: April 2014 - January 2017
Supplier-Log
abtm   aetm   s-id  s-nm      s-scfk  s-type
Apr14  Aug14  S1    Acme      SC1     T4
Aug14  Feb15  S1    Acme      SC1     T3
Feb15  Jan17  S1    Acme      SC1     T5
```

FIGURE 12.14

A Current Logfile Query - 4.

Assuming that a SORT clause is (although not shown) part of the query, the final result set is as shown in Figure 12.14.

This result set shows the assertion-time history of S1 in the single clock tick specified by the IN STATE INTERVAL clause, and nowhere else. In terms of semantics, it shows every assertion, from April 2014 up to January 2017, about the state of Acme on March 2017.

THE VERSION VIEW

By a *version view*, I mean a view which provides a history of changes to one or more specified referents. This view provides a state-time history of those referents.

A complete such history for any referent is what I have called the *life history* of that referent. It is a series of episodes of that referent extending from when it began to exist, and then either into the indefinite future (if its latest episode is open), or until it ceases to exist (if its latest episode is closed).[7]

The most important version table view will almost certainly be that in which a state-time history is provided for those referents for which there exists one or more current assertions. The following CREATE VIEW statement provides this history.

```
CREATE VIEW Supplier-Ver
SELECT sbtm, setm, s-id, s-nm, s-scfk, s-type
FROM Supplier-B
WHERE abtm ≤ Now() AND Now() < aetm
```

FIGURE 12.15

Version Table View Creation on a Bitemporal Table.

Other views providing a state time history, of course, might differ from this one, for example by including assertion begin time and assertion end time on the qualifying rows. But what I mean by a "current version" view is a history of changes of state to any referent which exists in current state time. It is a history of changes to things whose past, present, or future states we are currently keeping track of.

It is Now() March 2017. The view of Figure 12.15, on the Supplier-B table in Figure 12.6, makes the following rows from that table available for querying.

---

[7]Acme's existence as a corporate entity is an unbroken interval of time. But it is Acme's existence as one of our suppliers that I am referring to when I talk about the life history of that referent. Acme may have been one of our suppliers on several different occasions, those occasions separated by times when Acme, although continuing to exist as a corporate entity, was not one of our suppliers. Consequently, the life history of a referent is not always a single episode.

```
IN ASSERTION INTERVAL: March 2017
Supplier-Ver
sbtm  setm  s-id s-nm      s-scfk s-type
Feb14 Oct14 S1   Acme      SC1    T4
Oct14 Jan16 S1   Acme      SC1    T3
Jan16 9999  S1   Acme      SC1    T5
Jan15 9999  S2   Superior  SC2    T3
```

FIGURE 12.16

A Current Version View on a Bitemporal Table.

Figure 12.17 shows a query issued against the Supplier-Ver view, in which a state-time history for supplier S1, between April 2014 and January 2017, is requested.

```
SELECT
IN STATE INTERVAL (Apr14, Jan17)
s-id, s-nm, s-scfk, s-type
FROM Supplier-Ver
WHERE s-id = S1
```

FIGURE 12.17

A Current Version Query - 1.

The result of this query is shown in Figure 12.18.

```
IN STATE INTERVAL: April 2014 - January 2017
IN ASSERTION INTERVAL: March 2017
Supplier-Ver
sbtm  setm  s-id s-nm  s-scfk s-type
Feb14 Oct14 S1   Acme  SC1    T4
Oct14 Jan16 S1   Acme  SC1    T3
Jan16 9999  S1   Acme  SC1    T5
```

FIGURE 12.18

A Current Version Query - 2.

The IN STATE INTERVAL clause is first translated into the WHERE predicate

```
WHERE sbtm ≤ Apr14 AND Jan17 < setm
```

Next, it directs the DBMS to decoalesce rows which cross the query's temporal scope boundaries, as shown in Figure 12.19.

```
IN ASSERTION INTERVAL: March 2017
Supplier-Ver
      sbtm  setm  s-id s-nm  s-scfk s-type
SR1   Feb14 Oct14 S1   Acme  SC1    T4
SR2   Oct14 Jan16 S1   Acme  SC1    T3
SR3   Jan16 9999  S1   Acme  SC1    T5
SR4   Feb14 Apr14 S1   Acme  SC1    T4
SR5   Apr14 Oct14 S1   Acme  SC1    T4
SR6   Jan16 Jan17 S1   Acme  SC1    T5
SR7   Jan17 9999  S1   Acme  SC1    T5
```

FIGURE 12.19

A Current Version Query - 3.

The description of the decoalescence of the two rows in Figure 12.17 also describes the decoalescence of the two rows in Figure 12.19. The result is as shown in Figure 12.20.

```
IN ASSERTION INTERVAL: March 2017
Supplier-Ver
sbtm   setm   s-id  s-nm      s-scfk  s-type
Apr14  Oct14  S1    Acme      SC1     T4
Oct14  Jan16  S1    Acme      SC1     T3
Jan16  Jan17  S1    Acme      SC1     T5
```

FIGURE 12.20

A Current Version Query - 4.

As similar as Figures 12.14 and 12.20 are, they represent very different semantics. The three rows in Figure 12.14 tell us what the database said (asserted), anytime during each of three adjacent intervals of time whose concatenation [Equals] the temporal interval specified on the query, that the state of S1 was/is/will be on March 2017. So all rows in the result set are about one moment in the life history of supplier S1, the moment of March 2017, and of the different things the database said about it during the assertion-time intervals within the query's temporal scope.

The three rows in Figure 12.20 tell us what the database says, on March 2017, that three temporally adjacent states of supplier S1 whose concatenated temporal intervals [Equal] the temporal interval specified on the query, were/are/will be. So all rows in the result set are about that time-slice from the life history of supplier S1, and of the different states, during that time, that the database, on March 2017, says S1 was/is/will be in.

The previous two paragraphs are my best attempt at a straightforward description of the semantics of the two queries, against their respective views. And yet those descriptions are still complex and easily misunderstood. If speaking clearly about both what things are like and what our data says they are like is this difficult, it should be a warning to subject matter experts from the business community, and business analysts from the IT community, to be very careful in expressing and writing down temporal requirements for databases. It should be a warning to those requesting and those writing queries and reports about our past and current assertions about the past, present and future states of things, that requests and requirements can easily be misstated and/or misunderstood. Lacking a clear understanding of these distinctions, it is even easy for a person stating a requirement to not understand what she herself is asking for.

POINT-IN-TIME RANGE QUERIES

A query which specifies a point in assertion time and a range of state time, or vice versa, is a *point-in-time range query*. The queries which defined the logfile view and the version view are both point-in-time range queries. In this section, we look at one more point-in-time range query.

The current version and current logfile views are defined to make available to queries, respectively, an assertion-time history of all referents that are current in state time, and a state-time history of all referents that are current in assertion time. The former view shows us a history of what we used to say things that currently exist were like, up to and including what we say about them right now. The latter view shows us a history of what we currently say things used to be like, are like right now, and may be like in the future.

So clearly, queries can be directly written against bitemporal tables that will tell us what we asserted, at any time, that things were like, at any time. There is no obscure corner of bitemporal history that will not be recorded by bitemporal transactions. There is no obscure corner of bitemporal history that cannot be accessed by bitemporal queries.

Here's an example. This query is issued against the Supplier-B table in Figure 12.6.

```
SELECT
IN STATE INTERVAL (Jun14, Jan16)
IN ASSERTION INTERVAL (Jun16, Jun16)
s-id, s-nm, s-scfk, s-type
FROM Supplier-B
```

FIGURE 12.21

An Interval Query.

In the first step of processing this query, the DBMS can apply the IN ASSERTION INTERVAL assertion-time filter. The result is shown in Figure 12.22.

Supplier-B

abtm	aetm	sbtm	setm	s-id	s-nm	s-*scfk*	s-type
~~Feb14~~	~~Aug14~~	~~Feb14~~	~~9999~~	~~S1~~	~~Acme~~	~~SC1~~	~~T4~~
Aug14	9999	Feb14	Oct14	S1	Acme	SC1	T4
~~Aug14~~	~~Feb15~~	~~Oct14~~	~~9999~~	~~S1~~	~~Acme~~	~~SC1~~	~~T3~~
Feb15	9999	Oct14	Jan16	S1	Acme	SC1	T3
Feb15	9999	Jan16	9999	S1	Acme	SC1	T5
Jan15	9999	Jan15	9999	S2	Superior	SC2	T3

FIGURE 12.22

An Assertion-Time Filter on the Version Query.

Since only a single point in assertion time is specified on the query, there is no assertion-time decoalescing to do. A row either includes that point in time in its assertion-time interval, or it does not. In this example, the two rows that do not are the two rows in past assertion time, and so they are dropped out of the intermediate result set.

From this point forward, the DBMS drops the two assertion-time period columns because they are no longer needed to complete processing of the query.

In the second step of processing this query, the DBMS can apply the IN STATE INTERVAL state-time filter. The result is shown in Figure 12.23.

```
          IN ASSERTION INTERVAL: June 2016
          Supplier-B
          sbtm   setm   s-id  s-nm      s-scfk s-type
    SR1   Feb14  Oct14  S1    Acme      SC1    T4
    SR2   Oct14  Jan16  S1    Acme      SC1    T3
    SR3   Jan16  9999   S1    Acme      SC1    T5
    SR4   Jan15  9999   S2    Superior  SC2    T3
    SR5   Feb14  Jun14  S1    Acme      SC1    T4
    SR6   Jun14  Oct14  S1    Acme      SC1    T4
    SR7   Jan15  Jan16  S2    Superior  SC2    T3
    SR8   Jan16  9999   S2    Superior  SC2    T3
```

FIGURE 12.23

A State-Time Filter on the Version Query.

Since a *temporal range* is specified for state time, i.e. a temporal interval consisting of more than a single point in time, there is state-time decoalescing to do. Also, state time will be required in the final result set, so the two state-time period columns are retained in the intermediate result set.

In this step, SR1 is decoalesced into SR5 and SR6. SR1 is dropped as redundant. SR5 is dropped as outside the query's temporal scope. Next, SR3 is dropped because it is outside the query's temporal scope. Finally, SR4 is decoalesced, and then dropped as redundant. SR8 is outside the query's temporal scope, and so it is dropped.

Cleaning up the working storage area, and sorting the result set, the query returns the rows shown in Figure 12.24.

```
          IN ASSERTION INTERVAL: June 2016
          Supplier-B
          sbtm   setm   s-id  s-nm      s-scfk s-type
          Jun14  Oct14  S1    Acme      SC1    T4
          Oct14  Jan16  S1    Acme      SC1    T3

          Jan15  Jan16  S2    Superior  SC2    T3
```

FIGURE 12.24

Combining Filters on the Version Query.

If assertion time were a range rather than a point in time, then its two assertion-time columns would not have been dropped out of the result set. But when a single point in time is specified for either or both temporal dimension, I think it is better for the DBMS to drop the temporal dimension's columns, and add a one-line header to the result set, as shown in Figure 12.24.

RANGE QUERIES

A query which specifies a range of both assertion time and state time is a *range query*. It asks for a history of changes to the data about a history of states.

Here's an example. This query is issued against the Supplier-B table in Figure 12.6.

```
SELECT
IN STATE INTERVAL (Jun14, Jan16)
IN ASSERTION INTERVAL (Mar14, Mar15)
s-id, s-nm, s-scfk, s-type
FROM Supplier-B
```

FIGURE 12.25

A Range Query.

In the first step of processing this query, the DBMS will apply the IN ASSERTION INTERVAL assertion-time filter. The result is shown in Figure 12.26.

Supplier-B

	abtm	aetm	sbtm	setm	s-id	s-nm	s-scfk	s-type
S1	~~Feb14~~	~~Aug14~~	~~Feb14~~	~~9999~~	~~S1~~	~~Acme~~	~~SC1~~	~~T4~~
S2	~~Aug14~~	~~9999~~	~~Feb14~~	~~Oct14~~	~~S1~~	~~Acme~~	~~SC1~~	~~T4~~
S3	Aug14	Feb15	Oct14	9999	S1	Acme	SC1	T3
S4	~~Feb15~~	~~9999~~	~~Oct14~~	~~Jan16~~	~~S1~~	~~Acme~~	~~SC1~~	~~T3~~
S5	~~Feb15~~	~~9999~~	~~Jan16~~	~~9999~~	~~S1~~	~~Acme~~	~~SC1~~	~~T5~~
S5	~~Feb15~~	~~9999~~	~~Jan16~~	~~9999~~	~~S1~~	~~Acme~~	~~SC1~~	~~T5~~
S6	~~Jan15~~	~~9999~~	~~Jan16~~	~~9999~~	~~S2~~	~~Superior~~	~~SC2~~	~~T3~~
S7	~~Feb14~~	~~Mar14~~	~~Feb14~~	~~9999~~	~~S1~~	~~Acme~~	~~SC1~~	~~T4 from S1~~
S8	Mar14	Aug14	Feb14	9999	S1	Acme	SC1	T4 from S1
S9	Aug14	Mar15	Feb14	Oct14	S1	Acme	SC1	T4 from S2
S10	~~Mar15~~	~~9999~~	~~Feb14~~	~~Oct14~~	~~S1~~	~~Acme~~	~~SC1~~	~~T4 from S2~~
S11	Feb15	Mar15	Oct14	Jan16	S1	Acme	SC1	T3 from S4
S12	~~Mar15~~	~~9999~~	~~Oct14~~	~~Jan16~~	~~S1~~	~~Acme~~	~~SC1~~	~~T3 from S4~~
S13	Feb15	Mar15	Jan16	9999	S1	Acme	SC1	T5 from S5
S14	~~Mar15~~	~~9999~~	~~Jan16~~	~~9999~~	~~S1~~	~~Acme~~	~~SC1~~	~~T5 from S5~~
S15	Jan15	Mar15	Jan15	9999	S2	Superior	SC2	T3 from S6
S16	~~Mar15~~	~~9999~~	~~Jan15~~	~~9999~~	~~S2~~	~~Superior~~	~~SC2~~	~~T3 from S6~~

FIGURE 12.26

An Assertion-Time Filter on the Range Query: Intermediate Results.

These rows were decoalesced on the assertion-time boundaries of the query's temporal scope. Rows which were decoalesced into other rows were then dropped because original rows are redundant with the rows they are decoalesced into. Either one of the two rows resulting from a decoalesce, or two of the three rows resulting from a decoalesce, were dropped because they fell entirely outside the query's temporal scope.

To produce the results shown in Figure 12.26, the following decoalesce and drop transformations were applied.

- S1 was decoalesced into S7 and S8. S1 and S7 were dropped.
- S2 was decoalesced into S9 and S10. S2 and S10 are dropped.
- S3's assertion-time period is wholly contained in the query's temporal scope, and so S3 was not decoalesced.
- S4 was decoalesced into S11 and S12. S4 and S12 were dropped.
- S5 was decoalesced into S13 and S14. S5 and S14 were dropped.
- S6 was decoalesced into S15 and S16. S6 and S16 were dropped.

Removing the rows that were dropped, we have:

```
Supplier-B
        abtm   aetm   sbtm   setm   s-id  s-nm       s-scfk  s-type
S3      Aug14  Feb15  Oct14  9999   S1    Acme       SC1     T3
S8      Mar14  Aug14  Feb14  9999   S1    Acme       SC1     T4 from S1
S9      Aug14  Mar15  Feb14  Oct14  S1    Acme       SC1     T4 from S2
S11     Feb15  Mar15  Oct14  Jan16  S1    Acme       SC1     T3 from S4
S13     Feb15  Mar15  Jan16  9999   S1    Acme       SC1     T5 from S5
S15     Jan15  Mar15  Jan15  9999   S2    Superior   SC2     T3 from S6
```

FIGURE 12.27

An Assertion-Time Filter on the Range Query: Final Results.

In the second step of processing this query, the DBMS will apply the IN STATE INTERVAL state-time filter. The result is shown in Figure 12.28.

```
Supplier-B
        abtm   aetm   sbtm   setm   s-id  s-nm       s-scfk  s-type
S3      Aug14  Feb15  Oct14  9999   S1    Acme       SC1     T3
S8      Mar14  Aug14  Feb14  9999   S1    Acme       SC1     T4
S9      Aug14  Mar15  Feb14  Oct14  S1    Acme       SC1     T4
S11     Feb15  Mar15  Oct14  Jan16  S1    Acme       SC1     T3
S13     Feb15  Mar15  Jan16  9999   S1    Acme       SC1     T5
S15     Jan15  Mar15  Jan15  9999   S2    Superior   SC2     T3
S17     Aug14  Feb15  Oct14  Jan16  S1    Acme       SC1     T3 from S3
S18     Aug14  Feb15  Jan16  9999   S1    Acme       SC1     T3 from S3
S19     Mar14  Aug14  Feb14  Jun14  S1    Acme       SC1     T4 from S8
S20     Mar14  Aug14  Jun14  Jan16  S1    Acme       SC1     T4 from S8
S21     Mar14  Aug14  Jan16  9999   S1    Acme       SC1     T4 from S8
S22     Aug14  Mar15  Feb14  Jun14  S1    Acme       SC1     T4 from S9
S23     Aug14  Mar15  Jun14  Oct14  S1    Acme       SC1     T4 from S9
S24     Jan15  Mar15  Jan15  Jan16  S2    Superior   SC2     T3 from S15
S25     Jan15  Mar15  Jan16  9999   S2    Superior   SC2     T3 from S15
```

FIGURE 12.28

A State-Time Filter on the Range Query: Intermediate Results.

To produce the results shown in Figure 12.28, the following decoalesce and drop transformations were applied.

- S3 was decoalesced into S17 and S18. S3 and S18 were dropped.
- S8 was decoalesced into S19, S20 and S21. S8, S19 and S21were dropped.
- S9 was decoalesced into S22 and S23. S9 and S22 were dropped.
- S11's state-time period is wholly contained within the query's temporal scope, and so S11 is not decoalesced.
- S13's state-time period is completely outside the query's temporal scope, and so S13 is dropped.
- S15 is decoalesced into S24 and S25. S15 and S25 are dropped.

Removing the rows that were dropped, we have:

```
Supplier-B
          abtm   aetm   sbtm   setm   s-id  s-nm       s-scfk  s-type
    S11   Feb15  Mar15  Oct14  Jan16  S1    Acme       SC1     T3
    S17   Aug14  Feb15  Oct14  Jan16  S1    Acme       SC1     T3 from S3
    S20   Mar14  Aug14  Jun14  Jan16  S1    Acme       SC1     T4 from S8
    S23   Aug14  Mar15  Jun14  Oct14  S1    Acme       SC1     T4 from S9
    S24   Jan15  Mar15  Jan15  Jan16  S2    Superior   SC2     T3 from S15
```

FIGURE 12.29

A State-Time Filter on the Range Query: Final Results.

Cleaning up the working storage area, and sorting the result set, the query returns the rows shown in Figure 12.30.

```
          IN STATE INTERVAL: June 2014 - January 2016
          IN ASSERTION INTERVAL: March 2014 - March 2015

          Supplier-B
          abtm   aetm   sbtm   setm   s-id  s-nm       s-scfk  s-type
    S17   Aug14  Feb15  Oct14  Jan16  S1    Acme       SC1     T3
    S11   Feb15  Mar15  Oct14  Jan16  S1    Acme       SC1     T3

    S20   Mar14  Aug14  Jun14  Jan16  S1    Acme       SC1     T4
    S23   Aug14  Mar15  Jun14  Oct14  S1    Acme       SC1     T4

    S24   Jan15  Mar15  Jan15  Jan16  S2    Superior   SC2     T3
```

FIGURE 12.30

Combining Filters on the Range Query.

Blank lines have been inserted into the result set to emphasize certain groupings of rows. The result set has been split, first of all, by supplier, and so the row for supplier S2 is set apart from the rest of the result set. Then, within the four rows for S1, the two rows that exist in [Equal] state-time intervals are grouped and, finally, the last two rows form a group in which the assertion times [Meet].

These physical characteristics of the data reflect different semantics. First of all, the first two rows describe the same temporal state of Acme. Their state-time periods are [Equal]. As for the second two rows for Acme, their assertion-time periods [Meet], and both ascribe the same atemporal state to Acme. Also, S23's state-time period [starts] that of S20.

These semantic relationships among the four Acme rows can be represented in a more condensed form. First of all, rows S17 and S11 can be coalesced. They represent the same temporal state of Acme, in contiguous assertion-time periods. The result of coalescing these two rows is:

```
[Aug14|Mar15|Oct14|Jan16|S1|Acme|SC1|T3]
```

Next, S20 and S23 both agree that Acme was a T4 supplier from June 2014 up to October 2014. Since their assertion-time periods [Meet], we can derive the following row from them:

[Mar14|Mar15|Jun14|Oct14|S1|Acme|SC1|T4]

However, S20 also asserts that Acme was a T4 supplier from October 2014 up to January 2016. Since the previously derived row covers S20's assertion about the June to October state-time period, the next derived row we need is the following:

[Mar14|Aug14|Oct14|Jan6|S1|Acme|SC1|T4]

Together, these last two derived rows contain exactly the same information as rows S20 and S23. And so the query could instead have returned the result set shown in Figure 12.31.

```
IN STATE INTERVAL: June 2014 - January 2016
IN ASSERTION INTERVAL: March 2014 - March 2015

Supplier-B
abtm  aetm  sbtm  setm  s-id s-nm      s-scfk s-type
Aug14 Mar15 Oct14 Jan16 S1   Acme      SC1    T3
Mar14 Mar15 Jun14 Oct14 S1   Acme      SC1    T4
Mar14 Aug14 Oct14 Jan16 S1   Acme      SC1    T4
Jan15 Mar15 Jan15 Jan16 S2   Superior  SC2    T3
```

FIGURE 12.31

Coalescing a Range Query Result Set.

Presenting the information as shown in Figure 12.30 emphasizes the fact that, as of August 2014, we knew that Acme would no longer be a T3 supplier after October 2014. But presenting the information as shown in Figure 12.31 emphasizes the fact that throughout the query's assertion-time scope, we asserted that Acme was a T4 supplier from June to October. It was only during the first five months of that assertion-time scope that we also asserted that Acme would be a T4 supplier through the end of the query's state-time scope.

In the next chapter, I will analyze bitemporal queries that are more complex than the ones in this chapter. These more complex queries are range queries involving joins over multiple tables.

GLOSSARY LIST

assert	inscription	statement
assertion time	life history	temporal indexical
coalesce	referent	temporal interval
decoalesce	state time	temporal upward compatibility
fact	state	

ADVANCED TEMPORAL QUERIES 13

The series of steps involved in a DBMS processing each of the temporal queries described in the previous chapter or in this one, are algorithms for transforming those temporal queries into queries that can be carried out by standard SQL, i.e. by SQL that does not include any specifically temporal features. This approach to adding temporal functionality to queries and transactions against relational databases is possible because standard SQL is syntactic sugar for a restricted subset of typed first-order predicate logic, and because no extensions to that logic are required to manage temporal data. Given those two facts, it follows that there is nothing new, from a logical point of view, about querying and updating bitemporal data. Anything that can be done with the new temporal SQL can be done with the old, pre-temporal SQL.

An interesting consequence is that a bitemporal implementation which does not use the temporal extensions of either ISO 9075:2011 or TSQL2, i.e. the extensions implemented in, respectively, DB2 10 and Teradata 13, can be a vendor-neutral implementation. Given the differences between IBM's and Teradata's support for bitemporality, interoperability between those implementations, in such specific forms as cross-DBMS temporal queries, will be quite difficult. But if a vendor-neutral implementation of bitemporality is used, cross-DBMS interoperability will not be a problem.

Temporal range queries are queries whose temporal scope, whether state time or bitemporal, consists of more than a single clock tick. They are significantly more complex than queries which specify a single point in time. Temporal range multi-table queries are also more complex than single-table queries. This is because the referents in a joined pair of rows exist in temporal intervals whose Allen relationship to one another, and to the temporal interval specified in the query itself, must be taken into consideration.

A BASIC TEMPORAL RANGE MULTI-TABLE QUERY

In this section, the query I analyze will be a query issued against the two tables shown in Figure 13.1.

```
S-Cat-B
abtm   aetm   sbtm   setm   sc-id  sc-abbr  sc-desc
Jan14  May15  Jan14  9999   SC1    SCA      tier 1
May15  9999   Jan14  Jan15  SC1    SCA      tier 1
May15  9999   Jan15  9999   SC1    SCA      tier 2
Dec14  9999   Dec14  9999   SC2    SCB      tier 2


Supplier-B
abtm   aetm   sbtm   setm   s-id  s-nm      s-scfk  s-type
Feb14  Aug14  Feb14  9999   S1    Acme      SC1     T4
Aug14  9999   Feb14  Oct14  S1    Acme      SC1     T4
Aug14  Feb15  Oct14  9999   S1    Acme      SC1     T3
Feb15  9999   Oct14  Jan15  S1    Acme      SC1     T3
Feb15  9999   Jan15  9999   S1    Acme      SC1     T5
Jan15  9999   Jan15  9999   S2    Superior  SC2     T3
```

FIGURE 13.1

Bitemporal Supplier and Supplier-Category Tables.

Figure 13.2 graphically illustrates the example I will use in this section. "QTS", in that Figure, stands for "query temporal scope".

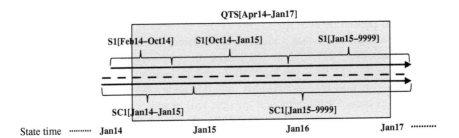

FIGURE 13.2

A Diagram of a Basic Temporal Range Multi-Table Query.

In Figure 13.2, three Supplier rows are shown above the dashed timeline, and two Supplier Category rows are shown below that timeline. The state-time timeline itself, with the four years of 2014, 2015, 2016 and 2017 marked at the bottom of the diagram, is shown as a dashed line. The query's temporal scope is shown by means of the shaded rectangle. The solid line above the dashed timeline represents one episode of supplier S1. The arrowhead on the right indicates that the episode is open, i.e. that its latest row has an open state-time period. The solid line below the dashed line represents supplier category SC1, and is similarly interpreted.

It is Now() March 2017. The query shown in Figure 13.3 is issued against the two tables shown in Figure 13.1.

```
SELECT
IN STATE INTERVAL (Apr14, Jan17)
S.sbtm, S.setm, S.s-id, S.s-nm, S.s-type,
C.sc-abbr, C.sc-desc
FROM Supplier-B AS S, S-Cat-B AS C
WHERE S.s-id = S1
AND S.s-scfk = C.sc-id
```

FIGURE 13.3

A Basic Temporal Range Multi-Table Query.

STEP 1: DECOALESCE AND RESTRICT ON ASSERTION TIME

The first step is to apply the query's temporal scope to both tables, beginning with the default assertion-time scope of [Mar17-9999].

Although assertion-time columns are not listed in the query's set of projected columns, they are included in these early-stage intermediate results in the query's working storage. They are needed because all data that lies outside the query's bitemporal scope must be dropped.

Figure 13.4 shows the result of dropping all data outside the query's assertion-time interval.

```
S-Cat-B
abtm   aetm   sbtm   setm   sc-id sc-abbr sc-desc
Jan14 May15 Jan14 9999  SC1    SCA    tier 1
May15 9999  Jan14 Jan15 SC1    SCA    tier 1
May15 9999  Jan15 9999 SC1    SCA    tier 2
Dec14 9999  Dec14 9999 SC2    SCB    tier 2

Supplier-B
abtm   aetm   sbtm   setm   s-id s-nm      s-scfk s-type
Feb14 Aug14 Feb14 9999  S1    Acme      SC1    T4
Aug14 9999  Feb14 Oct14 S1    Acme      SC1    T4
Aug14 Feb15 Oct14 9999  S1    Acme      SC1    T3
Feb15 9999  Oct14 Jan15 S1    Acme      SC1    T3
Feb15 9999  Jan15 9999 S1    Acme      SC1    T5
Jan15 9999  Jan15 9999 S2    Superior SC2    T3
```

FIGURE 13.4

A Basic Temporal Range Join Query: Intermediate Results - 1.

One row in S-Cat-B and two rows in Supplier-B are dropped because their assertion-time periods end prior to the assertion-time interval of the query, that interval being [Mar17-9999].

Next we restrict the assertion-time periods in the table to the assertion-time interval of the transaction. This happens in two stages. First, all rows are decoalesced on the March 2017 point in time. Next, the rows with assertion-time periods outside the [Mar17-9999] range are dropped. The results are shown in Figure 13.5.

```
S-Cat-B
abtm   aetm   sbtm    setm    sc-id   sc-abbr  sc-desc
Mar17  9999   Jan14   Jan15   SC1     SCA      tier 1
Mar17  9999   Jan15   9999    SC1     SCA      tier 2
Mar17  9999   Dec14   9999    SC2     SCB      tier 2


Supplier-B
abtm   aetm   sbtm    setm    s-id   s-nm       s-scfk  s-type
Mar17  9999   Feb14   Oct14   S1     Acme       SC1     T4
Mar17  9999   Oct14   Jan15   S1     Acme       SC1     T3
Mar17  9999   Jan15   9999    S1     Acme       SC1     T5
Mar17  9999   Jan15   9999    S2     Superior   SC2     T3
```

FIGURE 13.5

A Basic Temporal Range Join Query: Intermediate Results - 2.

In Figure 13.5, all the rows which are current in the transaction's assertion time interval of [Mar17-9999] are included. In addition, the only rows in Figure 13.5 are rows which are current in the transaction's assertion time interval.

STEP 2: DECOALESCE AND RESTRICT ON STATE TIME

This step filters out all rows based on the temporal predicate expressed in the IN STATE INTERVAL clause. These are rows whose *row temporal scopes* do not fall within the *query's temporal scope*, i.e. whose temporal areas do not share even a single clock tick with the query's temporal area. In Figure 13.5, this process filtered out data whose assertion time was outside the query's temporal scope. Now it will filter out rows whose state time is outside the query's temporal scope. The result is shown in Figure 13.6.

In this step of this example, I leave it as an exercise for the reader to account for the struck-through rows in Figure 13.6. Of course, we already know that every struck-through row will be a row that is either redundant with one or more non-struck-through rows, or that falls entirely outside the query's temporal scope.

Removing the struck-through rows, the result of Step 2 is shown in Figure 13.7.

STEP 3: DROP ASSERTION-TIME PERIOD COLUMNS

In Figure 13.7, all rows that remain in the query's working storage have the identical assertion time. This means that we can remove the assertion-time periods from these rows, since they will

S-Cat-B

abtm	aetm	sbtm	setm	sc-id	sc-abbr	sc-desc
~~Mar17~~	~~9999~~	~~Jan14~~	~~Jan15~~	~~SC1~~	~~SCA~~	~~tier 1~~
~~Mar17~~	~~9999~~	~~Jan14~~	~~Apr14~~	~~SC1~~	~~SCA~~	~~tier 1~~
Mar17	9999	Apr14	Jan15	SC1	SCA	tier 1
~~Mar17~~	~~9999~~	~~Jan15~~	~~9999~~	~~SC1~~	~~SCA~~	~~tier 2~~
Mar17	9999	Jan15	Jan17	SC1	SCA	tier 2
~~Mar17~~	~~9999~~	~~Jan17~~	~~9999~~	~~SC1~~	~~SCA~~	~~tier 2~~
~~Mar17~~	~~9999~~	~~Dec14~~	~~9999~~	~~SC2~~	~~SCB~~	~~tier 2~~
Mar17	9999	Dec14	Jan17	SC2	SCB	tier 2
~~Mar17~~	~~9999~~	~~Jan17~~	~~9999~~	~~SC2~~	~~SCB~~	~~tier 2~~

Supplier-B

abtm	aetm	sbtm	setm	s-id	s-nm	s-scfk	s-type
~~Mar17~~	~~9999~~	~~Feb14~~	~~Oct14~~	~~S1~~	~~Acme~~	~~SC1~~	~~T4~~
~~Mar17~~	~~9999~~	~~Feb14~~	~~Apr14~~	~~S1~~	~~Acme~~	~~SC1~~	~~T4~~
Mar17	9999	Apr14	Oct14	S1	Acme	SC1	T4
Mar17	9999	Oct14	Jan15	S1	Acme	SC1	T3
~~Mar17~~	~~9999~~	~~Jan15~~	~~9999~~	~~S1~~	~~Acme~~	~~SC1~~	~~T5~~
Mar17	9999	Jan15	Jan17	S1	Acme	SC1	T5
~~Mar17~~	~~9999~~	~~Jan17~~	~~9999~~	~~S1~~	~~Acme~~	~~SC1~~	~~T5~~
~~Mar17~~	~~9999~~	~~Jan15~~	~~9999~~	~~S2~~	~~Superior~~	~~SC2~~	~~T3~~
Mar17	9999	Jan15	Jan17	S2	Superior	SC2	T3
~~Mar17~~	~~9999~~	~~Jan17~~	~~9999~~	~~S2~~	~~Superior~~	~~SC2~~	~~T3~~

FIGURE 13.6

A Basic Temporal Range Join Query: Intermediate Results - 3.

S-Cat-B

abtm	aetm	sbtm	setm	sc-id	sc-abbr	sc-desc
Mar17	9999	Apr14	Jan15	SC1	SCA	tier 1
Mar17	9999	Jan15	Jan17	SC1	SCA	tier 2
Mar17	9999	Dec14	Jan17	SC2	SCB	tier 2

Supplier-B

abtm	aetm	sbtm	setm	s-id	s-nm	s-scfk	s-type
Mar17	9999	Apr14	Oct14	S1	Acme	SC1	T4
Mar17	9999	Oct14	Jan15	S1	Acme	SC1	T3
Mar17	9999	Jan15	Jan17	S1	Acme	SC1	T5
Mar17	9999	Jan15	Jan17	S2	Superior	SC2	T3

FIGURE 13.7

A Basic Temporal Range Join Query: Intermediate Results - 4.

have no further impact on completing the processing of the query. What remains is that assertion-time interval as a fact that characterizes the query results as a whole, and so I will represent it as a one-line statement about the query result set, as shown in Figure 13.8.

```
IN ASSERTION INTERVAL: March 2017 - 9999
S-Cat-B
sbtm  setm  sc-id sc-abbr sc-desc
Apr14 Jan15 SC1   SCA     tier 1
Jan15 Jan17 SC1   SCA     tier 2
Dec14 Jan17 SC2   SCB     tier 2


Supplier-B
sbtm  setm  s-id s-nm     s-scfk s-type
Apr14 Oct14 S1   Acme     SC1    T4
Oct14 Jan15 S1   Acme     SC1    T3
Jan15 Jan17 S1   Acme     SC1    T5
Jan15 Jan17 S2   Superior SC2    T3
```

FIGURE 13.8

A Basic Temporal Range Join Query: Intermediate Results - 5.

STEP 4: ALIGN ON STATE-TIME BOUNDARIES

Before a supplier row can be joined to a supplier category row, the two rows must be aligned on their state-time periods.

The alignment will be made by decoalescing the rows in one of the tables. It doesn't matter which of a pair of tables the decoalesce transformation is first applied to, so I will begin by decoalescing the S-Cat-B table.

The first row in the Supplier-B table needs an SC1 row in S-Cat-B with a state-time interval of [Apr14-Oct14]. To get this row, we decoalesce the first row in S-Cat-B in Figure 13.8, splitting it into two rows on the October 2014 clock tick.

The second row in the Supplier-B table needs an SC1 row with a state-time interval of [Oct14-Jan15]. Fortunately, the previous decoalesce transformation provided that row.

The third row in the Supplier-B table needs an SC1 row with a state-time interval of [Jan15-Jan17]. There already exists an SC1 row with that state-time interval, so no decoalesce transformation is needed.

The last row in the Supplier-B table needs an SC2 row with a state-time interval of [Jan15-Jan17]. A decoalesce transformation on January 2015 provides the needed row.

The result is shown in Figure 13.9.

Note that the original row in each decoalesce transformation has been carried over to the next step of the process. This does produce a situation in which two rows for the same referent have overlapping state-time intervals. Normally this would be a temporal entity integrity violation. But when this situation is created by a decoalesce transformation, it is not. The reason is that a decoalesce transformation always produces rows whose state description is identical to the state description of the original row. And so it will never be possible for a decoalesce transformation to result in a set of statements that contain a contradiction.

```
IN ASSERTION INTERVAL: March 2017 - 9999
S-Cat-B
sbtm   setm   sc-id  sc-abbr  sc-desc
Apr14  Jan15  SC1    SCA      tier 1
Jan15  Jan17  SC1    SCA      tier 2
Dec14  Jan17  SC2    SCB      tier 2
Apr14  Oct14  SC1    SCA      tier 1
Oct14  Jan15  SC1    SCA      tier 1
Dec14  Jan15  SC2    SCB      tier 2
Jan15  Jan17  SC2    SCB      tier 2


Supplier-B
sbtm   setm   s-id   s-nm      s-scfk  s-type
Apr14  Oct14  S1     Acme      SC1     T4
Oct14  Jan15  S1     Acme      SC1     T3
Jan15  Jan17  S1     Acme      SC1     T5
Jan15  Jan17  S2     Superior  SC2     T3
```

FIGURE 13.9

A Basic Temporal Range Join Query: Intermediate Results - 6.

ASIDE

This provides another example of the importance of understanding the semantics of the rules we implement in the program code that maintains data. The first and the fourth rows in the S-Cat-B table in Figure 13.9 appear to violate temporal entity integrity. So do the first and the fifth rows, the third and the sixth rows, and the third and the seventh rows.

But the purpose of the temporal entity integrity rule is to prevent contradictory statements in a database. And as I just noted, decoalesence can never result in contradictory statements. So no set of rows consisting of an original row and two or more rows decoalesced from that original row can ever contain a contradiction, and so they are an exception to the implementation mechanics for the temporal entity integrity rule.

But to call anything an exception to a rule is to miss an opportunity to understanding what is going on. Why is it an exception to the rule? How can the rule be reformulated so that there are no exceptions to it?

An example can be found in in two descriptions of temporal entity integrity that I provided in Chapter 9, in the section "Bitemporal Entity Integrity". First describing the bitemporal form of temporal entity integrity in terms of its implementation, I said that it is the requirement that "there can be no combination of an assertion-time clock tick and a state-time clock tick that is included in the time periods of multiple rows for the same referent." And yet, here in Figure 13.9, we have six pairs of rows which violate that requirement.

But in the very next paragraph, I went on to say that "(t)wo bitemporal cells in the same referent slice may (and often will) contain the same state description. But no bitemporal cell in a referent slice may contain more than one state description." This is a description of temporal entity integrity in terms of its semantics. And in Figure 13.9, no pair of rows violates this requirement since decoalesced rows always contain the same state description as the row from which they were decoalesced.

In fact, the same reasoning applies to (nontemporal) entity integrity. There is no reason why two rows, in a conventional relational table, with the same primary key, cannot concurrently exist in that table, as long as both rows make the same statement.

Any rule is stated in terms of its semantics. Its statement in terms of its implementation are the instructions given to someone whose job it is to apply the rule to its subject matter. The implementation statement is not the final word, as it is so often taken to be. The final word is what has to be done; an implementation is how that final word is carried out.

Looking at the two tables in Figure 13.9, we can easily identify those rows in the S-Cat-B table which do not match a corresponding row in the Supplier-B table. Dropping those rows from our intermediate result set, we arrive at Figure 13.10.

```
IN ASSERTION INTERVAL: March 2017 - 9999
S-Cat-B
sbtm  setm  sc-id sc-abbr sc-desc
Jan15 Jan17 SC1   SCA     tier 2
Apr14 Oct14 SC1   SCA     tier 1
Oct14 Jan15 SC1   SCA     tier 1
Jan15 Jan17 SC2   SCB     tier 2


Supplier-B
sbtm  setm  s-id s-nm      s-scfk s-type
Apr14 Oct14 S1   Acme      SC1    T4
Oct14 Jan15 S1   Acme      SC1    T3
Jan15 Jan17 S1   Acme      SC1    T5
Jan15 Jan17 S2   Superior  SC2    T3
```

FIGURE 13.10

A Basic Temporal Range Join Query: Intermediate Results - 7.

The *s-id* predicate in Figure 13.3 could have been applied at any time during the processing of the query. And often, the best performance will be achieved by applying the nontemporal predicates first. However, because the *s-id* predicate has not yet been applied in this example, let it be applied now, in which case our intermediate result set is as shown in Figure 13.11.

```
IN ASSERTION INTERVAL: March 2017 -9999
S-Cat-B
sbtm  setm  sc-id sc-abbr sc-desc
Jan15 Jan17 SC1   SCA     tier 2
Apr14 Oct14 SC1   SCA     tier 1
Oct14 Jan15 SC1   SCA     tier 1
Jan15 Jan17 SC2   SCB     tier 2


Supplier-B
sbtm  setm  s-id s-nm    s-scfk s-type
Apr14 Oct14 S1   Acme    SC1    T4
Oct14 Jan15 S1   Acme    SC1    T3
Jan15 Jan17 S1   Acme    SC1    T5
```

FIGURE 13.11

A Basic Temporal Range Join Query: Intermediate Results - 8.

All work preparatory to joining the two tables has now been done.

STEP 5: JOIN ON REFID AND STATE TIME

This step adds row temporal scope equality predicates to the original WHERE clause. The join internally drops its *s-id* predicate since it has already been applied, and augments its WHERE clause to include the following:

```
AND S.s-scfk = C.sc-id
AND S.sbtm = C.sbtm
AND S.setm = C.setm
```

Also, because of how the algorithm, to this point, has aligned temporal intervals, it isn't necessary to retain both temporal predicates in the internal WHERE clause. And so the internal WHERE clause can be:

```
WHERE S.s-scfk = C.sc-id
AND S.sbtm = C.sbtm
```

There will be one row in the final result set for each row in the table on which the Select operation is performed. The result is shown in Figure 13.12.

```
IN ASSERTION INTERVAL: March 2017 - 9999
sbtm   setm   s-id  s-nm   s-type   sc-abbr  sc-desc
Apr14  Oct14  S1    Acme   T4       SCA      tier 1
Oct14  Jan15  S1    Acme   T3       SCA      tier 1
Jan15  Jan17  S1    Acme   T5       SCA      tier 2
```

FIGURE 13.12

A Basic Temporal Range Join Query: Final Results.

Nothing in this result set is superfluous. Nothing has to be discarded, coalesced or decoalesced.

Temporal range joins involving three or more tables would be, of course, more complicated. But the same strategy will produce the correct results. That strategy is to restrict the working storage query results to the temporal scope of the transaction, and then do temporal scope *internal decoalesces* until all rows to be joined align on state-time temporal boundaries.

In describing an algorithm to carry out temporal range multi-table queries, I have made no attempt to consider performance issues. One such issue is the order in which the first two steps should be carried out. Is it more efficient to filter out rows which do not match the nontemporal WHERE clause predicates first, and then apply the temporal filter after that? Or is it more efficient to apply the temporal predicates first? That will likely depend on partitioning and indexing strategies employed for the tables, and the sparseness or density of the qualifying RefIds. These are aspects of performance that I have not considered in this book.[1]

In these temporal range examples, rows have been decoalesced so that they can be joined on [Equal] temporal ranges. I note, however, that all that is required is that rows be decoalesced so that the temporal ranges of the rows in the base table (the table that other tables are being joined to) are Allen relationship [Contained In] the temporal ranges of the rows that are being joined to them. And clearly, in all cases where a [Contained In] relationship can be used rather than an [Equals] relationship, there will be less decoalescing work to be done, and so the query will achieve better performance.

---

[1]For a discussion of bitemporal performance issues, see Chapter 15 of *MTRD*.

A COMPLEX TEMPORAL RANGE MULTI-TABLE QUERY

The temporal range multi-table query just considered is basic in the sense that the temporal foreign key joins are all 1:1 or 1:M; they are never M:1 or M:M. But when all cardinalities for temporal joins are considered, decoalescence may become an iterative process. That is, one or more rows resulting from a decoalescence of a row may themselves need to be decoalesced. This is an additional level of complication for temporal range multi-table queries.

To illustrate complex temporal range multi-table queries, I have created a different set of S-Cat-B and Supplier-B rows to begin with. These are shown in Figure 13.13.[2]

S-Cat-B

	abtm	aetm	sbtm	setm	sc-id	sc-abbr	sc-desc
Cat1	Jan14	May15	Jan14	9999	SC1	SCA	tier 1
Cat2	May15	9999	Jan14	Jan15	SC1	SCA	tier 1
Cat3	May15	9999	Jan15	9999	SC1	SCA	tier 2

Supplier-B

	abtm	aetm	sbtm	setm	s-id	s-nm	s-scfk	s-type
Sup1	Feb14	Aug14	Feb14	Dec15	S1	Acme	SC1	T4
Sup2	Aug14	9999	Feb14	Oct14	S1	Acme	SC1	T4
Sup3	Aug14	Feb15	Oct14	Dec15	S1	Acme	SC1	T3
Sup4	Feb15	9999	Oct14	Jun15	S1	Acme	SC1	T3
Sup5	Feb15	9999	Jun15	Dec15	S1	Acme	SC1	T5
Sup6	Apr14	Nov14	Apr14	Dec14	S2	Superior	SC1	T4
Sup7	Nov14	9999	Apr14	Nov14	S2	Superior	SC1	T4
Sup8	Nov14	9999	Nov14	Dec14	S2	Superior	SC1	T2
Sup9	Jun15	Dec15	Jun15	Feb16	S2	Superior	SC2	T2
Sup10	Dec15	9999	Jun15	Dec15	S2	Superior	SC1	T3
Sup11	Dec15	9999	Dec15	Feb16	S2	Superior	SC1	T4
Sup12	Jun14	9999	Jun14	9999	S3	Ace	SC1	T5

FIGURE 13.13

Suppliers and Supplier Categories.

It is Now() March 2017. The query shown in Figure 13.14 is issued against the two tables shown in Figure 13.13.

```
SELECT
IN STATE INTERVAL (Apr14, Jan17)
S.sbtm, S.setm, S.s-id, S.s-nm, S.s-type,
C.sc-abbr, C.sc-desc
FROM Supplier-B AS S, S-Cat-B AS C
WHERE S.s-scfk = C.sc-id
```

FIGURE 13.14

A Complex Temporal Range Join Query.

---

[2]Because of the relatively large number of rows in this example, I have added a unique tag to each row, listed at the left-hand edge of the illustration. These tags are not part of the data, of course. They are just to make the example easier to follow.

Once again, the IN STATE INTERVAL clause specifies the state-time interval. The point of using an IN STATE INTERVAL clause for this purpose, instead of just

```
sbtm  ≥  Apr14 AND setm  <  Jan17
```

is simplicity, and the distinction between data which is part of a statement and data which is about a statement. State begin time and state end time aren't just another pair of columns on a table. They are statement delimiters, not predicates within that statement. More precisely, they are temporal indexicals.

STEP 1: DECOALESCE AND RESTRICT ON ASSERTION TIME

The first step is to restrict both tables to the query's temporal scope, beginning with the default assertion-time scope of [Mar17-9999].

Although assertion-time columns are not listed in the query's set of projected columns, they are included in the early-stage intermediate results in the query's working storage. They are needed because, at this point in processing the query, all data that lies outside the query's bitemporal scope must be dropped.

First we filter the S-Cat-B table on the query's assertion-time period, as follows:

1. Drop Cat1 because its assertion-time interval is entirely out of scope.
2. Decoalesce Cat2 into Cat4 and Cat5.
3. Drop Cat2 because its assertion-time interval is partially out of scope.
4. Drop Cat4 because its assertion-time interval is entirely out of scope.
5. Decoalesce Cat3 into Cat6 and Cat7.
6. Drop Cat3 because its assertion-time interval is partially out of scope.
7. Drop Cat6 because its assertion-time interval is entirely out of scope.

Next we filter the Supplier-B table on the query's assertion-time period.

1. Drop Sup1 because its assertion-time interval is out of scope.
2. Decoalesce Sup2 into Sup13 and Sup14.
3. Drop Sup2 because it is redundant.
4. Drop Sup13 because its assertion-time interval is out of scope.
5. Drop Sup3 because its assertion-time interval is out of scope.
6. Decoalesce Sup4 into Sup15 and Sup16.
7. Drop Sup4 because it is redundant.
8. Drop Sup15 because its assertion-time interval is out of scope.
9. Decoalesce Sup5 into Sup17 and Sup18.
10. Drop Sup5 because it is redundant.
11. Drop Sup17 because its assertion-time interval is out of scope.
12. Drop Sup6 because its assertion-time interval is out of scope.
13. Decoalesce Sup7 into Sup19 and Sup20.
14. Drop Sup7 because it is redundant.
15. Drop Sup19 because its assertion-time interval is out of scope.
16. Decoalesce Sup8 into Sup21 and Sup22.
17. Drop Sup8 because it is redundant.

18. Drop Sup21 because its assertion-time interval is out of scope.
19. Drop Sup9 because its assertion-time interval is out of scope.
20. Decoalesce Sup10 into Sup23 and Sup24.
21. Drop Sup10 because it is redundant.
22. Drop Sup23 because its assertion-time interval is out of scope.
23. Decoalesce Sup11 into Sup25 and Sup26.
24. Drop Sup11 because it is redundant.
25. Drop Sup25 because its assertion-time interval is out of scope.
26. Decoalesce Sup12 into Sup27 and Sup28.
27. Drop Sup12 because it is redundant.
28. Drop Sup27 because its assertion-time interval is out of scope.

Figure 13.15 shows the result of dropping all data outside the query's assertion-time interval. And with the struck-through rows dropped out, the results are shown in Figure 13.16.

STEP 2: DECOALESCE AND RESTRICT ON STATE TIME

This step filters out all rows based on the temporal predicate expressed in the IN STATE INTERVAL clause. The result is shown in Figure 13.17.

The process is the same as the one we have used before. Starting with either assertion time or state time, the first step is to decoalesce rows which lie partially inside and partially outside a query's temporal area, replacing them with rows which lie entirely outside or entirely inside the query's temporal area. Next, the rows which were decoalesced, and the decoalesced rows which lie outside the query's temporal area, are dropped. This same process is then applied to the other temporal dimension.

The second step is to temporally align rows so that rows which are to be joined, based on a temporal foreign key to RefId match, are aligned on temporal boundaries. To achieve temporal alignment, some rows may need to be further decoalesced.

Finally, the join of rows with a temporal foreign key to RefId match, and with [Equal] assertion time and state time extents, is carried out.

It is interesting to note that the point of all these decoalesce transformations is to achieve a temporal state that conventional tables always and automatically have. Rows in conventional tables, every time they are accessed, have assertion-time and state-time values of [Now(!)-9999]. Also, queries against conventional tables are queries whose bitemporal scope is [Now(!)-Now(!)].

Therefore, any joins between any two conventional tables are joins on rows which are already bitemporally aligned. By a trivial decoalescence which takes their time periods from [Now()-9999] to [Now(!)-Now(!)], we can obtain, for each row, a decoalesced row which lies entirely within the temporal scope of the query.[3] At that point, a join operation can proceed by matching foreign key values to primary key values. With temporal tables, once temporal alignment is achieved, a join operation can proceed by matching temporal foreign key values to referent identifiers.

Removing the struck-through rows, the result of Step 2 is shown in Figure 13.18.

---

[3]This is trivial in the sense that there are no transformations to carry out to achieve the temporal alignment. There are no transformations because, in conventional tables, both assertion-time and state-time periods are implicit, and are not persisted by any data in the tables.

STEP 3: DROP ASSERTION-TIME PERIOD COLUMNS

In Figure 13.18, all rows that remain in the query's working storage have the identical assertion time. This means that we can remove the assertion-time periods from the rows, since they will have no further impact on completing the processing of the query. What remains is assertion time as a fact that characterizes the query results as a whole, and so I will represent it as a one-line statement about the query result set, as shown in Figure 13.19.

```
         S-Cat-B
         abtm   aetm   sbtm   setm   sc-id  sc-abbr  sc-desc
Cat1  Jan14 May15  Jan14 9999   SC1    SCA     tier 1
Cat2  May15 9999   Jan14 Jan15  SC1    SCA     tier 1
Cat3  May15 9999   Jan15 9999   SC1    SCA     tier 2
Cat4  May15 Mar17  Jan14 Jan15  SC1    SCA     tier 1
Cat5  Mar17 9999   Jan14 Jan15  SC1    SCA     tier 1
Cat6  May15 Mar17  Jan15 9999   SC1    SCA     tier 2
Cat7  Mar17 9999   Jan15 9999   SC1    SCA     tier 2


         Supplier-B
          abtm   aetm   sbtm   setm   s-id  s-nm      s-scfk  s-type
Sup1   Feb14 Aug14  Feb14 Dec15  S1    Acme      SC1     T4
Sup2   Aug14 9999   Feb14 Oct14  S1    Acme      SC1     T4
Sup3   Aug14 Feb15  Oct14 Dec15  S1    Acme      SC1     T3
Sup4   Feb15 9999   Oct14 Jun15  S1    Acme      SC1     T3
Sup5   Feb15 9999   Jun15 Dec15  S1    Acme      SC1     T5
Sup6   Apr14 Nov14  Apr14 Dec14  S2    Superior  SC1     T4
Sup7   Nov14 9999   Apr14 Nov14  S2    Superior  SC1     T4
Sup8   Nov14 9999   Nov14 Dec14  S2    Superior  SC1     T2
Sup9   Jun15 Dec15  Jun15 Feb16  S2    Superior  SC2     T2
Sup10  Dec15 9999   Jun15 Dec15  S2    Superior  SC1     T3
Sup11  Dec15 9999   Dec15 Feb16  S2    Superior  SC1     T4
Sup12  Jun14 9999   Jun14 9999   S3    Ace       SC1     T5
Sup13  Aug14 Mar17  Feb14 Oct14  S1    Acme      SC1     T4
Sup14  Mar17 9999   Feb14 Oct14  S1    Acme      SC1     T4
Sup15  Feb15 Mar17  Oct14 Jun15  S1    Acme      SC1     T3
Sup16  Mar17 9999   Oct14 Jun15  S1    Acme      SC1     T3
Sup17  Feb15 Mar17  Jun15 Dec15  S1    Acme      SC1     T5
Sup18  Mar17 9999   Jun15 Dec15  S1    Acme      SC1     T5
Sup19  Nov14 Mar17  Apr14 Nov14  S2    Superior  SC1     T4
Sup20  Mar17 9999   Apr14 Nov14  S2    Superior  SC1     T4
Sup21  Nov14 Mar17  Nov14 Dec14  S2    Superior  SC1     T2
Sup22  Mar17 9999   Nov14 Dec14  S2    Superior  SC1     T2
Sup23  Dec15 Mar17  Jun15 Dec15  S2    Superior  SC1     T3
Sup24  Mar17 9999   Jun15 Dec15  S2    Superior  SC1     T3
Sup25  Dec15 Mar17  Dec15 Feb16  S2    Superior  SC1     T4
Sup26  Mar17 9999   Dec15 Feb16  S2    Superior  SC1     T4
Sup27  Jun14 Mar17  Jun14 9999   S3    Ace       SC1     T5
Sup28  Mar17 9999   Jun14 9999   S3    Ace       SC1     T5
```

FIGURE 13.15

A Complex Temporal Range Join Query: Intermediate Results - 1.

S-Cat-B

	abtm	aetm	sbtm	setm	sc-id	sc-abbr	sc-desc
Cat5	Mar17	9999	Jan14	Jan15	SC1	SCA	tier 1
Cat7	Mar17	9999	Jan15	9999	SC1	SCA	tier 2

Supplier-B

	abtm	aetm	sbtm	setm	s-id	s-nm	s-scfk	s-type
Sup14	Mar17	9999	Feb14	Oct14	S1	Acme	SC1	T4
Sup16	Mar17	9999	Oct14	Jun15	S1	Acme	SC1	T3
Sup18	Mar17	9999	Jun15	Dec15	S1	Acme	SC1	T5
Sup22	Mar17	9999	Nov14	Dec14	S2	Superior	SC1	T2
Sup24	Mar17	9999	Jun15	Dec15	S2	Superior	SC1	T3
Sup26	Mar17	9999	Dec15	Feb16	S2	Superior	SC1	T4
Sup28	Mar17	9999	Jun14	9999	S3	Ace	SC1	T5

FIGURE 13.16

A Complex Temporal Range Join Query: Intermediate Results - 2.

S-Cat-B

	abtm	aetm	sbtm	setm	sc-id	sc-abbr	sc-desc
~~Cat5~~	~~Mar17~~	~~9999~~	~~Jan14~~	~~Jan15~~	~~SC1~~	~~SCA~~	~~tier 1~~
~~Cat7~~	~~Mar17~~	~~9999~~	~~Jan15~~	~~9999~~	~~SC1~~	~~SCA~~	~~tier 2~~
~~Cat8~~	~~Mar17~~	~~9999~~	~~Jan14~~	~~Apr14~~	~~SC1~~	~~SCA~~	~~tier 1~~
Cat9	Mar17	9999	Apr14	Jan15	SC1	SCA	tier 1
Cat10	Mar17	9999	Jan15	Jan17	SC1	SCA	tier 2
~~Cat11~~	~~Mar17~~	~~9999~~	~~Jan17~~	~~9999~~	~~SC1~~	~~SCA~~	~~tier 2~~

Supplier-B

	abtm	aetm	sbtm	setm	s-id	s-nm	s-scfk	s-type
~~Sup14~~	~~Mar17~~	~~9999~~	~~Feb14~~	~~Oct14~~	~~S1~~	~~Acme~~	~~SC1~~	~~T4~~
Sup16	Mar17	9999	Oct14	Jun15	S1	Acme	SC1	T3
Sup18	Mar17	9999	Jun15	Dec15	S1	Acme	SC1	T5
Sup22	Mar17	9999	Nov14	Dec14	S2	Superior	SC1	T2
Sup24	Mar17	9999	Jun15	Dec15	S2	Superior	SC1	T3
Sup26	Mar17	9999	Dec15	Feb16	S2	Superior	SC1	T4
~~Sup28~~	~~Mar17~~	~~9999~~	~~Jun14~~	~~9999~~	~~S3~~	~~Ace~~	~~SC1~~	~~T5~~
~~Sup29~~	~~Mar17~~	~~9999~~	~~Feb14~~	~~Apr14~~	~~S1~~	~~Acme~~	~~SC1~~	~~T4~~
Sup30	Mar17	9999	Apr14	Oct14	S1	Acme	SC1	T4
Sup31	Mar17	9999	Jun14	Jan17	S3	Ace	SC1	T5
~~Sup32~~	~~Mar17~~	~~9999~~	~~Jan17~~	~~9999~~	~~S3~~	~~Ace~~	~~SC1~~	~~T5~~

FIGURE 13.17

A Complex Temporal Range Join Query: Intermediate Results - 3.

```
        S-Cat-B
        abtm   aetm   sbtm   setm   sc-id  sc-abbr  sc-desc
Cat9    Mar17  9999   Apr14  Jan15  SC1    SCA      tier 1
Cat10   Mar17  9999   Jan15  Jan17  SC1    SCA      tier 2


        Supplier-B
        abtm   aetm   sbtm   setm   s-id   s-nm      s-scfk  s-type
Sup16   Mar17  9999   Oct14  Jun15  S1     Acme      SC1     T3
Sup18   Mar17  9999   Jun15  Dec15  S1     Acme      SC1     T5
Sup22   Mar17  9999   Nov14  Dec14  S2     Superior  SC1     T2
Sup24   Mar17  9999   Jun15  Dec15  S2     Superior  SC1     T3
Sup26   Mar17  9999   Dec15  Feb16  S2     Superior  SC1     T4
Sup30   Mar17  9999   Apr14  Oct14  S1     Acme      SC1     T4
Sup31   Mar17  9999   Jun14  Jan17  S3     Ace       SC1     T5
```

FIGURE 13.18

A Complex Temporal Range Join Query: Intermediate Results - 4.

```
            IN ASSERTION INTERVAL: March 2017-9999
        S-Cat-B
        sbtm   setm   sc-id  sc-abbr  sc-desc
Cat9    Apr14  Jan15  SC1    SCA      tier 1
Cat10   Jan15  Jan17  SC1    SCA      tier 2


        Supplier-B
        sbtm   setm   s-id   s-nm      s-scfk  s-type
Sup16   Oct14  Jun15  S1     Acme      SC1     T3
Sup18   Jun15  Dec15  S1     Acme      SC1     T5
Sup22   Nov14  Dec14  S2     Superior  SC1     T2
Sup24   Jun15  Dec15  S2     Superior  SC1     T3
Sup26   Dec15  Feb16  S2     Superior  SC1     T4
Sup30   Apr14  Oct14  S1     Acme      SC1     T4
Sup31   Jun14  Jan17  S3     Ace       SC1     T5
```

FIGURE 13.19

A Complex Temporal Range Join Query: Intermediate Results - 5.

STEP 4: ALIGN ON STATE-TIME BOUNDARIES

In this step, rows are decoalesced so that all state-time intervals for all suppliers can be equi-joined to state-time intervals for the supplier categories designated by their temporal foreign keys. I will describe this process for the Sup16 row in the Supplier-B table in detail, and then describe the process for the remaining Supplier-B rows in an abbreviated form.

First, note that Sup16 spans two supplier category rows which cannot be coalesced. So Sup16 must itself be decoalesced on the [Meet] point of those two supplier category rows. This results in Sup32 and Sup33, shown in Figure 13.20.

The temporal foreign key in these supplier rows designates supplier category SCA. But even after decoalescing Sup16 into Sup32 and Sup33, there are no SCA rows in Supplier-Category-B to which either Sup32 or Sup33 can be equi-joined.

```
               IN ASSERTION INTERVAL: March 2015 - 9999
               S-Cat-B
               sbtm  setm   sc-id sc-abbr sc-desc
         Cat9  Apr14 Jan15  SC1    SCA     tier 1
         Cat10 Jan15 Jan17  SC1    SCA     tier 2
         Cat11 Apr14 Oct14  SC1    SCA     tier 1
         Cat12 Oct14 Jan15  SC1    SCA     tier 1
         Cat13 Jan15 Jun15  SC1    SCA     tier 2
         Cat14 Jun15 Jan17  SC1    SCA     tier 2
         Cat15 Jun15 Dec15  SC1    SCA     tier 2
         Cat16 Dec15 Jan17  SC1    SCA     tier 2
         Cat17 Oct14 Nov14  SC1    SCA     tier 1
         Cat18 Nov14 Dec14  SC1    SCA     tier 1
         Cat19 Dec14 Jan17  SC1    SCA     tier 1
         Cat20 Dec15 Feb16  SC1    SCA     tier 2
         Cat21 Feb16 Jan17  SC1    SCA     tier 2
         Cat22 Apr14 Jun14  SC1    SCA     tier 1
         Cat23 Jun14 Jan15  SC1    SCA     tier 1


               Supplier-B
               sbtm  setm   s-id s-nm      s-scfk s-type
         Sup16 Oct14 Jun15  S1   Acme      SC1    T3
         Sup18 Jun15 Dec15  S1   Acme      SC1    T5
         Sup22 Nov14 Dec14  S2   Superior  SC1    T2
         Sup24 Jun15 Dec15  S2   Superior  SC1    T3
         Sup26 Dec15 Feb16  S2   Superior  SC1    T4
         Sup30 Apr14 Oct14  S1   Acme      SC1    T4
         Sup31 Jun14 Jan17  S3   Ace       SC1    T5
         Sup32 Oct14 Jan15  S1   Acme      SC1    T3
         Sup33 Jan15 Jun15  S1   Acme      SC1    T3
         Sup34 Jun14 Jan15  S3   Ace       SC1    T5
         Sup35 Jan15 Jan17  S3   Ace       SC1    T5
```

FIGURE 13.20

A Complex Temporal Range Join Query: Intermediate Results - 6.

So the next step is to obtain an SCA row that [Starts] either Sup32 or Sup33. This is done by decoalescing Cat9 into Cat11 and Cat12. Cat12 [Starts] Sup32; and in fact, it [Equals] Sup32. So Sup32 can be equi-joined with Cat12.

This leaves Sup33 to equi-join to some SCA row. Cat10 already [Starts] Sup33, and so the objective is to truncate Cat10 so it also [Ends] Sup33. This is done by decoalescing Cat10 into Cat13 and Cat14. The resulting Cat13 [Equals] Sup33, and so they can be equi-joined.

I will describe the equi-join preparation for the remaining Supplier-B rows in an abbreviated form. When the equals sign is used between Cat and Cat, or between Sup and Sup, it indicates a decoalesce transformation. When it is used between Sup and Cat, it indicates that the temporal intervals are [Equal].

1. Sup18: Cat14 = Cat15, Cat16. Sup18 = Cat15.
2. Sup22: Cat12 = Cat17, Cat18, Cat19. Sup22 = Cat18.
3. Sup24 = Cat15.

4. Sup26: Cat16 = Cat20, Cat21. Sup26 = Cat20.
5. Sup30 = Cat11.
6. Sup31: Cat9 = Cat22, Cat23. Sup31 = Sup34, Sup35. Sup34 = Cat23. Sup35 = Cat10.

The result is shown in Figure 13.20.

In Figure 13.21, we go back and drop all rows in S-Cat-B whose state-time interval does not [Equal] the state-time interval of a row in Supplier-B, and also the two supplier rows which had to be decoalesced.

```
           IN ASSERTION INTERVAL: March 2015 - 9999
              S-Cat-B
              sbtm   setm   sc-id  sc-abbr  sc-desc
       Cat10  Jan15  Jan17  SC1      SCA     tier 2
       Cat11  Apr14  Oct14  SC1      SCA     tier 1
       Cat12  Oct14  Jan15  SC1      SCA     tier 1
       Cat13  Jan15  Jun15  SC1      SCA     tier 2
       Cat15  Jun15  Dec15  SC1      SCA     tier 2
       Cat18  Nov14  Dec14  SC1      SCA     tier 1
       Cat20  Dec15  Feb16  SC1      SCA     tier 2
       Cat23  Jun14  Jan15  SC1      SCA     tier 1


              Supplier-B
              sbtm   setm   s-id  s-nm      s-scfk  s-type
       Sup18  Jun15  Dec15  S1    Acme       SC1     T5
       Sup22  Nov14  Dec14  S2    Superior   SC1     T2
       Sup24  Jun15  Dec15  S2    Superior   SC1     T3
       Sup26  Dec15  Feb16  S2    Superior   SC1     T4
       Sup30  Apr14  Oct14  S1    Acme       SC1     T4
       Sup32  Oct14  Jan15  S1    Acme       SC1     T3
       Sup33  Jan15  Jun15  S1    Acme       SC1     T3
       Sup34  Jun14  Jan15  S3    Ace        SC1     T5
       Sup35  Jan15  Jan17  S3    Ace        SC1     T5
```

FIGURE 13.21

A Complex Temporal Range Join Query: Intermediate Results - 7.

STEP 5: JOIN ON REFID AND STATE-TIME

This step adds row temporal scope equality predicates to the original WHERE clause. It also drops the IN ASSERTION INTERVAL clause and the nontemporal predicate from the query. The result is shown in Figure 13.22.

Note that only one of the delimiting clock ticks is used in the internally revised query. This is possible because the decoalesce algorithm guarantees that this will be sufficient for the match.

This step completes the join. It produces the result set shown in Figure 13.23. Sorted on *s-id* and time period, we get the result set shown in Figure 13.24.

Nothing less will do. Nothing more is needed. No fewer rows in the result set can tell the complete tale.

Clearly, joins involving three or more tables can be handled with this same algorithm.

```
SELECT
S.sbtm, S.setm, S.s-id, S.s-nm, S.s-type,
C.sc-abbr, C.sc-desc
FROM Supplier-B AS S, S-Cat-B AS C
WHERE S.s-scfk = C.sc-id
AND S.sbtm = C.sbtm
```

FIGURE 13.22

The Internal Form of the Complex Temporal Range Join Query.

```
          IN ASSERTION INTERVAL: March 2017 - 9999
          sbtm  setm  s-id  s-nm      s-type  sc-abbr  sc-desc
   Sup18  Jun15 Dec15 S1    Acme      T5      SCA      tier 2
   Sup22  Nov14 Dec14 S2    Superior  T2      SCA      tier 1
   Sup24  Jun15 Dec15 S2    Superior  T3      SCA      tier 2
   Sup26  Dec15 Feb16 S2    Superior  T4      SCA      tier 2
   Sup30  Apr14 Oct14 S1    Acme      T4      SCA      tier 1
   Sup32  Oct14 Jan15 S1    Acme      T3      SCA      tier 1
   Sup33  Jan15 Jun15 S1    Acme      T3      SCA      tier 2
   Sup34  Jun14 Jan15 S3    Ace       T5      SCA      tier 1
   Sup35  Jan15 Jan17 S3    Ace       T5      SCA      tier 2
```

FIGURE 13.23

A Complex Temporal Range Join Query: Intermediate Results - 8.

```
          IN ASSERTION INTERVAL: March 2017 - 9999
          sbtm  setm  s-id  s-nm      s-type  sc-abbr  sc-desc
          Apr14 Oct14 S1    Acme      T4      SCA      tier 1
          Oct14 Jan15 S1    Acme      T3      SCA      tier 1
          Jan15 Jun15 S1    Acme      T3      SCA      tier 2
          Jun15 Dec15 S1    Acme      T5      SCA      tier 2

          Nov14 Dec14 S2    Superior  T2      SCA      tier 1
          Jun15 Dec15 S2    Superior  T3      SCA      tier 2
          Dec15 Feb16 S2    Superior  T4      SCA      tier 2

          Jun14 Jan15 S3    Ace       T5      SCA      tier 1
          Jan15 Jan17 S3    Ace       T5      SCA      tier 2
```

FIGURE 13.24

A Complex Temporal Range Join Query: Final Results.

WHY TEMPORAL RANGE MULTI-TABLE QUERIES ARE COMPLEX

It is important to realize *why* range queries with joins are so much more complex than point-in-time queries with joins. The reason is that for a given RefId, a point in time will be found in at most one row with that RefId. Semantically, it is because, at any given point in time, a referent can be in at most one state.

So point-in-time joins will always be one row to one row, regardless of what Allen relationship exists between the two rows, as long as it is one of the [Includes] relationships, that is, as long as the two rows have at least one clock tick in common. There is no need to decoalesce or sub-interval rows to create [Equal] time periods for the joined rows.

This indicates that it is the grouping of multiple atomic temporal units by *RefId* + *State* that creates the complexity for range query joins. So suppose that all stored data was stored as *RefId* + *State* + *ATU* (atomic temporal unit). For example, every stored unit of bitemporal data would be *RefId* + *State* + *Bitemporal Cell*, bitemporal cells being a pair of single clock ticks, one in assertion time and one in state time. If this were done, then temporal range queries with joins would have no preparatory work to do. The join would be on temporal foreign key to RefId, and on equal bitemporal cells.

One further level of decomposition is also possible. It is the decomposition of a state into its component column values. This is attribute-level temporal data management. Statement schemas consisting of multiple column values would still be needed, so we can retrieve a *RefId* + *Temporal Interval* for a set of column values without having to specify each one individually. But there would not be one privileged statement schema and then all the others, the privileged schema being the schema for the physical base table. This is because there would be no physical base table. There would just be a collection of *RefId* + *Column Value* + *Bitemporal Cell* triples.

Each RefId designates an instance of a type of referent. Each column value designates an instance of a type of property or relationship. Consequently, each *RefId* + *Column Value* pair is a single-predicate statement which says that the specified referent has the specified property or relationship. In a normalized database, each row in a table is the conjunction of all RefId + Column Value pairs for the same RefId. So the table is a schema representing that conjunction. The addition of bitemporal cells to these pairs is a third dimension to their representation, allowing multiple RefId + Column Value pairs to exist, so long as they have different bitemporal cells. These different bitemporal cells distinguish different assertions of different states of the referent object or event.

I will return to this topic in Chapter 19.

GLOSSARY LIST

assertion-time interval	episode	temporal indexical
clock tick	state	temporal scope
coalesce	statement schema	withdraw
decoalesce	statement	

FUTURE ASSERTION TIME

The standard theory of bitemporal data is the set of concepts articulated by computer scientists, standardized in the ISO 9075:2011 temporal extensions to the SQL standard and in the TSQL2 standard, and implemented in several major DBMSs. In the standard theory, the assertion-time period of a row of data begins when the row is inserted into its target table, and ends when the row is deleted from that table. Of course, to preserve a history of the modifications made to that table, those deletions are logical deletions, not physical ones.

It is because the begin and end time of this time period is determined by this transactional activity that the standard theory's term "transaction time" seems so appropriate. But because the semantics implemented by means of these transactions are the semantics of asserting statements and withdrawing those assertions, I believe the term "assertion time" is more appropriate.

But as long as transactions against the same bitemporal database states result in the same consequent bitemporal database states, however, this difference is only terminological. And so far, that has been the case. But in this chapter, I will describe transactions which are undefined in the standard theory, in both SQL standards, and in all bitemporally-enabled commercial DBMSs. These are transactions for which the database user can specify assertion time and, in particular, future assertion time.

In the first section, I will discuss the semantics of future assertion time, and explain why it has been overlooked by the computer science community. In the second section, I will show how transactions that specify future assertion time, and that result in rows of data that exist in future assertion time, can be added to the standard theory without introducing any inconsistencies into that theory, and without altering the results of the temporal transactions it already supports. I will show, in other words, that future assertion time is a proper superset of the semantics of the standard theory, and that its implementation is a proper superset of the implementation of that standard theory. This will demonstrate that future assertion time is temporally upwards compatible with the standard theory of bitemporal data.

FUTURE ASSERTION TIME: SEMANTICS

In the standard theory, when rows of data are added to a bitemporal table, they are assigned an assertion time period of [Now(!)-9999]. Once a row is present in a bitemporal table, there is only one change that can take place to its assertion-time period. That change results from logically deleting the row, and that action is carried out by closing the row's assertion-time period. The 9999 end point in assertion time of the row is changed to the Now(!) of the transaction that logically deletes that row.[1] It follows that no row in a bitemporal table can ever have either a closed current assertion-time period or a future assertion-time period — a *closed current assertion-time period* being one which began in the past and ends in the future, i.e. on a non-9999 future point in time, and a *future assertion-time period* being one which begins in the future.

Since it is part of the standard theory that no assertion begin time can ever be altered, it follows that a standard theory bitemporal table can never contain a row with an assertion-time period that begins in the future. This commits the standard theory of bitemporal data to what I call the *Six-Fold Way*.

THE SIX-FOLD WAY

As shown in Figure 14.1, state-time periods indicate when the referent of a row was, is or will be in the state described by the row. A state-time period on a row, then, indicates whether the row tells us what something used to be like, or what it is currently like, or what it will be like sometime in the future. These three possibilities are represented as the three rows in Figure 14.1.

	what we used to assert	**what we currently assert**
what things used to be like	(1) what we used to assert things used to be like.	(4) what we currently assert things used to be like.
what things are like now	(2) what we used to assert things are like now.	(5) what we currently assert things are like now.
what things will be like	(3) what we used to assert things will be like.	(6) what we currently assert things will be like.

FIGURE 14.1

The Six-Fold Way.

More precisely, the first row in Figure 14.1 represents the category of all rows with past state-time periods, i.e. state-time periods that end in the past. These are statements about the past. The second row represents the category of all rows with current state-time periods, i.e. state-time periods that include the current moment in time. These are statements about the present. The third row represents the category of all rows with future state-time periods, i.e. with state-time periods that begin in the future. These are statements about the future.

All rows in bitemporal tables, in the standard theory, start out life with an *open assertion-time period*. But as we have already seen, a temporal Update and a temporal Delete transaction each result in one or more rows having their open assertion-time periods closed as of the Now(!) of that

---

[1]As we have already seen, a temporal Update transaction against a single row logical deletes that row, inserts a state-time decoalesced pair or triplet of rows, and then physically updates the one decoalesced row that falls within the transaction's scope. And a temporal Delete transaction against a single row logically deletes that row, inserts a state-time decoalesced pair or triplet of rows, and then ends the assertion-time period of the one row that is inside the transaction's scope.

Update or Delete transaction. And so, as soon as the first update or delete takes place, a bitemporal table will contain both past assertions and current assertions.

These are the values that assertion-time periods can take on, and how those values are set and altered. But this doesn't explain *why* things work this way. It doesn't explain what information is being managed by means of these constraints on data and on changes to that data. That is a matter of semantics.

The assertion-time period on a row is closed in order to end the assertion made by the row. Just as physically deleting a row from a conventional table is the way that the assertion made by that row is withdrawn from the set of current assertions in that table (those being the *only* assertions in a conventional table), logically deleting a row from a bitemporal table, by closing its assertion-time period, is the way that the assertion made by that row is withdrawn from the set of current assertions in that table. The only difference is that, in the latter case, a record of that once-asserted statement remains in the table, available to queries whose temporal scope includes any part of that past time.

The two columns in Figure 14.1 represent, respectively, rows in past assertion time and rows in current assertion time. I will call rows in past assertion time *past assertions*, and rows in current assertion time *current assertions*. Past assertions, in the standard theory, are rows with closed assertion-time periods. No row will have a closed assertion-time period that is not a past assertion. Current assertions are those with open assertion-time periods. No row will have an open assertion-time period that is not a current assertion.

Three kinds of state time and two kinds of assertion time give us six combinations, the ones shown in Figure 14.1.

CHALLENGING THE SIX-FOLD WAY

I have said that the standard theory always assigns a Henceforth-based value to the assertion-time period of every row added to a bitemporal table. In other words, the standard theory requires that all rows, when added to a table, are added as current assertions. But why is this? What is the semantics which this constraint implements? What is the semantics that justifies a user interface that makes it impossible for the author of a transaction to specify an assertion-time period for the data resulting from that transaction?

Here is a wrong answer. The assertion time of any row, *by definition*, starts when a transaction adds the row to its database, and ends when the row is logically deleted. That's just what assertion time *is*.

This attraction of this wrong answer is clearer if we use the standard theory's terminology instead of mine. Thus rephrased: the transaction time of any row, *by definition*, starts when a transaction adds the row to its database, and ends when a subsequent transaction deletes that row from the database. That's just what transaction time *is*.

In other words, this wrong answer is that every statement is added to a database as a current assertion. So to give the author of a transaction the ability to specify an assertion-time period is both unnecessary and inadvisable. It's unnecessary because the system can assign the correct value for that time period. It is inadvisable because the author of a transaction might assign an incorrect value.

What's wrong with this response is that it describes *how* things work, but doesn't explain *why* things work that way. Data structures are a syntax for their instances, and software implements a set of transformations on those instances. Those instances are valuable because they represent true statements about the things whose states they describe. What's valuable is what the data *means*. The implementation is a means to that end, or it is nothing of value at all.

Past Assertion Time

So a justification for letting the system assign (and update) assertion time, and preventing the author of a transaction from doing so, must be given in terms of the semantics supported by that functionality. In terms of semantics, then, we can begin by understanding why no row can be added to a bitemporal table in *past* assertion time.

The reason is that if rows could be added in past assertion time, i.e. with assertion-time periods that began in the past, then the result would be a row that the database then claimed began to be asserted *before* it was physically present to be asserted. For example, suppose that it is now January 2016, and that there is no row for supplier S8 anywhere in the Supplier-B table. If we then enter the row:

[Nov15|9999|Jul16|Jan17|S8|Parts Unlimited|*SC3*|T4]

into the Supplier-B table, the database would then indicate that during the last two months of 2015, it contained the assertion that, for the second half of 2016, there would be a supplier with name "Parts Unlimited", in category SC3, and with supplier type T4. But that's untrue, and so the system must prevent such falsehoods from being entered. We know that no query about Parts Unlimited, issued anytime during those two months, would have turned up that assertion because, at no time during those two months was that row physically present to be asserted.

So the standard theory is certainly correct to prevent rows from being added to a database with assertion-time periods that begin in the past.

Future Assertion Time

The standard theory of bitemporal data also includes the constraint that rows cannot be added to a table with assertion-time periods that begin in the future. And once again, there is an invalid justification which may come to mind, that the assertion time of a row, by definition, begins when the transaction that creates the row takes place. That, according to this justification, is just what assertion time *is*. Once again, the argument seems more persuasive if we use the standard theory's terminology: the transaction time of a row, by definition, begins when the transaction that creates the row takes place. That is just what transaction time *is*.

There is a closely-related invalid argument, one also based on terminology. It points out that a transaction is a physical event. It happens when it happens, not before it happens and not after it happens. So the transaction begin time of any row *must* be the point in time when the transaction takes place.

But a choice of terminology is not an argument. Call transaction time something else and the supposed argument reduces to terminological smoke and mirrors.

Of course a transaction, as a physical event, takes place when it takes place, and at no other time. And issued against conventional tables, those transactions do have immediate semantic impact. In a *conventional table*, the presence of a row *is* the assertion that the statement made by that row is true, and so that assertion begins the moment the row appears in the table. And the deletion of a row from a conventional table *is* the withdrawal of that assertion, and so that assertion ceases to be made the moment the row disappears from the table. Issued against tables which have no assertion-time period, physical assertion (transaction) time and semantic assertion (transaction) time are co-extensive.

But my proposed extension to the standard theory does not apply to conventional tables. It applies only to tables which have explicit assertion-time periods. My contention is that if a row in past assertion time is one that was asserted during that past time, and a row in current assertion time is one that is currently asserted, then a row in future assertion time is one that will be asserted when that future time comes to pass. If the first two are allowed in a bitemporal table, then why not the third as well?

We usually think of rows that once made statements but no longer do as rows that would be found in some kind of logfile. What about rows that don't yet make statements but eventually will (if nothing happens to them in the meantime)? Where would rows like that be found?

Well, we don't have far to look. Any Insert transaction written but not yet applied to its target table is a statement that is not yet asserted, because the presence of a row in a production table is required for there to be an assertion. The statements that a company asserts as being true descriptions of their referents are found in that company's production tables. An assertion doesn't exist the moment a business user writes down a transaction. An assertion doesn't exist until a statement ends up as a row in a table understood by everyone to be a table of true statements that the company "stands behind", "operates on the basis of", etc. − and these are the tables we commonly call "production tables" in a database.

A statement which is not yet an assertion might be a row in a set of tables in a staging area or a sandbox area. It might be a transaction held in a queue by an asynchronous transaction processer. Or it might be a transaction contained in a batch of transactions that will be applied later, when the database is next taken off-line.[2] The use of batch files, run when the database is off-line, makes it possible to use single-threaded no-locking processes which can run much faster than update processes which must take into account other possibly concurrently executing update processes, and must enforce a serial order on those concurrent processes that are attempting to alter the same data.

Clearly, we can create a batch of transactions each of which specifies a past, present or future state-time period. Suppose that, at a specified time t_1, a database is scheduled to be taken off-line, and a batch of transactions applied to it. After the batch file is processed, the database is scheduled to be brought back on-line.

Now suppose that there are too many transactions to apply in one off-line cycle, but the business requirement is nonetheless that those transactions must not appear in the database in stages. Instead, they must appear in the database all at once on, say, t_n.

Suppose five nightly batch processing runs will be required to load all the data − a situation that is not untypical when mergers and acquisitions are being implemented. So on each of the five nights leading up to t_n, one batch of transactions is run. All the rows created by these transactions are given an assertion-time period which begins on t_n. During the five days prior to t_n, the rows resulting from those transactions have future assertion-time periods, ones that will not begin until t_n. Finally t_n becomes the current moment in time. At that moment, all of the rows whose assertion-time periods begin on t_n will become current assertions.

There is no implementation reason why we can't do this. And doing it clearly does not violate the semantics of that data, which are the same whether those transactions are held apart in a batch

---

[2]To be precise, only queued Insert transactions are statements in waiting. Queued Delete transactions are withdrawals in waiting. Queued Update transactions are both.

file, or immediately applied to their target tables. One issue, however, which I will discuss later in this chapter, should be mentioned here. It is the issue of serialization and its implementation mechanism, locking.

Each of the batches of transactions described above were applied while the database was locked. It was locked by being taken off-line. However, the database was not locked between those nightly off-line periods of time. In those interims while the database was not locked, any of the target rows for those transactions might have changed. This means that the results of those transactions that were applied on any of the last four nights might be different from the results that would have been produced if they had all been applied on that first night.

The Incompleteness of the Six-Fold Way

A row of data is the inscription of a statement. During its assertion-time period, it is the assertion of that statement. After its assertion-time period, it is *no longer* the assertion of that statement. So before its assertion-time period, it is *not yet* the assertion of that statement.

After its assertion-time period, a row of data is the record of an assertion of a statement, telling us when that statement had been asserted. So before its assertion-time period, a row of data is the record of an anticipated assertion of that statement, telling us when, if nothing happens to the row in the meantime, that statement will be asserted. Before its assertion-time period begins, a row of data is a prediction that, when the time comes, the statement made by that row will indeed be true and asserted to be true.

So the Six-Fold Way is incomplete. It is incomplete because it cannot express anticipated assertions. It does not include future assertion time.

I have described a consistent semantics for assertion time which, as it applies to the past and present, is identical to the semantics which is implemented in the standard theory for what that theory calls transaction time. This consistent semantics extends to include future assertion time which, as we have just seen, can belong to rows which describe the past, present, or future states of things.

This extension is what I call the Nine-Fold Way.

THE NINE-FOLD WAY

With three possibilities for state-time periods, and three possibilities for assertion-time periods, we have nine combinations of possibilities. These are illustrated in Figure 14.2.

	what we used to assert	what we currently assert	what we will assert
what things used to be like	(1) what we used to assert things used to be like.	(4) what we currently assert things used to be like.	(7) what we will assert things used to be like.
what things are like now	(2) what we used to assert things are like now.	(5) what we currently assert things are like now.	(8) what we will assert things are like now.
what things will be like	(3) what we used to assert things will be like.	(6) what we currently assert things will be like.	(9) what we will assert things will be like.

FIGURE 14.2

The Nine-Fold Way.

It is important to clearly understand the semantic difference between future state time and future assertion time, between statements about the future and future assertions of statements. A row of data, as an inscription, is a physical object. A row of data, as a statement, is a disambiguated existentially-quantified declarative sentence whose normal use is to assert that something exists and to describe the state of that thing. A row of data with a state-time period is a temporally explicit existentially-quantified statement whose normal use is to assert that something existed, exists and/ or will exist during that period of time, and to describe the state that thing was/is/will be in during that period of time. This *normal use* of a row of data is to assert that something was, is or will be the case. The assertion-time period of a row of data tells us when that row was, is or will be used in that normal way.

Future Assertion Time and Future State Time

To clarify the difference between future assertion time and future state time, consider the following example. In this example, it is Now() November 2015. The CEO of the Acme company, which is acquiring the Superior company, tells Superior's CEO: "Starting on January 2016, your entire Parts table will be merged into our Parts table. This includes your scheduled mid-year price increases."

Let us suppose that the Superior Company's Parts table is too large to be completely loaded in a single batch window. We can't, in that case, wait until the night before January 2016 to load Superior's Parts data. Acme's CEO, however, wants none of Superior's Parts data to be visible until January 2016, and so we can't load any of that data prior to that time, even data about price increases that won't take effect for six months. Acme's CEO wants none of Superior's Parts data to become visible before January 2016, and all of it to become visible on January 2016. So it's no good for the CIO to suggest that they load as much of that data as they can the night before January 2016, and then load the rest of it as soon as possible after that.[3]

Future state time is no solution to this problem. What is needed is future assertion time.

To simplify the example, I will concentrate on one row in Superior's Parts data. Let that row have part id P25, part number S43, part name "Leaf Springs", and a unit price of $135.00, and let that row be for part S43 in the second half of 2016.

If Acme's Parts table were a state-time table, that row would look like this:

```
[Jul16|Jan17|P25|S43|Leaf Springs|$135.00]
```

But since Acme's Parts table is a bitemporal table, there is also an assertion-time period on that row. Given the standard theory of bitemporal data, the insert transaction that adds this row to the table must give the assertion-time period a Henceforth value. In that case, if the row were loaded on November 2015, the row would look like this:

```
[Nov15|9999|Jul16|Jan17|P25|S43|Leaf Springs|$135.00]
```

Of course, as soon as the transaction is complete and the database is opened for business the next morning, this row will be a current assertion. Like any other row with a current assertion-time period, it will be eligible to be included in the result set of any normal query, i.e. any query that does not explicitly exclude currently asserted rows.

---

[3]The example reads better if we think of timestamps as delimiting these time periods, rather than my ersatz datatype of month plus year.

Note that this row has a future state-time period, but that this future state-time period doesn't do what Acme's CEO wants. Acme's CEO wants this row, and all the other Acme rows, to be invisible in the database, i.e. unavailable for querying or updating, until January 2016. But rows with future state-time periods are queryable and updatable rows just as much as rows with past or present state-time periods are.

But suppose that Superior's data could be added using a user-specified assertion-time period, in this case one with the value [Jan16-9999]. In that case, the row added to the Parts database (i.e. table) on November 2015, would be:

```
[Jan16|9999|Jul16|Jan17|P25|S43|Leaf Springs|$135.00]
```

Other rows added to the database on November 2015, ones not from the M&A of the Superior Company, would have the default assertion time of [Nov15-9999]. Since all standard queries are written against rows in current assertion time, these other rows will be immediately available for queries, while Superior's rows will be automatically excluded from those queries for two more months.

Once again, however, there is a plausible but invalid objection. It is that any time prior to January 2016, [Jan16-9999] is not a valid assertion time. A valid assertion time always begins when the transaction takes place — not before, and not after that time. And once again, the point seems more persuasive when rephrased: any time prior to January 2016, [Jan16-9999] is not a valid transaction time. A valid transaction time always begins when the transaction takes place — not before, and not after that time.

The objection is irrelevant, however, because it simply restates the implementation constraint which the standard theory associates with this kind of time period, and ignores the semantics behind that constraint. As we have seen, the semantics of a conventional table is that a row asserts that the statement it makes is true for as long as that row is physically present in its table. So to assert a statement, a row is physically added to the table. And to withdraw the assertion, that row is physically removed from the table.

Making and withdrawing assertions is the behavior that must be, and is, preserved as we move from conventional tables to the standard theory's bitemporal tables. In conventional tables, it must be, and is, possible to tell, at any time, what the current assertions made by that table are. They are the assertions made by every row present in the table. In bitemporal tables, it must also be, and is, possible to tell, at any time, what the current assertions made by that table are. They are the assertions of statements made by rows with current assertion-time periods. The standard theory permits, indeed requires, that rows which are logically deleted remain physically present in the table (or in an associated history table). But it marks them as rows which no longer are assertions by setting the assertion-time end point to the time when those rows were logically deleted.

Asserted Versioning's proposed extension to the standard theory permits rows which are *not yet* asserted to also exist in a bitemporal table. And it too preserves the semantics carried over from conventional tables because it is still possible to distinguish assertions from non-assertions. Past assertions are rows with assertion-time periods that have already ended. Future assertions are rows with assertion-time periods that have not yet begun. Current assertions are all the rest. Therefore, a row with a [Jan16-9999] assertion-time period, present in a bitemporal table prior to January 2016, is semantically valid because, in such a table, it is still possible to identify this row as one which is not an assertion. All we have to do now is make it operationally valid by describing a consistent implementation mechanism for future assertion time.

A past assertion-time period on a row tells us when the authors of that data were once willing to assert that the row made a true statement, whether that true statement was about the state time past, present or future. A future assertion-time period on a row tells us when the authors of that data will be willing to assert that the row makes a true statement, whether that true statement will be about the state time past, present or future.

What Acme's CEO demanded, expressed in these terms, is that none of Superior's data would be currently asserted statements in his database until January 2016, at which point in time all of Superior's data would be currently asserted statements. And he didn't want to be told that it was impossible to do what he wanted because there was too much data from Superior to load it all on the night before it was to become currently asserted.

With the current temporal SQL standards, and current bitemporally-enabled DBMSs, the CIO cannot satisfy the CEO's demands. But when future assertion time is included in the standards and in their implementations, the CIO will be able to satisfy those demands.

Future assertion time, then, is a consistent extension to the semantics of standard theory assertion time. The invalid objection mentioned above is simply that the implementation of standard theory assertion time does not handle future transaction-time periods — an objection which becomes an admission once "assertion" is substituted for "transaction".

FUTURE ASSERTION TIME: IMPLEMENTATION

It is Now() May 2015. The transaction shown in Figure 14.3 is submitted to the DBMS.

```
INSERT INTO Part-B
VALUES (P1, W45, wheel, $3.25)
```

FIGURE 14.3

A Bitemporal Insert.

If the Part-B table is empty at the time of the transaction, the result is as shown in Figure 14.4.

```
Part-B
```

abtm	aetm	sbtm	setm	ibtm	p-id	p-nbr	p-nm	p-upr
May15	9999	May15	9999	May15	P1	W45	wheel	$3.25

FIGURE 14.4

The Bitemporal Part Table - 1.

The column heading *ibtm* stands for "inscription begin time". It is the point in time at which the row is written to the database. In the standard theory, it would always have the same value as transaction begin time. In the Asserted Versioning theory, as we are about to see, it does not always have the same value as assertion begin time.

It is Now() November 2015. The following transaction is issued.

```
UPDATE IN Part-B
IN STATE INTERVAL (Jul17, 9999)
IN ASSERTION INTERVAL (Jan17, 9999)
SET p-upr = p-upr + $0.75
WHERE p-id = P1
```

FIGURE 14.5

A Future Assertion Update - 1.

The IN ASSERTION INTERVAL clause is used to specify an assertion-time period on a transaction. The result of this transaction is shown in Figure 14.6.

Part-B								
abtm	aetm	sbtm	setm	ibtm	p-id	p-nbr	p-nm	p-upr
May15	Jan17	May15	9999	May15	P1	W45	wheel	$3.25
Jan17	9999	May15	Jul17	Nov15	P1	W45	wheel	$3.25
Jan17	9999	Jul17	9999	Nov15	P1	W45	wheel	$4.00

FIGURE 14.6

The Bitemporal Part Table - 2.

A conventional table contains one current assertion for each row in the table. A table with an assertion-time period contains one current assertion for each row in the table that has a current assertion-time period. In the table in Figure 14.6, there is one current assertion after the transaction of Figure 14.5 completes. That is the assertion expressed by the first row. That row will remain a current assertion for fourteen months (from November 2015 up to January 2017), at which time it will become a past assertion, and the last two rows will become current assertions.

This should be, by now, a familiar pattern. The implementation of future assertion-time transactions is just as smooth an extension to the implementation of standard temporal transactions as the semantics of future assertion time is to the semantics of the standard theory.

THE TIME TRAVEL PARADOX

The well-known paradox of being able to travel back in time is that one could thereby alter one's own past. In one scenario, someone travels back in time, and murders his father before he himself was conceived, thereby making his own existence impossible. The paradox is that if he did that, he couldn't have done that because he wouldn't have existed to do it in the first place.

An analogous paradox is possible using future assertion time — unless we take steps to prevent it. So I'll first describe that analogous paradox in order to motivate the following discussion of assertion-time locking.

It is Now() December 2016, and we issue the transaction shown in Figure 14.7.

```
UPDATE IN Part-B
IN STATE INTERVAL (Jul17, 9999)
SET p-upr = p-upr * 1.05
WHERE p-id = P1
```

FIGURE 14.7

A Future Assertion Update — 2.

This is a standard theory temporal update, i.e. one which does not specify an assertion-time period. It uses the assertion begin time from the transaction to end the assertion-time period of the one row for P1 that is Now() current in assertion time. That row is the first row in Figure 14.6. It uses the same clock tick to begin the assertion-time period of the row or rows which it will add to the table.

Since assertion time is not specified on this transaction, the assertion begin time is December 2016. The update specifies a state time of [Jul17 — 9999], and so the original row is first decoalesced on July 2017. Finally, the price increase is applied to the decoalesced row whose state time matches that of the transaction.

This transaction is applied to the table of Figure 14.6, with the following results.

```
Part-B
abtm   aetm   sbtm   setm   ibtm   p-id  p-nbr  p-nm    p-upr
May15  Dec16  May15  9999   May15  P1    W45    wheel   $3.25
Dec16  Jan17  May15  Jul17  Dec16  P1    W45    wheel   $3.25
Dec16  Jan17  Jul17  9999   Dec16  P1    W45    wheel   $3.41
Jan17  9999   May15  Jul17  Nov15  P1    W45    wheel   $3.25
Jan17  9999   Jul17  9999   Nov15  P1    W45    wheel   $4.00
```

FIGURE 14.8

The Bitemporal Part Table - 3.

But already, things aren't working out very well. For one thing, we have lost the information that, in November 2016, row 1's assertion end time was January 2017. But there's a more serious problem. Not only has information been lost. Incorrect results have been introduced.

Every transaction is applied to the state of the database current when the transaction takes place. Since transactions are applied to an in-memory copy of the data they are modifying, and then written out to persistent storage, transactions will, if necessary, lock the persistent storage copy of that data to prevent other concurrently executing transactions from retrieving their own in-memory copy of that same data, altering it, and then writing their results out to persistent storage. This locking, as is well-known, serializes transactions against that data. In the absence of that serialization, whichever of two concurrently executing transactions against the same row happens to write its updates to persistent storage first, will have its results overwritten when the second transaction writes out its results. It will be as if the former transaction had never happened.

In the absence of future assertions, the physical state of the database immediately prior to a transaction is also the semantic state of the database immediately prior to that transaction. But in the table of Figure 14.8, something is wrong. In the *physical* sequence in which the transactions were applied, the unit prices for P1, for state time [Jul17-9999], are first $4.00 (row 5) and, thirteen months later, $3.41 (row 3). But in assertion-time sequence, the unit prices for P1, for that same state-time period, are first $3.41 (row 3) and, one month later, $4.00 (row 5).

And things are even worse than this. Starting on January 2017, the result of one of the transactions will disappear from the database. The transaction that will disappear is the five percent price increase, effective beginning July 2017. That transaction was applied on December 2016, and applied to the then current unit price (from row 1) of $3.25. But what the database will show, starting on January 2017, is a seventy-five cent price increase. That seventy-five cent price increase was applied on November 2015, but was not applied to the $3.41 unit price which included the five percent price increase. Instead, it was applied to the then still current unit price of $3.25.

In this scenario, two transactions have both updated the same referent. One increased its unit price by seventy-five cents. The other increased its unit price by five percent. What has happened is that these two update transactions were serialized in one sequence in physical (inscription) time, but were serialized in the opposite sequence in semantic (assertion) time. And the result of this lack of semantic serialization is, like the result of a lack of physical serialization when future assertions are not involved, that the results of the transaction which persisted its update last are lost. From January 2017 onwards, it will be as if the 5% increase in unit price had never taken place.

In the absence of future assertion time, semantic serialization is identical to physical serialization. With future assertion time, physically serialized transactions may still result in contradictions and lost data occurring in databases. The solution is to use the same locking mechanisms that enforce physical serialization to also enforce semantic serialization. It is for each transaction to lock the semantic state of the database against which it executes. The most visible difference between physical locking and semantic locking is that physical locks typically last for milliseconds, i.e. for as long as a single physical transaction takes to complete. Semantic locks, on the other hand, typically last for days or even years.

FUTURE ASSERTION TIME LOCKING

In conventional tables, rows which have been deleted can never be altered. Once they are deleted, they aren't there any longer to be altered. In tables with assertion time, rows with past assertion-time periods can never be altered. They are rows whose assertion end time is in the past. In both the standard theory and Asserted Versioning, those rows are forever locked. In both cases, the semantics are the same. The past is the past, and can never be altered.

Put another way, only rows in current assertion-time periods can be altered. These rows are not locked. In the absence of rows with future assertion-time periods, rows with current assertion-time periods are the most recent assertions about their referents. Therefore, the physical sequence in which updates to these rows are made corresponds to the semantic sequence of updating the most recent assertions about the referents of those rows.

As we see in Figure 14.6, carrying out a future assertion-time update results in a row which remains in current assertion time, but whose assertion-time period is closed. After the transaction of Figure 14.5 is applied, row 1 in Figure 14.6 has an assertion-time period that will remain current for fourteen months. It will remain current until the rows resulting from the update become current assertions, on January 2017.

Then, on January 2017, everything is back to normal. The table, at that time, looks exactly like a table in which a standard theory update was applied on January 2017.

The fly in the ointment is the 5% price increase that was applied on December 2016. That is what resulted in incorrect data being introduced. And it did this because it altered the state of the database to which the seventy-five cent price increase was applied. It altered the *semantic past* of that transaction.

The solution is to prevent the semantic past from being altered. The implementation of this solution is to prevent updates or deletes to any row whose assertion-time period does not end in 9999. The reason is that rows with current assertion-time periods are part of the semantic past of rows, for the same referent and state time, which have future assertion-time periods.

With assertion-time locking being enforced, the DBMS will reject the update of December 2016. The current assertion for P1 in state time [Jul17-9999] is row 1, and its assertion-time period is [May15-Jan17]. Like all rows with non-9999 assertion end times, this row is locked. It is locked in current assertion time, and it will carry its lock with it into past assertion time.

FUTURE TRANSACTIONS WITH ASSERTION-TIME LOCKING

The standard theory of bitemporal data treats all rows with closed transaction (assertion) time periods as locked. In that theory, the transaction (assertion) time periods of all such rows lie entirely in the past, i.e. the end time clock tick of those time periods is always a past point in time.

To extend this standard theory locking to work with future assertions, all that is required is that the software continue to treat, as temporally locked, all and only those rows whose assertion-time periods are closed. With this extension, future assertions introduce no semantic errors into a database. This is because temporal locking, as thus extended, serializes transactions in assertion time. It provides semantic serialization, even when that serialization differs from the physical serialization of the same transactions.

To illustrate, I begin with the table of Figure 14.4, copied here as Figure 14.9.

```
Part-B
abtm   aetm   sbtm   setm   ibtm   p-id  p-nbr  p-nm    p-upr
May15  9999   May15  9999   May15  P1    W45    wheel   $3.25
```

FIGURE 14.9

The Bitemporal Part Table - 4.

It is Now() September 2015.

```
DELETE FROM Part-B
IN STATE INTERVAL (Jul17, 9999)
IN ASSERTION INTERVAL (Jan7, 9999)
WHERE p-id = P1
```

FIGURE 14.10

A Future Assertion Delete.

Applying the future assertion Delete transaction shown in Figure 14.10, we get the table shown in Figure 14.11.

Part-B

abtm	aetm	sbtm	setm	ibtm	p-id	p-nbr	p-nm	p-upr
May15	Jan17	May15	9999	May15	P1	W45	wheel	$3.25
Jan17	9999	May15	Jul17	Sep15	P1	W45	wheel	$3.25

FIGURE 14.11

The Bitemporal Part Table - 5.

It is Now() August 2016, and the transaction shown in Figure 14.12 is issued.

```
UPDATE IN Part-B
IN STATE INTERVAL (Jul15, 9999)
SET p-upr = $3.90
WHERE p-id = P1
```

FIGURE 14.12

A Current Assertion Update.

The default assertion time for this transaction is [Aug16-9999]. However, until January 2017, the first row in Figure 14.11 is locked and so the DBMS would reject this transaction. If it did not, the following contradictions would be introduced into the database.

For part P1, from August 2016 up to January 2017, the database would assert two things about the state of P1 from July 2015 until further notice. With the first row in Figure 14.11, it would assert a unit price of $3.25. With the row created by the update, it would assert a unit price of $3.90. Thus, for five months, the database would contain a contradiction.

Then, starting on January 2017, another contradiction would become currently asserted. In this case, it is a continuation of the first contradiction in which the database, from January 2017 until further notice, would continue to assert those two unit prices from May 2015 up to July 2017.

So to prevent these semantic anomalies, the first row in the table is locked while it is still a current assertion. It is the current assertion, but it is not the latest assertion. During that time, updates and/or deletions against that assertion will be prevented. Until January 2017, the database will say that, from May 2015 until further notice, there was/is/will be a part P1, with part number W45, part name "wheel", and a unit price of $3.25, and it will say nothing else about the state of that part during that time.

In implementation terms, the difference between these two rows is that the first row has a closed assertion-time period and the second row has an open assertion-time period. So an Asserted Versioning-enabled DBMS will consider any row whose assertion-time period is closed as a locked row, one which cannot be removed from its assertion-time interval, or altered within that interval.[4]

Note again that this constraint is already present in the standard theory of bitemporal data. In that theory, no row with a closed transaction-time period can be updated or deleted. But in that theory, the only rows with closed transaction-time periods are rows whose transaction-time periods are entirely in the past. In the Asserted Versioning theory, rows may also have closed transaction-time (assertion-time) periods that are current, i.e. that began in the past but that will not end until sometime in the future. Indeed, the Asserted Versioning theory permits rows to have closed transaction-time (assertion-time) periods that lie entirely in the future.

The point of locking all closed assertion-time period rows is to enforce *semantic serialization*. As we saw in the section "The Time Travel Paradox", above, the standard kind of serialization available with all DBMSs is not sufficient to keep semantic errors from being introduced into a database, if we permit transactions to be applied to the database which specify a future assertion-time period. That is because the purpose of serialization is to prevent any transaction from altering the state of any part of a database that another transaction has already relied on. So once a future assertion-time transaction has been applied to a row of data, we must prevent a later transaction, carried out by a DBMS sometime prior to the start of that future assertion-time period, from being applied to the still-currently-asserted row that the future assertion-time transaction has already updated.[5]

The standard theory of bitemporal data recognizes past, present and future statements, and past and present assertions. In this chapter, I have extended the standard theory to include future assertions as well. I have shown that future assertions are a semantically consistent extension of the standard theory, and that the standard theory's Six-Fold Way is a semantic proper subset of my proposed Nine-Fold Way. I have also shown that the mechanisms which implement the Nine-Fold Way replace the mechanisms that implement the Six-Fold Way, but give exactly the same results when the same transactions are used to transform the same database states.

---

[4] A more in-depth discussion of the implementation details of future assertion time can be found in *MTRD*, Chapter 12. There I discuss how semantic serialization is enforced when future assertion-time transactions update or delete rows which are themselves in future assertion time. I also discuss the very useful capability of moving one or more rows in future assertion time forwards or backwards in future assertion time.

[5] Alternatively, if serialization were not enforced, the results of multiple updates to the same row could nonetheless be preserved if the DBMS supported a branching temporal record (in assertion time, in state time, or in both temporal dimensions). In effect, any update in a database is a step along a temporal branch. Serialization guarantees that there is only one temporal branch, the one we think of as reflecting the temporal series of events that happen in the real world. If different temporal branches were supported in a database, that would provide a straightforward implementation of Kripke's possible world semantics for modal logic, and of Hugh Everett's branching time solution to the Schrodinger's Cat quantum conundrum.

GLOSSARY LIST

assertion
bitemporal
conventional table
current assertion
decoalesce
future assertion time
future assertion

future state time
inscription time
open assertion-time
   period
past assertion
physical serialization
referent

semantic past
semantic serialization
statement
temporal indexical
temporal locking
transaction time
withdraw

TEMPORAL REQUIREMENTS

The most important thing a business analyst must understand, in gathering and clarifying temporal requirements, is that a request for "history" with respect to one or more tables is an ambiguous request. Nearly always, the response to this request is to build *state-time tables*. Nearly always, this falls short of what the business users would have requested, if they had only known what they really wanted, and how to express it.

There is another serious problem with the use of state-time tables. It is this: if corrections are made to the data in state-time tables, then those corrections are either applied to the wrong temporal intervals, or those tables become *ambiguous-time tables*. In the former case, the corrections will both introduce incorrect information into those tables and also remove important information from them. In the latter case, we will no longer know what the time period attached to any row in those tables means.

Ambiguous-time tables have been used in commercial databases for decades. And as far as I have been able to determine, no one has pointed out this problem with them. Another indication of the widespread failure to recognize this problem is that the ISO 9075:2011 temporal SQL standard (although not the TSQL2 standard) supports ambiguous-time tables. That is, it supports tables in which either corrections to data cannot be made, or in which if those corrections are made, they either remove information and also introduce falsehoods into those tables, or else they substitute assertion time for state time.

UPDATES AND CORRECTIONS TO CONVENTIONAL TABLES

We have seen in earlier chapters that some modifications are made to a database because the things represented in the database have changed, while other modifications are made to improve the data in the database. There is a great deal that follows from this difference.

In accordance with standard usage, I will call any modification to a database an update. To make this distinction, I will use the terms *reflection update* and *correction update*.

Suppose that the current state of the Part table is as shown in Figure 15.1.

```
            Part
            p-id p-nbr p-nm      p-upr
      R1    P1   W45   wheel    $3.25
      R2    P2   A02   axle     $5.50
      R3    P3   C01   chassis $13.25
```

FIGURE 15.1

A Conventional Part Table - 1.

W45's name has just changed from "wheel" to "wheel-X".[1] To reflect this change to part W45, we submit the update shown in Figure 15.2.

```
      UPDATE IN Part
      SET p-nm = wheel-X
      WHERE p-id = P1
```

FIGURE 15.2

A Reflection Update.

This is a reflection update. This update was made because something about part W45 changed. The result is shown in Figure 15.3.

```
            Part
            p-id p-nbr p-nm      p-upr
      R1    P1   W45   wheel-X $3.25
      R2    P2   A02   axle     $5.50
      R3    P3   C01   chassis $13.25
```

FIGURE 15.3

The Conventional Part Table - 2.

But sometimes we update data because the data is incorrect, incomplete, or in some other way less than optimal. Suppose we learn that the unit price for part A02 is actually $4.50. To correct this mistake, we submit the update shown in Figure 15.4.

```
      UPDATE IN Part
      SET p-upr = $4.50
      WHERE p-id = P2
```

FIGURE 15.4

A Correction Update.

---

[1]Row numbers (R1, R2, etc.) in these Figures are not part of the tables shown in those Figures. But they will sometimes prove to be a convenient way of referring to the rows in those tables.

This is a correction update. The data is being updated even though the unit price for P2 has not changed. The unit price is what the business said it was, and that hasn't changed. It's the unit price *data* that is being adjusted, not the unit price itself.

The result of this update is:

```
        Part
        p-id p-nbr p-nm     p-upr
    R1   P1   W45   wheel-X $3.25
    R2   P2   A02   axle    $4.50
    R3   P3   C01   chassis $13.25
```

FIGURE 15.5

The Conventional Part Table - 3.

There is nothing in the table in Figure 15.5 that tells us that the P1 change was made because the name of that part changed, while the P2 change was made because its price was originally entered incorrectly. But the former update was a reflection update, and the latter update was a correction update.

The distinction between these two types of updates can also be expressed in a way that makes the contrast even more explicit. A reflection update is made because what the data is about changed, while a correction update is made in spite of the fact that what the data is about did *not* change. Certainly so fundamental a distinction must be important. And it is. However, in conventional tables, it is a distinction without a difference. The importance of the distinction manifests itself in temporal tables, not in conventional tables.

Insert transactions and Delete transactions are also updates, and either of them can be a reflection update or a correction update. This may seem, however, to be wrong. How can an insert be a correction? It isn't correcting any data in a table. It's adding new data to that table and altering nothing that was already there. And how can a delete be a correction? It isn't correcting any data in the table. It's removing data from the table and leaving no correction behind in its place.

To see in what sense inserts and deletions can be corrections, let's suppose that P2 should have been deleted last week, and that a row for a new part should have been inserted yesterday. Let those two transactions be these:

```
DELETE FROM Part
WHERE p-id = P2
```
and
```
INSERT INTO Part
VALUES (P8, B02, body, $18.50)
```

FIGURE 15.6

A Correction Insert and a Correction Delete.

The result of these two transactions is this:

```
         Part
         p-id p-nbr p-nm     p-upr
   R1    P1   W45   wheel-X  $3.25
   R2    P3   C01   chassis  $13.25
   R3    P8   B02   body     $18.50
```

FIGURE 15.7

The Conventional Part Table - 4.

If this correction Insert transaction and this correction Delete transaction had happened on time, then they would have been reflection transactions. But an insert which is late in being applied is always a correction because it always corrects a mistake in the data. The mistake is that the to-be-inserted row should have already been there. So from the time that the insert should have taken place up to the time it actually did take place, the database contained a mistake. In this case, the mistake was that the database said, during that time, there was no part B02 during that time, because the database contained no row for B02 during that time.

Similar considerations explain why a late Delete transaction is a correction, not a reflection.

Another reason to correct data is to provide additional information that had not been previously entered. For example, suppose the person doing the original data entry for the Insert transaction for B02 had all the information about B02 except the new part's name. A quick search in her inbox failed to find the email that authorized adding B02 to the Part table, an email that would have included the name for B02. Under pressure to get the new part listed in the Part table, she skipped the name and entered all the other data. As a result, the system added the new part, but set its part name to null. It wasn't until three days later that an update was submitted to add the name for the new part.

Adding the name was not a correction in the strict sense of the word, because there was no incorrect name to correct. But it was an improvement to the data, and so the update that added the name was a correction update, not a reflection update. It changed the data even though nothing about the part had changed.

Other kinds of corrections could be described, but the essential point is this: a correction either alters data in a table when what that data is about has not changed, removes data that should have already been removed, or adds data that should have already been added. Transactions that don't happen on time are always corrections because they make a change to the database that should have already been made. As for transactions that do happen on time, Insert and Delete transactions that happen on time are never corrections because it is only the lack of timeliness that makes these transactions corrections. It is not the data values they place in the table or remove from the table. As for Update transactions that happen on time, they may or may not be corrections. If an on-time Update transaction is applied to a row of data, but the referent of that row has not changed state, then the transaction is a correction, and otherwise is a reflection.[2]

---

[2]An on-time Update transaction which is a correction really isn't on-time, of course. It is a transaction which reflects management's decision that it isn't necessary to correct past state-time data, that applying the correction as a current update is good enough for the purposes to which the data is being put.

But as we have seen, nothing in the history of transactions against a conventional table, or in the results of those transactions, can tell us if data was being updated to reflect what it represents, or if data was being corrected. And this shouldn't surprise us. Corrections have something to do with time. When we correct data, we are playing catch-up to real changes in the real world. But time is mentioned nowhere in conventional table transactions, and appears nowhere in their results.

Nor, when dealing with conventional tables, is it important to distinguish corrections from reflections. Conventional tables include no record of past states, and include no record of anticipated future states either. They tell us only what things are like Now(), to the best of our knowledge right Now(). Both kinds of updates — reflections and corrections — create new database states. Both are our best attempts to make the database as complete and accurate a current description as possible of what things are currently like. If the only database states recorded in a table are current states, then it doesn't really matter how we got to those current states — via reflections, corrections, or a mixture of the two.

But the reflections vs. corrections distinction does begin to play an important role in transactions and tables as soon as time is introduced. When the business specifies temporal requirements for a conventional table, it usually specifies them in the form of a request for "history" to be retained for that table. Experienced business analysts will have heard similar requests before. Experienced developers will have implemented similar requests before.

Let's look at some of those implementations and see how the reflections vs. corrections distinction is involved with them. The reason for doing so is that a long-standing best practice for satisfying such requests is fundamentally flawed, and that the use of bitemporal tables eliminates this flaw. The flaw almost always begins in the requirements definition process.

TIMESTAMPED TABLES

The two most common responses to a request for "history" on a table are to add a timestamp, or a pair of timestamps, to the primary key of the table for which history has been requested, or else to keep the original table and create a paired history table that has an identical schema except for that added timestamp or pair of timestamps. But in terms of the rows of data in the database, and the column values in those rows, the only difference between these two responses is that one response physically partitions historical from current data and the other does not. In both cases, a row to be updated is first copied, and the copy is given a current timestamp. Then the update is applied to the copy.[3]

It should be clear why part-timestamp (*p-ts*) is part of the primary key of the table in Figure 15.8. If it were not, duplicate primary keys would prevent us from retaining a history of changes to the table.

	Part				
	p-id	p-ts	p-nbr	p-nm	p-upr
R1	P1	9999	W45	wheel	$3.25
R2	P2	9999	A02	axle	$5.50
R3	P3	9999	C01	chassis	$13.25

FIGURE 15.8

A Timestamped Part Table - 1.

[3]For an analysis of four common design patterns for history tables, see *MTRD*, Chapter 4.

In Figure 15.8, there are three current rows to which we will re-apply the four transactions discussed above.

It is Now() May 2014, and the Update transaction shown in Figure 15.9 is applied.

```
UPDATE IN Part
SET p-nm = wheel-X
WHERE p-id = P1
```

FIGURE 15.9

An Update to the Timestamped Part Table - 1.

As shown in Figure 15.10, after this update, there are two rows for part W45, rows R1 and R4.

	Part				
	p-id	p-ts	p-nbr	p-nm	p-upr
R1	P1	May14	W45	wheel	$3.25
R2	P2	9999	A02	axle	$5.50
R3	P3	9999	C01	chassis	$13.25
R4	P1	9999	W45	wheel-X	$3.25

FIGURE 15.10

The Timestamped Part Table - 2.

ASIDE

Of course, in standard SQL the Update transaction in Figure 15.9 will not produce the results shown in Figure 15.10. Instead, it will simply change *p-nm* on row R1 to "wheel-X", and will not add row R4. To get the result shown in Figure 15.10 requires, instead, a delete of R1 in Figure 15.8 and then an insert of R1 and R4 in Figure 15.10.

One way to achieve these results is to code those three transactions directly, to write one Delete and two Insert transactions. But that would be tedious, and would inevitably lead to the occasional error. It is, however, the do-it-yourself approach, and there will certainly be some IT organizations who will want to take that approach, at least for now.

A variation on this do-it-yourself approach is to put all the hard work in a before-update trigger. This trigger would retrieve the row specified on the update and then, as an atomic unit of work, would delete that row and insert rows R1 and R4 in Figure 15.10.

A further complication is that, on the Update transaction in Figure 15.9, only *p-id* is specified in the WHERE clause. If there were multiple rows with that same part id, the update would modify all of them. So the before-update code must assume that when the timestamp part of a primary key is not specified on the transaction, a 9999 value for the timestamp is intended.

The update finds the current row for part P1, which is row R1 in Figure 15.8. If there were no current row, the update would fail, even if there were one or more rows for P1 with non-9999 part timestamps.

Row R1 has been preserved in history by being deleted and inserted with a new primary key whose timestamp indicates the end of the *period of effectivity* of the row. (In our terminology, the state-time period of that row has come to an end.) The new data from the update is applied to a copy of the original row R1, resulting in row R4.

Any row with a 9999 *p-ts* value is a row representing the current state of its referent, so when this transaction completes, the table then tells us that the current name of part W45 is "wheel-X".

The history of part W45 shown in this table is that on May 2014, W45 ceased to be in the state shown by row R1, and that currently, W45 is in the state shown by row R4. But that's all we know. We don't know when or for how long W45 was in the state shown by R1. And when we look at this table later on, i.e. after May 2014, we also won't know when W45 took on the name "wheel-X". In this example, it was on May 2014, by means of an Update transaction. But it might have been as a result of a delete to row R1 on May 2014, and then a later insert of row R4.[4]

It is Now() October 2014, and the following transaction is applied to the database:

```
UPDATE IN Part
SET p-upr = $4.50
WHERE p-id = P2
```

FIGURE 15.11

An Update to the Timestamped Part Table - 2.

As shown in Figure 15.12, there are two rows for part A02 after this transaction completes. The update finds the current row for part A02, which is row R2 in Figure 15.10. If there were no current row, the update would fail, whether or not there were one or more rows for A02 with non-9999 part-timestamps.

	Part				
	p-id	p-ts	p-nbr	p-nm	p-upr
R1	P1	May14	W45	wheel	$3.25
R2	P2	Oct14	A02	axle	$5.50
R3	P3	9999	C01	chassis	$13.25
R4	P1	9999	W45	wheel-X	$3.25
R5	P2	9999	A02	axle	$4.50

FIGURE 15.12

The Timestamped Part Table - 3.

The history of part A02 shown in Figure 15.12 is that row R2 ended its period of effectivity on October 2014, i.e. that starting on October 2014, A02 was no longer in the state described by row R2. Row R5 now represents the current state of that part. The same comments that applied to the update of W45 apply here to the update of A02.

It is Now() February 2015.

---

[4]These examples assume that *p-ts* marks the *end* of the period of time during which the row was current. The reader may want to rework these examples based on the assumption that *p-ts* marks the *beginning* of that period of time. This will help to make the point that with only one timestamp, there will be some temporal information that cannot be expressed, whichever interpretation is given to that one timestamp.

The Insert transaction shown below in Figure 15.13 looks for a current row for a part B02. If one were found, the insert would fail, whether or not there were one or more rows for B02 with non-9999 *p-ts* values. The Delete transaction finds the current row for part A02, which is row R5 in Figure 15.12. If there were no current row, the delete would fail, even if there were one or more rows for A02 with non-9999 part-timestamps.

```
INSERT INTO Part
VALUES (P8, B02, body, $18.50)

DELETE FROM Part
WHERE p-id = P2
```

FIGURE 15.13

An Insert and a Delete to the Timestamped Part Table.

Both transactions succeed, and the results are shown in Figure 15.14.

	Part				
	p-id	p-ts	p-nbr	p-nm	p-upr
R1	P1	May14	W45	wheel	$3.25
R2	P2	Oct14	A02	axle	$5.50
R3	P3	9999	C01	chassis	$13.25
R4	P1	9999	W45	wheel-X	$3.25
R5	P2	Feb15	A02	axle	$4.50
R6	P8	9999	B02	body	$18.50

FIGURE 15.14

The Timestamped Part Table - 4.

In the table shown in Figure 15.14, we can see that part A02 was a part as far back as October 2014. But we don't know how much farther back than that it was a part. So this is clearly not a very good solution to the requirement to provide history for the Part table. And it seems that the source of the inadequacy is that only an end timestamp has been provided.

To correct this problem, we might add another primary key column, one indicating whether the timestamp marked the end of a period of effectivity, i.e. of a state-time period, or the beginning of one. In that case, we would have something like this:

	Part					
	p-id	p-ts	p-be	p-nbr	p-nm	p-upr
R1	P1	May14	e	W45	wheel	$3.25
R2	P2	Oct14	e	A02	axle	$5.50
R3	P3	9999	x	C01	chassis	$13.25
R4	P1	9999	x	W45	wheel-X	$3.25
R5	P2	Feb15	b	A02	axle	$4.50
R6	P8	9999	x	B02	body	$18.50

FIGURE 15.15

A Begin/End Timestamped Part Table.

Column *p-be* (part-begin-end) indicates whether the value in *p-ts* is a begin timestamp or an end timestamp. The value "x" is associated with part-timestamp values of 9999.

But this is to start down a dark and dangerous road. The part-begin-end column is the means by which two different points in state time are expressed by means of one column. So one column now corresponds to two properties — begin time and end time.

In Figure 15.15, The part-timestamp on the second P2 row (R5), marks the beginning of that row's state-time period. Since the part-timestamp on the first P2 row (R2) marks the end of that row's state-time period, we know that for the intervening three months, part A02 was not present in the table.

But do we want to put the burden of figuring this out on all queries against this table that want to know the life history of A02, as recorded in the table? If this table is to be queried only by programmers skilled in SQL, it is still not likely that this is a cost-effective solution. And if this table is to ever be queried by business users, it is simply an unacceptable solution.

If the business is satisfied with being unable to query this table directly, then this solution will satisfy the same requirements that are satisfied by a state-time table. For each part which has been deleted, there will be two rows — one with a begin-timestamp and one with an end-timestamp. But since each such pair of rows is equivalent to one row in a state-time table, it is at least an inelegant solution and, more importantly, a much more difficult solution to query.

DOUBLE-TIMESTAMPED TABLES

Having clarified the business requirements, the business analyst happily goes back to the IT department, and specifies a requirement to record both the begin and end time of data in the Part table.

If we assume that, in the starting state of the Part table, all rows had been added effective January 2012, that starting state of the state-time Part table looks like this.

	Part					
	p-id	p-bts	p-ets	p-nbr	p-nm	p-upr
R1	P1	Jan12	9999	W45	wheel	$3.25
R2	P2	Jan12	9999	A02	axle	$5.50
R3	P3	Jan12	9999	C01	chassis	$13.25

FIGURE 15.16

A Double-Timestamped Part Table - 1.

Note that there is no requirement that rows be added with a 9999 end timestamp. If we happen to know when the period of effectivity of a row will end, we can include that end time when we create the row.[5]

---

[5]I call this kind of table a "double-timestamped" table, because as this chapter has progressed, we have inched our way towards this kind of table, one timestamp at a time. But it is what I call a "state-time table" everywhere else in this book. It is what is usually called a "valid-time table" by everyone else, and what is called an "application time period table" in the ISO standard.

So we have three current rows. Now let's re-apply the four transactions discussed above. It is Now() May 2014.

```
UPDATE IN Part
SET p-nm = wheel-X
WHERE p-nbr = W45
```

FIGURE 15.17

An Update to the Double-Timestamped Part Table - 1.

The update finds the current row for part W45. If there were no current row, the update would fail, even if there were one or more rows for W45 with non-9999 part-end timestamps. But the update finds its current row, and is applied to the table. The result is as shown in Figure 15.18.

```
       Part
       p-id  p-bts  p-ets  p-nbr  p-nm     p-upr
R1     P1    Jan12  May14  W45    wheel    $3.25
R2     P2    Jan12  9999   A02    axle     $5.50
R3     P3    Jan12  9999   C01    chassis  $13.25
R4     P1    May14  9999   W45    wheel-X  $3.25
```

FIGURE 15.18

The Double-Timestamped Part Table - 2.

Row R1 in Figure 15.16 has been preserved in history by being deleted and re-inserted with a new primary key whose part-end timestamp indicates the end of the state-time period of the row. For any part, the row whose begin and end timestamps include Now() between them, is the row representing the current state of its referent, so when this transaction completes, the table will then tell us that the current name of W45 is "wheel-X".

We now have a little more history than we did with the first solution. Unlike the first solution, this one shows us when and for how long W45 was in the state shown by row R1. Unlike the first solution, this one also shows us that W45 has been a part continuously from January 2012 up to right now, May 2014.

It is Now() October 2014.

```
UPDATE IN Part
SET p-upr = $4.50
WHERE p-id = P2
```

FIGURE 15.19

An Update to the Double-Timestamped Part Table - 2.

As shown in Figure 15.20, after the update of Figure 15.19, there are two rows for part A02, rows R2 and R5.

	Part p-id	p-bts	p-ets	p-nbr	p-nm	p-upr
R1	P1	Jan12	May14	W45	wheel	$3.25
R2	P2	Jan12	Oct14	A02	axle	$5.50
R3	P3	Jan12	9999	C01	chassis	$13.25
R4	P1	May14	9999	W45	wheel-X	$3.25
R5	P2	Oct14	9999	A02	axle	$4.50

FIGURE 15.20

The Double-Timestamped Part Table - 3.

The history of part A02 shown in this table is that row R2 ended its period of effectivity on October 2014, that row R5 now represents the current state of that part, and that part A02 has been represented continuously in the table since January 2012.

It is Now() February 2015.

```
INSERT INTO Part
VALUES (P8, B02, body, $18.50)

DELETE FROM Part
WHERE p-id = P2
```

FIGURE 15.21

An Insert and a Delete to the Double-Timestamped Part Table.

The Insert transaction in Figure 15.21 looks for a current row for part B02. If one were found, the insert would fail, whether or not there were one or more rows for B02 with non-9999 part-end-timestamps.

The Delete transaction in Figure 15.21 finds a current row for part A02. If there were no current row, the delete would fail, even if there were one or more rows for A02 with pairs of timestamps that did not include Now().

But both transactions succeed, and the result is shown in Figure 15.22.

	Part p-id	p-bts	p-ets	p-nbr	p-nm	p-upr
R1	P1	Jan12	May14	W45	wheel	$3.25
R2	P2	Jan12	Oct14	A02	axle	$5.50
R3	P3	Jan12	9999	C01	chassis	$13.25
R4	P1	May14	9999	W45	wheel-X	$3.25
R5	P2	Oct14	Feb15	A02	axle	$4.50
R6	P8	Feb15	9999	B02	body	$18.50

FIGURE 15.22

The Double-Timestamped Part Table - 4.

This is clearly a better solution to the requirement to provide history for the Part table than the previous solution. With this double-timestamp solution, the business can tell the exact period of effectivity of every row. It can tell when a row was inserted. It can follow a chronological history of when a row was updated. It can tell when a row was deleted.

Or can it?

The pair of timestamps on each row in a double-timestamped table delimits the period of effectivity of that row. But what is that period of effectivity? I said earlier that, "...the row whose begin and end timestamps include Now() between them, is the row representing the current state of its referent". So these timestamps delimit a state-time period.

The interest of the business is almost certainly in when each part was in the state ascribed to it by each row. It wants to know the life history of the parts represented in the Part table. Does this solution provide that information? Appearances perhaps to the contrary, it unfortunately does not.

Let's see why this is the case.

DOUBLE-TIMESTAMPS AND CORRECTIONS

It is Now() August 2015. We realize that we should have updated the unit price on P8 to $20 effective last June. What can we do?

There are two options. One is to apply the following update:

```
UPDATE IN Part
SET p-upr = $20.00
WHERE p-id = P8
```

FIGURE 15.23

A Correction Update to the Double-Timestamped Part Table.

And the result is as shown in Figure 15.24.

Part

	p-id	p-bts	p-ets	p-nbr	p-nm	p-upr
R1	P1	Jan12	May14	W45	wheel	$3.25
R2	P2	Jan12	Oct14	A02	axle	$5.50
R3	P3	Jan12	9999	C01	chassis	$13.25
R4	P1	May14	9999	W45	wheel-X	$3.25
R5	P2	Oct14	Feb15	A02	axle	$4.50
R6	P8	Feb15	Aug15	B02	body	$18.50
R7	P8	Aug15	9999	B02	body	$20.00

FIGURE 15.24

A Problem With the Double-Timestamped Part Table - 1.

But this is wrong. This introduces incorrect information into the table. It says that the unit price of B02, in June and July 2015, was $18.50. But the new unit price of $20.00 was effective starting in June 2015.

The second option is to use the true effective date.[6] The transaction is shown in Figure 15.25.

```
UPDATE IN Part
SET p-bts = Jun15, p-upr = $20.00
WHERE p-id = P8
```

FIGURE 15.25

A Different Correction to the Double-Timestamped Part Table.

And the result is as shown in Figure 15.26.

```
         Part
         p-id p-bts p-ets  p-nbr p-nm    p-upr
R1       P1    Jan12 May14  W45   wheel   $3.25
R2       P2    Jan12 Oct14  A02   axle    $5.50
R3       P3    Jan12 9999   C01   chassis $13.25
R4       P1    May14 9999   W45   wheel-X $3.25
R5       P2    Oct14 Feb15  A02   axle    $4.50
R6       P8    Feb15 Jun15  B02   body    $18.50
R7       P8    Jun15 9999   B02   body    $20.00
```

FIGURE 15.26

A Problem With the Double-Timestamped Part Table - 2.

This seems to be the correct result. And so this seems to be the way to handle a retroactive correction update. This solution to the business requirement seems to work.

But there is a problem. The problem is that we have lost information. The information that has been lost is that during June and July 2015, the database said that the unit price of P8 was $18.50. This information is important because executives may have made business decisions based on that incorrect data. This information would be especially important if that table had been available to decision-makers outside the business, who may also have based business decisions on it. In that case, there may be legal liabilities involved. So as far as the contents of the table itself is concerned, the retroactive update has perpetrated a cover-up.

THE DOUBLE-TIMESTAMPED DILEMMA

This dilemma — that with double-timestamped history tables, corrections either introduce erroneous data (as did the update in Figure 15.23) or eradicate all traces of the mistake they are

---

[6]Of course, the physical SQL that carries out this command is the Delete of the (R7) row shown in Figure 15.22, followed by the Insert of the (R7) row shown in Figure 15.26.

correcting (as did the update in Figure 15.25) — is the foundational issue which makes bitemporal data necessary. It should be clear that this issue arises when any retroactive transaction is issued — Inserts, Updates or Deletes. It can also arise when current Update transactions are issued. It arises whenever data is changed although what the data is about has not changed.

Another way of stating this dilemma is this. If corrections are made correctly (i.e. assigned the correct state-time period), then double-timestamped tables will lose history because the corrections will overwrite the data they are correcting. If corrections are instead applied with a Henceforth value, then although history will be preserved, the resulting pair of timestamps will not indicate the correct state time for the row with the correcting data, but will instead indicate the assertion time of that row. This means that the time periods of some rows in the table will indicate state time, the time periods of other rows in the table will indicate assertion time, and we will have no way to tell, on any row, which is which.

Such tables are no longer state-time tables. They have become *ambiguous-time tables*. We can never be sure, on any row retrieved from those tables, that the time period on that row tells us when the referent of the row was in the state described by the row. It might tell us that; or it might tell us, instead, when the row was added to the table.

This dilemma is no less real for the fact that double-timestamped tables are probably the most ubiquitous response to a business request to "add history" to a table. Yet every double-timestamped table contains this flaw. No double-timestamped table can record corrections correctly and also preserve a record of the mistakes which those corrections fixed.

THE BITEMPORAL DATA SOLUTION

State time is likely what the business analyst had in mind when he finalized the requirements for a Part table history. So by intention, at least, the columns *p-bts* and *p-ets* in the double-timestamped Part table are state-time columns. But as we saw, if corrections are entered with the temporal interval to which they really apply, then the data being corrected will be overwritten and therefore removed from the table. The table will remain a state-time table, however. The time period on all of its rows will be the time during which the referent of those rows was/is/will be in the state described by those rows.

On the other hand, to preserve history, users may choose to enter corrections with a start time of Now(). In this case, the incorrect data will not be overwritten, and so the history that includes that incorrect data will not be lost.

If users choose this option, they preserve history in the table, but at a high price. First of all, they introduce false information into the table. In the example just considered, the update to the Part table results in a table which continues to incorrectly state that P8's unit price was $18.50 in June and July of 2015, and which incorrectly indicates that the new unit price of $20.00 took effect in August of that year.

In addition, in the example just considered, a row has been added to the table whose two time-stamps indicate the assertion-time period of the row rather than the state-time period of the part. Since rows which are not the result of corrections have state-time periods, and since there is no indication which kind of time period is being used for each row, the result is that we now don't know, for *any* row in that table, which time period its two timestamps indicate.

> **ASIDE**
>
> During a career of working with databases in approximately eighteen different enterprises, I have seen perhaps a dozen double-timestamped tables, usually referred to as "history tables" or "version tables". But I have never seen a case in which the business users of that data realized that correcting bad data in those tables would result either in lost information (in the form of history being overwritten) or in the addition of incorrect information (in the form of corrections being made effective on the date they were entered rather than on the date on which the change they record actually took place).
>
> I admit that, as an IT professional, I myself did not notice this problem until I was researching my first book on bitemporal data. But it is not the IT staff who will typically have the detailed knowledge of the business needed to recognize lost or incorrect information. It is, rather, the business users of the data. And so I find it remarkable that in none of those enterprises was there ever any indication that business users noticed the lost information, or the inclusion of incorrect information, or the consequent transformation of state-time history tables into ambiguous-time tables.
>
> So pervasively unrecognized has this problem been, indeed, that the authors of the ISO 9075:2011 standard's temporal features went out of their way to make it possible for ISO-compliant databases to include tables flawed in precisely this manner. For details, see the section "Remove the Ability to Correct Data in State-Time Tables" in Chapter 20.

To solve this problem, we obviously need to introduce something else into the primary keys of double-timestamped tables. This something else should sequence corrections to erroneous data so we could always pick out the most recent correction, and thus pick out our current understanding of what is really the case.

A sequence number would do quite nicely for this purpose. But a sequence number will not tell us when the correction was made. Since a sequence number will not provide the temporal information we want to preserve, perhaps we should use a timestamp. A timestamp can both sequence the corrections, and tell us when each one took effect. The next question is whether two additional timestamps are needed. It might seem that only one additional timestamp is needed because to distinguish two statements about the same or about overlapping state-time periods for the same referent, all we need to know is a single point in time.

But the correct answer is that two additional timestamps are needed. The short explanation is that the assertion of a false statement may be withdrawn without replacing it with another statement. To expand on this explanation just a little, suppose that we attempted to use only a single assertion timestamp. Clearly it must represent the start of an assertion-time period, or we would never know when the first statement in an episode began to be asserted. If an assertion could only be ended by replacing it with a better assertion of the same state time of the same referent, then a start timestamp for assertion time would suffice. But clearly, we sometimes want to withdraw a statement without making another statement about the same thing, i.e. about the same state-time interval of the referent of our statement. We just want to stop claiming as true what, up to then, we had been claiming as true.

So this must be possible with databases also. It must be possible to withdraw a statement in a database, and just leave things at that. And in that case, assertion time requires both a start time and an end time.

Figure 15.27 shows the initial state of a bitemporal Part-B table. Its two pairs of timestamps (rendered as mmmyy values here and throughout this book) delimit two time periods, assertion time and state time. State time, the reader will recall, is what everyone else calls valid time; and with future assertions not an issue, assertion time is what everyone else calls transaction time.

I assume, once again, that all rows in this Part-B table have been added on January 2012, and so the initial state of the bitemporal Part-B table looks like this.

```
            Part-B
            abeg   aend   sbeg   send   p-id p-nbr p-nm     p-upr
    R1      Jan12  9999   Jan12  9999   P1   W45   wheel    $3.25
    R2      Jan12  9999   Jan12  9999   P2   A02   axle     $5.50
    R3      Jan12  9999   Jan12  9999   P3   C01   chassis  $13.25
```

FIGURE 15.27

A Bitemporal Part Table - 1.

So we have three current rows. Now we will re-apply the four transactions discussed above. It is Now() May 2014.

```
                    UPDATE IN Part-B
                    SET p-nm = wheel-X
                    WHERE p-id = P1
```

FIGURE 15.28

An Update to the Bitemporal Part Table - 1.

The update in Figure 15.28 finds the current row for part W45, which is row R1 in Figure 15.27.

The results of applying this Update transaction are shown in Figure 15.29.

```
            Part-B
            abeg   aend    sbeg   send    p-id p-nbr p-nm     p-upr
    R1      Jan12  May14   Jan12  9999    P1   W45   wheel    $3.25
    R2      Jan12  9999    Jan12  9999    P2   A02   axle     $5.50
    R3      Jan12  9999    Jan12  9999    P3   C01   chassis  $13.25
    R4      May14  9999    Jan12  May14   P1   W45   wheel    $3.25
    R5      May14  9999    May14  9999    P1   W45   wheel-X  $3.25
```

FIGURE 15.29

The Bitemporal Part Table - 2.

Row R1 in Figure 15.27 has been preserved in history as row R1 in Figure 15.29. There we see it as a row which was asserted to make a true statement from January 2012 up to May 2014 but which, on May 2014, was withdrawn. Starting on May 2014, rows R4 and R5 together replaced R1. The assertion-time period of those two rows continues the assertion-time period of R1. Together, the state-time periods of those two rows [Equal] the state-time period of row R1. Row R4 preserves the state time of R1 that was outside the scope of the update. Row R5 is assigned the state-time period of the update, and its state description reflects the results of that update applied to that time in the life history of part W45.

We now have a complete history. We know that, prior to May 2014, row R1's state-time period extended to 9999. With the double-timestamp table, we had lost that information.

It is Now() October 2014.

```
UPDATE IN Part-B
SET p-upr = $4.50
WHERE p-id = P2
```

FIGURE 15.30

An Update to the Bitemporal Part Table - 2.

As shown in Figure 15.31, after the update of Figure 15.30, there are three rows for part A02.

	Part-B abeg	aend	sbeg	send	p-id	p-nbr	p-nm	p-upr
R1	Jan12	May14	Jan12	9999	P1	W45	wheel	$3.25
R2	Jan12	Oct14	Jan12	9999	P2	A02	axle	$5.50
R3	Jan12	9999	Jan12	9999	P3	C01	chassis	$13.25
R4	May14	9999	Jan12	May14	P1	W45	wheel	$3.25
R5	May14	9999	May14	9999	P1	W45	wheel-X	$3.25
R6	Oct14	9999	Jan12	Oct14	P2	A02	axle	$5.50
R7	Oct14	9999	Oct14	9999	P2	A02	axle	$4.50

FIGURE 15.31

The Bitemporal Part Table - 3.

Row R2 has been withdrawn into past assertion time and replaced, in current assertion time, by rows R6 and R7. Row R6 takes care of the state-time interval of R2 that was outside the scope of the update. Row R7 takes care of the state-time interval of R2 that was within the scope of the update.

The history of part A02 recorded in this table shows us that row R2 was withdrawn on October 2014. It was withdrawn, as all rows are, because what it said was no longer true. One of the things that row R2 said was that the unit price of part A02 was the unit price of that part starting on January 2012 and continuing on to the latest time the DBMS could record. It follows, for example, that row R2 said that the unit price of A02 will be $5.50 on December 2014.

Of course, when row R2 was placed into the table, we had no way to know how long part A02 would be in that state, e.g. how long the unit price of A02 would continue to be $5.50. So we had no way to assign a specific state end time to the row. The semantically straightforward thing to do would have been to set that end time to null. But DBMSs in general perform better on range predicates with specific values than with nulls, and so a widespread convention — included in the ISO 9075 and TSQL2 SQL standards — is to use the latest time a DBMS can record instead of null.

Because everyone understands that statements about the contingent future may turn out to be incorrect, no one will be misled by this convention. Everyone understands that change is all around us and that predictions about the future often turn out to be wrong.

It is Now() February 2016.

```
INSERT INTO Part-B
VALUES (P8, B02, body, $18.50)

DELETE FROM Part-B
WHERE p-id = P2
```

FIGURE 15.32

An Insert and a Delete to the Bitemporal Part Table.

The Insert transaction of Figure 15.32 looks for a current row for part B02. Finding none, it proceeds. The Delete transaction of Figure 15.32 looks for a current row for part A02. Finding one (row R7 of Figure 15.31), it too proceeds. Unlike row R6, row R7 in Figure 15.31 is about the current state of A02. Unlike row R2, It is a currently asserted statement about that part. It is our currently best statement about what part A02 is currently like.

The insert creates row R8 in Figure 15.33. The delete *decoalesces* row R7 into one row outside the transaction's scope, and one row within that scope. It withdraws row R7 by setting its assertion end time to February 2016, and adds back the decoalesced row that is outside the transaction's scope as row R9.

With the next transaction to be applied, the double-timestamp implementation of the requirement to keep history on the Part table ran into trouble. When it became necessary to apply a correction, there were only two options. Either the correction would be entered with an incorrect state-time period, or the correction would overwrite the incorrect statement. In the first case, the state-time table became an ambiguous-time table, and it was no longer possible to tell, for any row, what its time period really meant. In the second case, IT broke its promise to keep a complete history for the Part table.

Part-B

	abeg	aend	sbeg	send	p-id	p-nbr	p-nm	p-upr
R1	Jan12	May14	Jan12	9999	P1	W45	wheel	$3.25
R2	Jan12	Oct14	Jan12	9999	P2	A02	axle	$5.50
R3	Jan12	9999	Jan12	9999	P3	C01	chassis	$13.25
R4	May14	9999	Jan12	May14	P1	W45	wheel	$3.25
R5	May14	9999	May14	9999	P1	W45	wheel-X	$3.25
R6	Oct14	9999	Jan12	Oct14	P2	A02	axle	$5.50
R7	Oct14	Feb16	Oct14	9999	P2	A02	axle	$4.50
R8	Feb16	9999	Feb16	9999	P8	B02	body	$18.50
R9	Feb16	9999	Oct14	Feb16	P2	A02	axle	$4.50

FIGURE 15.33

The Bitemporal Part Table - 4.

It is Now() August 2016. We realize that we should have updated the unit price on P8 to $20 effective last June. What can we do?

As before, there are two options. One is to apply the following update:

```
UPDATE IN Part-B
SET p-upr = $20.00
WHERE p-id = P8
```

FIGURE 15.34

A Semantically Invalid Correction to the Bitemporal Table.

But that would introduce incorrect information into the table. After the update, the table would say that the unit price of B02, in June and July 2016, was $18.50. But the new unit price of $20.00 was effective starting in June 2016. So this never was a real option, if we believe that databases should contain only true statements.

IT professionals responsible for the maintenance of double-timestamped tables (or single-timestamped ones, for that matter) should realize that if they insert data after it became effective, or delete data after it is no longer effective, or update data after the change they are recording actually took place, then if they assign Now() as the start timestamp for those transactions, they are introducing false data into the database.

The second option, which does not introduce false data, is to use the date on which the price change actually went into effect. The transaction is:

```
UPDATE IN Part-B
IN STATE INTERVAL (Jun16, 9999)
SET p-upr = $20.00
WHERE p-id = P8
```

FIGURE 15.35

A Semantically Valid Correction to a Bitemporal Table.

And the result is:

```
Part-B
```

	abeg	aend	sbeg	send	p-id	p-nbr	p-nm	p-upr
R1	Jan12	May14	Jan12	9999	P1	W45	wheel	$3.25
R2	Jan12	Oct14	Jan12	9999	P2	A02	axle	$5.50
R3	Jan12	9999	Jan12	9999	P3	C01	chassis	$13.25
R4	May14	9999	Jan12	May14	P1	W45	wheel	$3.25
R5	May14	9999	May14	9999	P1	W45	wheel-X	$3.25
R6	Oct14	9999	Jan12	Oct14	P2	A02	axle	$5.50
R7	Oct14	Feb16	Oct14	9999	P2	A02	axle	$4.50
R8	Feb16	Aug16	Feb16	9999	P8	B02	body	$18.50
R9	Feb16	9999	Oct14	Feb16	P2	A02	axle	$4.50
R10	Aug16	9999	Feb16	Jun16	P8	B02	axle	$18.50
R11	Aug16	9999	Jun16	9999	P8	B02	body	$20.00

FIGURE 15.36

The Bitemporal Part Table - 5.

The bitemporal Part-B table has been updated with a correction that is assigned to the correct state-time period. So no falsehood has been introduced into the database. Row (R8) preserves our mistake. It shows that during June and July, this table said that B02 had a unit price of $18.50 during those two months. Row R11 is the correction. It says that, starting in June, B02 had a unit price of $20.00. Row R10 preserves the information content of the now withdrawn row (R8) that was not affected by the transaction, the information that part B02 had a unit price of $18.50 until June 2016. In spite of the fact that the update was applied two months late, this is the truth, the whole truth, and nothing but the truth. And no other kind of temporal table can do this.

So to the query "What did the database say, at any time between February 2016 and August 2016, that the unit price of B02 was at any time from February 2016 until further notice", the answer is "$18.50". To the query, "What does the database currently say that the unit price of B02 was at any time from February 2016 until further notice", the answer is "Prior to June 2016, $18.50. After that, $20.00".

I confess that this chapter provides no new facts about bitemporal data that were not already provided in earlier chapters. My purpose in writing this chapter is to make it clear that when the business requests history to be kept for any table, an implementation which uses only a single time period in its primary key is not adequate because there are two orthogonal histories running through any database. One is a history of the states that, in sequence, constitute the life history of an object. Another is a history of the states of the database itself.

GLOSSARY LIST

ambiguous-time table
assertion time
assertion
bitemporal table
conventional table
correction

decoalesce
life history
referent
reflection
state description
state time

state
statement
state-time table
withdraw

BITEMPORAL DATA AND THE INMON DATA WAREHOUSE

A BRIEF HISTORY OF THE DATA WAREHOUSE

In the 70s and well into the 80s, computerized data existed in files. Files consisted of records, and records consisted of fields. Over time, collections of files were assembled into databases. The file/record/field distinction survived the migration from files to databases, but was renamed. It became the table/row/column distinction.

Hierarchical and network DBMSs provided means to navigate these collections of data to find where to insert new data, to find existing data to update or delete, and to find data to assemble into results to be passed back to the user. But navigation is a procedural matter, and is specified as an algorithm. Although assisted by some built-in functionality of these early DBMSs, that navigation still required programmers to write procedural code, for example code to initialize a counter, to loop through a list, to increment the counter, and to determine when to end the loop. This is, obviously, a highly procedural way to produce a list of records/rows.

Relational theory provided a declarative way to do the same thing. Pre-relational DBMSs required you to specify *how* to select the rows you were interested in. Relational DBMSs only required you to specify *what* rows you were interested in. This is one of the reasons why relational DBMS eventually replaced, for the most part, hierarchical and network DBMSs.

ASIDE

Before proceeding with this reconstructed history of data warehouses, it will be useful to summarize key elements in the Relational Paradigm and to assemble some of the concepts we will need to analyze Inmon's position on data warehousing and, later on, to analyze Kimball's position as well.

One of the key concepts of the Relational Paradigm is that of a *set*. To the well-defined operations on sets such as Cartesian Product, union and intersection, Dr. Ted Codd added an operator to select members from a set, to join members of different sets, and to select a subset of columns from the union of the columns of the joined members. These are the well-known Select, Join and Project operators implemented in relational DBMSs.

Another of the key concepts of the Relational Paradigm is that of a *functional dependency*. In terms of the Relational Paradigm's ontology, a functional dependency exists between *referents* and their *attributes*, their attributes being their *properties* and *relationships*. In terms of the Relational Paradigm's mathematics, a functional dependency exists between a set of values which constitute the domain of the function and, for each attribute, a set of values which

---

represents the range of that function. That function is, in each case, a function from a *referent type* to an *attribute type*. And in terms of the Relational Paradigm's semantics, a functional dependency is the association of a *subject* with a *predicate* in a row which is an instantiation of a *typed, existentially-quantified statement*.

The *domain* of each function is a set of referents of a given type, each referent type associated with a relational table. For example, a set of customers is such a domain. Each of the columns in that table represents a type of property or a type of relationship of the members of that domain. The valid values for each attribute constitute the *range* of the function whose domain is the set of referents. For example, a set of customer status codes is such a range.

Each functional dependency associated with a table specifies that for each member of the domain, there is one member of the corresponding range. In terms of databases, it specifies that for each primary key of a table, there is at most one attribute value in each of its non-primary-key columns.

As implemented in the instances of these types, a functional dependency exists between the identifier of a referent (a *RefId*) and one or more columns which represent properties and relationships of the referent identified by that RefId. As implemented in the rows of these tables, a functional dependency exists between the primary key of a row and one value for each of that row's columns.

Object tables consist of one row for each instance of the type they represent. The same is true for *event tables*. Object tables and event tables are the two types of *referent tables*, since the two immediate subtypes of Referent are Object and Event.

As we have seen, there is only one *state* for each event. This is because an event cannot undergo change. An event happens, and then it's over with. The properties and relationships of the event describe the event's single state.

But objects are different. There can be many states for an object, because an object can remain the same object throughout a series of changes, each change placing that object in a new state. Of course, after a series of one or more changes, an object may revert to an earlier state, i.e. to a set of properties and relationships identical to a set in an earlier state.

This fact is important enough to require a terminological distinction. An *atemporal state* of an object is a set of property and relationship values for that object. A *temporal state* of an object is a *temporal interval*, or *time period*, during which the object is in an atemporal state. In these terms, the last sentence in the previous paragraph can be rephrased like this: "after a series of one or more changes, an object may revert to the same atemporal state it was in during an earlier temporal state".

When the term "state" is used without qualifiers, I always mean a temporal state.

Now we can return to the 70s and 80s. More broadly, we can think of this as the period of time before, in 1988, Devlin and Murphy introduced the concept of a data warehouse. This concept gained traction with the work of Bill Inmon who, in the early 90s, defined a data warehouse as "a subject-oriented, integrated, time-variant, nonvolatile database whose data is primarily used to support management decision-making". (Inmon, 1992, p. 29.)

Prior to the introduction of data warehouses, most tables in a database were referent tables, i.e. either object tables or event tables.[1] For example, *transaction tables* are event tables. An example of a transaction table is a table of all the debits and credits to all the personal checking accounts managed by a bank.

Object tables are all the other tables. For example, a table of customers who hold personal checking accounts with a bank is an object table. This table is updated as changes to customer information are recorded.

The checking accounts themselves are instances of the Personal Checking Account object table. (This table is not, as it might seem, an event table. The reason is that the rows in this table are account

---

[1]Referent tables, not reference tables.

balance records, and unlike events, balances change over time.) At the end of each accounting period, final adjustments are made to account tables, after which that accounting period is *settled*.

Tables which define the financial terms for checking accounts, and tables of other regulatory or descriptive information about them, are also object tables, but they are generally updated less frequently than customer tables or account tables.

But all these object tables have one thing in common: modifications to them are *destructive*. Updates overwrite the data they update. Deletes remove rows from these tables. This is what Inmon meant by saying that these tables are *volatile*. At all times, these object tables inscribe the *current state* of the objects represented by their rows, and no other states.

At the end of each accounting period, after the accounts for that period were settled with any necessary adjustments, a tape backup was made of the account tables and all the tables associated with them — customer tables, terms tables, etc. This backup copy was timestamped to identify that accounting period. And this process was repeated as each new accounting period was settled and then faded into the past.

Then, as the cost of disk space fell, and later began to plummet, the first act of the data warehouse opened. This opening is usually associated with Inmon's name. In this first act, it was realized that data for past accounting periods was in many cases still valuable enough that if those past periods were moved back online, business users might be able to find additional useful information in that data.

So these past accounting periods were restored to disk, where online access was available for them. All the tables (or files) that were backed up for one period constituted a *snapshot* of that data, a snapshot of those tables (or files) as they existed at the end of that time period. But it soon became apparent that instead of associating a time period with a snapshot of a set of tables (or files), the data would be more useful if we instead made that time period the low-order component of the primary keys of the rows (or records) in each of those tables.[2]

Moving the timestamps from entire multi-table snapshots to individual rows of individual tables was not simply a matter of convenience, however. For example, if that hadn't been done, then those historical on-line tables could not have been consolidated. If that hadn't been done, then if twenty-four accounting period snapshots were moved onto disk, there would have had to be twenty-four customer tables, twenty-four terms tables, twenty-four personal checking account tables, and so on. But with the time period moved into the primary keys of those tables, all twenty-four customer tables could be consolidated into one table, and similarly for all the other sets of twenty-four tables.

Another benefit of moving time periods from multi-table snapshots to each table itself is that temporal intervals could then be recorded at whatever frequency was most appropriate for each table. For example, a Customer table could be snapshotted once a month, an accounts table twice a month, and a reference table once a year. For a finer-grained history, a Customer table might be snapshotted once each day, and an accounts table several times during the course of a day.

---

[2]For convenience, I'll drop the dual language of "tables (or files)" and "rows (or records)" in the rest of this section, and speak only of tables and rows. The reader should understand, however, that in those ancient times of which I am now speaking, most data was stored in files and records. Databases had just begun to appear on the scene towards the end of that time.

The next step was to replace periodic snapshots of an entire table or group of tables with time-stamped copies of individual rows made after individual Insert, Update or Delete transactions. That had two benefits. One was that *every* modification to the data could be copied, timestamped, and sent to the warehouse. No modifications would be missed if that were done whereas, with periodic snapshots, no matter how frequent, there was no guarantee that every change would be captured. The second benefit was that timestamped copies of only modified rows, i.e. copies made only when a row was inserted, updated, or deleted, would in most cases take up less space in the warehouse than periodic snapshots in which all rows in a set of tables were copied to the warehouse, whether or not they had changed.

In this way, the straightjacket of multi-table snapshots was removed. And with it, the dependency of the historical data warehouse on snapshots ended. Updates to historical warehouse tables could now happen in as close to real-time as desired.[3]

At this point, we have described an apparently time-variant and nonvolatile database, the early manifestation of the data warehouse. Because of the most prominent feature distinguishing it from operational databases, that of keeping an historical record of objects of interest, it was often called an *historical* data warehouse.

These developments were not just a matter of finding a use for increasingly inexpensive disk space, a use which brought selected historical data back online. From the point of view of the Relational Paradigm Ontology, here is what happened in this first act of the data warehouse. Transaction tables remained event tables. They always had a time period (sometimes consisting of a single clock tick) associated with each of their instances. But object tables ceased to be object tables. They became *state tables*.

This was a fundamental change. In object tables, each object is represented by one row, and each row represents one object. Based on the assumption that the relationship between rows and the objects they represent is one-to-one, relational DBMSs enforced entity integrity, which is a semantic concept, by means of enforcing primary key uniqueness, which is an implementation mechanism for that semantic concept. Based on that same assumption, relational DBMSs enforced referential integrity, which is also a semantic concept, by means of foreign keys each of which pointed to a single parent row, this being the DBMS' implementation mechanism for that semantic concept. All this changed when object tables became state tables because, in state tables, the relationship between rows and the objects they represent is no longer one-to-one. It is many-to-one.[4]

---

[3]This brief history of data warehouses has not been given in terms that were used by the contributors to that history, at the time that history was unfolding. Instead, it is what philosophers call a *rational reconstruction* of that history. A rational reconstruction is an internally coherent story that is consistent with the facts, but that also keeps certain facts in the foreground and moves others to the background. Of course, all history that attempts to explain why things happened as they did is a rational reconstruction, more or less. All facts are a selection from an ocean of facts, a selection of those facts which the historian considers most important. And few are the facts that relate directly, without interpretation, to the things and events being described. Nearly all facts rest on an interpretative basis.

[4]We saw how profound those changes were in the chapters on temporal entity integrity and temporal referential integrity. We saw that primary key uniqueness did not guarantee the semantics of temporal entity integrity in state tables. We also saw that, in state tables, it would often require several parent rows to satisfy one temporal foreign key reference from a child row.

WHAT IS AN INMON DATA WAREHOUSE?

Because Devlin and Murphy's introduction of the data warehousing concept is not well-known, and because Inmon's work on data warehousing is widely known, I will focus my discussion on Inmon's work. In 1992, Inmon defined a *data warehouse* as "a subject-oriented, integrated, time-variant, nonvolatile collection of data in support of management's decisions." (Inmon, 1992, p.29)

Inmon has never rescinded this definition nor, to the best of my knowledge, has he ever modified it. In particular, the five criteria used in this definition reappear in the book which introduced his next generation data warehouse architecture – Data Warehouse 2.0, usually referred to as DW2.0. (Inmon, 2008, p.7)

I will examine each of Inmon's five criteria, in turn. However in describing these criteria, I will *not* rely on Inmon's own published statements about them. From my point of view, most of those statements are too general to help develop the highly analytical treatment of data warehousing that I am attempting to provide here.

What I need for this analytical treatment, and what I will use, are the concepts and the terminology which make up the Relational Paradigm, as presented in Part 1 of this book. Using those concepts and that terminology, I will present each of Inmon's criteria in the best light possible so that when, later on, I reject some of those criteria, I will not be rejecting straw men.

This approach leaves me open to the charge of misrepresenting Inmon's own account of these criteria, of course. If so, so be it, and I would expect to be corrected. But my intention is to express these criteria of Inmon's in the best possible light.

SUBJECT ORIENTATION

A subject-oriented database is one whose data structures reflect the meaning of the data rather than the exigencies of any specific use of that data. This requires that, in a subject-oriented database, there is little or no denormalization. The reason this is so is that normalization is based on functional dependencies, and functional dependencies identify, for each referent, those properties and relationships that belong to it, and only those properties and relationships. So what each column value, in each column of each row in a normalized table *means*, is that the referent designated by that row has that specific property or relationship, for example that what a status code of Platinum means on a row for customer Smith is that that very customer has that very status code. That's what normalization does, and that's why a subject-oriented database is a normalized one.

A subject-oriented database is also one whose *scope* is determined by the meaning of the data, and is not restricted to just the data needed for a specific purpose. As any *enterprise data model* (*EDM*) will show, every important entity in an enterprise is related, directly or indirectly, to every other important entity. To include only some of those entities in a database is to draw boundaries where the meaning of the data itself does not indicate boundaries. Those boundaries are what restrict the scope of a database that is not subject-oriented, and they reflect the specific purpose a business has for an operational database. And so operational databases are not *subject-oriented*; they are *purpose-oriented*.

Here's an example. An invoice management database will certainly include customer data. But it will not include every attribute and relationship about those customers, because not every customer attribute or relationship is needed to manage invoices. That inventory management database may even exclude data on some customers entirely, ignoring, for example, customers with an inactive status.

These restrictions on a Customer table in an invoice management system are purpose-oriented restrictions, not subject-oriented ones. Customers are the subject. Issuing invoices to them is the purpose. A subject-oriented database will include all the data of enterprise significance, about all the customers of the enterprise. A purpose-oriented database will include only that data that is needed for its specific purpose.

Most of us are familiar with Inmon's distinction between an *operational data store* (*ODS*) and an *enterprise data warehouse* (*EDW*). ODS databases are purpose-oriented. EDWs are subject-oriented. In Inmon's *DW2.0*, the ODS/EDW distinction appears as the boundary between *Interactive Sector* databases and *Integrated Sector* databases. Databases in the Interactive Sector are purpose-oriented. Subject-oriented databases are found in the Integrated Sector, and in sectors downstream from that sector.

However, subject orientation and normalization do not always clearly distinguish operational databases from EDWs. For one thing, operational databases are often highly normalized, with specific denormalizations introduced only when data retrieval performance requires it. For another thing, many operational databases are robust enough that the data in them can be used for more than a single purpose. For example, operational data is increasingly being used to support real-time decision-making.

Perhaps we could say that subject orientation means that an EDW is a collection of data whose ultimate end-state is a fully normalized representation of all the important data in an enterprise. It is, to put it more succinctly, a collection of important data with a neutral structure and unlimited scope. As normalized, the data is not structured to support any specific use. With "all the important data in an enterprise" (as vague as that is) as the intended scope, that scope is not restricted to support any specific use.

INTEGRATION

Integration is, in my opinion, the most important function of an EDW. But Inmon seems to believe that data cannot be *semantically integrated* without also being *physically integrated* into a single database instance – the enterprise data warehouse. A virtual data warehouse, Inmon says, is "a supremely bad idea". (Inmon, 2009).

What Inmon is objecting to is the idea that we can semantically integrate data from multiple operational databases each time a query is run or each time a message is exchanged between databases. Inmon never explains why this is not possible. But since real-time decision making often requires integrating real-time data, it better be possible. As I will attempt to show in the next chapter, it is possible.

The point I wish to emphasize is that the *semantic integration* of data from multiple databases is distinct from and independent of the *physical instantiation* of that data in a single database. In the next chapter, I will describe how data from operational systems which has not yet been integrated and persisted in a physical EDW can nonetheless be integrated "on the fly". This transformation of data into a consistent representation of a standard semantics can be applied to messages between databases as well as to data assembled from one or more databases into a query result set.

But what *is* this integration we have been talking about? Specifically, what does Inmon mean by "integration", what do I mean by "semantic integration", and how are the two related?

Inmon and others explain integration by means of examples. Repeatedly, the example of different currencies is used. Inmon points out that we cannot add up invoice total amounts across U.S. dollars, Canadian dollars, Australian dollars, and so on. So to integrate across different currencies, a standard currency for the enterprise should be decided on. Then, integrated in the data warehouse, all currencies should be expressed as that standard currency.

This will indeed make it possible for business users to sum invoice totals across invoices that use different currencies, to compare them to purchase order totals on purchase orders to suppliers in different countries, and so on, but with one important proviso. These comparisons must be comparisons as of a single point in time. We cannot sum totals in a standard currency, originally expressed in different currencies, that are computed at different times. Totals expressed in the standard currency for invoices issued on one day cannot be compared to totals expressed in the standard currency for invoices issued on any other day, because the currency conversion factor will probably not be the same on those two days.

On the other hand, if all totals were persisted in the warehouse in their original currencies, then any summarizations of those numbers, across different currencies and across invoices issued at different times, would be summarizations based on a single value for the conversion factor. Those summarizations would be valid because the standard currency numbers they were composed of would not be based on different conversion factors. They would summarize apples and apples, not apples and oranges.

The conversion factor used might be today's conversion factor, or a factor used on the last day of a given year, or even a conversion factor made up for some special purpose (such as what-if scenarios for currency trading). But my point is that virtualization, in this instance, trumps physical persistence. A standard currency, except for its use as a native currency, should be a *virtual* currency, not one which regiments all the persisted currency values in a database. An EDW in which financial numbers are physically stored in their original currencies is superior to an EDW in which those numbers are converted to a standard currency before being stored.

Two other frequently-used examples of integration are the different date formats used by different countries, and the different values used to represent gender. In these cases, it does seem appropriate to impose a standard representation on the data persisted in an integrated warehouse.

As this book should have made clear by now, the concept of semantic integration which I have described is a more extensive concept than the concept Inmon describes. Defining a consistent set of domain values, or using a standard datatype, is a relatively simple step in establishing semantic integration. A much more difficult step involves establishing a consistent set of definitions of the entities, attributes and relationships which are expressed as the shared structures of the data being integrated.

These definitions, as I have argued in this book, must be formal definitions. Each must state the set membership criterion for the type being defined and, as part of doing that, must situate each type in one or more type hierarchies. In those hierarchies, each immediate parent type defines a *universe of discourse*. Each set membership criterion for an immediate subtype of that parent type specifies what subset of that universe of discourse belongs to that subtype. Because type hierarchies define universes of discourse, the existentially-quantified statements made by the rows in relational databases can be typed existentially-quantified statements.

Turning now to semantic integration, what do I mean by that? To begin with, semantic integration includes what Inmon calls integration. For example, it includes standardization of currency amounts, date formats, and gender codes. In the terminology of the Relational Paradigm, this means that the set of valid values making up the currency domain, the date domain, and the gender domain, will be the same for all columns in a semantically integrated database that uses those domains.[5,6]

I have already indicated what semantic integration means, beyond the standardization of domain values. I refer the reader to the section "Reading Ontologies" in Chapter 5 of this book. I briefly described, in that section, how different definitions of what a customer is might be integrated, not just in terms of standard values presented to end users, but — far more powerfully —in a manner that could be used by software to mediate federated queries across the Semantic Web, queries which assemble customer data from the databases of different enterprises.

Semantic integration is an important concept. And, in the vast majority of cases, when data about the same things appears in multiple operational databases, that data is not integrated. My issue with Inmon concerns whether or not semantic integration requires physical integration. My contention is that it does not. And that will be the subject of the next chapter.

TIME-VARIANCE

A time-variant table is one that records history. In a Customer table which is time-variant, for example, each row tells us what, to the best of our knowledge, the customer was like during the time period associated with that row. In a conventional Customer table, there is only one row for each customer, and it tells us what, to the best of our knowledge, each customer is currently like. It tells us nothing about what customers used to be like, nor can it record our anticipations of what customers are going to be like.

Source-system and ODS data, according to Inmon, is primarily current data, used to manage ongoing processes. Data warehouse data is a collection of historical data, used to discover and analyze patterns of change. But as IT professionals should already know, time-variant capability in a table is not restricted to the enterprise data warehouse. In the insurance industry, for example, claims could not be processed without historical information about policies. The reason is that whether or not a claim is paid depends on the policy specifics that were in effect at the time the costs on the claim were incurred, and not on the policy specifics in effect at the time the claim was processed. For example, if someone submits a claim for a sleep study that was conducted on the fifteenth of last month, the question isn't whether or not that person's policy currently covers sleep

---

[5]As I pointed out above, financial transactions should be physically stored in their original currencies. A standard currency should be defined, of course. But this should not be the currency in which foreign transaction amounts are physically stored. It should be the currency to which foreign transaction amounts are converted, at the point in time when those transactions are pulled into result sets and their currency amounts are combined.

[6]In Part 1, I wrote as if there were a one-to-one relationship between domains as types, and columns of relational tables as types. It was as if each different date column had its own domain, its own set of valid values. But type hierarchies are a well-articulated part of the Relational Paradigm Ontology, and so a date domain type, for example, should be assumed to be incorporated into that ontology as a supertype of the column-specific domains of all columns storing dates.

studies. The question is whether or not that person's policy covered sleep studies on the fifteenth of last month.

But an even more important issue with time-variance is this: as I will attempt to show, Inmon's data warehouse tables cannot be time-variant when making corrections to erroneous data, without introducing further errors.[7] No temporal tables, unless they are bitemporal tables, can do that.

NONVOLATILITY

Nonvolatility is closely related to time-variance. ODS data is usually updated by being overwritten, and deleted by being physically removed. But data warehouse data is never overwritten. Instead, periodic copies of that ODS data are made and timestamped, and moved into the data warehouse, where they are preserved.

However, the problem with any unitemporal table, including those used in Inmon data warehouses, is this: they can be nonvolatile only by mis-stating the time period to which corrections are applied. If a correct begin time is assigned to a correction, then the correction will overwrite the data it is correcting because the time period on the original row will be identical to or included in the time period on the correction, and so the correction will not be distinguishable, within that time period, from the original. In that case, the update is necessarily an overwrite; and so, in that case, nonvolatility is lost. In order to preserve the original error (which is information that also must not be overwritten in a data warehouse), a correction must be entered, like a normal update, with a begin time of Now(). But as soon as that is done, we will have created a row whose start time is wrong, and we will have added to the intended use of that time period as state time, a specific row in which that time period is actually assertion time.

If there is any way around this conundrum, other than the use of bitemporal tables, three decades of computer science research have failed to find it. Nonvolatile or time-variant: neither Inmon nor anyone else can have both without assigning incorrect time periods to corrections. But if the time-variant tables in an Inmon data warehouse were bitemporal, he could have it both ways. Corrections could be entered correctly without overwriting the mistakes they are correcting.

SUPPORT FOR MANAGEMENT DECISION-MAKING

Inmon distinguishes between databases which support operational processes and databases which support management decisions. This distinction is clear enough, but it has become obsolete. Inmon distinguishes between current data in operational systems used to carry out business processes, and historical data in a data warehouse used to analyze those processes in order to support management decision making. But on the one hand, decision-making is no longer an activity that relies solely on historical data. Data in operational systems is often needed for real-time decision making. And on the other hand, historical data, especially in the insurance industry, is often needed to carry out real-time operational processes such as claims processing.

---

[7]I have already explained why unitemporal tables — which all of Inmon's time-variant and nonvolatile tables are — must either lose information when corrections are made, or else enter those corrections erroneously. This is the issue to which Chapter 15 was devoted, and the problem was summarized in the section "The Double-Timestamped Dilemma".

WHY UNITEMPORAL TABLES CANNOT BE BOTH TIME-VARIANT AND NONVOLATILE

The basic point — in a way perhaps the basic point of this book — is this: history tables and other kinds of unitemporal tables don't work. Those tables would work if we were willing to never change anything we said about the past. But erroneous data will eventually make its way into any table. If the table is a conventional table, there is no pretense about retaining any history in the table. And so in that case, correcting erroneous data creates no problems. We just fix the mistake and move on.

This shortcoming of all non-bitemporal ways of persisting history is not widely recognized. For example, Inmon himself says "There is an interesting effect of tracking historical changes to data as it is done in the Integrated Sector. Namely, once a question is asked, it will always get the same answer, even if it is asked at a later point in time." (Inmon, Strauss, Neushloss, 2008, p.67.) But that's not quite right, and it is misleading. For it is only true provided that all corrections are entered with a Henceforth value for their time periods; and as we have already seen, if we handle corrections that way, we knowingly introduce incorrect information in the process of purportedly correcting other incorrect information.

A correction applies to all or part of the time period specified on the row or rows it corrects. But no matter how that time period is represented on the row or rows being corrected, if the correction is (correctly) given the time period to which it applies, it will overwrite all or part of the original data. The table, purportedly being an improvement on a corresponding conventional table because it retains historical data while a conventional table does not, is not what it claims to be, and is not what its business users probably think it is. Corrections to data describing the past, in non-bitemporal tables, do not and cannot retain both corrections associated with their proper time periods, and the original data that they correct.

This loss of information can be as serious a matter as you care to imagine because what is lost is any trace, in the table to which the correction was made, of incorrect information on which important decisions may already have been made. If the incorrect information was used in decisions made by parties outside the enterprise itself, there may well be legal liabilities associated with erroneous data. There may well be legal liabilities also associated with the incorrect time period assigned to the correcting data.

The original erroneous data can be found in database backups and/or transaction logs, of course, but that isn't the point. Any data can be found in database backups and/or transaction logs, in which case why do we bother to keep any of that data in relational databases? One important reason is certainly the ready availability of important information, which backups and logfiles do not provide. And my point here is that the information provided by that erroneous data which, until it was discovered to be in error, was presented to its business users as the truth about things, can sometimes be just as important as information which is based on data which is not in error.

The only way to preserve erroneous data is to replace it without overwriting it, and to delete it without removing it. And this leads far too many enterprises to employ a sleight of hand when applying corrections to a table. Instead of entering the correcting data with the time period to which it in fact applies, they enter the data with a different time period. They enter the correcting data as though it were data which describes a time period which begins right now, when the transaction applying it to the database takes place.

For most temporal tables, most data is entered with that current time period, one which I have called Henceforth. But what Henceforth means is that the row entered into the table describes the new current state of its referent, and will continue to describe it until further notice. In other words, the Henceforth time period in these cases, is *state-time* Henceforth. It describes when the referent began to be in that state. But if corrections are also entered with a Henceforth time period, they are themselves in error. They do not tell the truth, because they say that the data they contain describes the new current state of their referent. But it does not. It describes a state-time period which began in the past, not one which began at the moment the correcting transaction was entered.

This is the dilemma summarized in the section "The Double-Timestamped Dilemma" in Chapter 15. Corrections to unitemporal tables either overwrite data and therefore destroy information, or else they tell a lie. And it is important to understand that even a single correction made by using Henceforth destroys the semantic integrity of *all* the rows in the table to which it is applied. That is because we then have no way to know, for any row in that table, whether or not the referent of that row really did begin to be in the state described by the row at the begin time of its time period. The entire table becomes an *ambiguous-time table*, and is no longer a state-time table. And therefore the information in the table is unreliable. We can no longer be sure when any referent was in the state described by any row.

How bitemporal data solves this problem was described in "The Bitemporal Solution", also in Chapter 15.

TWO SENSES OF "AS-WAS"

A distinction is often made between *as-is* reports and queries, and *as-was* reports and queries. But as we should all know by now, there are two distinct senses of both as-is and as-was. With respect to as-is, we can be talking about either what things are currently like, or about what the data currently is. With respect to as-was, there is *as-was data about things* and *as-was states of things* For example, if the business requests a report on who its customers were two weeks ago, an Inmon time-variant table or a Kimball slowly-changing dimension can provide that information. But that information is information about the *as-was states of things*, based on *as-is data* about those states. Now suppose that for regulatory reasons, the business needs a report showing who its customers were two weeks ago, according to who the database said they were last week. What the database said last week about what things were like two weeks ago is week-ago *as-was data* about the two-weeks-ago *as-was states* of those things. That week-ago data may or may not be the same as what the database said, two weeks ago, that things were like two weeks ago. That week-ago data may or may not be the same as what the database currently says things were like two weeks ago.

This distinction correlates with the two important business needs mentioned above. One need is to keep track of the history of changes to an object, from when it first appeared in the database to when it ceased to be represented there. That is the *life history* of the object, and it is tracked in state time by attaching state-time periods to rows of relational data. State time supports the as-was states of things sense of as-was. An added benefit of state time is that it can also be used to record the future states of things.

Another need is to keep track of a history of modifications to data which does not reflect changes to what the data is about. Typically these modifications are corrections to erroneous data.

But they may also be late-arriving data which replaces nulls or default values, or which provides more accurate estimates that replace earlier less accurate ones.

This history is tracked in assertion time, by attaching assertion-time periods to rows of relational data. Assertion time supports the as-was data sense of as-was. But a unitemporal table for which the database user can specify time periods on transactions, is a state-time table. And assertion-time history cannot be tracked in a state-time table. The attempt to do so turns a state-time table into an ambiguous-time table.

Neither the Inmon nor the Kimball architecture can support reporting on what things were/are/will be like at any point in time, as described by the database at any past or present point in time. This is what bitemporal data can do. Asserted Versioning's bitemporal data can also report on what things were/are/will be like at any point in time, as described by the database at some future point in time.

THE ENTERPRISE DATA WAREHOUSE REDEFINED

What is left of Inmon's definition are four of his five criteria.

Subject orientation, as I have interpreted this criterion of Inmon's, means a database that is fully normalized and, at least in its idealized end-state, whose scope is not limited to any specific operational purpose. It is a database whose structures and scope are not influenced by any non-semantic considerations.

Integration of data across databases is indeed important. But Inmon's examples of integration illustrate only the simplest kind of integration, that being the standardization of domain values and datatypes. Semantic integration, as I call it, also includes the standardization of object, event, property and relationship types. Ultimately, all these standardizations should be formalized so that they can be used by software to make *semantic interoperability* among databases possible.

Nonvolatility means that data is not lost because of maintenance to that data. Updates copy rows and apply their changes to the new copy. Deletions mark rows as deleted rather than physically removing them. Unfortunately, if the data in an Inmon EDW (or any other type of non-bitemporal EDW) is nonvolatile, it is because all corrections to data have been made incorrectly.

Time-variance is a consequence of nonvolatility. Since updates are applied to copies of their target rows, and deletes do not remove rows from tables, by retaining those original rows, the data in those tables constitutes an historical record. However, there are two independent historical records, and they must be kept distinct. One is a record of the changes to the things represented by those rows. The other is a record of changes to the data itself. These two historical records must be kept distinct because if they are not, the timestamps and/or time periods in those tables will represent a confused chronology of changes to things and changes to data. And unfortunately, the tables in an Inmon EDW have this confused chronology. Fortunately, as we have already seen, it doesn't have to be this way.

Being used for management decision-making is not a distinguishing feature of data warehouses. It is simply a use to which a data warehouse may be put. And increasingly, operational data is also used for management decision-making. This last of Inmon's five criteria no longer distinguishes data warehouses from operational databases.

So this is the Inmon enterprise data warehouse, based on my interpretation of his definition. On my interpretation, subject orientation is satisfied by the scope of the database, and by the data structures that it uses being determined only by the semantics of the data. Semantic integration includes the standardization of datatypes and domain values, but goes well beyond that. With the introduction of bitemporal tables, it will be possible, for the first time, to satisfy the two criteria of time-variance and nonvolatility without introducing errors into the data. And as for Inmon's last criterion, supporting management decision-making is no longer a distinguishing feature of the EDW.

THE SEMANTICS OF THE EDW AND THE QUESTION OF ITS PHYSICAL INSTANTIATION

The basic requirement that justifies the costs of creating and managing any collection of data is this: business users should have access to the information they need.

It follows that that collection of data should be expressive enough to represent all the information those users need. That data should be represented in a standard form because otherwise we will not always be able to tell when data from multiple sources is or is not data about the same things, and about the same properties and relationships of those things.

An EDW helps to meet this basic requirement. Its ultimate objective is to include data representing all information of enterprise importance. Since this includes historical data and even data about the anticipated future, that data is time-variant. Since that time-variant data must be accessible throughout its period of usefulness, it must also be nonvolatile. To be semantically integrated, that data must have a standard representation in terms of the types of its objects and events and the types of the properties and relationships of those objects and events. A standard set of datatypes and a standard set of domain values for each type of referent and each type of attribute is the minimum requirement for semantic integration; but as we have seen, semantic integration is much more than that.

An EDW is one component in the data infrastructure needed to support this information requirement. But unless its temporal tables are bitemporal, it will not provide both time-variance and nonvolatility.

I have also noted that a traditional EDW cannot include up-to-the-moment real-time data because, by the time that data is retrieved, transformed and stored in the EDW, it will no longer be real-time. This is important because for real-time decision-making, real-time data is needed. To overcome this limitation, we need time-variant and nonvolatile data in our operational databases. And fortunately, bitemporal tables can be used in operational databases just as easily as in an EDW.

But we also need to be able to semantically integrate data in operational databases. Until all operational databases are transformed into partial implementations of an enterprise data model, this means that the semantic integration of operational data will have to be done "on the fly". Any query assembling data from two or more operational databases will, by definition, be a federated query. If we choose to use the term "virtual data warehouse" to refer to the ability of federated queries to assemble and semantically integrate data from multiple databases, then those queries imply the need for a virtual data warehouse.

But as we are about to see, Inmon doesn't think much of federation or of data virtualization.

INMON'S ARGUMENTS FOR A PHYSICAL EDW

One place Inmon makes the case for a physical EDW is in his article "The Elusive Virtual Data Warehouse" (Inmon, 2009). A virtual data warehouse, of course, is one that isn't itself a physical database.

Inmon begins by telling us where he stands. After saying "I believe virtual data warehouses are inane", he adds that they are "a supremely bad idea". Fortunately, he also tells us what he thinks a virtual data warehouse is. He says that "….. a virtual data warehouse occurs when a query runs around to a lot of databases and does a distributed query. With a distributed query, the analyst does not have to face the dreadful task of integrating data."

By that last sentence, Inmon does not mean that some "behind the scenes" work *will* carry out that dreadful task for the analyst. He means that a distributed query either doesn't include any integration at all, or includes some kind of data transformation that represents a serendipitous choice among integration options that would probably be different if a different analyst were writing the query. As Inmon says, "(w)hen every analyst is free to integrate data as he or she sees fit, then there is no integrity of data. There is no single corporate system of record — there is no corporate single version of the truth." (Inmon, 2009).

For example, if a federated query sums currency amounts from two different databases, and those databases use different currencies, any integration will depend on whether or not the analyst realizes that different currencies are involved and, if she does realize it, how she decides to resolve the currency differences. Does she pull a currency conversion factor from a real-time outside source? Does she pull the conversion factor from an internal table that is updated once a month? Does she go out on the Internet and find the currency conversion number in effect on the stroke of the most recent midnight and then hardcode that number in a query that may be run several more times over the coming weeks and months? Regardless of what she decides to do, does the business user looking at a report based on her query understand the rules she used for the conversion?

These are valid concerns. Realistic examples like these make it clear that the lack of semantic integration is a real problem in countless numbers of queries — federated or not — that return results to the business user that may be as important as you care to imagine. In all these cases, the business user literally does not know what he is looking at. What's worse, he usually doesn't know that he doesn't know what he's looking at. Instead, he usually looks at data with a set of background assumptions. Perhaps, in the example just considered, he assumes that a real-time conversion factor is used, and that it is current each time the query is run and its report is produced. Perhaps, even probably, he's wrong.

But integration is a semantic issue. Inmon argues that it requires a physical database. If it does, the semantic integration of real-time data from operational databases will be impossible because reconciliation and consolidation in a single physical database takes time. In the next chapter, however, I will show that the semantic integration of real-time data from operational databases *is* possible, and that it does not require copying that data from one database to another.

Nonetheless, Inmon does have several reasons other than semantic ones for advocating a physical EDW. I emphasize again that these reasons have nothing to do with the semantics of data. They are purely implementation considerations, although not unimportant for all that. Inmon says:

- "A query that has to access a lot of databases simultaneously uses a lot of system resources. In the best of circumstances, query performance is a real problem.

- A query that has to access a lot of databases simultaneously requires resources every time it is executed. If the query is run many times at all, the system overhead is very steep.
- A query that has to access a lot of databases simultaneously is stopped dead in its tracks when it runs across a database that is down or otherwise unavailable.
- A query that has to access a lot of databases simultaneously shuffles a lot of data around the system that otherwise would not need to be moved. The impact on the network can become very burdensome.
- A query that has to access a lot of databases simultaneously is limited to the data found in the databases. If there is only a limited amount of historical data in the databases, the query is limited to whatever historical data is found there. For a variety of reasons, many application databases do not have much historical data to begin with." (Inmon, 2009).

These are not unimportant points, although they are relative to the amount of stress that federated queries place on the specific system resources that they use. And more and more, advances in platform technologies are making these kinds of points moot − advances such as processing speeds, main memory sizes, disk storage capacities, the gradual replacement of spinning disks with solid-state nonvolatile memory, fiber optic bandwiths in the network, parallelism in the system software, system abilities to coordinate asynchronous processes, and so on. In the not too distant future, the demands that classical business data, i.e. character set data generated by operational processes, places on platform resources will become insignificant compared to the demands of such tasks as extracting useful information from semi-structured data streams, or managing volumes of Big Data.

As these objections do become increasingly moot, the idea of semantically integrating data "on the fly" will begin to seem less and less unrealistic. This is fortunate because there is a growing need to be able to semantically integrate real-time data.

Nonetheless, there will probably always be value in integrating as much time-variant and non-volatile data as possible in a single data repository simply because it is always easier to manage one physical object than to coordinate the management of multiple physical objects. This one data repository might as well be thought of as an Inmon EDW, now properly understood.

I want to suggest, however, than an Inmon EDW faces a second data integration issue that Inmon does not discuss, and that I have not mentioned so far. That is the issue of *schema evolution*. For any given database, its schema definitions may evolve over time. A table may be horizontally or vertically partitioned. One set of subtype tables for a given supertype table may be replaced by a different set. The datatype for a column may change. The set of values constituting the domain for one or more columns may be extended to include new values. A column may be dropped and replaced by two new columns.

Together, these and other types of schema change result in both different ways of representing the same information, and in adding to or subtracting from the information represented in a database. How is semantic consistency to be maintained as schemas evolve? With bitemporally persisted data, it is likely that an EDW will contain data from different points or periods of time that can be combined or compared only by resolving semantic integration problems due to schema evolution which are every bit as great as those already discussed.

One solution is to continue as we have begun, to address this semantic integration issue just as we have suggested we should address the ones we have already considered − by mapping from old schemas to new ones, from source schemas to target ones.

But there are more radical solutions. One is to include, in all messages, not only the data being sent, but also a description of the schema for that data. XML is the most important technology supporting schema self-description.

Another more radical solution is what is often called a *no-schema* approach, although a "very abstract schema" approach would be a more appropriate name. The most important of these very abstract schemas are the Resource Description Framework RDF triples defined by the W3C.

A third more radical solution is to make all schemas the same, and never change any of them. This can be done by storing all data as atomic statements consisting of the ascription of one predicate to one subject. The statement schemas for these statements would all define binary tables in a relational database. An associated ontology would identify all binary tables whose RefIds are for the same types of objects or events, thus allowing fully normalized tables in those databases to be defined dynamically, as the union of all binary tables with identical RefId types. I will discuss this approach to solving the schema evolution problem in Chapter 19.

GLOSSARY LIST

ambiguous-time table	instance	state
assertion time	life history	statement
as-was data about	object table	state-time table
things	Object	subject
as-was states of things	object	temporal interval
atemporal state	predicate	temporal state
attribute	property	time period
clock tick	referent table	transaction table
conventional table	referent	type
correction	reflection	unitemporal table
current state	relationship	universe of discourse
event table	semantic	
Event	interoperability	
event	state time	

INMON TERMS

Following is a list of Inmon technical terms used in this chapter, and more general terms also used by Inmon, and discussed in this chapter.

Data Warehouse 2.0	historical data	physical EDW
data warehouse	warehouse	subject-oriented
DW2.0	Integrated Sector	time-variant
EDW	integrated	virtual data warehouse
enterprise data	Interactive Sector	volatile
warehouse	nonvolatile	
federated data	ODS	
warehouse	operational data store	

SEMANTIC INTEGRATION VIA MESSAGING

In this chapter, I will develop the concept of semantic integration via *messaging* by discussing a new role for the *enterprise database* (*EDB*) and the *enterprise data model* (*EDM*) which it is based on.[1] This involves leaving Inmon's terminology of warehouses behind, but its relevance to the previous chapter's discussion of enterprise warehouses will be apparent.

The motivation for this new concept was mentioned at the end of the previous chapter. It is that the semantic integration of real-time or near real-time data cannot be achieved by copying that data into a consolidating database. There just isn't enough time to do that.

This new role for the EDB is as the hub in a *hub-and-spoke* architecture, one in which data is exchanged, not *point-to-point*, but rather sent to a hub and retrieved from that hub. However, the hub I will describe is not a physical hub; it is a semantic one. While this leaves the concept of federation behind, it embodies the concept of virtualization. While this focusses the discussion on the exchange of data between databases, its relevance to the queries discussed in the previous chapter is direct. We can just think of the result sets of those queries as equivalent to the results of queries against this virtual EDB itself.

THE OBJECTIVES OF AN ENTERPRISE DATABASE

In this chapter, I will talk about enterprise databases, and not specifically about enterprise data warehouses. Enterprise databases are a generalization. Enterprise databases which are used as data warehouses are one kind of EDB.

In the previous chapter, I revised Inmon's definition by discarding the last of his five criteria — support for decision-making — and revising the other four — subject orientation, time variance, nonvolatility, and integration. I defined subject orientation as a semantic concept, one in which the data structures of a collection of data, and the scope and boundaries of that data, are determined on a purely semantic basis. I demonstrated that time variance and nonvolatility are jointly possible

---

[1]The material in this chapter is adapted from (Johnston, 2011a-c) by permission of the editor.

if *and only if* data is bitemporal. I also demonstrated that Inmon's discussions of standardized currencies illustrate only a very small part of what is involved in semantically integrating data.

To begin this chapter, I will define the concept of an EDB in my own terms, not Inmon's. In my terms, an EDB is a stable, complete, and semantically well-formed collection of data that records information of enterprise value.

Stability means that information will not be lost. Given that operational policies and procedures will preserve data against loss due to quotidian events like memory crashes, disk crashes, and simple operator error, stability means that updating data will not destroy any of that data. It means that updates will not overwrite data, and deletes will not remove data.

Completeness means that this stable data will preserve all the information we need. Let's stipulate that, at any point in time, the data kept by the totality of an enterprise's operational systems is current-state complete. By that I mean that operational databases have current-state data on all the properties and relationships of all the objects and events that they need to do their work.

With this stipulation, we can focus on the temporal aspect of information completeness. In this sense, completeness means that if we need information about some past state of affairs, that information will be found somewhere in the data we have kept. It also means that we will have the ability to record what we anticipate future states of affairs will be like, and can provide that information on demand, as well.

Stability and completeness are provided by bitemporal data, and by no other kind of data.

Information is *semantically well-formed* when it is free of what are called *semantic anomalies*. The information recorded in a relational database is semantically well-formed — and, by extension, we may say that that data itself is semantically well-formed — when all the sets are clearly defined, all the relationships among the sets are clearly defined, and the implementation of those sets contains no homonyms or synonyms.

ASIDE

The concepts needed to elaborate on this definition of "semantically well-formed" can be found in Chapters 3–6. But a few brief comments might be in order here.

Functional dependencies relate a pair of sets. One set defines the *domain* of the functional dependency; the other set defines the *range* of the functional dependency. A functional dependency is a rule for assembling any number of columns into a table. They are the columns each of which is a range of that table's domain.

A table represents a *type*; the domain of the type is the set of all its possible instances. The *set membership criterion* for the type is the rule which unambiguously states, for every member of the *universe of discourse* for the type (which I have suggested is defined by the immediate supertype of that type), which of those set members are eligible to be members of the type represented by that table. So, for example, if the supertype of Invoice is Financial Document, then Financial Document defines the universe of discourse for Invoice, and the set membership criterion for Invoice is a rule for picking out those financial documents which are invoices.

The other set in a functional dependency defines the range of the function. This range is a set of values for a column of the table. The column properly belongs to the table only if, for every member of the table's domain, there is associated one and only one member of that range. The domain is a set of *referents*, i.e. *objects* or *events*; the range is a set of *attributes*, i.e. *properties* or *relationships* of those referents. So, for example, if department number and department name are two columns of an Employee table, the reason department name doesn't belong there is that department name is not a property of an employee, nor does it establish a relationship in which the employee participates. It is, in the common parlance, only transitively dependent on the primary key of the Employee table.

We all know about transitive dependencies, of course. That is, we all know how to carry out the normalization process that removes them from tables. We all know that if transitive dependencies aren't removed, it becomes possible for the unnormalized table to keep multiple copies of the same information, copies which will can become inconsistent with one another unless always updated as a single unit of work.

But what we don't all understand, and what I explained in the paragraph just prior to the previous one, is the semantics by virtue of which transitive dependencies make database inconsistencies possible. Those semantics are that tables represent things, and non-primary key columns represent properties or relationships of those things. A column which does not represent a property or relationship of the type of thing represented by the table is a column which violates the Relational Paradigm Ontology, especially that aspect of it shown in Figure 5.5.

So given a type of object or a type of event, each functional dependency in which that type is the domain picks out a type of property or a type of relationship of that type of object or event.

Implemented as tables and columns in a relational database, i.e. at the level of types associated with the mathematical structures of the Relational Paradigm, that database is *homonym* free if and only if no table represents more than one type of object or event, and no column represents more than one type of property or relationship. And that database is *synonym* free if and only if no two tables represent the same type of object or event, and no two columns represent the same type of property or relationship of the same type of referent. At the instance level, a table is homonym free if and only if no row represents more than one object or event of the type designated by the table. And a table is synonym free, at the instance level, if and only if no two rows represent the same object or event of the type designated by the table.

The question is whether data can have a consistent semantics, across a collection of multiple databases, without copying that data into a consolidating database, and mapping source types and domains onto a standardized representation of consolidating database types and domains. Inmon to the contrary, the answer is that it can be.

TWO PATHS TO SEMANTIC INTEGRATION

Integration, for Inmon, as we saw in the last chapter, is what you get when domains for columns which mean the same thing are standardized, that is, when all those columns which mean the same thing use the same set of values for their domains. But that is only one specific way to achieve domain-level semantic integration – to make a copy of the data to be integrated, and to transform the differently-valued domains representing the same event, object, property or relationship type into a single standardized set of domain values for that type. However, that is the only way to achieve integration that Inmon thinks is not "inane" or "seriously misguided".

Note that this is a more detailed account of what Inmon means by integration than he provides himself. When Inmon provides examples like currency conversion, or gender codes, for example, he assumes that we already know which columns are the candidate columns for conversion to a standard set of values, for example that across a set of tables and databases, we already know which columns represent gender codes. In terms of the Relational Paradigm Ontology, he assumes that we already know which columns represent the same types, and also which tables represent the same types. But that is a precarious assumption. Let me illustrate.

The fact, for example, that two different columns are both labelled "gender-code" does not confirm that we should integrate them by assigning a standard set of values for the warehouse columns onto which they will be mapped. For example, it might well be that one of those columns labelled "gender-code" is actually a column that indicates sex, not gender. The point here is that while there are two sexes, male and female, there are three genders, masculine, feminine and neuter. Sex and gender are not the same type, although they are often confused with one another.

So the *real* work of integration, in even the simplified cases that Inmon discusses, is not mentioned by him. Mapping two sets of values onto a common set of values is easy — once you know what you are doing. Knowing what you are doing is the hard part. And in this case, knowing what you are doing means knowing what columns represent the same types, and what domain values represent the same instances of those types.

But the Inmon method of integrating domain values — the method of copying data from source tables which use different sets of values for the same concept into a target table which uses one set of values for that concept — is not the only way to achieve domain-level integration. Another way is to *virtually* integrate that data, to do the integration "on the fly". If one database is sending data to one or more other databases, values in the columns being sent can be translated into the equivalent values used by each of the receiving databases. If data from one or more databases appears in a query result set or on a report, data values as stored can be translated into the values that the enterprise assigns as the standard values for the types being reported on.

So our objective is a stable, complete and semantically well-formed record of the important information in the enterprise. The Inmon approach to achieving this objective is to copy columns from source databases onto columns in a consolidating database in which referent types and attribute types are those defined as standard throughout the enterprise, in which the relationships among those referent types are the ones defined in the enterprise's *enterprise data model* (*EDM*), in which the associations between referent types and attribute types are the ones defined (as normalized tables) in the EDM, and in which the domains for each of the types are well-defined.

I propose that this objective can be realized as a collection of databases which have been individually bitemporalized and semantically integrated. Databases have been bitemporalized when all their data is bitemporally persisted. A pair of databases have been semantically integrated when data can be exchanged between them without loss of information. The collection of an enterprise's semantically integrated bitemporal databases is what I call a *virtual enterprise database*, a *virtual EDB*.

I turn now to this second way of achieving semantic integration. I situate the semantic mapping that will be involved, in the messaging layer of a *Service-Oriented Architecture*. There, the enterprise data model, instead of being the data model for a physical EDB, becomes the data model for a *CMM*, a *Canonical Message Model*.

THE ENTERPRISE DATA MODEL AS A CANONICAL MESSAGE MODEL

The term "*canonical*" originates in the Greek term *kanon*. In Xenophanes and Euripides, it referred to "a rule used by carpenters and masons" (Liddell and Scott, 1994, p. 399). Later uses include "Canon Law" (the legal code of the Catholic Church), music canons (compositions with a particularly regular structure), "canonical form" (used in logic), and the general use of the term "canonical" to mean "standard" or "authoritative."

The term *canonical message model* (*CMM*) appears in discussions of *service-oriented architecture* (*SOA*), where it refers to the use of a message-specific common data model to mediate data exchanges between one database and another. A message from a source database is translated into the representation defined by this data model. On the receiving end, the message is translated from this representation into the representation used by the target database. Being the standard representation into and out of which the data in messages is translated, the data model common to these messages is the canonical model for the data they exchange, and the message formats it defines are canonical formats.

The term "enterprise data model" (EDM) is widely used by data architects and data modelers to refer to a normalized logical data model of the entire enterprise. In most cases, the EDM will include only those entities whose significance extends outside the confines of any one department or division within the enterprise.

THE FAILED MISSION OF THE ENTERPRISE DATA MODEL

The principal use of the EDM has always been to define the approved way that any enterprise data, in any database, should be modeled. Each database in the enterprise should be, in this view, a fully consistent implementation of that part of the EDM which it instantiates. Exactly what this means is not completely clear, but we can think of it as meaning that if all EDM-conformant databases in the enterprise were logically combined, and all consequent redundancies eliminated, the result would be a fully attributed implementation of the EDM free of any semantic anomalies (especially homonyms and synonyms).

However, in point of fact, there are very few enterprises most of whose databases implement data models that are consistent instantiations of their EDMs. Although all enterprises have projects to create and extend working databases, few have ever had a project whose sole or principal purpose was to revise those databases so that their data models would be consistent instantiations of their EDMs. Because many of the important databases in an enterprise have existed longer than the EDM for that enterprise, those databases are not (and show no inclination to ever become) consistent instantiations of those EDMs.

The main reason for this sad state of affairs is cost. Working databases have an extensive codebase to maintain their data and an extensive set of queries to assemble information from that data. Changing the schemas for those databases would have a ripple effect out to that codebase and those queries. It might be possible to protect many of those queries by means of views, but it is unlikely that views can or should protect all the code that maintains the data. If we were to rewrite those databases to be EDM-consistent, we would incur a significant cost, and there would be no user-visible results from the rewrite — or at least none that business management would accept as justifying that cost.

This is why rewrites of those databases to make them consistent with their EDMs don't happen. In the real world, an EDM is just a paper reference model that may or may not be consulted by a project's data modeler during development of a model designed to meet the objectives for that specific project. If IT policy mandates oversight reviews to guarantee consistency with the EDM, that oversight is usually resented because it generates project costs and consumes project time to achieve an objective that the project customer doesn't see and doesn't care about.

Consequently, across the multiple databases in an enterprise, there are significant differences in how data about the same things is structured and represented. As a result, when data is exchanged across these databases, and when queries assemble results from across these databases, those data messages and queries must handle differences in physical representations of the same information, and resolve semantic differences among those representations.

A NEW MISSION FOR THE ENTERPRISE DATA MODEL

Data has always been exchanged between databases, and those exchanges have almost always required mapping. The mapping has usually been a point-to-point mapping between two specific databases, implemented in application code and queries, where it is inextricably intertwined with all the other work done by that code and those queries (for example, the work of expressing business logic as data is created and transformed, the work of assembling data into information results, the work of managing the user interface, and so on).

In SOA-governed collections of databases, on the other hand, data exchanges are isolated in their own architectural layer, called the *SOA messaging layer*. The work done in this layer is not merely data transport. Rather, it includes data mapping which, besides straightforward translations from one datatype to another, or from one set of values to another, often includes the more formidable task of resolving deeper type differences between source and target. In SOA environments, the code that does this mapping is segregated from the code and the queries that do the other work, the work of acquiring, managing, and presenting information to business users.

In this way, an EDM can have a real impact on software and database design and development. It can be more than just a paper reference model. It can be a model that defines the standard data formats and the standard semantics for the data being exchanged between systems. It can be a physically implemented model, but one that is implemented in code rather than in database schemas. It can be a *canonical model* for messages exchanged between a data source and a data target.

The idea here is that since inertia (in the form of cost) prevents the extensive transformation of established databases into instantiations of an EDM, why not use the EDM, instead, as a *virtual* standard representation of data? It would be as if all point-to-point data exchanges would be carried out as spoke-to-hub and then hub-to-spoke exchanges, in which the hub is a virtual enterprise database, a virtual instantiation of the EDM. In this way, the EDM could be brought out of the back office of enterprise data management, into the front office of software and database design and development. In this way, the EDM could begin to do real work.

Point-to-Point Messaging

Mapping messages from a source database to a target database incurs costs. There are the costs of writing and managing the code that does the mapping and of running that code every time a message requires it. If a source database sends the same message to n target databases, and if each of those databases formats the data in a slightly different way, then n translations will be required. But if a single format is used to mediate the data exchange, then the source database will only have to map from its proprietary format into the canonical format for the data in the message.[2]

---

[2] In this chapter, I am using the term "same format" to mean both "same datatype" and "same semantics", so that a mapping from one format to another means the semantic integration of those formats so that no information is lost in the messaging.

Conversely, if *m* source databases send the same message to a target database, and if none of those databases uses the same format for the data in the message, then *m* translations will be required. But if a single format mediates the data exchange, then the target database will only have to map from the canonical format for the data in the message into its own proprietary format.

Figure 17.1 shows a point-to-point architecture for the messaging layer. One message leaves X, passes through messaging nodes (1) - (3), and arrives at Z. Another message leaves Y, passes through messaging nodes (4) and (5), and also arrives at Z.

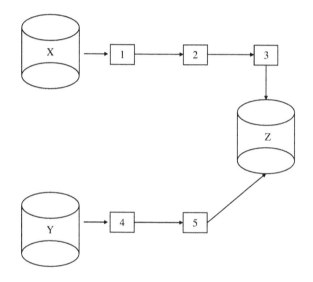

FIGURE 17.1

Point-to-Point Messaging.

If the formats that X and Z have for this data are different, then code must map the data from X's format into Z's format. If the same message content is sent to Z from a different source, say Y, and Y's format is not identical to the format used by either X or Z, then new code must be written to map the data from Y's format into Z's format, and so on for every message sent from a source to a target database.

Hub-and-Spoke Messaging

Figure 17.2 shows a hub-and-spoke architecture for the messaging layer. The message leaves X, passes through messaging nodes (1) − (3), and arrives at the hub database W. If the format that X uses for the data in the message is not identical to the canonical format for that data, then the data in the message must be mapped into canonical format before the data is stored in W.

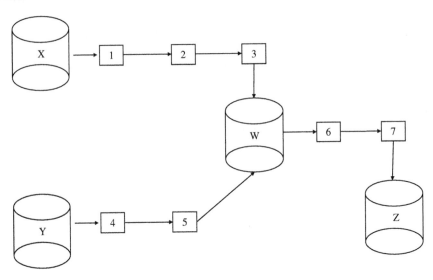

FIGURE 17.2

Hub-and-Spoke Messaging.

After being stored in W, the message is reconstituted and sent on, via nodes (6) and (7), to its target Z. If the same message is sent from Y, there is another translation from Y's format into W's format, but the same code that maps the message into Z's format will work no matter which source database created the message.

As a physical database, W decouples source and target databases. It makes X, Y, and Z independent of one another as far as the different formatting of message content is concerned. X and Y may be radically modified, or even completely replaced, and Z will remain unaffected, just as long as the modifications to — or replacements for — X and Y continue to support the messages which they send to W.

X and Y are sources of one or more messages that supply data to W. Those messages continually update the contents of W. When Z wants data, it obtains it from W, not from X or Y. This supports the ability, across a system of data-sharing databases, for any database to *pull* the data it wants from a shared repository. If instead the communication between a source and target database, say X and Z, is a *push* from X to Z, then X must send its data to W as a store-and-forward message, not just as a "store" message.

The data model for W is the EDM. The schemas used by W to store data define the formats for all data exchange messages received by all target databases. Those schemas instantiate the canonical message model for the system of inter-communicating databases.

But if the whole point of having W is to facilitate messages among a set of databases, then why bother storing the contents of those messages in an intermediate database? Why not just drop the "store" function altogether?

The answer is that the "store" function in any "store-and-forward" transmission exists to allow the transmission to be asynchronous. However, if messages between databases must be transmitted asynchronously, this does not mean that application developers must construct and manage a hub database. Commercial software that facilitates asynchronous messaging is readily available.

We can envision the hub database in Figure 17.2 fading away, in which case the step from (3) to W to (6) (in this case) is replaced by a direct step from (3) to (6), or a step mediated by asynchronous messaging software. The translation of X's data into canonical format can take place at any point along the transmission. Since W no longer physically exists, this diagram then becomes equivalent to Figure 17.1.

What is important is the translation into canonical format, not the storing of that mapped data in a physical database.

As I pointed out earlier, EDMs are almost always used only as a paper reference model, and therefore most databases within an enterprise are imperfect and incomplete instantiations of their EDMs, storing data about the same things in different ways. Consequently, when that data is exchanged between those databases or assembled from multiple databases in query result sets, those differences must be resolved.

For many years, a point-to-point approach to resolving those differences has been taken, more by default than by conscious choice. For any data exchanges between a sending and a receiving database, resolving differences meant mapping the source data into the format required by the target database. Consequently, the two databases were *tightly coupled*. A change in how the data was stored in either database meant that the data exchanges involving that data would fail unless the point-to-point mapping was revised.

Employing a hub-and-spoke paradigm, in which point-to-point translations are replaced by translations into and out of a canonical format, the messaging layer of Service-Oriented Architectures reduces the number of translations required for databases to communicate with one another.

The EDM takes on this message-mediating role by defining a complete canonical format for enterprise data to which each canonical message must conform. Because asynchronous messaging no longer requires a physical store-and-forward database, and because synchronous messaging never required one in the first place, the EDM becomes realized as a virtual enterprise database, not as a never-to-be-attained physical one. Its physical realization is in the messages which conform to it.

I point out again that the hub-and-spoke architecture in which an EDB is a virtual hub, is a *semantic architecture*, not a physical one. Suppose that all the connections between a set of communicating databases are physically implemented as point-to-point connections, some connections exchanging data as real-time messages, others as asynchronous messages, and yet others as batch extract, transform, and load processes. As long as all these exchanges translate all data from source systems into an EDM-defined canonical format, and send only data in canonical format as input flowing into target systems, the benefits of canonical format messaging will be realized. Thus, the architecture mediating the semantics may be completely different from the architecture mediating the physical exchanges.

Because the EDB is now a messaging model as well as a database model, it should include the definition of the mappings that mediate message exchanges between databases and not just the definition of an idealized database. Let's call this the "Extended EDM", and the new part that includes mapping definitions the "Mapping Rules Dictionary" component of the Extended EDM.

A Mapping Rules Dictionary

Each mapping rule describes a translation either from a source database to the virtual EDB, or else from the virtual EDB to a target database. These rules are illustrated in Figure 17.3, in which the EDB is marked as the underlined database.

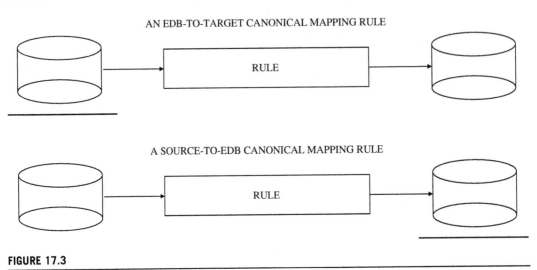

FIGURE 17.3

Mapping Rules.

A source-to-target mapping combines a source-to-EDB rule and an EDB-to-target rule. This is illustrated in Figure 17.4.

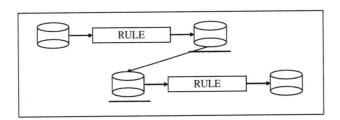

FIGURE 17.4

A Source-to-Target Mapping.

A useful heuristic for designing end-to-end rules is to proceed from both ends back towards the middle. First, there is usually a preferred source for the data needed by the target database. All messages from that source that include some or all of that data are selected. These are candidates for the mapping from the source database to the EDB. Next, all messages whose target format is used by the target database, and which include some or all of the data needed for that message, are selected. These are candidates for the mapping from the EDB to the target database. Finally, source-to-EDB and EDB-to-target mappings are matched such that the information content of the former fully contains the information content of the latter. The result is a complete source-to-target mapping of the desired message content from the source system, delivering the data in a format recognizable to the target system.

Frequently, however, no such pair of rules can be found. In those cases, one option is to write a new source-to-EDB mapping and/or a new EDB-to-target mapping. But with a sufficiently robust set of rules already in the Rules Dictionary, another option is to chain together a set of already-existing rules. This second option is illustrated in Figure 17.5.

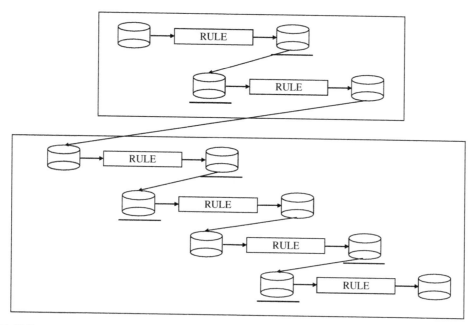

FIGURE 17.5

Chained Mapping Rules.

Other topologies of mapping rules are also possible. For example, a rule may use multiple sources to produce one EDM-compliant target, or multiple EDM-compliant sources to produce one non-EDM-compliant target. However, it is beyond the scope of this discussion to examine such additional topologies.

The Extended Enterprise Data Model

Figures 17.6 shows the major components of an EDM extended to include a Mapping Rules Dictionary. The EDM diagram is more than a diagram, of course, because it includes the semantics that distinguish primary keys from all other attributes, foreign keys from all other attributes, that express the minimum and maximum cardinality of relationships, that define datatypes for attributes, and whose entities represent interpreted mathematical relations. It is the model which maps the ontology of the database onto its physical representation, albeit in the limited way in which current relational databases can express that ontology.

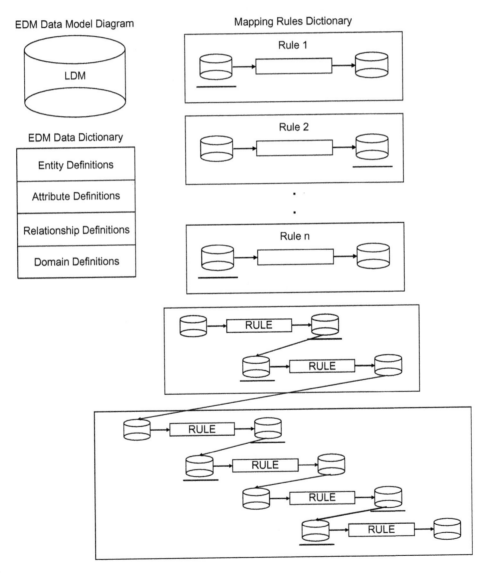

FIGURE 17.6

An Enterprise Data Model Extended to Include Mapping Rules.

The EDM Data Dictionary in Figure 17.6 provides definitions for all instances of the major components of the data model. In data modeling terms, those components are entities, attributes, relationships, and domains. In terms of the Relational Paradigm Ontology, those components are objects, events, properties and relationships.

The Mapping Rules Dictionary has already been described, although far too briefly. For every message sent from a specific database, the Extended EDM's Mapping Rules Dictionary includes the rule required to translate the message into an EDM-consistent format. For every message received by a specific database, the Extended EDM Mapping Rules Dictionary includes the rule required to translate that message from an EDM-consistent format into one recognizable by the target database. This set of rules constitutes a *semantic web* which makes a semantically consistent whole out of the set of communicating databases.[3]

The use of an EDM as a canonical message model breaks the semantic integration problem between two databases into a set of more manageable pieces. Each piece is a transformation of one format into another format. Each message exchanged between databases, or presented as a result set to a query, is provided by a chain of one or more mapping rules. This set of canonically-compliant messages provides semantic integration across operational databases. It allows data to be exchanged without loss of information. It is the implementation of a virtual EDB. It is an implementation which does not require an Inmon physical enterprise data warehouse to provide time variance, nonvolatility or semantic integration.

GLOSSARY LIST

attribute	instance	semantic architecture
bitemporal	object	synonym
current state	property	type
event	referent	universe of discourse
fact	relationship	
homonym	semantic anomaly	

---

[3]This is not to be confused with the Semantic Web as an Internet superstructure, although both uses of the term refer to a web of semantic relationships.

BITEMPORAL DATA AND THE KIMBALL DATA WAREHOUSE

18

I will begin with a summary statement of both the Inmon and Kimball data warehouse architectures, in order to establish their similarities and differences. Of course, comparing these two architectures is something of a cottage industry among IT authors. But the Relational Paradigm, I believe, allows us to compare these two architectures in a way that hasn't been done before.

First of all, Inmon's preferred representation of an enterprise's data is as a normalized set of relational tables. Relationally normalized data does not privilege any one way of looking at that data. Relational data structures are intuitively natural because they reflect the folk ontology we all share, that the world is made up of things (which are either objects or events), and that these things are described by saying what kind of things they are, what properties they have, and what relationships they have to other things.

An Inmon enterprise data warehouse (EDW) provides a semantically integrated record of things and of changes to things. Those changes happen to *objects* in the course of their involvement with other objects in events. Those *events* are the occasions on which those changes happen. If those changes are recorded in our data in a non-destructive way, then we can accumulate a history of those changes, recorded either as a sequence of states of the things changed, or as a sequence of events that the things participated in.

For changes recorded as a sequence of *states*, my recommended improvement to Inmon's EDW architecture is to use *bitemporal tables* to provide what Inmon calls time variance and nonvolatility. Of course, event tables should also be bitemporal. But with event tables, there can be only one state. If there are multiple rows for the same event in an event table, it is because those rows have non-overlapping assertion-time periods. The later of two such consecutive rows is always a correction to the earlier one.

When Inmon EDWs begin using bitemporal tables, they will embody a permanent record of the *life history* of the things we are interested in and of the events those things have taken part in, as well as a record of all corrections and adjustments made to the data itself. They will provide a dual history of how things used to be, and what the data used to say about how things used to be.

In the Inmon architecture, *semantic reconciliation* of data from multiple operational systems is emphasized, and for this objective, my recommended improvement to Inmon's EDW is to use a *canonical messaging model* to support semantic reconciliation for real-time data, as described in the previous chapter.

Semantic reconciliation should also include reconciliation at the level of *type definitions*, expressed as set-membership criteria for those types which distinguish instances of those types from all other instances drawn from the universe of discourse defined by their immediate super-types. These more complete semantics can be initially provided as human-readable definitions of types of *things* and *properties* of those types, of *relationships* among types of things, of *type hierarchies*, and of *universes of discourse, datatypes*, and *domains* of those types. In addition, those definitions should be formalized in some convenient form of *typed predicate logic*. When that is done, those type definitions will be machine-readable, and available for use in federated queries. At that point, and not before, the foundation for *semantic interoperability* across the Semantic Web will have been established.

This emphasis on semantics is one of the most important things about the Inmon architecture. It emphasizes the data itself, and the meaning it has, rather than any particular perspective on that data. This way of representing data maximizes the business uses to which that data can be put. It maximizes the value of that data.

But Kimball will have none of this neutrality. For Kimball, fact tables are the focus of everything, and all other data exists to provide supporting detail for the metrics recorded in fact tables. Once fact tables and dimension tables are conformed, semantics has had its due, and the developer can get down to the important work of building star schemas and the ETL that populates them.[1]

Here is how I believe the world of enterprise data looks to those who have adopted the Kimball point of view on that data, as described in the terminology provided by the Relational Paradigm.

An enterprise's operational databases record the *events* in which the enterprise takes part, each event being recorded as a transaction. Kimball and Ross usually call these events *business processes*. Examples of events include issuing a purchase order, hiring an employee, signing a contract, receiving a shipment from a supplier, palletizing bundles of finished goods, issuing an insurance policy, exchanging goods in transit at a cross-dock facility, enrolling a student in a class, scanning a can of soup at a check-out register, crediting or debiting a checking account .... clearly, the list is endless. *Transactions* record the events that an enterprise engages in, and *dimensions* record the objects which participate in those events.

Examples of objects involved in events include parties to transactions, in such roles as contributor of something of value and/or recipient of something of value, the thing or things of value exchanged in the transactions, facilitators of the transactions, as well as regulations governing the transactions, calendars which provide temporal groupings of the transactions, categories that define collections of transactions of interest to the enterprise ..... clearly, this list is also endless. Dimensions are the record of the *participants* in events. Transactions are the record of those events themselves.

Sometimes an enterprise will choose a more succinct way of recording events than to list every single transaction. One of these more succinct ways is to record periodic summarizations of those transactions. Another is to record periodic snapshots of the effects of those transactions. But the focus is still on the events. The perspective is not that things change by taking part in events. It's that events are not fully described without describing the things that take part in them.

---

[1]By "star schema", I mean a fact-dimension structure, whether or not recursion appears in the dimension tables of those structures. For Kimball and Ross, of course, recursion in dimension tables is anathema.

This focus on an enterprise's business processes puts the things involved in those processes in the role of supporting actors to the transactions the enterprise engages in. In Kimball's view of things, events are fundamental, and objects are important because they provide additional information about events. In Inmon's view of things, on the other hand, objects and events are of equal importance.

Kimball took an important step when he created a design pattern that reflects his event-centric view. In that pattern, transactions are the focus. They (or summarizations of groups of them, or snapshots of their effects) are represented in *fact tables* in which each table corresponds to one type of fact.

Dimensions are the participants in facts. Some participants are unaffected by their participation, such as facilitators, regulations, and categorizations. But in all transactions, one or more of their participants is altered, or else a relationship between them and other participants is altered.

When a relationship is altered, the enterprise will maintain data that records the ongoing cumulative effect of those transactions. That data is usually called something like a *balance record*. A bank account, with debit and credit transactions against it, is one such balance record. In a store, there will be balance records that record the on-hand and on-order inventory of each type of item sold in the store.

From this point of view, an enterprise data warehouse is a record of the important transactions an enterprise has been involved in, and of the effect those transactions have had on the things that took part in them. Since the same things may take part in many different types of business processes, it is important to be sure that, in describing their participation in those various types of processes, those descriptions of those things are consistent. Those descriptions must be, in Kimball and Ross' terms, *conformed*.

STAR SCHEMAS AND RELATIONAL DATABASES

It is important to emphasize, to begin with, that star schemas are a design pattern within relational databases, not an alternative to relational databases. The foreign keys in star schema tables are relational foreign keys. The tables in star schemas are relational tables, and the mathematical rigor of relational tables accrues to them because of that. SQL can be used to access star schema data only because SQL is an implementation of the logical and set-theoretic operators of the Relational Paradigm, and star schema tables are objects defined in that paradigm, i.e. relational tables.

Any result set derived by applying those operators is a well-formed object to which those operators can be applied, recursively. In other words, the operations of logic and set theory are closed. They never take you outside the system of those things to which those operators can be applied. Even when the benefits of relational closure are not directly visible to end-users, or recognized by star schema designers, DBAs, and programmers, those benefits are there. The task of populating star schemas and of retrieving information from them would be far more difficult if they were not.

In short: anyone who believes that star schemas are an alternative to relational databases is mistaken. They are a design pattern which exists within the framework of some kind of database; and when that framework is relational, they benefit from the mathematical and logical rigor which relational theory provides.

THE STAR SCHEMA DATA WAREHOUSE ARCHITECTURE

A new version of Kimball's data warehouse architecture was introduced in (Kimball and Ross, 2013). As with Kimball's original architecture, introduced in the mid-90s, this architecture is based on and exists to support the star schema design pattern. In this architecture, star schemas are periodically refreshed by ETL processes, during which the necessary logic is applied to conform facts and dimensions across those star schemas.

In a Kimball warehouse, each star schema serves the business needs of a different segment of the user community. Common dimensions across different star schemas must be consistent, and when they are, those dimensions are said to be conformed. Interdependent sets of facts, too, must be conformed. If two star schemas both have a Customer dimension, for example, the two dimensions will either be identical, or it will be possible to identify one as a horizontal and/or vertical subset of the other, or to otherwise map one onto the other. The two conformed tables will never provide conflicting information about the same customers.

THE STAR SCHEMA DESIGN PATTERN

A star schema consists of one fact table, and one or more dimension tables. The fact table contains information about changes. In the most basic kind of fact table, each row represents a transaction. A transaction is an event in which something changes something else, or changes the relationship between itself and something else. For example, each step in a manufacturing process changes the thing being manufactured. Each monthly mortgage payment by a homeowner decreases the balance due on her mortgage account.

Fact tables have foreign key relationships to dimension tables. Some of these dimensions don't change very much. Tax tables change once a year. The payroll calendar used by a store, or by the corporation which owns the store, may remain the same for many years. But other dimensions change more frequently, and it may be important to retain a history, however limited, of those changes. On-hand and on-order inventories are constantly changing. Salespersons often move from one sales team to another. Customers change addresses, and may be assigned to different demographic categories over time. Unit prices of items for sale change frequently.

Sometimes we construct fact tables that don't contain one row for each event. Instead, we may populate those fact tables with periodic snapshots of the balance records that those events affect. For example, instead of recording every movement of items into and out of in-store inventory, we may simply choose to record the on-hand quantity of each item in that inventory at store-closing each night.

The value of star schemas, besides recording a history of important events, is that they provide an elegant way to aggregate the numbers that measure those events from the point of view of anything affected by those events. In a retail sales star schema in which store, product and calendar are dimensions, each sale is directly linked by foreign key to the store where the sale took place, to the product sold, and to the calendar period in which the sale took place. If there are ten stores, a hundred products and 52 lowest-level calendar periods, for example, then there would be 52,000 different aggregations if every store sold at least one unit of every product each week. And it is likely that there is an organizational hierarchy in which stores are grouped by region, and perhaps region by division, with corporate as the root node of the hierarchy. There is probably also a two- or three-level product hierarchy, as well as a calendar hierarchy. And a business user might want to see aggregations at any levels of any combination of these hierarchies.

But what *are* fact tables? Aren't dimensions facts as well? In a Customer dimension table, for example, if there is a customer C123 who lives in Oregon and falls into demographic category XYZ, aren't those facts about that customer? And for that matter, what are dimension tables? What is dimensional about them?

RECONCEPTUALIZING STAR SCHEMAS: FACT TABLES AND DIMENSION TABLES

In a star schema, the most basic kind of fact table is a table of transactions. This is the sense of "transaction" I described in a footnote in Chapter 1, the sense in which it refers to an event in which something takes place — usually an exchange of some sort between or among parties involved in the transaction. These transactions, in these fact tables, represent these events.

So fact tables would be more accurately called *event tables*, especially since dimension tables have an equal claim to the title of "fact table". It is a fact that part W45 currently has a unit price of $3.50, for example. It is a fact that Acme is currently a type 4 supplier. These are facts, but in star schemas, these tables would be dimension tables.

In a star schema, a dimension table is a table of things that *participate* in events, by changing and/or being changed by other things in the course of those events, by regulating or categorizing those events in various ways, and so on. The instances of those dimensions represent objects that take part in those events. But when those dimensions must be historicized, a transformation takes place. Rows in those tables then represent, not those objects themselves, but *states* of those objects.

EVENTS AND OBJECTS

In Chapter 5, I developed the concepts of events and objects. Events have no history because they do not change. Once they are over with, nothing else happens to them. But objects can have a history because they can remain the same object over an extended period of time in which a series of changes happens to them.

These changes to objects happen in time and, therefore, in sequence. The result of each change to an object, including the changes of its coming into existence and ceasing to exist, is that the object enters and/or leaves a given state. Each state is described by the set of attribute values the object has during a given period of time. Each time an object changes state, it is as the result of that object's participation in an event in which another object affected it. The series of states of an object constitute the *life history* of that object. Between each consecutive pair of states of an object, there is an event in which the object changed from the previous state to the new state. (I refer the reader to Figure 5.3. "Objects and the Events in Which They Change", and the accompanying discussion, in Chapter 5.)

Kimball and Ross say that a row in a fact table represents a "business process event" (p.10).[2] Various objects may be involved in that event, such as objects which cause one object to change

---

[2]All page references in this chapter, unless otherwise indicated, refer to (Kimball and Ross, 2013).

state, or which are instruments which the agent object uses to effect that state change, or regulatory mechanisms, or various types of categorizations of such changes.

In the ontology of the Relational Paradigm, an event is a referent which cannot change states. Because it is a referent, it has properties and/or relationships. Because it is an event, it cannot change. Because it is not an object, it cannot be the cause of any change. In star schemas, a fact table represents events of one specific type. The transactions in that fact table are instances of that type.

As the term "transaction" suggests, many of those events are ones in which the changes are *exchanges*, events in which one party gives something of value to another party and receives something else of value in return. These changes and exchanges are often measurable, and when they are, it is often useful to accumulate various statistical results on sets of those transactions, results such as sums, averages, standard deviations and − often most important of all − changes in these metrics over time. Those statistical results are usually accumulated along hierarchies of relationships to which the participants in those events belong, and are often even more usefully accumulated along combinations of those relationships.

ASIDE

The two other kinds of fact tables are periodic snapshot tables and cumulative snapshot tables. These two kinds of fact tables are ways of representing the results of business processes in a more condensed way than by using one row for each transaction. In these tables, one row represents many transactions, either by being a consolidation of them, or by being a snapshot of the effect of those transactions on a balance record. In the first case, these fact tables are still event tables, but in the second case they are not. Balance records can change over time, and so they are objects, not events.

The difference between these two additional kinds of fact table is that, in the first case, these events are periods of time during which a possibly large number of individual transactions may have occurred. In the second case, these fact tables become *state tables*. The states are states of the objects affected by the transactions in the fact tables. Those objects are things like on-hand inventories, the financial relationship between a company and a supplier, the financial relationship between a company and a customer, and so on.

Kimball and Ross say that dimension tables "contain the textual context associated with a business process measurement event" (p.13). This is vague enough to be non-contentious, but it also misses the most important point about dimensions, a point which our ontological perspective makes clear. Dimension tables are object tables. Objects participate in events. In those events, some objects change state. If those changes are recorded in dimension tables, those dimension tables cease being object tables, and become state tables. Those state tables are what Kimball and Ross call *slowly-changing dimension tables*.

Some objects, however, do not change state. Mathematical formulas, for example, do not change state. If they change, they become a different formula. Other objects change state infrequently. Tax codes, for example, change at most once a year. The calendar used by an enterprise as a dimension in most or all of its star schemas may not change for many years.

Other objects change state more frequently. Clearly, the frequency with which objects change states is distributed across a continuum. From this point of view, to call the dimensions for these types of objects "slowly changing" is not accurate. They change at whatever speed they change at.

I suspect that the source of the term "slowly-changing" lies in the observation that, compared to fact tables, there are relatively few physical updates to dimension tables. Of course, compared to fact tables, there are relatively few rows in dimension tables to begin with, so it seems a little off the mark to say that dimension tables change slowly compared to fact tables. Moreover, fact tables of transactions are event tables, and events don't change at all. So there is really nothing for the frequency of changes in dimension tables to be compared to.

So fact tables aren't the only tables which record facts. They are tables of events, but there are other kinds of facts. Dimension tables may be tables of dimensions, but only because "dimension" is so vague a term. Dimension tables are actually object tables or, in the case of slowly-changing dimensions, state tables; and so dimension tables record facts just as much as event tables do. It is equally much a fact that an object is in a given state as it is that an event has occurred.

Slowly-changing dimension tables aren't tables that change particularly slowly. They are state tables that record states of objects.

Dimension tables do more than provide "textual descriptions". The dimension tables in any star schema are tables of those objects that participate in the events recorded in the schema's fact table.

This is more than just a substitution of new terms for a set of terms that are already well-understood by their users. Because events, objects, and states are concepts in an explicit ontology, these new terms tell us what fact tables and dimension tables really are. The terminology of Kimball and Ross, as well-established as it is, does not tell us that.

There are two more components of star schemas which I believe need to be explained. They are what Kimball and Ross call *surrogate keys* and *natural keys*.

SURROGATE KEYS AND NATURAL KEYS

Kimball and Ross use the terms "surrogate key" and "natural key" in a way which fails to bring out what these two types of key represent. I need to clarify what these two kinds of keys really are, before going on to discuss bitemporal tables as an alternative to slowly-changing dimension (SCD) tables. So in the following discussion, I will use the term "K&R surrogate key" to represent Kimball and Ross's use of the term "surrogate key", and the term "K&R natural key" to represent Kimball and Ross's use of the term "natural key".

Kimball and Ross state that "(s)urrogate keys are simply integers that are assigned sequentially as needed to populate a dimension. . . . . The actual surrogate key value has no business significance." (p.98)

First of all, although they don't say so, it's clear that K&R surrogate keys are primary keys. It's also clear that K&R surrogate keys are single-column primary keys. They say that "(a) pseudo surrogate key created by simply gluing together the natural key with a time stamp (sic) is perilous." (p.100) This last statement also suggests that Kimball and Ross think that the primary value of surrogate keys is their use in slowly-changing dimensions. And indeed, elsewhere they say that "smart keys" may be appropriate for dimensions that change hardly at all, such as a Calendar dimension.

However, there is no reason why the values for surrogate keys must be "assigned sequentially". The only requirement is that those values be system-assigned. As such, they lack any business meaning, and consequently they can remain stable because there will never be any business reason to change them. This is not the case with natural keys.[3]

Kimball and Ross also state that ". . .(the) operational system identifier (is) known as the *natural key*." (p.98) But even by their own usage, this is not exactly correct. Operational system tables often

---

[3]A discussion of surrogate vs. natural keys, and the advantages of using surrogate keys, may be found in (Johnston, 2000a-c) which, as of late 2013, was still available in the archives at InformationManagement.com.

use surrogate primary keys themselves. If they do, they should also include, as a non-key attribute, the unique identifier used by the business. That unique identifier is what I have called the natural key of the table, and have referred to as the RefId of the rows in that table. So in cases where an operational system table has a surrogate-valued primary key, does "operational system identifier" refer to the primary key of the table, or to its natural key? Kimball and Ross don't say.

Suppose the operational system table is a history table. Its primary key might still be a surrogate-valued single column. In that case, as non-primary key attributes, the table should also include a natural key (RefId) and at least one timestamp. In fact, as discussed in Chapter 15, any history table is better off using a pair of timestamps to delimit a time period. So in any or all of these configurations, what is the K&R natural key of a history table in an operational system database? Kimball and Ross don't say.

As I noted above, a K&R natural key is also what I call a natural key. It is the unique identifier of an object which can change over time. That unique identifier may or may not be all or part of the primary key of the operational system table.

Kimball and Ross say that "One of the primary techniques for handling changes to dimension attributes relies on surrogate keys to handle the multiple profiles for a single natural key." (p.101) What are these "multiple profiles" for a "single natural key"? They are the multiple states of a single object, the object identified by that natural key.

It's worth quoting more extensively what Kimball and Ross say about natural and surrogate keys.

> In a dimension table with attribute change tracking, it's important to have an identifier that uniquely and reliably identifies the dimension entity across its attribute changes ..... If the dimension's natural keys are not absolutely protected and preserved over time, the ETL system needs to assign permanent durable identifiers, also known as *supernatural keys*. A persistent durable supernatural key ..... remains immutable for the life of the system. ..... And like the natural keys discussed earlier, the durable supernatural key is handled as a dimension attribute; it's not a replacement for the dimension table's surrogate primary key. (p.101)

We can paraphrase this as follows.

> In a state table, it's important to have an identifier that uniquely and reliably identifies the object whose state each row represents. ..... If the state table's RefIds are not absolutely protected and preserved over time, the ETL system needs to assign permanent durable RefIds. A persistent durable RefId ..... remains immutable for the life of the system. ..... And like the RefIds discussed earlier, the durable RefId is handled as a non-primary key column of its state table; it's not a replacement for the state table's primary key.

Of course, a RefId *couldn't* be a replacement for a state table's primary key, because it is the unique identifier of an object, not of a state of an object. By the same token, a supernatural key *couldn't* be a replacement for a dimension table's surrogate primary key.

What Kimball and Ross mean, I think, is that a K&R natural key (RefId) should never appear as part of the primary key of a slowly-changing dimension table (a state table). While I too prefer to include RefIds as non-key attributes in state tables, I note that the ISO 9075:2011 standard permits the primary key of a state table to consist of a RefId plus a time period, and uses that style of state table in most of its examples. So the ISO doesn't consider this technique to be as "perilous" as do Kimball and Ross. Nor does IBM, who utilizes it in DB2's implementation of state tables. Nor do I, who utilize it in the sample tables used in this book.

As we saw above, Kimball and Ross' account of fact tables and dimension tables doesn't provide any insight into what those tables are, and what they represent. Similarly, what they say about K&R surrogate keys and K&R natural keys doesn't give us any insight into what those keys are.

The significant thing about K&R surrogate keys is not that their values are system-assigned. It is that their values identify object states rather than objects, temporal intervals during which things like customers and products have a specific set of values for their attributes. As such, there is no reason why K&R surrogate keys must be surrogate-valued. And the significant thing about K&R natural keys is not that their values are not surrogate values, or even that their values are recognizable as identifiers to business users. It is that their values identify objects rather than object states, things that persist over time and through a series of state changes. As such, there is no reason why K&R natural keys can't be surrogate-valued.

A BITEMPORAL STAR SCHEMA

I have said that all dimension tables that require history, i.e. all slowly-changing dimension tables, should be implemented as bitemporal tables. To illustrate the expressive power and ease-of-use of bitemporal dimensions, I will use as an example a fact table of sales events and a dimension table of salespersons and sales teams. The dimension table is a recursive hierarchy, with salespersons belonging to sales teams, and with sales teams belonging to a single corporate root node. In my examples, I will use this table with its recursive hierarchy, rather than adopt any of the Kimball and Ross work-arounds for the recursion. Since SQL99, CTEs (common table expressions) have been defined to support recursive structures, and have been implemented in several DBMSs, so the work-arounds are not necessary.

An alternative representation of this Sales Group table is as a pair of tables. In that snowflake representation, a Sales Team table would be the parent table, and a Salesperson table would be the child table. Kimball and Ross, in their determination to avoid either snowflake structures or recursive ones, propose two major alternatives. One is a flattened hierarchy in which the entire sequence of parent rows for each child row is copied onto each child row. The other is a bridge table.

One thing to note about these Kimball and Ross recursion work-arounds is that no one other than a SQL expert should be allowed to write SQL directly against flattened hierarchies or bridge tables. They are not intuitive, and bridge tables in particular are difficult to navigate.

For those who would like to see an example scenario that uses a flattened hierarchy or a bridge table instead of a recursive hierarchy, I leave the construction of those parallel scenarios to the reader. Indeed, I recommend it. It will assure the reader than "official" flattened hierarchy or bridge table dimensions indeed cannot represent the information that can be represented in bitemporal tables, that this information gap exists whether a slowly changing dimension uses a recursive hierarchy, a flattened hierarchy or a bridge table.

Although the issue of how recursive hierarchies are represented in dimension tables is orthogonal to the issue of the inability of slowly-changing dimensions to persist the information that bitemporal tables persist, I would like the reader to notice the ease with which changes can be made to a recursive hierarchy, and the considerable difficulty in making those changes to a flattened hierarchy or a bridge table. I also note that maintaining flattened hierarchies and bridge tables is something that will require procedural code, with all its concomitant design, coding, testing and maintenance costs. Maintaining the normalized form of recursive hierarchies, by contrast, is something that can be done without procedural code, using only SQL.

All of the conclusions reached in this analysis will also apply, of course, to more typical star schemas in which there are several dimensions for the fact table and, in particular, a calendar dimension. I have chosen to simplify this example as much as possible, aware that the price paid for the simplification is a loss of real-world verisimilitude.

A BITEMPORAL DIMENSION CASE STUDY

Figure 18.1 is an object-level representation of a Sales Group dimension table. The nodes in this illustration represent objects, not states of objects. To represent states of objects in this example, we would have to use the diagrams developed in Chapter 8. Indeed, it would be another excellent exercise for the reader to draw bitemporal diagrams of these sample tables, and to note that there is no way to place the data in any slowly-changing dimension on these diagrams, since slowly-changing dimensions represent only one temporal dimension, not two.

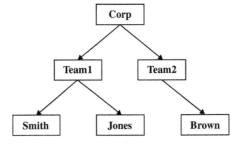

FIGURE 18.1

A Sales Group Hierarchy.

Figure 18.2 is a sample table representation of a bitemporal Sales Group dimension table (Dim-Sales-Group-B). It shows the state of the table at the start of the series of transactions we will discuss. The fact table of sales events (Fact-Sales-Event) for which this is the dimension table will be shown later.

```
Dim-Sales-Group-B
row     asr-tm        state-tm      sid snm    cat psfk
sg301 Jan14-9999    Jan14-9999    S00 Corp    -   ---
sg779 Jan14-9999    Jan14-9999    S01 Team-1  -   S00
sg828 Jan14-9999    Jan14-9999    S02 Team-2  -   S00
sg520 Jan14-9999    Jan14-9999    S16 Smith   1   S01
sg334 Jan14-9999    Jan14-9999    S37 Jones   2   S01
sg542 Jan14-9999    Jan14-9999    S26 Brown   1   S02
```

FIGURE 18.2

A Bitemporal Sales Group Dimension - 1.

The column *row* (i.e. the column named "row") is the primary key of the table. It is a surrogate-valued key (although, obviously, not one whose values are sequential integers). The next two columns are assertion time (*asr-tm*) and state time (*state-tm*). The column *sid*, in Kimball and Ross nomenclature, is the *durable identifier*. It is the identifier of the objects represented in the table. It identifies the corporation, Team 1, Team 2, Smith, Jones, and Brown. It is the RefId of the table. The columns *snm* and *cat* are, respectively, salesperson name and salesperson category. Finally, the column *psfk* is the recursive foreign key of the table.

The sample data starts its bitemporal existence on January 2014. We may assume that prior to that date, this was a nontemporal dimension, a type 1 SCD. A requirement was given to the IT department to begin keeping a complete history on sales groups and their salespersons, beginning in 2014. Since no history was maintained prior to that time, the rows in the dimension table start their bitemporal existence with a Henceforth default value for both assertion time and state time, as shown in Figure 18.2.

Dimension Update #1

It is Now() March 2014. Smith is being changed from category 1 to category 2, effective immediately. The bitemporal transaction is shown in Figure 18.3, and the results of the transaction in Figure 18.4.

```
UPDATE IN Dim-Sales-Group-B
SET cat = 2
WHERE sid = S16
```

FIGURE 18.3

A Bitemporal Update - 1.

```
Dim-Sales-Group-B
row    asr-tm        state-tm       sid snm    cat psfk
sg301 Jan14-9999    Jan14-9999     S00 Corp    -   ---
sg779 Jan14-9999    Jan14-9999     S01 Team-1  -   S00
sg828 Jan14-9999    Jan14-9999     S02 Team-2  -   S00
sg520 Jan14-Mar14   Jan14-9999     S16 Smith   1   S01
sg334 Jan14-9999    Jan14-9999     S37 Jones   2   S01
sg542 Jan14-9999    Jan14-9999     S26 Brown   1   S02
sg183 Mar14-9999    Jan14-Mar14    S16 Smith   1   S01
sg934 Mar14-9999    Mar14-9999     S16 Smith   2   S01
```

FIGURE 18.4

The Bitemporal Sales Group Dimension - 2.

The row sg520 was the currently asserted statement about Smith until this transaction completed. It was withdrawn because this transaction tells the database that Smith stopped being a category 1 salesperson on March 2014. That means that what sg520 in Figure 18.2 tells us is no longer correct, since its state-time period extends to 9999.

Instead, two things are now claimed to be true about Smith. The first is that he *was* a category 1 salesperson from January up to March 2014. The second is that he *is* a category 2 salesperson as of March 2014. The rows sg183 and sg934 make those currently asserted statements. Together they cover the same state-time period that row sg520 did. Their assertion-time period [Meets] that of the withdrawn row they are replacing. No information has been lost.

This is a prototypical bitemporal update. If a corresponding update were applied to a type 1 dimension table, the update would simply physically overwrite category 1 with category 2 on the one row representing Smith. But in that case, no information on the state of Smith prior to the update would have been preserved.

Dimension Update #2

It is Now() April 2014. We are told that Jones will be changed from category 2 to category 1, effective two months from now, i.e. beginning on June 2014. The bitemporal transaction is shown in Figure 18.5, and the results of the transaction in Figure 18.6.

```
UPDATE IN Dim-Sales-Group-B
IN STATE INTERVAL (Jun14, 9999)
SET cat = 1
WHERE sid = S37
```

FIGURE 18.5

A Bitemporal Update - 2.

```
Dim-Sales-Group-B
row    asr-tm       state-tm      sid snm     cat psfk
sg301 Jan14-9999  Jan14-9999   S00 Corp    -   ---
sg779 Jan14-9999  Jan14-9999   S01 Team-1  -   S00
sg828 Jan14-9999  Jan14-9999   S02 Team-2  -   S00
sg520 Jan14-Mar14 Jan14-9999   S16 Smith   1   S01
sg334 Jan14-Apr14 Jan14-9999   S37 Jones   2   S01
sg542 Jan14-9999  Jan14-9999   S26 Brown   1   S02
sg183 Mar14-9999  Jan14-Mar14  S16 Smith   1   S01
sg934 Mar14-9999  Mar14-9999   S16 Smith   2   S01
sg119 Apr14-9999  Jan14-Jun14  S37 Jones   2   S01
sg200 Apr14-9999  Jun14-9999   S37 Jones   1   S01
```

FIGURE 18.6

The Bitemporal Sales Group Dimension - 3.

This is a proactive update, one that does not take effect until sometime after the row is physically created. The first step is to withdraw row sg334 by ending its assertion-time period. (Withdrawing a row is what the standard theory calls *logically deleting* that row.) The second step is to add row sg119 to replace the part of sg334 that is not affected by the update. The final step is to add row sg200. This is the part of the original row that is affected by the update, and so the update is applied to it. Even though it is currently April 2014, the table correctly tells us that Jones will not become a category 1 salesperson until June.

Dimension Update #3

It is Now() August 2014. We have learned that Smith remained a category 1 salesperson until three months ago, i.e. until last May. The bitemporal transaction which records this new information is shown in Figure 18.7, and the results of that transaction are shown in Figure 18.8.

```
UPDATE IN Dim-Sales-Group-B
IN STATE INTERVAL (May14, 9999)
SET cat = 1
WHERE sid = S16
```

FIGURE 18.7

A Bitemporal Update - 3.

Note that this update corrects an error in the table. Prior to this transaction, the Sales Group table said that, in May, June and July of 2014, Smith was in category 2. After this transaction, the Sales Group table says that, in May, June and July of 2014, Smith was in category 1.

What this dimension table does, that no SCD can do, is to record the fact that this information was not available in the database until August, *and also* to record the fact that from March to August, what was available in the database, and what was presented as the truth about Smith for those three months, was the incorrect information that Smith was a category 2 salesperson during that time. The first fact is recorded by means of the assertion begin time on row sg204. The second fact is recorded by means of the assertion end time and the state description on row sg934.

The row sg934 correctly tells us that from March to August 2014, the table said that Smith was a category 2 salesperson from March onwards. That statement is now withdrawn. In its place, and covering the same extent of state time, row sg756 tells us that Smith was a category 2 salesperson from March to May, and row sg204 tells us that Smith was a category 1 salesperson from May onwards.

```
Dim-Sales-Group-B
row    asr-tm       state-tm     sid snm   cat psfk
sg301 Jan14-9999   Jan14-9999   S00 Corp   -   ---
sg779 Jan14-9999   Jan14-9999   S01 Team-1 -   S00
sg828 Jan14-9999   Jan14-9999   S02 Team-2 -   S00
sg520 Jan14-Mar14  Jan14-9999   S16 Smith  1   S01
sg334 Jan14-Apr14  Jan14-9999   S37 Jones  2   S01
sg542 Jan14-9999   Jan14-9999   S26 Brown  1   S02
sg183 Mar14-9999   Jan14-Mar14  S16 Smith  1   S01
sg934 Mar14-Aug14  Mar14-9999   S16 Smith  2   S01
sg119 Apr14-9999   Jan14-Jun14  S37 Jones  2   S01
sg200 Apr14-9999   Jun14-9999   S37 Jones  1   S01
sg756 Aug14-9999   Mar14-May14  S16 Smith  2   S01
sg204 Aug14-9999   May14-9999   S16 Smith  1   S01
```

FIGURE 18.8

The Bitemporal Sales Group Dimension - 4.

This correction will show up in various sales totals, such as by salesperson and category, or perhaps by salesperson and category within sales team. There are, in fact, three noteworthy sets of totals, not just two. One set of totals for Smith is based on what the table said, at the time of each sale, about what category and sales team Smith was in at the time of each sale.

A second set of totals are based on what the table currently says about what category and sales team Smith was in at the time of each sale. These totals, like the first ones, are based on the category and sales team Smith was in at the time of each sale he was credited with. But these totals will differ from the first set of totals if, at the time of any sale he was credited with, the table showed him in the wrong category and/or sales team.

A third set of totals are based on what the table currently says about what category and sales team Smith is in right now, which is after all the sales events have occurred.

Dimension Update #4

It is Now() September 2014. Jones will be moved from Team 1 to Team 2, effective next month. The result of the change is shown as an object diagram in Figure 18.10. The bitemporal transaction is shown in Figure 18.9, and the results of the transaction in Figure 18.11.

```
UPDATE IN Dim-Sales-Group-B
IN STATE INTERVAL (Oct14, 9999)
SET psfk = S02
WHERE sid = S37
```

FIGURE 18.9

A Bitemporal Update - 4.

This transaction carries out what is called a "prune and graft" operation in graph theory. The node for Jones is "pruned" from the Team 1 "branch" and "grafted" onto the Team 2 branch.

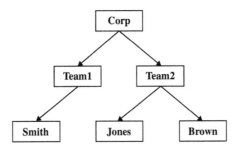

FIGURE 18.10

The Sales Group Hierarchy - 2.

The effect of this transaction on the Sales Group table is shown in Figure 18.11.

The update will ignore row sg334, even though its state time includes the state-time interval specified on the transaction. It will ignore row sg334 because that row is in past assertion time. It will ignore row sg119 because that row's state-time period falls outside the state-time interval specified on the transaction. Thus, although several rows have sid = S37, it is only row sg200 which is still in current assertion time, and is also contained in the transaction's state-time interval.

This is no accident. For any referent, and any point or period of state time, there can never be more than one row that is currently asserted.

```
Dim-Sales-Group-B
row    asr-tm        state-tm      sid snm    cat  psfk
sg301  Jan14-9999    Jan14-9999    S00 Corp   -    ---
sg779  Jan14-9999    Jan14-9999    S01 Team-1 -    S00
sg828  Jan14-9999    Jan14-9999    S02 Team-2 -    S00
sg520  Jan14-Mar14   Jan14-9999    S16 Smith  1    S01
sg334  Jan14-Apr14   Jan14-9999    S37 Jones  2    S01
sg542  Jan14-9999    Jan14-9999    S26 Brown  1    S02
sg183  Mar14-9999    Jan14-Mar14   S16 Smith  1    S01
sg934  Mar14-Aug14   Mar14-9999    S16 Smith  2    S01
sg119  Apr14-9999    Jan14-Jun14   S37 Jones  2    S01
sg200  Apr14-Sep14   Jun14-9999    S37 Jones  1    S01
sg756  Aug14-9999    Mar14-May14   S16 Smith  2    S01
sg204  Aug14-9999    May14-9999    S16 Smith  1    S01
sg692  Sep14-9999    Jun14-Oct14   S37 Jones  1    S01
sg177  Sep14-9999    Oct14-9999    S37 Jones  2    S02
```

FIGURE 18.11

The Bitemporal Sales Group Dimension - 5.

The prune and graft is carried out like this. First, row sg200 is withdrawn, because the new truth about Jones from June 2014 onwards is that he belonged to Team 1 until October, at which time he was switched to Team 2. Next, row sg692 is added to restore the information about the state of Jones prior to next month. Finally, row sg177 is added. It supplies the information that Jones will be part of Team 2 beginning next month.

ASIDE

Suppose that the Sales Group hierarchy went several levels deeper, that, for example, there were a total of four more levels and twenty more nodes under Jones as of September 2014. Note that none of the nodes at any of the levels would have to be updated to reflect this change to Jones. Totals for all of those nodes would automatically roll up to Team 2 starting in October, as they should. All of those nodes would be moved to Team 2 by the single action of updating the foreign key on the node for Jones to point to Team 2.

Note that Kimball and Ross claim that it is "impractical to maintain organizations as type 2 slowly-changing dimension attributes because changing the key for a high-level node would ripple key changes down to the bottom of the tree". (p.216)

However, if the ripple effect they are referring to is the need to individually update a foreign key on every row from that high-level node "down to the bottom of the tree", then they are mistaken. On the contrary, by maintaining any recursive hierarchy, such as salespersons and sales teams, or organizational structures, in its normalized recursive form, changes do *not* have to be individually applied "down to the bottom of the tree". In a table with a recursive foreign key, changing the foreign key on one node not only moves that node under a new parent node. It automatically moves every node under it as well. None of those other nodes need to be updated. That is what a prune and graft operation does.

On the other hand, if the ripple effect they are referring to is the fact that by physically changing the foreign key on one row, all rows under that row are automatically moved to the new location indicated by the new foreign key on the high-level node, that is hardly "impractical". On the contrary, the ability to relocate millions or more rows in a subtree to a new location by changing one pointer on the one root node of that subtree, is highly practical. So the point that Kimball and Ross appear to be making is a point against their own recursive hierarchy work-arounds, and in favor of using the normalized representation of a recursive hierarchy in dimension tables.

Dimension Update #5

It is Now() December 2014. We must correct a pair of errors in the data. The table currently says that Jones was moved from Team 2 to Team 1 as of last October and, at the same time, was promoted to salesperson category 2. We just now learned that these two changes did indeed take place on October, but that both were reversed for November, and then reinstated beginning in December.

The bitemporal transaction is shown in Figure 18.12, and the results of the transaction in Figure 18.13.

```
UPDATE IN Dim-Sales-Group-B
IN STATE INTERVAL (Nov14, Dec14)
SET psfk = S01, cat = 1
WHERE sid = S37
```

FIGURE 18.12

A Bitemporal Update - 5.

The result of the change is shown in Figure 18.13.

```
Dim-Sales-Group-B
```

row	asr-tm	state-tm	sid	snm	cat	psfk
sg301	Jan14-9999	Jan14-9999	S00	Corp	-	---
sg779	Jan14-9999	Jan14-9999	S01	Team-1	-	S00
sg828	Jan14-9999	Jan14-9999	S02	Team-2	-	S00
sg520	Jan14-Mar14	Jan14-9999	S16	Smith	1	S01
sg334	Jan14-Apr14	Jan14-9999	S37	Jones	2	S01
sg542	Jan14-9999	Jan14-9999	S26	Brown	1	S02
sg183	Mar14-9999	Jan14-Mar14	S16	Smith	1	S01
sg934	Mar14-Aug14	Mar14-9999	S16	Smith	2	S01
sg119	Apr14-9999	Jan14-Jun14	S37	Jones	2	S01
sg200	Apr14-Sep14	Jun14-9999	S37	Jones	1	S01
sg756	Aug14-9999	Mar14-May14	S16	Smith	2	S01
sg204	Aug14-9999	May14-9999	S16	Smith	1	S01
sg692	Sep14-9999	Jun14-Oct14	S37	Jones	1	S01
sg177	Sep14-Dec14	Oct14-9999	S37	Jones	2	S02
sg345	Dec14-9999	Oct14-Nov14	S37	Jones	2	S02
sg809	Dec14-9999	Nov14-Dec14	S37	Jones	1	S01
sg156	Dec14-9999	Dec14-9999	S37	Jones	2	S02

FIGURE 18.13

The Bitemporal Sales Group Dimension - 6.

Row sg177 is withdrawn effective December by the transaction because we now know that it is not true that Jones was in Team 2 in November. That row, like all withdrawn rows in bitemporal tables, physically remains in the table. The information it contains — that from September up to December 2014, the table said that Smith belonged to Team 2 from October 2014 until further notice — remains in the table, accessible to queries.

Three rows together replace row sg177, and each of them "takes over" as a current assertion at the same moment that sg177 is withdrawn. The middle of those three rows — row sg809 — is the one that contains the correction. The first and third of those rows — rows sg345 and sg156 — restore the assertions that, except for November, Jones has indeed been on Team 2 since October, in category 2, and remains on that team and in that category until further notice.

If we are asked what team Jones belonged to in, say, November of that year, there are two answers. Originally, the table said that Jones was on Team 2 in November; but currently it says that Jones was on Team 1 that month. More precisely, if a query about what the database currently says what sales team Jones was on in November 2014 was submitted anytime from September through November, the answer would be "Team 2". But for any query submitted anytime from December onwards, the answer will be "Team 1". But because of the expressive power of bitemporal data, we can always recreate the response to a past query. If it is now December 2014, for example, we can recreate the query run in, say September, that asked "what team will Jones be on next month, according to current data"? We simple issue a query with these two WHERE clause predicates:[4]

```
WHERE asr-tm CONTAINS Sep14 AND state-tm CONTAINS Oct14
```

If the question actually asked is simply "What team was Jones on in November 2014?", it might be a question about what the database said at the time the question was asked, since that is always our best knowledge, at that point in time, about what things were, are, or will be like. On the other hand, the business user may want to see the information she is requesting to be shown to her on a rerun of a report that was originally run last October, and wants that report reproduced exactly as it was originally run. In that case, the question is not about what team the database currently says Jones was on last November. It's about what team the database said, last October, that Jones was on last November.

FACT TABLE ANALYSIS

It is Now() January 2015. Figure 18.14 shows the Fact-Sales table as of that date. The column whose heading is "row", as indicated, is the primary key of the table. Its values are surrogate values. Like Kimball and Ross, I believe that the best primary key for any table is a single column with surrogate values.

To keep the example simple, I have not shown time periods on the fact table. Instead, *s-tm* indicates the point in time on which the sales event took place. The column *s-amt*, of course, is the amount associated with the sale. It is the only metric on this simplified fact table.

With bitemporal dimension tables, any bitemporal cell, i.e. any set of bitemporal coordinates, can be specified. So we can see the accumulation of metric totals for any bitemporal dimension, and any combination of bitemporal dimensions with other dimensions. We simply need to specify the temporal coordinates of the bitemporal cell, i.e. the point in assertion time and the point in state time we are interested in.

In this fact table, there are three bitemporal coordinates that are given a privileged representation. I will call them *then-then*, *now-then*, and *now-now*. The first element in each pair represents assertion time, and the second element represents state time. "Then" means "at the time of the sale", and "now" means "now".

---

[4]The ISO standard, however, does not have a time period datatype, and uses begin and end points in time instead. In that format, the predicates would be: WHERE (abtm ≤ Sep14 AND Sep14 < aetm) AND (sbtm ≤ Oct14 AND Oct14 < setm).

```
Fact-Sales-Event
row   s-tm  s-amt  ttfk   flag1  ntfk   flag2  nnfk   reffk
s143  Feb14 $355   sg334  y      sg119  n      sg156  S37
s336  Feb14 $298   sg542  y      sg542  y      sg542  S26
s307  Apr14 $150   sg934  y      sg756  n      sg204  S16
s521  May14 $572   sg119  y      sg119  n      sg156  S37
s464  Jun14 $224   sg200  y      sg692  n      sg156  S37
s376  Jun14 $476   sg934  n      sg204  y      sg204  S16
s462  Jul14 $390   sg542  y      sg542  y      sg542  S26
s500  Aug14 $721   sg204  y      sg204  y      sg204  S16
s922  Sep14 $126   sg204  y      sg204  y      sg204  S16
s771  Oct14 $778   sg177  y      sg177  y      sg156  S37
s556  Oct14 $624   sg177  y      sg177  y      sg156  S37
s302  Nov14 $334   sg177  n      sg809  y      sg809  S37
s318  Dec14 $417   sg542  y      sg542  y      sg542  S26
s491  Dec14 $492   sg156  y      sg156  y      sg156  S37
```

FIGURE 18.14

The Sales Event Fact Table.

Column *ttfk* represents the then-then bitemporal coordinate. By using *s-tm*, the time the sale took place, as the value for both clock ticks, *ttfk* selects a row for the salesperson credited with the sale. That is the row that tells us who the database then said was associated with the sale, and what state that salesperson was then in. For example, for sales event s143, that row is sg334.

The referent of each row is a salesperson, and the referent identifier is *sid*. Each row represents a bitemporal interval during which its referent was/is/will be in a specific state. So, for example, row sg119 tells us that starting in April 2014, the database said that, for the five months starting in January 2014, the salesperson identified as sid S37 was named "Jones", was a category 2 salesperson, and was on Team 2. Row sg809 tells us that starting in December 2014, the database said that, in November 2014, this same salesperson was a category 1 salesperson and was on Team 1.[5]

Column *ntfk* represents the now-then temporal coordinate. By using Now() as the value for "now", and *s-tm* as the value for "then", *ntfk* selects a row for the salesperson credited with the sale. That is the row that tells us what the table currently says that the state of the salesperson then was. For example, for sales event s143, that row is sg119.

Column *nnfk* represents the now-now temporal coordinate. By using Now() as the value for both clock ticks, *nnfk* selects a row for the salesperson credited with the sale. That is the row that tells us what the table currently says that the state of that salesperson currently is. For example, for sales event s143, that row is sg156.

The column *flag1* provides important additional information. *Flag1* compares the state descriptions of the then-then row and the now-then row for the salesperson and state description associated with that sale at the time the sale took place. If flag1 = "y", then the two state descriptions about that single point in time are identical. Since the now-then row is the currently asserted row about that point in state-time, the flag indicates that the sales event is still associated with the salesperson

---

[5]At any point in time, the database will "say" that a statement is true if and only if the corresponding row's assertion-time period is current at that point in time. So the colloquialism "the database said, at time t_n" means the same thing as "was asserted at time t_n". In other words, the totality of what a database "says", at any time t_n, is the collection of the statements made by all the rows which are asserted at that point in time.

and state description it was originally associated with. Conversely, if flag1 = "n", then a correction has been made. A different salesperson and/or salesperson state is now associated with that sale and that point in time.

So *flag1* tells us whether or not a correction has been made. *Flag2*, on the other hand, tells us if the current state of the salesperson currently associated with that sale is the same as the state of that salesperson on the date of the sale.

For example, the then-then Sales Group row for sale s143 is:

[sg334|Jan14-Apr14|Jan14-9999|S37|Jones|2|S01]

But we can see that, as of April 2014, this row was withdrawn. Between January and April, the sales amount for this sale would be credited to Jones, to category 2 and to Team 1. But starting in April, what happened? The following two rows from Dim-Sales-Group-B show us:

[sg119|Apr14-9999|Jan14-Jun14|S37|Jones|2|S01]

[sg200|Apr14-Sep14|Jun14-9999|S37|Jones|1|S01]

Jones changed from a category 2 salesperson to a category 1 salesperson on June 2014. So from January to June, there was no change. Therefore, in spite of the fact that sg334 was withdrawn, the sales event was not affected. The sales event occurred on February of that year, and as *flag1* indicates, on that clock tick, the two state descriptions agree. Therefore, if code has retrieved either sg119 or sg200 in association with sales event s143, *flag1* tells us that we don't have to retrieve the other row if we want the information provided by that other row; the information will be the same.

Flag2 gives us different information. The now-now row for sale s143 is sg156.

[sg156|Dec14-9999|Dec14-9999|S37|Jones|2|S02]

sg156 tells us what we currently believe the salesperson currently associated with that sale is currently like. And *flag2* tells us that something about that salesperson has changed. We can see what that change is. At the time of the sale, Jones was on Team 1. But currently, he is on Team 2.

Of course, because this is a bitemporal dimension, we are not limited to just these three perspectives on the salesperson associated with each sale. We can pick any point in assertion time and any point in state time, and the bitemporal table will tell us, first, whether or not the database said/says, at that point in assertion time, that the salesperson existed/exists/will exist at that point in state time. And if the salesperson did/does/will exist at that point in state time, the bitemporal dimension table tells us what salesperson category he is in, and what sales team he is assigned to.

SUMMARY OF THE CASE STUDY

This bitemporal dimension will answer to any set of bitemporal coordinates whatsoever, for any Sales Group referent. That is, for any set of bitemporal coordinates, it will say whether or not the database, at that (first coordinate) time, said that the designated referent existed at that (second coordinate) time and, if it did exist at that time, what state the referent was in at that time. That is, it will say what the sid, name, salesperson category, and parent referent was, for that referent, at that time.

But in this case study, I have privileged three bitemporal coordinates by including three foreign keys in the fact table. Say that the clock tick on which the sale took place is stm_x. Then the coordinates for the first foreign key — *ttfk* — are (stm$_x$, stm$_x$). The coordinates for the second foreign key — *ntfk* — are (Now(), stm$_x$), and the coordinates for the third foreign key — *nnfk* — are (Now(), Now()).

The totals for these sales, by category, at these three points in bitemporal space, are shown in Figure 18.15.

Salesperson Categories			Then/Then		Now/Then		Now/Now	
row	**s-tm**	**s-amt**	**Cat 1**	**Cat 2**	**Cat 1**	**Cat 2**	**Cat 1**	**Cat 2**
s143	Feb2014	$355		sg334		sg119		sg156
s336	Feb2014	$298	sg542		sg542		sg542	
s307	Apr2014	$150		sg934		sg756	sg204	
s521	May2014	$572		sg119		sg119		sg156
s464	Jun2014	$224	sg200		sg692			sg256
s376	Jun2014	$476		sg934	sg204		sg204	
s462	Jul2014	$390	sg542		sg542		sg542	
s500	Aug2014	$721	sg204		sg204		sg204	
s922	Sep2014	$126	sg204		sg204		sg204	
s771	Oct2014	$778		sg177		sg177		sg156
s556	Oct2014	$624		sg177		sg177		sg156
s302	Nov2014	$334		sg177	sg809		sg809	
s318	Dec2014	$417	sg542		sg542		sg542	
s491	Dec2014	$492		sg156		sg156		sg156
		Totals:	**$2,176**	**$3,781**	**$2,986**	**$2,971**	**$2,912**	**$3,045**

FIGURE 18.15

Three Sets of Salesperson Category Totals.

Comparing then-then and now-then totals, $810 was reallocated from category 2 to category 1. Of that, sale s376 accounted for $476, and sale s302 for $334. These reallocations were due to corrections. The data had originally said that, allocated as of the point in time at which each sale occurred, $2,176 belonged in category 1 and $3,781 belonged in category 2. After the corrections, the data says that, allocated as of the point in time at which each sale occurred, $2,986 belongs in category 1 and $2,971 belongs in category 2.

One category correction was made with transaction #3. This correction changed salesperson Smith from category 2 to category 1 for the months of May, June and July 2014. This affected sale s376, which was credited to Smith, and which took place in June.

The other category correction was made with transaction #5. This correction changed salesperson Jones from category 2 to category 1 (and also from Team 2 to Team 1) for the month of November 2014. This affected sale s302, which was credited to Jones, and which took place in November.

Comparing now-then and now-now totals, there is $74 less in category 1 and $74 more in category 2. Of that, $150 from sale s307 that was allocated to category 2 as of the point in time of each sale, is now allocated to category 1 based on the category each salesperson is currently in. $224 from sale s464 that was allocated to category 1 as of the point in time of each sale, is now allocated to category 2 based on the category each salesperson is currently in. These reallocations were due to changes in the salesperson category for Smith and Jones, respectively. Based on the categories the salespersons were in at the time of each sale they were credited with (taking corrections into account), $2,986 belongs in category 1 and $2,971 belongs in category 2. Based on the categories the salespersons are currently in, $2,912 belongs in category 1 and $3,045 belongs in category 2.

The totals for these sales, by sales team, at these three points in bitemporal space, are shown in Figure 18.16.

Sales Teams			Then/Then		Now/Then		Now/Now	
row	s-tm	s-amt	Team 1	Team 2	Team 1	Team 2	Team 1	Team 2
s143	Feb2014	$355		sg334		sg119		sg156
s336	Feb2014	$298	sg542		sg542		sg542	
s307	Apr2014	$150		sg934		sg756	sg204	
s521	May2014	$572		sg119		sg119		sg156
s464	Jun2014	$224	sg200		sg692			sg156
s376	Jun2014	$476		sg934	sg204		sg204	
s462	Jul2014	$390	sg542		sg542		sg542	
s500	Aug2014	$721	sg204		sg204		sg204	
s922	Sep2014	$126	sg204		sg204		sg204	
s771	Oct2014	$778		sg177		sg177		sg156
s556	Oct2014	$624		sg177		sg177		sg156
s302	Nov2014	$334		sg177	sg809		sg809	
s318	Dec2014	$417	sg542		sg542		sg542	
s491	Dec2014	$492		sg156		sg156		sg156
		Totals:	$2,176	$3,781	$2,986	$2,971	$2,912	$3,045

FIGURE 18.16

Three Sets of Sales Team Totals.

BITEMPORAL DIMENSIONS VERSUS SLOWLY-CHANGING DIMENSIONS

Nothing like this is available with slowly-changing dimensions. The only case that could now be made for using a slowly-changing dimension instead of a bitemporal dimension is that the complete information provided by the bitemporal form of the dimension isn't needed, and that the cost of using a slowly-changing dimension is less than the cost of using the bitemporal form of that dimension.

But neither point can withstand scrutiny. First of all, where is the business that would prefer to have less information rather than more information? In particular, where is the business that will be satisfied with a solution that cannot guarantee the same results when a report is rerun at a later time? And yet even with the new slowly-changing dimension types that Kimball and Ross introduced in 2013, none of those types can reproduce the same results every time a query is run when that query accesses data about the past that was subsequently corrected.[6]

---

[6]The type 5 SCD provides a limited exception to this, because type 5 SCDs preserve the original, uncorrected dimension row even if a later row says something different about what a dimension object (i.e. the thing that a "durable key" identifies) was like at that past point in state time. This, however, is a far cry from the unlimited ability of bitemporal dimensions to respond to a query about *any point* in the state-time history of an object as the database recorded that information at *any point* in the assertion-time history of that database.

As to the point about cost, where can slowly-changing dimensions produce the same information at lower cost than an equivalent bitemporal dimension? For one thing, access to bitemporal data is now built into the SQL language, as defined in the ISO 9075:2011 and TSQL2 standards. The reader should consider the cost of updating a bitemporal dimension table with these straightforward SQL statements, and compare it to the cost of updating an SCD-implementation of that same dimension with ETL code. Hand-coded updates of SCDs cannot compete on a cost basis with the ability to update bitemporal dimensions with simple SQL statements for which the DBMS manages the temporal complexity.

The other point about cost, that might seem to favor SCDs over bitemporal dimensions, is the amount of disk space required to store the dimension. Most SCD types clearly attempt to minimize the amount of space required to store the limited history supported by those types.[7]

The simple response to this point is that the disk storage required for dimensional data is already a non-issue, except possibly for Alice-in-Wonderland scenarios. First of all, dimension tables consume only a small fraction of the storage that fact tables consume, often several orders of magnitude less. Secondly, classical character-set business data about objects and events is becoming an increasingly insignificant part of the total data that an enterprise is willing to persist, often *many* orders of magnitude less than the storage required for Big Data.

Finally, there is the simple fact that, in late 2013, the cost of a terabyte of disk storage was about forty dollars! Where is the realistic use case for a dimension so large that it is worth bothering about the extra storage that it will consume as a bitemporal dimension compared to some space-saving SCD type?

In addition, any reduced-terabyte cost savings must be paid for with the cost of designing the SCD, writing, debugging and maintaining the ETL code required to transform source data into data that will populate the SCD, and writing, debugging and maintaining the native SQL or tool-assisted code required to extract useful information from the SCD. Any incremental costs over and above the cost of deploying a bitemporal and SQL-standard solution, most of whose functionality is already built in to major DBMSs like DB2 and Teradata, must be counted as offsets to any terabyte-based cost savings. The major part of those incremental costs, of course, is the man-hour cost of the IT personnel required to design, implement, use and support the SCD and its associated ETL. Clearly, even a single man-hour of incremental effort more than offsets the cost savings of a terabyte of storage saved by the SCD.

Are the incremental costs of space-saving SCD types insignificant? Clearly they are not. For example, besides the incremental man-hour costs of all types of SCDs, another cost of the SCD technique of storing past values of selected attributes in additional columns of a dimension lies in the inflexibility of the technique. If the business wants to store two past values instead of one, the dimension must be redesigned and ETL rewritten. If the business wants to store a past value of another attribute, the dimension must again be redesigned and ETL again rewritten.

Another significant incremental cost of most SCD types lies in their complex design. These include the use of bridge tables, pathstring attributes, mini-dimensions, outrigger dimensions, dual-type dimensions, and the various permutations and combinations of these techniques. SCDs which use these techniques will have immensely higher design, coding and maintenance costs than will DBMS-supported bitemporal dimensions.

---

[7]I refer to disk space. But, of course, other forms of persistent storage are increasingly replacing spinning disks. The relevant fact, however, is that the cost of persistent storage in any form is declining at a precipitous rate.

In addition, fact-dimension structures which use SCDs that employ these techniques are effectively isolated within their OLAP tools. No business user should attempt to query such rococo dimensional structures. By contrast, the SQL standard defines straightforward bitemporal queries, and major DBMSs now support those queries. So the use of bitemporal dimensions in fact-dimension structures, instead of SCDs, has the additional benefit that it makes access to those dimensions and that structure available to native SQL, written by business users.

Kimball and Ross introduced a new and extended set of slowly-changing dimension types in the 2013 edition of their toolkit book. But slowly-changing dimensions preserve and make available less information than do bitemporal dimensions. The cost of slowly-changing dimensions is much higher than the cost of bitemporal dimensions. Finally, the disk space savings that slowly-changing dimensions may provide, in comparison to bitemporal dimensions, is insignificant. Kimball and Ross introduced these new SCD types just in time for them to become obsolete. There is no use case, anywhere, that can justify the continued use of SCDs in preference to bitemporal dimensions.

GLOSSARY LIST

assertion time	instance	state table
assertion-time period	life history	state time
attribute	object	state
bitemporal cell	ontology	temporal interval
bitemporal table	participate in	thing
change	property	time period
clock tick	referent	transaction
correction	relationship	type
event table	semantic	universe of discourse
event	interoperability	withdraw
fact	state description	

KIMBALL AND ROSS TERMS

Following is a list of Kimball and Ross technical terms used in this chapter.

bridge table	natural key	slowly-changing
business process	object	dimension
conformed dimensions	operational database	smart key
cumulative snapshot	operational system	snapshot
dimension table	identifier	snowflake
dual-type dimension	outrigger dimension	star schema
durable identifier	pathstring attribute	supernatural key
fact table	periodic snapshot	surrogate key
flattened hierarchy	pseudo surrogate key	unique identifier
mini-dimension	SCD	

TIME, TYPES AND THE FUTURE OF RELATIONAL DATABASES

19

Relational databases associate types with the mathematical structures of tables and columns, resulting in a framework of existentially-quantified statement schemas, and instantiations of those schemas represented as rows in those tables. But those types are represented, in today's databases, simply as suggestive names to which, in a logical data model, free-form text "definitions" may be attached. Types are definitely second-class citizens in relational databases.

However, we have done quite well with this limited conceptual framework. Relational databases are the principal form in which the business data of an enterprise is persisted. I begin with a summary description of that framework, expressed with the concepts of the Relational Paradigm. The rest of this chapter will describe extensions to that framework, and to its implementation in relational databases, that will significantly enhance the expressive power of those databases.

In today's relational databases:

1. Each row of data in a relational table is an instantiation of the statement schema for that table, and each row is identified by a primary key.
2. The thing referred to by each row is an instance of the type represented by the table, and each thing referred to is represented by a referent identifier.
3. The attributes of those things are instances of the types represented by the non-surrogate-valued columns in those statement schemas.
4. The referent of each row is the thing one of whose states is the subject of the statement made by the row.
5. Each attribute is a predicate in that statement.
6. Each predicate is an instance of the type represented by the column of its attribute.
7. The combination of a row's referent identifier and state-time period identifies each temporal state of each thing. In conventional tables, the state-time period is implicit. Each time a row in a conventional table is accessed, its state time takes on the value of Henceforth determined by the then-current moment in time.

To this current framework I recommend the following three enhancements.

1. First, I recommend that the bitemporal theory of data be extended to become a *tritemporal* theory, and that the Asserted Versioning concept of assertions and withdrawals be understood

as *speech acts* that persons or groups of persons make during specific periods of time. In the first section below, I sketch such a tritemporal theory of time.

2. Second, I recommend that an enterprise-level instantiation of the Relational Paradigm Ontology be formally expressed, together with constructs to link the application-specific tables, rows and columns of specific databases in the enterprise to that ontology. In the second section below, I sketch a framework that can be used by all application databases to achieve that linkage.

3. Third, I recommend that the statement schema of each normalized table be managed as the union of all and only those *atomic statement schemas* whose referent types are identical. From this point of view, normalized relational tables are collections of *binary tables* each of which associate one attribute with one referent, one predicate with one subject. In the third section below, I sketch a theory of atomic statements and binary tables in which relational tables are views over the unions of sets of those binary tables.

TRITEMPORAL DATA AND STATEMENT PROVENANCE

Data is managed in order to preserve important information and make it available when it is needed. As we have seen, that information exists in the form of full instantiations of existentially-quantified statements, i.e. statements that something exists, during an (implicitly or explicitly) specified period of time, in a specified state.

But these statements are not the same thing as the rows which are their inscriptions. The same statement may exist as an inscription in several of an enterprise's databases. It may seem that when we no longer wish to assert that a statement is true, we can simply delete the statement. But in fact, all that we will be deleting is an inscription of that statement. If there happen to be other inscriptions of that same statement, that deletion will not delete those other inscriptions. And as long as there is even one inscription of an asserted statement in the production databases of an enterprise, that statement has not been removed from the set of statements asserted by that enterprise. It will be the job of the end-user IT staff to find the other inscriptions of any statement that the enterprise no longer wishes to assert and, if there are any, to delete them as well.[1] And all of this, of course, should be done as a single atomic unit of work.

The problem of managing multiple inscriptions of one statement is not restricted to single enterprises. Statements have an authoritative source which may or may not be the enterprise itself. If it is not, then what should happen when that authoritative source wishes to withdraw a statement it has made? Clearly, all the derivative copies of the original inscription of that statement, in all downstream databases across all downstream enterprises, should also be deleted. More precisely, we should be able to define a multi-enterprise *statement space* within which the act of deleting an inscription of a statement should trigger a process in which all downstream inscriptions of the same statement are also deleted.

---

[1] Of course, and as always, to delete the inscription of a statement in a bitemporal table is to end the assertion-time period of that statement on that inscription. And to delete the assertion of that statement by the enterprise, *all* inscriptions under the management of that enterprise must be deleted in this manner.

But we currently have no means to do this because we have never bothered to create and maintain a means of managing the dynamic *provenance* of a statement, a provenance which is added to every time a new inscription of that statement is created or moved about. As we will see, the first step in implementing the capability to track *statement provenance* is to represent statements as managed objects distinct from their inscriptions, with a one to many relationship between the statement and its inscriptions.

It is not surprising that the standard theory of bitemporal data does not distinguish statements from their inscriptions. Relational theory itself, as originally developed by Dr. Ted Codd and as continually deepened and extended by decades of computer science work, does not make this distinction. This is one thing I found wrong in the standard theory of bitemporal data, from the beginning of my interest in temporal data, and that, by extension, I now find wrong in standard relational theory.

Based on the fact that DBMSs manage rows of data, but do not directly manage the statements that those rows represent, I have, up to now, accepted the standard theory's premise that there are only two temporal dimensions applicable to the management of relational databases. I have differed from the standard theory primarily in what I have interpreted one of those dimensions to be.

Specifically, the standard theory's transaction time is a time associated with *inscriptions*, a time which tells us when each inscription was initially created and when, if ever, that inscription was marked as deleted. But Asserted Versioning's assertion time is a time associated with *statements* — with when a statement represented by an inscription was first asserted to be true and when, if ever, the assertion of that statement was withdrawn.

Since the standard theory operates on the tacit assumption that statements and inscriptions are one-to-one, and since up to this point I have not challenged that assumption, my re-interpretation of this temporal dimension did not alter anything about how standard theory DBMSs manage bitemporal data.[2] It did, however, lead me to propose an *extension* to the standard theory's account of that temporal dimension. That extension was to replace the Six-Fold Way of the standard theory with the Nine-Fold Way of Asserted Versioning, thereby introducing future assertion (transaction) time to the standard theory.

And here we see the reason why future assertion (transaction) time was never recognized by computer scientists. A *transaction-time period* on a row provides information about that *inscription*. And so no row's transaction-time period could begin in the future, because that would be to say that the row would not begin to exist until after it already did exist in the table. But an *assertion-time period* on a row provides information about the *statement* physically represented by an inscription. And a row's assertion-time period *can* begin in the future, because that would be only to say that the statement made by that inscription would not be asserted to be a true statement until sometime after that inscription was written down. And there is nothing wrong with that. It happens in ordinary language all the time.

---

[2]I said that the standard theory of bitemporal data "operates on the tacit assumption that statements and inscriptions are one-to-one", which does emphasize the point that they are, of course, *not* one-to-one. But it might be more accurate to say that the standard theory, like *all* of database theory, never concerned itself with anything other than data, i.e. than inscriptions. By interpreting those inscriptions as statements, human beings record information as data and retrieve information from that data. But computer science never thought it had anything to do with that interpretive activity. In this chapter, I disagree. In this chapter, I try to show how we can use data to manage statements as semantic objects, distinct from their individual inscriptions.

INSCRIPTION TIME, STATE TIME, SPEECH ACT TIME

Inscription time, one of the tritemporal dimensions I referred to above, begins when a row is physically created. It ends when a row is marked as physically deleted. The transaction time of the standard theory substituted logical deletion for physical deletion (in order to preserve history), but was otherwise a concept of inscription time. In my Extended Relational Paradigm Metamodel ("the metamodel", for short), shown in Figures 19.2, 19.3 and 19.4, inscriptions are associated with the actions of persons or groups of persons. The first inscription of a statement, in a defined multi-database inscription space, is associated with a *create* action. Subsequent inscriptions are associated with *copy*, *move*, and *delete* actions.

State time, another of the tritemporal dimensions I referred to above, is, as we know, the time the statement is about. It is the time that the referent of the statement was/is/will be in the state ascribed to it by the statement. Since nothing can be in two states at the same time, a statement is uniquely identified by a referent identifier (RefId) and a state-time period.

Statement time, as shown in the statement time column of the Statement-Schema metadata table in Figures 19.2 and 19.4, is the time that extends from the earliest to the latest inscription of that statement. This information could be derived from other data already available in the metamodel. Nonetheless, I have recorded it as a column in the Statement-Schema metadata table, for convenient access to so useful a piece of information. But statement time is *not* one of the three temporal dimensions of a tritemporal theory of time. It is a time period derived entirely from inscription time.

Speech act time is the third of the tritemporal dimensions. It is what Asserted Versioning originally called *assertion time*. But I now recognize that asserting a statement and withdrawing an assertion are not the only two relationships people can have to statements. They can also have other *propositional attitude* relationships such as believing or doubting a statement, and the expressions of such propositional attitudes about statements are also speech acts. So asserting that a statement is true, and withdrawing an assertion, are speech acts, as are expressions of other propositional attitudes. They are some of those things that, as Austin said, people *do* with words. The speech acts I have explicitly included in the metamodel, besides asserting and withdrawing a statement, are assenting to or dissenting from the assertion of a statement, and noticing a statement. One asserts a statement as the author of the statement. One assents to, dissents from, or takes notice of, a statement made by someone else.

Since speech acts are the actions of persons, the metamodel relativizes this temporal dimension to persons (or groups of persons). One person might assent to a statement at the same time (or at any other Allen relationship related time) that another person might dissent from that same statement.

Speech acts are implemented, as managed objects, in the Speech-Act associative table in this metamodel.

ONTOLOGIZING RELATIONAL DATABASES

What we know, we express in statements. Each statement made by a row in a relational table picks out a particular, and says something about it. If we didn't know what type the particular was, we wouldn't know what the statement meant. The statement "This frobble is over seven feet tall" doesn't tell us anything because we don't know what frobbles are. We don't know the relevant Referent type. The statement "Supplier S123 is sarny" doesn't tell us anything about that supplier because we don't know what the property of being sarny is. We don't know the relevant Attribute type.

So in order for any statement to be meaningful, we have to know what type of thing it refers to, and what type of attribute each of that thing's properties and/or relationships are. We have to be able to identify the subject of each statement as an instance of a Referent type, and to identify the predicate of each statement as an instance of a Property or Relationship type.

But from their inception, relational databases have not provided us the means to say much about the *types* of the subjects and predicates of the statements in those databases. They let us assign datatypes to each of the columns of a table; but often this does not suffice to define the domain for the column. They let us define foreign keys to implement relationships, and to define the cardinalities of those relationships. But the name a data modeler gives to a relationship is just a name, and at that a name that never makes it into the database catalog. The name given to a foreign key, or to any other column or to any table in a database, can be changed to any other name, or even to a meaningless string of characters. If that name is changed in all the SQL and all the code using the name, then everything will work as before. The names may be different, but that difference doesn't *make* any difference.

We are so familiar with this sad state of affairs that we don't realize how sad it is. We listen to the promise of the Semantic Web without realizing that, lacking formal definitions of the types in our databases, the promise is empty. Federated queries across the Internet cannot gather instances of the same types until structures in different databases are identified as structures for the same types.

We can do better than this. We can do better by linking the types represented by application-specific database tables and by the columns of those tables to the types of the Relational Paradigm Ontology — seldom directly, of course, but rather linked through a chain of intermediate types.

The Relational Paradigm Ontology is an ontology of objects, events, properties, and relationships. It is our folk ontology, so we all understand it. It is the upper-level ontology common to all relational databases, so it is the foundation for semantic interoperability among those databases. Therefore, all other ontologies, in order to be relevant to application databases, should converge on the Relational Paradigm Ontology. Without that convergence, different ontologies can at best provide fragmented perspectives on those databases.

Some converging ontologies will introduce clusters of important additional upper-level concepts into the Relational Paradigm Ontology, clusters and concepts such as:

- *Space.* Spatial concepts, such as region, dimensionality, location, distance, relative position, containment, surfaces and interiors.
- *Mind.* Mental concepts, such as mind itself, perception, belief, other propositional attitudes, knowledge, plans and goals.
- *Thematic roles.* Roles such as agent, patient, instrument, donor and recipient, cause and effect.

Other converging ontologies will provide and interrelate increasingly specific subtypes of the types in the Relational Paradigm Ontology. Some of them will be ontologies created by industry groups in such areas of endeavor as medicine, insurance, manufacturing, finance and accounting, telecommunications and other utilities, law and education. At a finer-grained level of specificity, leading edge enterprises will create their own enterprise-level ontologies which will mediate between industry ontologies and the ontologies of the tables and columns of specific databases within those enterprises, as expressed in the database catalogs of those databases.

The extended Relational Paradigm Ontology created by this convergence will remain a structured ontology in which all types of Referent and all types of Attribute are defined as sets. It is not enough to create, in some graph structure, a node "Supplier" and a node "Supplier Name" and a link labelled "has" between them. What's needed is to define Supplier as a set, not just to assemble a collection of statements about suppliers. This means locating Supplier in a hierarchy of Referent types. That hierarchy of Referent types is sometimes called a *taxonomy* of those types. These taxonomies and their predicate logic supporting structures are what makes the difference between a *structured ontology* and an unstructured one. Taxonomies are the *bones* of an ontology.

The immediate supertype of any type, called by Aristotle the *genus* of that type, constitutes the universe of discourse for that type's set definition. In other words, every type is itself typed.[3] Each set's set membership criterion, called by Aristotle the *specific difference* for that type, is a rule for distinguishing, among members of that universe of discourse, those that are members of the set being defined from those that are not.

Note that this is not true of many concepts in many ontologies. Many concepts in an ontology are not expressed as well-defined sets with a clear universe of discourse from which a clear set membership criterion selects set members. But the core concepts of the extended Relational Paradigm Ontology are such concepts. The introduction of concepts into an ontology which lack such clear universe of discourse plus clear set membership criterion specificity, takes us away from the clarity needed to implement semantic interoperability across the Semantic Web. It takes us into the semantic haze of Wittgensteinian family resemblances and fuzzy logic.

In the extended ontology, each table definition in a database catalog corresponds to a subtype of Referent in the ontology. As we know by now, these ontology entries situate these types in one or more type hierarchies, and provide a formal set-theoretic definition of each one. In addition, both universally and existentially-quantified statements will be able to link the definitions of these types into a rich semantic network, integrating an *ontology* of Referents and Attributes with a *knowledge base* of referents and attributes — the referents and attributes which are so important to an enterprise that the enterprise has created tables in relational databases to organize statements about them.

ASIDE

The extended Relational Paradigm Ontology, described all too briefly here, is not some objective whose achievement necessarily lies far in the future. In no more time and at no more cost than a typical database project, an enterprise could produce an initial release of its own extended ontology. In that initial release, catalog entries from specific databases would be linked directly into upper-level ontological categories as shown, for example, in Figures 5.1, 5.4 and 5.5 of Chapter 5, or linked to those categories via the intermediaries shown below in Figure 19.1.

In successive releases, the links between database tables and columns, and those upper-level categories, would be increasingly mediated by middle-level ontological categories, enriching the formally expressed semantics which will make table and column names much more than simply names. It will make them concepts about which software can do automated reasoning. And by turning table and column names into concepts, it will establish the foundation on which the ontology expressed in an enterprise's structured data can be seamlessly integrated with the ontology expressed in an enterprise's less structured data.

---

[3]Except for the highest level type, of course, the one type that everything is an instance of, and that every other type is a subtype of. This type is called by Aristotle *ousia* which is usually translated as "substance". It is also called Being, What-There-Is, Root, Thing, Stuff, and other names which suggest an "everything-ness". In the Relational Paradigm Ontology, Aristotle's *ousia* corresponds to the type Object. He has no type Event. Nor does he have a type corresponding to Attribute; that is, he does not organize his list of nine properties of *ousia* and relationships among them under their own highest level supertype.

Definitions of types supplied by subject matter experts are not definitions in the strict sense that a formal ontology requires. They are, rather, informal statements that help us interpret the sets defined in the formalism, and help us understand the formal definitions. They are *glosses* on formal definitions, and should be recognized as nothing more than that. They are nothing like the final, authoritative statements of what those types *are* that they are usually taken to be. They are part of the metalanguage that we use to talk about those types. They are not part of the object language which defines them in a set-theoretically precise way. They are statements available to *us*, but not to the software which will provide semantic interoperability among databases.

THE EXTENDED RELATIONAL PARADIGM ONTOLOGY

Figure 19.1 shows the extended ontology at work. The group of boxes pointed to by the uppermost right-pointing arrow is a representation of the *basic* Relational Paradigm Ontology, as described in Chapter 5, and as illustrated in Figures 5.1, 5.4 and 5.5.

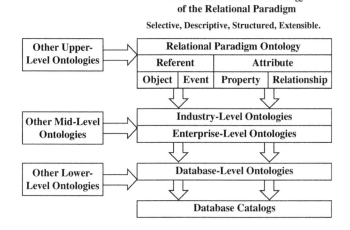

FIGURE 19.1

The Extended Relational Paradigm Ontology.

The extension of that ontology "downwards" creates additional categories which *inherit* the semantics of the components of the basic Relational Paradigm Ontology. This inheritance relationship was already described in Chapter 5, where I explained that, through the intermediaries of middle-level ontologies, including the ontologies of specific enterprises, upper-level ontological categories can be mapped onto the constructs defined in the database catalogs of those databases. In this way, the Relational Paradigm Ontology is an *extensible ontolo*gy.

An example of another upper-level ontology can be found in (Sowa, 2000). Although somewhat dated, it is still an impressive sketch of an upper-level ontology, not lacking in detail, and I frequently reread parts of that excellent book. Other examples of upper-level ontologies, for example SUMO and DOLCE, are available on the Internet.

The Relational Paradigm Ontology itself is an upper-level ontology. But as I said in the Preface, it is a *selective ontology*. It does not attempt, for example, to ontologize such concepts as space and time, topological relationships, minds and ideas, or thematic roles such as agent, patient and instrument. That is because those concepts are not part of the relational theory defined by Dr. Codd, and my purpose has been to define the ontology common to all relational databases. *The* ontology, note, not *an* ontology. My intention has been to present a *descriptive ontology*, not a prescriptive one.

An example of a middle-level ontology is the ontology of organizations developed by the World Wide Web Consortium. (W3C, 2013a). Other examples of middle-level ontologies are available on the Internet. At one level, they are ontologies corresponding to industries, and several such ontologies have been developed. Many industry groups have also developed industry data models, and for these groups, my recommendation is to integrate the ontologies and the data models of their industries using the extended Relational Paradigm Metamodel.

At a slightly lower level, middle-level ontologies are ontologies specific to an enterprise. These ontologies can be linked to the databases of those enterprises by the Extended Relational Paradigm Metamodel, described below. Indeed until ontologies are linked to database catalogs, any claim on the part of business ontologists to have integrated the semi-structured data of an enterprise, such as emails, spreadsheets and documents, with the structured data found in the relational databases of that enterprise, will be at best a superficial claim.

Frequently, the integration of two ontologies in which one is not a straightforward inheritance from the other, requires the development of a *bridge ontology* to map between them. However, a discussion of bridge ontologies, and other implementations of the right-pointing arrows in Figure 19.1, is beyond the scope of this book.

Nonetheless, I and other ontologists have some idea how the right-pointing and downward-pointing arrows in Figure 19.1 could be implemented. The same set-theoretic, propositional and predicate logic operators that link both quantified and unquantified statements within an ontology, also link statements across ontologies.

This formalization and integration of ontologies can be implemented, in a straightforward way, as a set of relational tables residing in an ontology database, with links in application databases connecting the ontology tables in the ontology database to the catalogs of those application databases.[4] The other tables in those databases can continue to be accessed directly, as they are now. But with these links, queries can be written against the ontologies of specific application databases. Queries can be written that reference both metadata and non-metadata. In some cases, the metadata could be displayed as type definitions associated with result sets. In more interesting cases, the results of metadata queries could be intermediate result sets that assign values to variables in non-metadata sections of those queries, thus directing those queries whose job it is to return instance-level data.

---

[4]That is to say, I consider ontology management tools and languages to be syntactic sugar for functionality that is a subset of that provided by relational databases and standard SQL, just as SQL itself is syntactic sugar for functionality that is a subset of that provided by predicate logic. ("Syntactic sugar", to remind the reader, is a phrase used by computer scientists to refer to a means of making certain functionality easier to use, but not to a means of providing any new functionality.)

THE EXTENDED RELATIONAL PARADIGM METAMODEL

Figures 19.2, 19.3 and 19.4 are logical data models. They use standard IEF notation. Their conventions, such as those for representing minimum and maximum cardinalities, for separating primary keys from all other columns of data by means of a horizontal line, and for annotating foreign keys with an "FK", will be well-known to most data modelers.[5]

Figure 19.2 shows the *semantic component* of the metamodel. This component relates the tables and columns of specific databases to the Relational Paradigm Ontology which is common to all relational databases. This relationship is what transforms the names we give to tables and columns into an ontologically informed set of concepts, showing us what we specifically mean by those names, and enabling software to carry out automated inferences about those types.

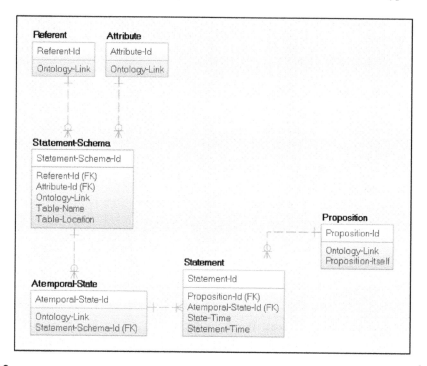

FIGURE 19.2

The Extended Relational Paradigm Metamodel: Semantics.

Figure 19.3 shows the *pragmatic component* of the metamodel. This component describes the individual actions, and types of actions, that constitute what we *do* with words, as Austin put it. It is worth noting that the speech act subset of this component provides a specific database model for implementing the "basic conversation for action" described in 1986 by Terry Winograd and

---

[5]As many data modelers will recognize, the diagrams in Figures 19.2, 19.3 and 19.4 were produced with the community edition of Computer Associate's Erwin data modeling tool.

Fernando Flores. It also provides the means to relativize the assertions and assertion withdrawals of the Asserted Versioning theory to persons and groups of persons. The inscription act subset of this component provides the means for implementing a mechanism to track the data provenance of statements along a branching structure of copies of a statement's originating inscription, within a defined multi-database and multi-enterprise inscription space.

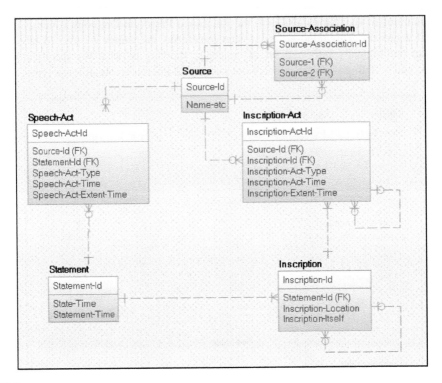

FIGURE 19.3

The Extended Relational Paradigm Metamodel: Pragmatics.

Figure 19.4 represents the complete metamodel. This metamodel implements the tritemporal theory of time discussed above. It interprets assertions and withdrawals as speech acts performed by people. These speech acts establish a person's cognitive stance to the statements those speech acts are about, a stance which persists throughout the temporal interval bracketed by an assertion and a withdrawal made by a specific person or group. Inscriptions also have their own time, which extends from when they are created to when they are deleted. And statements have their own time, which extends from when their first inscription is created within an inscription space to when their last inscription is deleted from that space. Also, since all statements in databases are about the states of referents, every such statement has, implicitly or explicitly, a state-time period associated with it. This is the familiar state time. Speech act time, inscription time and state time are the three temporal dimensions of this tritemporal theory of time.

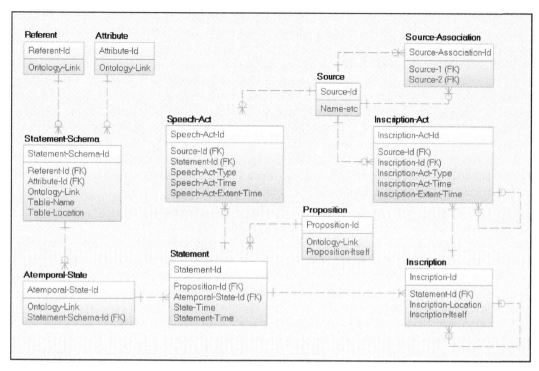

FIGURE 19.4

The Extended Relational Paradigm Metamodel: Semantics and Pragmatics.

The Semantic Component of the Extended Relational Paradigm Metamodel

The statements we have been concerned with in this book are the statements represented by rows in tables in relational databases. And we know a lot about these statements now.

Each statement is the instantiation of an existentially-quantified statement schema in a typed predicate logic. The subject of the statement is a referent, either an event or an object. The one or more predicates of the statement are properties of the referent, or relationships the referent has to other referents (or, perhaps, to itself).

An existentially-quantified statement schema expresses a mathematical relation on the Cartesian Product of a sequence of sets. Each column in a relational table corresponds to one of those sets, and the members of those sets are the domains of those columns.

One of those sets is the set of referents which have those properties and/or relationships. In a normalized relational table, there is a functional dependency from that set of referents to each of those sets of properties and/or relationships.

These statements are a more regimented form of the statements we make in ordinary conversation and in writing. When we make a statement, we pick something out, and then say something about it. We pick it out either by proper name, or by referring to it as an identifiable instance of a type, e.g. as a specific invoice, or product, or employee, and so on.

What we pick out is an object or event. What we say about it is that it is in a particular state. That state is the set of properties and relationships it has at that time. When we mean what we say, we assert that statement.

Type definitions can change over time, of course, and that suggests that this metamodel should itself be a temporal model. But a better approach, I think, is to treat types as timeless. The relations defined on the set of types making up a relational table are indeed time-varying. And the term "schema evolution" does refer to changes in the type-level definitions of relational tables and their constituents. But we can think of schema evolution, not as a set of types changing, but as one set of types giving way to a successor set of types.[6]

In the following discussion of the semantic component of the metamodel, I will describe the specific entities, attributes and relationships shown in Figure 19.2. The underlined name of each entity, attribute and relationship heralds each discussion.

Referent

This entity is not the familiar Referent of the Relational Paradigm Ontology, whose two immediate subtypes are Object and Event. It is, rather, a collection of links to the types in the ontology each of which corresponds to a table in the database being ontologized. Thus the primary key *Referent-Id* is not to be confused with the familiar RefId. A RefId is the unique identifier of an instance of a type; a *Referent-Id* is the unique identifier of a type, specifically of a subtype of Referent.

For a Customer database table, for example, there is a row in this table which links that Customer table to the database-specific concept Customer in the associated ontology. There would likely also be an enterprise-specific concept of Customer to which all database-specific concepts would be subtypes. There might also be an industry-level concept of Customer in the ontology as well, and so a hierarchy culminating in some cross-industry "universal" concept of what a customer is.[7]

In this way, in every relational database, every relational table represents one and only one subtype which, through a hierarchy of subtypes, is ultimately a subtype of Referent. Invoices, Products, Employees, Purchases, Sales, and so forth are all typical referent types, and typical tables in a database.

Attribute

This is not the familiar Attribute of the Relational Paradigm Ontology, whose two immediate subtypes are Property and Relationship. It is a collection of links to the type in the ontology which corresponds to a column of a table in the database. That type, in a database-level ontology, will have a supertype in an enterprise-level ontology, both being subtypes in the type

---

[6]This puts all the semantic burden on the notion of *type succession*, but since I will say nothing more about it here, I don't mind doing that. A more serious reason for saying nothing more about schema evolution, at this point, is that instead of solving the problem, we can *eliminate* it by making statement schemas entirely derivative managed objects, as described below in the section "Atomic Statements and Binary Tables".

[7]However, in this metamodel, the database tables that are linked to nodes in a hierarchy in an ontology are binary tables, tables with only a single Attribute column. A real-life Customer table, of course, would have more than one Attribute column. But as described below, real-life tables are managed, in this metamodel, as virtual constructs on all the binary tables with the same function domain, i.e. all the binary tables with the same Referent type. So the links of "real-life" tables to ontology categories are still supported. But they are indirect links, mediated by the binary tables all of which are about the "same kind of things".

hierarchy eventually culminating in the Attribute type of the Relational Paradigm Ontology. So in a relational database, every non-identifier column of a relational table represents one and only one attribute type. For example, supplier name and supplier type are two properties of suppliers, and thus two subtypes of Property. The Supplier table used in examples in this book also contains a foreign key which represents a relationship to supplier categories which is a subtype of Relationship.

Statement-Schema

This is the type whose instances are the familiar statement schemas of the Relational Paradigm's logic and semantics. In a relational database, every relational table defines a statement schema. However, as we will see shortly, the schemas recorded in this metamodel are the schemas of only binary tables. *Referent-Id* represents the type of subject of each statement schema, and *Attribute-Id* represents the type of predicate of each statement schema.

Referent-Id + Attribute-Id identifies a specific statement schema. It is the RefId of the Statement-Schema table. And so it follows that every row in the Statement-Schema table represents an *atomic statement schema*, a statement schema that consists of one subject and one predicate, not one subject and any number of predicates. This kind of table is often called a *binary table*. It associates one Attribute with one Referent.

Given atomic statements, and the binary tables that implement them, a normalized table in a relational database is a *dependent table* which corresponds to the union of all the atomic statement schemas that have the same Referent type. (I will have more to say about atomic statements and binary tables in the next section.)

Each row in this metadata table, by means of its two foreign keys, is directly linked to a binary table definition in a database catalog. *Table-Name + Table-Location* are attributes of convenience, identifying the normalized table in the database which is derived from the union of this binary table with all and only those other binary tables in the database which are for the same Referent (i.e. which have the same Referent-Id). The attribute *Table-Name* points to the catalog entry of that corresponding table in the database catalog of the database. The attribute *Table-Location* specifies where this table is. Assuming that an enterprise has an identity in some kind of universal namespace, then a table's location is specified by identifying the table itself, the database that contains it, and the enterprise that owns that database.

Atemporal State

An atemporal state is an instance of a Referent together with an instance of each of the Properties and Relationships defined in a statement schema. Each atemporal state consists of an ordered set of values such that each value is a member of the domain of the corresponding column in the statement schema. Thus, each atemporal state is one tuple from the Cartesian Product of the ordered set of Attributes on which the corresponding table is defined. With binary tables, of course, each atemporal state is a 2-tuple consisting of an instance of a Referent together with an instance of one and only one of its Attributes.

In a nontemporal table, there is a one-to-one correspondence between an atemporal state and a row. In a state-time or bitemporal table, however, the same referent can be in the same atemporal state at different times, and so the correspondence is many-to-one.

Proposition

A proposition is what a statement says. It is the information content of a statement. If two statements are *synonymous*, they express the same proposition. If they are not synonymous, they express different propositions. Chapter 6 contains a discussion of the concepts of statements and propositions.

ASIDE

The management of propositions is the Holy Grail of the quest to manage information by managing data, a quest in which we continue to extend our data management technologies to express more and more of the information we need.

For example, suppose that one email contained the text "Acme told us yesterday that they would sign the 2014 Supplier Agreement by the end of the month." And that another email contained the text "On Monday the 21st, we learned that Acme intended to sign the 2014 Supplier Agreement with us before the end of August."

These two statements don't necessarily "say the same thing". For example, if the first email was written sometime in March 2014, and the second on August 21st, 2014, then the two statements do not say the same thing. But if the first email was written on August 22, 2014, and the second email the day before, then the two statements do say the same thing. These two statements, in those circumstances, express the same proposition.

In organizing and cataloging the information in our semi-structured data, we don't just want these two statements copied from emails and put into lists, perhaps organized by keywords. If that's all we want, we certainly don't need ontologies to help us do it. What we really want, I suggest, is *one* entry on a list somewhere that says that Acme informed us, on August 21st, that they intend(ed) to sign the indicated agreement before the end of August 2014, and that would point to *both* emails as statements to that effect.

So in the implementation of this 1:M relationship from Proposition to Statement, we must imagine a very powerful database of formally defined terms and of formally expressed statements. Some of these statements will be definitions of those terms, these statements known as *analytic statements*. Other statements will be statements of fact, these statements known as *synthetic statements*.[8,9]

Statement

For a given statement schema, each statement is the result of instantiating the schema with the values from one tuple of the Cartesian Product on which the table for the schema is defined. That set of values constitutes one atemporal state of one object or event of that referent type. The state-time period associated with that statement makes the state described by that statement a temporal instance of that atemporal state.

A statement is a declarative sentence which attributes one or more properties and/or relationships to an object or an event. This set of properties and/or relationships is a state description. Since an event happens at a specific time, there is a state-time period associated with it. Since an object can be in many states, but in only one state at one time, there is a state-time period associated with it too. This time period is recorded in the *State-Time* attribute of the Statement table.

---

[8]This also provides a satisfying way to distinguish between ontologies and knowledge bases. Ontologies are (for the most part) collections of analytic statements. Knowledge bases are (for the most part) collections of synthetic statements. Analytic statements are true by definition. Synthetic statements are true, if they are, because the world is how they say it is.

[9]Another way of making this distinction is to say that ontologies consist of formal statements about types, while knowledge bases consist of formal statements about instances of those types.

The rows in nontemporal tables, since they too are about either objects or events, are also state descriptions, and those tables are implicit state tables. For those tables, the state time associated with each statement is based on the value of Henceforth at each time the statement is accessed.

Statement-Time is derived information. It is a time period that begins when the first inscription of a statement is created within an *inscription space*, and ends when the last inscription of that statement is removed from that space. (The related concepts of inscription spaces and statement spaces are discussed below.) It is entirely derived information, and is not one of the three tritemporal dimensions.

Before turning to a discussion of the specific relationships in this part of the metamodel, consider how those relationships together help to define what a statement is. A statement identifies something, and says something about it. What it identifies, and what it says about it, is the information content of the statement. Logicians call that information content the proposition expressed by the statement. Statements with the same information content are synonymous, and thus synonymous statements are those that express the same proposition.

The statements recorded in the Statement table of this metamodel are atomic statements. They pick out one thing, and ascribe one property or one relationship to it. The association of one thing — which is one instance of the type identified by the *Referent-Id* of the statement's schema — with one property or relationship — which is one instance of the type identified by the *Attribute-Id* of the statement's schema — is one 2-tuple of the Cartesian Product of the corresponding binary table. Each 2-tuple of that Cartesian Product represents one atemporal state of one referent of the indicated type.

Referent/Statement-Schema

One of the relationships in the semantic component of the metamodel is that between Referent and Statement-Schema. It has the minimum and maximum cardinalities indicated — optional/required and one-to-many from Referent to Statement-Schema. For every atomic statement schema, *Ontology-Link* in Referent links it to its Referent type in the ontology. If a non-binary table has ten attribute columns, for example, there will be ten binary tables corresponding to it, and thus ten rows in the Statement-Schema table with a foreign key to the same row in the Referent table.

In today's relational databases, the only information we have about a Referent is the name of the table that represents it. And that information is available only to human beings, not to software. Unless we know and can formally express more about the Referents associated with relational tables than the names of those tables, software-mediated semantic interoperability across databases will not be possible. To know that two tables in different databases, perhaps in different enterprises, represent the same Referent, we need to know more than the names of those tables.

Attribute/Statement-Schema

Comments here are exactly parallel to the comments for Referent / Statement-Schema.

Statement-Schema/Atemporal-State

This optional/required one-to-many relationship from Statement-Schema to Atemporal-State is a metatable which contains, for every binary table in an application database, one row for every tuple of that table's Cartesian Product which is or ever has been instantiated in a row in that application table. This means that this metatable keeps track, for every application table, of every state that any of its referent instances has ever been in. This restriction to tuples that have actually been used in tables is necessary because it would be impractical, even with the storage capacities associated with Big Data, to store all the tuples of the Cartesian Products of all the tables in an application database.[10]

Atemporal-State/Statement

Every statement describes the temporal state of a referent. Each temporal state is the logical intersection of an atemporal state with a state-time period. (For the sake of keeping the metamodel simple, I do not include metatables for any of the three tritemporal dimensions, and instead treat the entities, attributes and relationships of this metamodel as themselves timeless.)

Proposition/Statement

A proposition is expressed by one or more statements. For example, the proposition that John loves Mary is expressed by the statement "John loves Mary" and also by the statement "Mary is loved by John". The formal expression of the relationship between propositions and statements is the greatest challenge in the field of formal ontologies.

I turn next to a description of the pragmatic component of the Extended Relational Paradigm Metamodel.

The Pragmatic Component

Ontologies are fine things. But, as Austin might have asked, what are we going to *do* with them? The branch of linguistics that studies what we do with language is known as pragmatics, and an important perspective on and subject area within pragmatics is the speech act theory invented by Austin and extensively developed by John Searle. Speech act theory has strong affinities with H. P. Grice's account of rules implicit in conversations, rules without which conversations could hardly get started and, if once started, would soon fall apart.

In my first book, assertions and withdrawals played an important role; but at that time, I did not identify them as speech acts. In that book, I proposed that statements could be physically entered into databases prior to the time at which their authors would later assert them to be true. Only while writing *this* book did I come to realize that making and withdrawing assertions are two of the things people do with words, specifically two of the things that they do with statements. In this section, I sketch a more general theory of speech acts, and situate speech acts involving statements within that general theory.

A second aspect of the pragmatics of managing databases is the use of inscriptions to record statements. A statement doesn't exist until someone makes it; and to make a statement, one must speak it or write it down. Being concerned with databases, I have discussed inscriptions, not utterances.

The common thread relating inscriptions and speech acts are that both are things that people do with words. Inscriptions are physical things that people create and manage in order to record,

---

[10] I refer the reader to Chapter 3, in which we saw that the number of instances of a name with thirty or fewer characters, even assuming a restricted character set of 53 characters, is 53 million trillion trillion possible names. These kinds of numbers can quickly get out of hand.

The association of that name attribute with other attributes in a real-life application table would result in a literally *exponential* increase, over these already immense numbers, in the number of tuples for that table. Fortunately, as long as only 2-tuples populate this metatable, that exponential increase will not be an issue.

manage and access the information in statements. Speech acts express the propositional attitude relationships between people and the statements they inscribe, attitudes such as believing or not believing that a statement is true, or withholding judgment on whether or not it is.

Speech acts connect people to statements.[11] Inscriptional acts connect people to inscriptions. Every inscription is the inscription of a statement. Every statement is embodied in at least one inscription.

As previously, I discuss each entity, attribute and relationship in this component of the Extended Relational Paradigm Metamodel.

Source

A source is any object that is capable of performing any of the actions indicated by the action type columns in the two tables to which Source is the parent table. Only a human being, or an organization of human beings, can be the source of a speech act. Only people can assert that a statement is true, or later withdraw an assertion, or assent to or dissent from the assertion of a statement, or even simply notice a statement, i.e. read and understand it. Only a human being, or an organization of human beings, can be the source of an inscription, because while even monkeys at a keyboard will eventually create strings of characters that are orthographically identical to declarative sentences keyed in by a human being, it is only the character strings created by people that will be recognized as the inscriptions of statements.

Source-Association

The main purpose of this associative relationship is to form groups of persons, since groups as well as individuals can be the source of speech acts and inscriptional acts. Certainly a more robust implementation of groups is needed, but this serves to get the idea across.

Inscription-Act

This table relates a source to an inscription, e.g. a person inserting a row into a table to that row itself. Its action types are defined by the set {create, copy, move, destroy}. For every statement, only one inscription is associated with the create action. This is the first inscription of that statement. Subsequent inscriptions of the same statement are produced by the copy or move actions. A copy does what it says; it increases the count of statement inscriptions by one. A move does what it says; it changes the location of an inscription, but leaves the inscription count unaffected. A row in this table with the destroy action tells us that the inscription no longer exists within a defined inscription space.

Every time a new inscription is produced (created, copied, moved), an open inscription time period (*Inscription-Extent-Time*) is associated with it whose begin time is the *Inscription-Act-Time* of that action. If and when an inscription is destroyed, that action is given a closed time period whose begin time is the begin time of the action which produced it, and whose end time is the *Inscription-Act-Time* of that event itself.

---

[11]Austin himself was concerned primarily with speech acts other than those involved in making statements, with "sociological" speech acts such as asking for directions, performing a ceremony, making a promise, and so forth. Indeed, there seems to be very little discussion, in the philosophical literature, about *statement-constituting speech acts*, those being the speech acts without which declarative sentences fail to be statements.

Inscription

An inscription is a row in a table in a relational database. It is identified by its location. That *Inscription-Location* is the location of that row. That location is described by a string of identifiers of an inscription's nested containers. In a relational database, one such set of identifiers would be enterprise-id:database-id:table-id:row-id. Other ways of locating an inscription might be based, for example, on the X.500 namespace convention. This is what the column *Inscription-Location* represents.

An inscription is a physical object, normally a string of characters. Inscriptions are inscriptions of statements, and so sometimes it is convenient to refer to them as statements. But if a row is copied from one table to another, the result is two inscriptions of one statement, not two statements.

The begin time of an inscription is the associated *Inscription-Act-Time* of a create, copy or move action. It is the same thing as the standard theory's transaction begin time. That is because the standard theory of bitemporal time manages inscriptions, not statements. The inscription time of a row is the time from when a transaction physically creates that row to when a transaction logically deletes it. In this metamodel, it is the time between the create, copy or move action that put that inscription somewhere in its associated inscription space, and the delete action that logically removed it from that inscription space.[12]

Speech-Act

This table relates a source to a statement. The speech act types I have defined here for this relationship are types in the set {assert, withdraw, assent, dissent, notice}. Only one source may assert a statement. If other people or organizations agree, they will *assent* to the statement. If they disagree, they will *dissent* from the statement. If they are aware of the statement and have considered it, but are not prepared to either assent to it or dissent from it, they will *notice* the statement. A source may also withdraw its assertion, assent or dissent.

As acts, each speech act is an event, and so it is associated with the point in time recorded in *Speech-Act-Time*. *Speech-Act-Extent-Time* is the open or closed temporal interval formerly referred to, in the Asserted Versioning theory, as assertion time, but now generalized to be the time between any speech act and its withdrawal, and in addition relativized to the source performing the speech act. On an assert, assent, dissent or notice speech act, it is an open time period whose begin time is identical to its speech act time. On a withdraw speech act, it is a closed time period whose begin time is the action time of the speech act it is withdrawing, and whose end time is identical to its own speech act time.

Inscription/Inscription

The inscription to inscription relationship implements a hierarchical series of inscriptions. Any inscription can be copied many times, and each copy begins a new branch in the hierarchy. The root node of the hierarchy is the first inscription of a statement, the one made by the authoritative source of that statement. The hierarchy is acyclic because every inscription is temporally later than its parent inscription.

---

[12]In the world of today's databases, an inscription space is equivalent to a physical database instance. But I see considerable value in extending the concept of a managed inscription space to include multiple databases, across multiple enterprises.

This hierarchy establishes the *provenance* of the statement expressed by each inscription in the hierarchy. For each inscription of a statement other than the first one, it points to the inscription from which that inscription was copied or moved. For each inscription anywhere in the hierarchy, it seems a reasonable default policy to cascade a delete operation on an inscription down all chains emanating from that inscription, since all inscriptions on all those chains were made only because the inscription being destroyed was present and was relied on. It also seems a reasonable non-overridable policy to prevent a delete operation on any inscription from affecting any inscriptions not in the subtree under the inscription being deleted.

Source/Speech-Act
This relates a source to the zero or more speech acts he performs.

Source/Inscription-Act
This relates a source to the zero or more inscriptions she creates, copies, moves or deletes.

Inscription/Inscription-Act
This relates an inscription to the one or two inscription acts associated with it. An inscription does not exist until a create, copy, or move inscription act puts that inscription into a database table. The second inscription act associated with some inscriptions is the delete action in which the inscription is logically deleted from its database table. Since every inscription is related to one and only one source, there can be no more than two inscription acts associated with any inscription. SQL Insert and Delete transactions carry out these inscription acts in a relational database.

The Integrated Metamodel: Semantic and Pragmatic Components
Figure 19.4 shows both the semantic and pragmatic components of the Extended Relational Paradigm Metamodel, and the relationships between the entities in each component.

Statement/Inscription
A statement does not exist unless there is at least one inscription of that statement. Every inscription is the inscription of a statement. Thus this relationship is required for both the related entities.

Statement/Speech-Act
This relates a statement to a source by means of zero or more speech acts associated with it. Note that the standard theory of bitemporal time requires an assertion speech act to be associated with a statement. That is because the *semantics* of the standard theory's transaction time (as shown in Chapter 6) is the semantics of an assertion. Because of this, the standard theory's transaction time is a homonymous concept. It is both the time an inscription is created, and also the time it is asserted as a statement. The problem for the standard theory is that these two events do not have to occur at the same time (although the latter can only occur after the former has taken place). As for the Extended Relational Paradigm Metamodel, because of its support for future assertion time, it does not require a speech act to be associated with a statement.

Thus, one set of tables in this metamodel relates statements to the ontology which formally defines the type-level components of which the subject and predicate of any statement are instances. The other set of tables in this metamodel relates statements to the evolving provenance of their inscriptions, and to the speech acts which express the propositional attitudes of people towards those statements. Those propositional attitudes are what determine how people respond to statements, for example by relying on them or by disregarding them, by passing them on or by taking a stand against them.

ATOMIC STATEMENTS AND BINARY TABLES

Normalized relational tables have always been constructs consisting of the property and relationship types for a given referent type. And there continues to be a role for normalized tables in this future for relational databases that I am describing of ontologically enhanced and tritemporally located statement inscriptions.

These normalized relational tables are the tables I earlier called *dependent tables*. In databases for which this metamodel is implemented, they will be managed objects which are views or equivalently derived structures created by unioning all the binary tables for the same referent.

For example, here is a sample row from the Supplier table used in examples throughout this book.[13]

$$[\text{S2} \,|\, \text{Superior} \,|\, \mathit{SC3} \,|\, \text{T22}]$$

This is a three-predicate statement. We may also view it as a row in a table with three non-primary key attribute columns. Its representation as a set of single-predicate atomic statements is shown in Figure 19.5. Its representation as a set of three rows, one in each of three binary tables, is shown in Figure 19.6

$$[\underline{\text{S2}} \,|\, \text{Superior}]$$
$$[\underline{\text{S2}} \,|\, \mathit{SC3}]$$
$$[\underline{\text{S2}} \,|\, \text{T22}]$$

FIGURE 19.5

Three Atomic Statements.

Sid	s-nm
S2	Superior

Sid	s-scfk
S2	SC3

Sid	s-type
S2	T22

FIGURE 19.6

Three Binary Tables.

---

[13]These tables, against my own recommendations, use the same column for a primary key and a RefId. I have done this with several of the tables used for examples in this book, and my reason has always been brevity, specifically my concern to be able to display one row of data as one line of print on the page.

Notice that there is no table name for these tables. I also assume here that every value in the column *sid* is unique across all RefId types. In that case, in all three binary tables, it identifies the Supplier type, a subtype of the Object subtype of Referent. Since the only ontological role a table name plays is to suggest a type (which is never, in the database, defined anywhere), then unique names for RefId types makes table names unnecessary.

I also assume that the attribute column names in binary tables are unique across all attribute types. With this true for both of the columns in binary tables, their links to the Extended Relational Paradigm Ontology are established. The Statement-Schema metadata table in Figures 19.2 and 19.4 is a repository for binary table schemas, so those Figures show exactly how those relational database tables are linked to the extended ontology.

Now suppose we had a database full of binary tables, some with the same RefId type, others with different RefId types. With this collection of binary tables, normalization is a simple process. Create one group of binary tables for each different RefId type. Drop the duplicate RefId columns, and concatenate the remaining columns. Add a (non-RefId) primary key. The result is a normalized multi-attribute table utilizing a surrogate (non-RefId) primary key.

The value of an atomic statement representation of information is that it is the simplest statement form possible. It picks out one instance of a type of object or event, and attributes one property or one relationship to it. If all information were expressed in this basic form, then there would be no limitations on how the formal operations of logic and set theory could work on the information thus expressed. If a non-atomic statement form could not be expressed as a set of atomic statements, on the other hand, then that non-atomic statement form might prevent formal mechanisms from carrying out at least some semantically valid operations on the information expressed in those statements.

We now have the three extensions of the basic Relational Paradigm which I recommended at the start of this chapter, and the Extended Relational Paradigm Metamodel integrates all three of them. That metamodel is a set of metadata tables that can be included in any relational database. The ontology components which the metamodel references can be external to the database, internalized with it, or partially external and partially internal. Regardless, that metadata is the bridge between the Extended Relational Paradigm Ontology shown in Figure 19.1 (with further details shown in Figures 5.1, 5.4 and 5.5), and the database catalog of specific application databases.

That metamodel also associates state time with binary tables in its Statement-Schema metadata table, in which atemporal states become temporal states when associated with state-time periods. That metamodel associates inscription time with the inscriptions of these atomic statements, and speech act time with the speech acts that associate people or groups of people with these state-time situated atomic statements.

LOOKING AHEAD

Today's databases manage inscriptions. The recognition of those inscriptions as statements is a matter of human beings interpreting that data. In relational databases, statements are not managed objects; only inscriptions are.

This is how computers have been used to manage information since the earliest days. The distinction between one statement and its possibly many inscriptions was simply never considered to be within the scope of what a DBMS could or ought to manage.

Tritemporal time distinguishes between statements and inscriptions. So accompanying this tritemporal theory, I have described a set of metadata tables which implements the distinction between statements and inscriptions in relational databases. I have described metadata which allows us to keep track of each inscription of a statement, to recognize inscriptions which inscribe the same statement and distinguish them from other inscriptions, and to track the provenance of a statement from its first inscription to its terminal inscriptions along the one or more branches of that statement's provenance hierarchy.

The last step in the evolution of the semantics of relational databases will be to distinguish in them between propositions and statements, one proposition being the information content of a set of one or more synonymous statements. We will then have the progression from any number of inscriptions to the one statement they all express, and from any number of statements to the one proposition they all express.

The formalization of the semantic connections between propositions and statements is the most difficult step of all. The semantics of propositions about types is what a *formal ontology* will ultimately express, although for the present, it is only the semantics of statements about types that are expressed in a formal ontology. The semantics of propositions about instances is what a *formal knowledge representation system* will ultimately express, although for the present, it is only the semantics of statements about instances that are expressed in a formal knowledge representation system. In this next stage in the evolution of relational databases, ontologies and knowledge representation systems will be integrated with the database catalogs of relational databases. Speech act theory will relate persons to statements. Normalized tables will be managed as dependent objects, derived from the binary tables each of which expresses an atomic statement.

In short: the ultimate objective I am proposing is to evolve relational databases into databases of tritemporalized, ontologized, atomic statements on the basis of which normalized relational tables are useful views.

GLOSSARY LIST

assert	inscription time	state description
assertion time	inscription	state time
assertion-time period	object	state
atemporal state	ontology	statement identifier
atomic statement	open time period	statement space
Attribute	predicate	statement provenance
attribute	property	statement schema
binary table	Property	statement space
closed time period	proposition	statement time
event	referent	statement
existentially-quantified	Referent	state-time period
statement	relationship	subject
formal ontology	Relationship	synonym
future assertion time	semantic	temporal dimension
future assertion-time	interoperability	transaction time
period	source	transaction-time period
homonym	speech act extent time	tritemporal
inscription act time	speech act time	type
inscription extent time	speech act	withdraw

RECOMMENDATIONS

In the previous chapter, I described three directions in which I believe relational databases should evolve. But more generally, my intention was to describe an evolutionary path for any technology that manages information by managing data. Since statements are the way in which we express what we know, they are the fundamental units of recorded information. So any comments about technologies that manage statements are comments about a very important topic.

From this perspective, *Big Data* is a completely orthogonal topic. Big Data is about data. If Big Data is to provide *Big Information*, then somehow statements must be derived from that data. Once they are, those statements can be represented in conventional relational databases, in bitemporal relational databases, and eventually in tritemporalized and ontologized collections of atomic statements.

In the rest of this chapter, I make some recommendations for the deployment of bitemporal functionality in end-user IT organizations, and for the improvement of the ISO's bitemporal data standard and its implementation in DBMSs. So these recommendations have nothing to do with the prospective future of relational databases described in the previous chapter. That prospective future is on the far horizon. These recommendations are for what we can do right now that will have a direct impact on the use of bitemporal technology by IT professionals and database users.

RECOMMENDATIONS FOR IT PROFESSIONALS IN END-USER IT ORGANIZATIONS

For those IT professionals working in end-user organizations that have, or will soon acquire, a bitemporally-enabled DBMS, I have attempted to develop the concepts you will need to understand what you are doing when you use the bitemporal tools that these vendors are making available to you. In the simplest of terms, when you read the examples provided in their manuals and associated technical publications, you should now have a deep understanding of what is going on. You should be able to look at these DBMSs and understand not only what bitemporal functions each provides, but also what functions each has not yet provided. Among that latter set of functions, if some are more important to you than others — for example, the ability to provide a single go-live event for a large volume of data that has been loaded over several off-line sessions — you can make your priorities known to your vendors.

As for how you should make use of the bitemporal functionality of these DBMSs, my recommendations are easily stated. First of all, you should stop implementing requirements for Inmon's two criteria of time variance and nonvolatility by means of anything other than bitemporal tables. You should use only bitemporal tables in Inmon data warehouses, and you should use bitemporal tables rather than slowly-changing dimensions in Kimball star schemas. And in whatever priority sequence is most appropriate for your own enterprise, you should begin to replace all history tables, version tables and slowly-changing dimension tables with bitemporal tables.

Keep in mind that, in these replacements, you will not be substituting a new complex piece of application code for an old one. Rather, you will be replacing application code point solutions with an enterprise-standard solution the details of whose implementation is embedded in the DBMS and accessible by means of standards-defined SQL. By replacing point solutions with an enterprise-standard solution, joins involving temporal tables will not have to overcome different designs for the same temporal requirements, or for almost identical temporal requirements. By utilizing bitemporal SQL, you will not have to write complex temporal join logic.

Your next step should be to make *every* table in a production database a bitemporal table, including conventional nontemporal tables. There is no longer any need to overwrite data when updating it, or to remove data when deleting it. These tables can continue to be updated and queried as conventional tables, with the same SQL. But a complete bitemporal history of all modifications to those tables will then become available. It will then become possible to enter retroactive modifications — inserts, updates or deletes that correct mistakes — and to have them marked with their correct effectivity dates while at the same time preserving the information that, until those corrections were made, the database said something wrong about how things were at those past times.

RECOMMENDATIONS FOR STANDARDS COMMITTEES AND VENDORS

Computer scientists have attempted for over two decades to add support for bitemporal data to the SQL standard. Finally, in late 2011, the ISO 9075:2011 SQL standard was issued, which defined bitemporal functionality, and extensions to SQL DDL and DML to support that functionality. At about the same time, IBM implemented many of these bitemporal extensions in DB2 UDB.

Following is a list of specific recommendations I have for vendors and the standards committees. Some of these recommendations are to correct mistakes in the ISO standard. Other recommendations are modifications that I believe will improve both standards. One recommendation, for the inclusion of future transaction time, is for an extension to both standards.

I also urge those readers who agree with these recommendations (and also those who do not) to make their views known to the standards committees. Those of us who understand what bitemporal data is are fully qualified to enter into conversations with the members of those committees, if only by commenting on proposals and draft standards. Standards exist to serve us and to help us serve our business users. We need to let the committees in charge of those standards know what will best help us to do that job, and we need to discuss with them how to generalize (or specialize) those recommendations to arrive at the best statement of the recommendation as a standard.

Each of my recommendations is presented in summary form. But each one is based on material presented in this book, and many of them are also supported by material in my earlier book, *MTRD*.

REMOVE THE ABILITY TO CORRECT DATA IN STATE-TIME TABLES

The ISO standard permits corrections to rows in unitemporal state-time tables. As I have already shown, especially in Chapter 15, this is a mistake. It is a semantic mistake, forcing us to either lose information or to enter it incorrectly. It is a mistake because when history is maintained, it will inevitably be necessary to occasionally correct that history, and because with unitemporal tables, corrections either lose information by overwriting the data being corrected, or else are entered with Henceforth-valued time periods, which are clearly wrong. Moreover, a single Henceforth-valued correction means that the temporal semantics of the entire table is compromised because it is then no longer possible to tell which rows have time periods that record state time, and which rows have time periods that record assertion time.

Krisna Kulkarni, an IBM representative who participated in defining the temporal features in the ISO 9075:2011 SQL standard, said that it was important to support retroactive transactions against unitemporal tables. He wrote:

> In previous proposals, query expressions, constraint definitions, and insert/update/delete statements expressed without the statement modifier prefixes were assumed to operate only on the current rows. This applied to both transaction time tables and valid time tables. *While this made sense for transaction time tables, it did not make much sense for valid time tables.* For instance, users were allowed to insert into valid time tables only those rows whose valid time period started with the current time. In fact, there was no way for users to insert rows into valid time tables whose validity periods were either in the past or in the future. In contrast, query expressions, constraint definitions, and insert/update/delete statements on application-time period tables in SQL:2011 operate on the entire table content and follow the standard semantics. Also, *SQL:2011 allows users to specify any time values they desire for the application-time period start and end columns as part of the INSERT statement on application-time period tables.* (Kulkarni, 2012, pp. 42-43. Italics added.)

This is the mistake I am referring to. Kulkarni says that, in previous proposals, "there was no way for users to insert rows into valid time tables whose validity periods were either in the past or in the future". He indicates that this was an oversight, and that it is corrected in the 9075:2011 standard.

But the past-time constraint was not an oversight. Allowing users to "insert rows into valid time tables whose validity periods (are) . . . in the past" is what is the mistake. It is a mistake that should be removed from the ISO SQL standard, and from the DBMSs that implement that mistake. What this means, in practice, is that SQL:2011 must *not* allow users to "specify any time values they desire for the application-time period start and end columns as part of the INSERT statement on application-time period tables". The standard must be modified to prevent users from doing that.

SPECIFY REFERENT IDENTIFIERS IN SQL TABLE DEFINITIONS

I recommend to the standards committees that they add a clause to DDL table definition statements for state-time and bitemporal tables that designates the referent identifier for each table. The function of a primary key is to uniquely identify a row. It is *not* to uniquely identify what the row stands for (although, of course, for nontemporal tables, rows and referents must be one-to-one). But for state-time tables, primary keys and referent identifiers are many-to-one since each row represents one state of an object which can have any number of states. And for bitemporal tables, primary keys and referent identifiers are also many-to-one since each row represents one of possibly many assertions about one of possibly many states of an object.

Data modelers often include referent identifiers in relational tables, as they should. Sometimes those identifiers will also be used as the primary keys of those tables. Sometimes those identifiers will be non-key columns of those tables. Sometimes one or more columns in a multi-column referent identifier will be primary key columns while the remaining columns will be non-key columns. Whether they are used as all, or part, or none of a table's primary key, the purpose of a referent identifier is to identify what it is that a row is talking about, *not* to identify the row itself. Playing so important a role, referent identifiers should be explicitly stated on all table definitions, or else those tables should be explicitly marked, in the DDL, as tables that are *not* relational tables even though they have unique primary keys.

The mistake I am addressing here is that today's DBMSs regiment the management of *data* by using SQL DDL to define row identifiers, i.e. primary keys. But those DBMSs leave the management of *semantics* to the haphazard and idiosyncratic care of end-user-organization data modelers and developers, since those DBMSs do not use SQL DDL to define referent identifiers. And so while relational DBMSs manage *inscriptions*, they do not manage *statements*.

SPECIFY TEMPORAL UNIQUE IDENTIFIERS IN SQL TABLE DEFINITIONS

I recommend to the standards committees that they add a clause to DDL table definition statements for state-time and bitemporal tables that identifies the temporal unique identifier for each table, an identifier which may or may not be all or part of the primary key of those tables. For state-time tables, this is the referent identifier plus the state-time period. For bitemporal tables, this is the referent identifier plus both time periods. Primary keys, to emphasize the point once more, are row identifiers. They are not referent identifiers or state identifiers.

PACKAGE THE BITEMPORALIZATION OF CONVENTIONAL TABLES

DBMS vendors and data model tool vendors should package a function to bitemporalize nontemporal tables. There is every reason to convert nontemporal tables, as well as best practice unitemporal tables, to a bitemporal form. Views and Instead Of triggers can then provide temporal upward compatibility. Without any modification to existing transactions, a bitemporal history of those transactions would then automatically begin to be accumulated. Corrections would automatically be distinguishable from "normal" updates in this history.

This conversion does not involve any requirements clarification by business analysts, since any requirements to "preserve history" specified by the business will be a subset of the functionality provided by bitemporal data. Nor does this conversion require any design work by data architects, DBAs or data modelers since the target data structure is already determined.

It does, however, require the data modeler to enter metadata that describes the components of the source table in the transformation, that maps those components onto their target components, and that specifies one-time load default values for time periods. Among the pieces of metadata information that need to be provided are the following:

- source and target table name;
- source and target DBMS and release number;
- one-time load state-time period;
- one-time load assertion-time period;
- table type of foreign key target table;
- for each column:
  - source and target column name;
  - source column primary key yes/no flag;
  - source column within primary key sequence number;
  - source column RefId yes/no flag;
  - source column within RefId sequence number;
  - source column foreign key yes/no flag;
  - source column in foreign key sequence number.

If the source table is itself a temporal table, it will also be necessary to such additional information as the following:

- the column or columns that define the source table time period;
- whether the source table time period is being used as an assertion (transaction) time period or a state (valid) time period (or, regrettably, as often enough occurs, both);
- whether the source table time period is represented by a begin time only, an end time only, a begin and an end time, or some other method (such as begin time plus elapsed time); and
- the level of granularity used for the source table time period.

From this information, a target bitemporal table can be constructed. A standard SQL view can be defined on that table that has the same name as the source table, and whose columns have the same name as the corresponding source table columns, thus insuring upward compatibility for existing queries and updates. This standard view would make available to the DBMS user all and only those rows which would have been available in the original source table, had that original source table not been replaced by that bitemporal table. From this information, a generic Instead Of trigger routine can obtain the metadata description necessary to do its work for each specific table.[1]

MODIFY SQL QUERY SYNTAX TO CLARIFY SEMANTICS

I recommend to the standards committees that they utilize the IN STATE INTERVAL and IN ASSERTION INTERVAL clauses (or the equivalent clauses as already defined in the standards) as header information in query result sets. I defined this use of these clauses in Chapters 12 and 13.

---

[1]This means that a universal Instead Of trigger can be built-in to the DBMS. Without this metadata information, different Instead Of triggers would have to be hand-written by end-user developers, one for each table.

ADD WHENEVER TEMPORAL TRANSACTIONS TO THE STANDARD

I recommend to the standards committees that they define the functionality and the syntax of Whenever temporal transactions, as I defined them in Chapter 11, including temporal merge transactions. The practical value of these transactions should be apparent from that discussion.

ADD FUTURE TRANSACTION TIME TO THE STANDARD

I recommend to the standards committees that they extend transaction time (my assertion time) to permit rows to be added to bitemporal tables with future transaction-time periods. I presented, in Chapter 14 of this book, and in *MTRD*, the basics of semantic serialization in those instances in which the semantic sequence of assertions differs from the physical sequence in which those assertions were added to their bitemporal tables.

Once again, as with several of the preceding suggestions, the theme of semantics versus implementation is the heart of the issue. For as long as there have been relational databases and the entity integrity constraint, IT professionals have been able to assume a one-to-one correlation between rows and what they represented, and more generally between the mechanics of implementation and the semantics of what is being implemented. With temporal tables, that one-to-one correlation has been broken, and as a community of academicians and practitioners, we do not yet, I believe, fully realize how deeply the breakdown of that correlation affects the representation of data in databases.

I began my career working on a very large mainframe computer that had 256K of main memory (at that time consisting of ferromagnetic "cores" strung on a lattice of wires, and given the name "core memory"). Often, a file to be processed existed as a deck of punch cards (with sequence numbers in columns 72-80 for those who didn't like to live dangerously). Today we have come to bitemporal data as the current state of the database art. What tomorrow should bring, in my opinion, is the use of relational databases to manage tritemporal binary tables in association with a formal ontology of those tables and their types, all supporting fully normalized tables as the basic views against which updates will be written and to which queries will be directed.

And we've just gotten started.

GLOSSARY LIST

assertion time
assertion
atomic statement
bitemporal table
correction
future assertion time
future transaction time
inscription

object state
object
ontology
referent identifier
reflection
row identifier
semantic serialization
state identifier

state time
statement
state-time table
temporal unique
  identifier
tritemporal

Afterword: Reflections on Mindfulness and Bitemporality

This book began with a quotation from T. S. Eliot which expresses a Buddhist awareness of time. That Buddhist awareness of time is often called "mindfulness", which is a translation of the Sanskrit word *smrti*, which is also translated as "remembrance". In the latter sense, we have an immediate connection to data, since data is what we write down in order to be reminded of what we originally had in mind.

Mindfulness is an awareness in which the familiar distinctions of past, present and future seem an almost arbitrary construct imposed on our temporal experience. An example is provided by the anthropologist Benjamin Lee Whorf, co-creator of the Sapir-Whorf hypothesis that our linguistic and conceptual background deeply influences our most basic experiences of the world around us and within us. And I can say, with some authority, that later work in both Anglo-American analytic philosophy from Quine, Sellars and the later Wittgenstein, through to Davidson, Rorty, McDowell and Brandom, and also later work in European continental philosophy from phenomenology, through hermeneutics and deconstructionism, to contemporary metapsychology and philosophy in the works of Lacan, Zizec, Badiou and Johnston (my son, in fact), seems to both deepen and confirm the Sapir-Whorf hypothesis.

The example I am referring to is Whorf's interpretation of the stories told to him by the Hopi Native Americans he worked with, about their religious rituals and their reverence for their ancestors. The ancestors were consulted for their advice on important decisions, and much of the remembrance of ancestors took place in what the Hopi described as conversations with them. In contrast, the closest the Anglo Christian tradition comes is the practice of remembering our deceased family and friends in our prayers – although Hispanic Christian traditions, especially in such practices as *El Dia de Los Muertos*, are perhaps closer to a Hopi than an Anglo relationship with the dead.

Whorf concluded that, for the Hopi, their understanding of time is fundamentally different from ours. For us, what is past is over and done with. Agency is restricted to the present, and the future is the temporal realm of anticipation. But for the Hopi, Whorf concluded, time divides reality into two categories - the real, and the not yet real. For them, past and present are both real, and the difference between them is less important than that similarity. And agency is a property of the real, and therefore of the past as well as the present.

Later anthropological work, especially on how different languages split up the color spectrum, lends some support to the hypothesis. An excellent discussion and analysis of that work can be found in (Gardenfors, 2004). And although modern philosophers do not refer to the Sapir–Whorf hypothesis, I view their work as an extended clarification and confirmation of it.

So mindfulness is an awareness of the world in which, although the distinction of past, present and future (or the Hopi distinction of past/present and future) can indeed be made, those distinctions seem to recede into the background, and one's awareness is of a seamless woven fabric of reality from the moment of the Big Bang (or before it) into a far future with a limitless capacity to absorb the oncoming wave of what is, and to reflect it back onto the present and onto our understanding of the past. In fact, I think this is a description of reality not inconsistent with the long-accepted thermodynamic interpretation of entropy, and also with current work by physicists on string theory and loop quantum gravity, two theories which attempt to heal the breach between classical relativism and quantum mechanics.

Here is what Eliot said:

> Time present and time past
> Are both perhaps present in time future,
> And time future contained in time past.

This seems to be a comment on the ontological time of bitemporality, the time in which what there is, is. But there is epistemological time, as well, the time in which our statements of what we believe to be true exist. The Asserted Versioning theory of bitemporal data is distinguished from the standard theory primarily by the fact that the Asserted Versioning theory recognizes that data can exist not only in past and present epistemological time, but in future epistemological time as well. We can write down statements about what we may eventually be willing to claim is true about how things used to be, currently are, or may become in the future. And since we can do this, and since we find it useful to do so, we should be able to write down such statements in our databases, and we should be able to manage the inscriptions of those statements, and retrieve the information they contain on demand.

So mindfulness is not just an awareness of the world. It is an awareness in which the distinctions of past, present and future fade into the background of both ontological time and epistemological time.

In the former fading away, reality itself seems to become a temporally seamless garment. In the latter fading away, our awareness of that reality also seems to become a temporally seamless garment in which the distinctions between myself then and myself now, and indeed between my-self and other-self, and even between my-self and no-self, attain the status of insignificance. In this way, the quotation from Eliot, above, seems to apply to epistemological time as well as to ontological time.

This fading away of boundaries leaves us with an awareness in which these lines from Tennyson's poem *Ulysses* seem to be more literally true than merely metaphorically true:

> I am a part of all that I have met;
> Yet all experience is an arch wherethrough
> Gleams that untravelled world, whose margin fades
> For ever and for ever when I move.

In our everyday awareness of things, poetry is usually understood as something like significant metaphor. In mindfulness, there is a reversal of foreground and background in which those metaphors seem to be our very best insights into what is most fundamentally and most literally true, and our quotidian experience of ordinary life seems to be something more like a grainy movie than an engagement with reality.

And so we reach the theory of time developed in this book which, albeit expressed in the language of databases, is a Buddhist theory, a theory about the seamless weaving of the past, present and future of our beliefs about the seamless weaving of the past, present and future of ourselves and the world we are a part of, and of the ever-enlarging inscriptional record of those beliefs. And in writing this book, as I hope your reading of it will confirm, mindful data — the management of data with the constructs of the Extended Relational Paradigm — reveals itself as the management of the physical artifacts which embody our mindfulness, and as being pre-eminently practical in a business bottom-line sense. It is the immediate availability of data about what the things of importance and interest to us were like, are like and may become like, of what we once believed about those things, of what we currently believe about them and also of what we may eventually come to believe about them, and about the trail left by the inscription of those beliefs in our databases and in other less-regimented forms of written language such as legal documents, narrative and poetry.

Bibliography

With the exception of a couple of survey articles of work done on bitemporal data, all references in this bibliography are to publications that I have read, and that I consider relevant to the topics discussed in this book. One benefit of a bibliography thus restricted is that my comments on each reference are my own comments, and not glosses on the comments of others. Another is that this bibliography may provide clues to any conceptual biases I may have, since these references indicate where the influences on my thought lie.

For example, I have been much influenced by the work of Richard Snodgrass on bitemporal data. On the other hand, in spite of their prominence, I fail to see much importance in work done by Chris Date and his co-authors on bitemporal data.

The major drawback of this restriction, of course, is that this bibliography is not a neutral, balanced list of readings. Following bibliographies in the works cited, or consulting compendia like the ACM Digital Library, are the obvious correctives.

To avoid some otherwise confusing uses of the phrase "this book" in these bibliographical comments, I will refer to the book in which this is the bibliography, as *BDTP* (*Bitemporal Data: Theory and Practice*). The phrase "this book" will always refer to the book to which the comment applies. It will not refer to *BDTP*.

Adamson, C., 2006. Mastering Data Warehouse Aggregates. Wiley Publishing.

In *The Data Warehouse Toolkit, 3rd edition*, Kimball and Ross state that "aggregates are the single most dramatic way to affect performance in a large data warehouse environment." (p.481.) So I find it puzzling that Kimball and Ross mention aggregates only a few times in their book, and provide no detailed account of what aggregates are or how they affect performance.

This may be a good thing, however, because it would be difficult to improve on the comprehensive and in-depth treatment of star schema aggregates — aggregate fact tables, aggregate dimension tables, and even hybrid aggregate tables — provided by Adamson.

Because of its failure to explain aggregates, I do not consider the Kimball and Ross book to be a comprehensive statement of the Kimball approach to data warehousing. But with Adamson's book as a companion volume, I think that it is.

Al-Kateb, M., Ghazal, A., Crolotte, A., Bhashyam, R., Chimanchode, J., Pakala S.P., 2013. Temporal Query Processing in Teradata. *EDBT/ICDT '13* March 18−22, Genoa, Italy. (Copyright 2013 ACM 978-1-4503-1597-5/13/03), pp. 573−578.

This article describes how bitemporal queries are supported in Teradata databases, beginning with Teradata 13.10. It is based on the TSQL2 proposal of Richard Snodgrass and others, which differs from the ISO 2011 standard particularly in its distinction between current, sequenced, and non-sequenced queries, and in its support for a time period datatype.

Allen, J.F., 1983. Maintaining Knowledge About Temporal Intervals. Comm. ACM 26 (11), 832−843.

This article defined a set of thirteen positional relationships between two time periods along a common timeline. These relationships are a partitioning of all possible positional temporal relationships. Therefore, they are mutually exclusive and jointly complete.

Allwood, J., Andersson, L., Dahl, O., 1977. Logic in Linguistics. Cambridge University Press.
A brief introduction to set theory, to propositional, predicate, modal, and intensional logic, and to category theory. Written by linguists, this book about logic relates the logical formalisms it discusses to semantics, and illustrates important points with the use of examples taken from ordinary language.

Austin, J.L., 1961. (a). Philosophical Papers. Oxford University Press.

Austin, J.L. (b). Performative Utterances. In (J.L. Austin (a)), pp. 220−239.
J. L. Austin is the father of speech act theory which is about, as expressed in the title of a later book of his, "how to do things with words". Speech act theory has been extensively developed by Austin's most famous student, John Searle. Together with Paul Grice's work on rules of what he called "conversational implicature", I consider speech act theory the foundation of an eventual formalization of pragmatics, the fourth branch of linguistics (after phonology, syntax, and semantics) and the branch, at this time, least formalized.

Brachman, R.J., Hector, J.L., 2004. Knowledge Representation and Reasoning. Morgan-Kaufmann.
A formal ontology is a set of data structured so that software can carry out propositional and predicate logic-based inferences on that data, in order to answer queries. Knowledge representation is the representation of data in such structures, and the "reasoning" of this title refers to inferences (deductive proofs whose last lines are the answers to queries) carried out by software.
This book is written by two prominent authors in the field. However, some competence in set theory, and in propositional and predicate logic, will be needed to make headway with this book.

Burton, S., Dechaine, R.M., Vatikiotis-Bateson, E., 2012. Linguistics for Dummies. John Wiley.
Introduces many of the key concepts in syntax, semantics and pragmatics. Useful as a primer for (Saeed, 2003).

Chierchia, G., McConnell-Ginet, S., 1990. Meaning and Grammar: An Introduction to Semantics. MIT Press.
An introduction which emphasizes formal logic-based semantics, such as Montague grammar. Best read after reading (Saeed, 2003). For a comprehensive overview, I recommend reading Chierchia and McConnell-Ginet together with (Lyons, 1995), who surveys the field of semantics from the point of view of a linguist, and not a logician.

Clifford, J., Dyreson, C., Isakowitz, T., Jensen, C.S., Snodgrass, R.T., 1997. On the Semantics of 'Now' in Databases. ACM Transact. Database Syst. 22 (No. 2), 171−214.
This article discusses databases which contain variables, in particular temporal variables such as Now(). These are not the standard databases that are managed by today's relational DBMSs or defined by the current SQL standard. Therefore, these variable databases are currently of academic interest only.
The approach to managing Now() in standard bitemporal databases is to pretend that both valid-time and transaction-time periods extend to the end of time unless the database user indicates otherwise for valid-time periods or the DBMS indicates otherwise for transaction-time periods.
In this article, the authors argue that because we can't know what statements will be current in a database at any future time, a transaction-time period with a 9999 end time makes a statement about the far future which is certainly false. But it seems to me that, by the same token, valid-time periods with a 9999 end time are similarly flawed, and nobody objects to them. Everyone understands that statements about how things (including databases) may be in the future, are predictions which may or may not turn out to be true. And so I see no semantic flaws in representing open time periods in either valid time or transaction time by using a 9999 end time.

Colodny, R., 1962. Frontiers of Science and Philosophy. University of Pittsburgh Press, Pittsburgh, PA.

Cooke, H.P., Hugh T. *Aristotle: Categories, On Interpretation, Prior Analytics.* (Loeb Classical Library No. 325, 1938).
Early logical works of Aristotle, in Greek and English. Most relevant to the topics discussed in Chapter 5 of *BDTP* is the work *Categories*.

Date, C.J., 1982. An Introduction to Database Systems. Third Edition. Addison-Wesley.
A book, now in its eighth edition, which well deserves the accolades heaped on it. It was reading the chapter on advanced normalization, in this third edition of this book, that introduced me to the mathematical foundations of databases.

Date, C.J., Darwen, H., Lorentzos, N.A., 2003. Temporal Data and the Relational Model. Morgan-Kaufmann.
While the main focus of (Snodgrass, 1999) and (Johnston, 2010) is row-level bitemporality, the main focus of Date, Darwen and Lorentzos' book is column-level unitemporal versioning. While the main focus of Snodgrass' 1999 book and my 2010 book is on implementing temporal data management with current DBMSs and SQL, the main focus of Date, Darwen and Lorentzos' book is on describing language extensions that contain new operators for manipulating unitemporal data.

Darwen, H. Date, C.J., 2005. An Overview and Analysis of Proposals Based on the TSQL2 Approach (Date of this DRAFT: March 10th). http://isearch.avg.com/search?q = TSQL2%20%22temporal%20upward% 20compatibility%22&pid = avg&sg = 0&cid = {7d680489-457b-442b-8452-b2046cc00704}&mid = 46f0ff b82fa747d1bd9ad15f926a0bc8-45cf5985fd238be60643a5658809b1ca09b31e15&ds = AVG&v = 15.5.0.2& lang = en&pr = pr&d = 2011-11-26%2017%3A21%3A25&sap = nt&snd = hp&sap_acp = 0
Since it was primarily the British ISO committee that objected to the TSQL2 proposal, it seems likely that the objections to TSQL2 presented in this paper are among the reasons that the ISO never adopted TSQL2. But as the Teradata DBMS continues to evolve in its support for bitemporal data, we may eventually be able to decide whether or not the objections raised in this paper to TSQL2 are substantive, and we will eventually have good grounds on which to compare TSQL2 and the ISO 9075:2011 standards in terms of their expressive power, their flexibility, extensibility, ease of use, and other criteria of goodness.

Davis, E., 1990. Representations of Commonsense Knowledge. Morgan-Kaufmann.
Representations of folk ontology concepts in data structures on which software can perform automated inferencing. There are individual chapters on time, space, physics, minds, plans and goals, and society.
I consider these discussions to be about a level of ontology just below the upper-level ontology of the Relational Paradigm, describing a set of concepts which, in folk ontology, would be organized under the Relational Paradigm's ontology of (i) types and instances, (ii) referents, objects and events, (iii) object states and event states, and (iv) attributes, properties and relationships.

Devlin, B.A., Murphy, P.T., 1988. An Architecture for a Business and Information System. IBM Syst. J. 27 (1), 60−80.
To the best of my knowledge, this article is the origin of data warehousing in just as incontrovertible a sense as Dr. E. F. Codd's early articles were the origins of relational theory.

Devlin, Dr. B., 2013. Business (sic) unIntelligence. Technics Publications, LLC.
By the co-author of the paper which introduced data warehouses in 1988 (and the author of the Foreword to *BDTP*). This book discusses, among many other issues, what remains useful in the concept of a data warehouse, and what enterprise data warehouses can and cannot do in today's world of Big Data − big "hard data" generated by machines, and big "soft data" generated by social media and other sources of human expression.

Fong, P., Snyder, D., 2008. Temporal Versioning. BeyeNetwork http://www.b-eye-network.com/view/7921.
An article published on Inmon's website that provides a basic introduction to bitemporal data. In the same year, Inmon, Strauss and Neushloss published the book which introduced DW2.0, but in that book, the concept of bitemporality is absent. Also, with the exception of a passing mention in one other article (Jiang, 2012), I find no references to bitemporality in other publications on Inmon's BeyeNetwork website.

Gao, D., Jensen, C.S., Snodgrass, R.T., Soo, M.D., 2005. Join Operations in Temporal Databases. VLDB J. 14, 2−29.
This article describes temporal extensions to various types of joins, including Cartesian Product (cross join), several types of inner join (theta, equi-, natural), and several types of outer join (left, right, full). Section 2 describes each type of join operator, and shows the semantic equivalence of Now()-restricted temporal joins to conventional nontemporal joins. However, the non-academic reader should be aware that this article relies heavily on the notations of set theory and predicate logic, as well as notations specific to relational theory.

In my opinion, these notations, in widespread use throughout the computer science community, are the primary obstacle standing between computer scientists and IT practitioners. This is unfortunate for two reasons.

First, there is much that computer scientists could learn from IT practitioners about the complexities of applying computer science formalisms to real-world problems. But from their point of view, many accounts of real-world problems by IT practitioners, lacking logical and set-theoretic formalization, may seem to be too fuzzy to learn anything from. And on the other hand, there is much that practitioners could learn from computer scientists about generalizing and formalizing narrowly-focused solutions to specific problems. But the specialized mathematical vocabulary of computer science stands in their way.

Secondly, the obstacle is primarily one of notation only. IT practitioners who are already expert in SQL will find little conceptual difficulty in understanding the applicability of set theory and predicate logic to the management of data. So I recommend to my fellow practitioners those already-mentioned sources for introductions to set theory and to predicate logic, found elsewhere in this bibliography.

Gardenfors, P., 2004. Conceptual Spaces: The Geometry of Thought. MIT Press.
A brilliant attempt to relate the concepts of mathematics and logic to neurological constructs and processes in the human brain by means of an intermediate level of representation in terms of perceived shape patterns and the (hypothesized) neural correlates of their geometrical relationships.

Gensler, H.J., 2002. Introduction to Logic. Routledge.
This book is the best introduction to logic that I know of, far better for the beginning student than introductions by more prominent logicians such as Copi, Montague, or Quine. Besides covering standard propositional and predicate logic, it also introduces the student to Aristotle's logic of syllogisms, to the several systems of modal logic, and to deontic and epistemic logic as well.

Since SQL is a restricted form of propositional and predicate logic, some knowledge of logic will be invaluable for anyone who writes (or reads) SQL. I know of no better way to begin learning formal logic than with this book.

Grandy, R., Warner, E., 2009. Paul Grice. The Stanford Encyclopedia of Philosophy (Summer 2009 Edition), Edward N. Zalta (ed.), URL = http://plato.stanford.edu/archives/sum2009/entries/grice/
The importance of Grice's work is that, together with speech act theory, it is the origin of relatively recent attempts to formalize pragmatics, the last of the major branches of linguistics (the others being phonology, syntax, and semantics) to be formalized. The importance to the study of bitemporal and tritemporal data is that asserting and withdrawing statements are speech acts.

Gruber, T.R. A Translation Approach to Portable Ontology Specifications. Knowledge Acquis., 5, pp. 199–220.

This is the article in which Gruber gave his famous definition of ontology as "a formal, explicit speci-fication of a shared conceptualisation". This definition, and Sellars' definition of "philosophy", are birds of a feather. Both are uncontroversial and satisfyingly terse to experts, and uninformative to everyone else.

Hayes, P.J. A Catalog of Temporal Theories. Florida Institute for Human and Machine Cognition 1. Originally published as University of Illinois Technical Report UIUC-BI-AI-96-01.

This, and (Davis, 1990), are the principal sources used for the early sections of Chapter 2.

IBM, 2010. DB210 for z/OS. Technical Overview. IBM.

An IBM Redbook which contains a good presentation of IBM's early implementation of the temporal features of the ISO 9075:2011 SQL Standard.

Can usefully be read in conjunction with (Kulkarni, K., Michels, J.E., 2012).

Inmon, W., 1992. Building the Data Warehouse. John Wiley.

With this book, Inmon began his work of introducing the concepts of data warehousing to the rest of the IT profession, in the process extending the concept into several iterations of his own Corporate Information Factory architecture and then, in 2008, into his Data Warehouse 2.0 architecture.

Inmon, W.H., Hackathorn, R.D., 1994. Using the Data Warehouse. John Wiley.

The original definition of "data warehouse", except in wording, remains the same. Compare p.2 of this book with (Inmon, 1992), p.29.

Inmon, B., 1996. Virtual Data Warehouse: The Snake Oil of the '90s. Data Management Review, 50–54.

In this article, Inmon calls the virtual data warehouse "snake oil". Thirteen years later, he was saying "I believe virtual data warehouses are inane." (Inmon, March 2009). And indeed, what Inmon describes as a virtual data warehouse, here and in his 2009 article, cannot stand up to his objections. But for a more robust sketch of the virtualization of the enterprise data warehouse, see Chapter 17 of *BDTP*.

Inmon, B., 2008. The Virtual Data Warehouse (Again). BeyeNetwork http://searchdatamanagement.techtarget.com/news/2240037003/The-virtual-data-warehouse-again.

Inmon doesn't like virtual data warehouses. However, the virtual data warehouses he doesn't like are fed-erated queries, in which any semantic integration must be hardcoded into each query. That is indeed a bad idea, for all the reasons Inmon enumerates. But I consider his description of virtual data warehouses to be a description of a straw man, and consequently I do not accept his conclusion that the only valid embodi-ment of an enterprise data warehouse is as a physically integrated collection of data.

Inmon, W.H., Strauss, D., Neushloss, G., 2008. DW2.0. The Architecture for the Next Generation of Data Warehousing. Morgan-Kaufmann.

I cannot recommend this book. For more informative, and more recent, work on DW2.0, I recommend Inmon's website, the BeyeNetwork.

I also note that DW2.0. is said to extend the data warehouse to include the management of text data (documents and emails) and of metadata. But in (Inmon, 1992), for example, metadata is discussed on sev-enteen pages; and in (Inmon, 1994), metadata is discussed on twenty-six pages. So it is a topic Inmon paid more than passing attention to in earlier books. In addition, I find nothing remarkably new in the discus-sions of metadata in this book.

Inmon, B., 2009. The Elusive Virtual Data Warehouse. BeyeNetwork, http://www.b-eye-network.com/view/9956.

See (Inmon, 2008). Same straw man, same objections.

Inmon, B., 2009. Different Kinds of Data Warehouses. BeyeNetwork, http://www.b-eye-network.com/view/10416.
More on DW2.0 and text data. Nothing on DW2.0 and metadata, however. After promoting metadata as a major extension to the scope of data warehousing, in (Inmon, Strauss, Neuschloss, 2008), metadata in DW2.0 seems to have fallen off the map, at least as far as publications on the BeyeNetwork are concerned.

Inmon, B., 2009. Managing the Unstructured Volume. BeyeNetwork, http://www.b-eye-network.com/view/10553.
More on DW2.0 and text data. Still nothing on DW2.0 and metadata.

Inmon, B., 2011. Data Warehousing — The Vision. BeyeNetwork, http://www.b-eye-network.com/view/15518.
More on DW2.0 and text data. Still nothing on DW2.0 and metadata.

ISO. *ISO/IEC 9075-2, Fourth edition 2011-12-15. Information technology — Database languages — SQL — Part 2: Foundation (SQL/Foundation)*.
This is Part 2 of the 9075:2011 edition of the ISO SQL standard, in which the standard is extended to include concepts and implementation issues related to the management of bitemporal time.

Jensen, C.S., Clifford, J., Gadia, S.K., Segev, A., Snodgrass, R.T., 1992. A Glossary of Temporal Database Concepts. ACM Sigmod Record 21 (No. 3), 35—43.
Superceded by (Jensen and Dyreson, 1998).

Jensen, C.S., Dyreson, C.E., 1998. The Consensus Glossary of Temporal Database Concepts — February 1998 Version. In: Etzion, O., Jajodia, S., Sripada, S. (Eds.), Temporal Databases- Research and Practice. LNCS 1399, Springer-Verlag, Berlin, Heidelberg, pp. 367—405.
This is what it says it is — a consensus glossary of temporal database concepts. It is the de jure standard reference for the computer science community's use of such terms as "valid time", "transaction time" and "bitemporal".

Jiang, B. PhD. Is Inmon's Data Warehouse Definition Still Accurate? BeyeNetwork, 2012. http://www.b-eye-network.com/view/16066.
Contains a passing comment that very few data warehouses are bitemporal.

Johnston, T., 2000. Primary Key Reengineering Projects: The Problem. Information Management, http://www.information-management.com/issues/20000201/1866-1.html.

Johnston, T., 2000. Primary Key Reengineering Projects: The Solution. Information Management, http://www.information-management.com/issues/20000301/2004-1.html.
These two articles explain why I believe that all relational tables should use surrogate keys rather than business keys, even associative tables. For anyone contemplating the idea of writing their own bitemporal data management code, in which they intend to use business keys rather than surrogate keys as primary keys, I recommend that they read these articles first.

Johnston, T., Weis, R., 2010. Managing Time in Relational Databases: How to Design, Update and Query Temporal Data. Morgan-Kaufmann.
The book in which I and Randy Weis introduced the Asserted Versioning method of managing bitemporal data, including the extension of transaction time to include rows of data with future transaction-time periods.

Johnston, T., 2011. Integrating Canonical Message Models and Enterprise Data Models (Part 1 of 3). Enterprise Syst. J. http://esj.com/articles/2011/11/01/integrating-message-models.aspx.
The first in a three-part series from which Chapter 17 has been adapted.

Johnston, T., 2011. Integrating Canonical Message Models and Enterprise Data Models (Part 2 of 3). Enterprise Systems Journal http://esj.com/articles/2011/11/15/integrating-message-models-2.aspx.

Johnston, T., 2011. Integrating Canonical Message Models and Enterprise Data Models (Part 3 of 3). Enterprise Systems Journal http://esj.com/articles/2011/11/29/integrating-message-models-3.aspx.

Johnston, T., Weis, R. *The Management of Data by Means of a Canonical Schema.* U.S. Patent 8,219,522. 2012. http://www.google.com/advanced_patent_search.
The first of two patents by myself, and my *Managing Time in Relational Databases* co-author, in which we describe software that provides a semantically integrated implementation of nontemporal, unitemporal, and bitemporal data by using a universal ("canonical") schema to persist these temporally different kinds of data.

Johnston, T.M., Weis, R.J. *The Management of Data by Means of a Canonical Schema.* U.S. Patent 8,713,073, April 29, 2014. Publication number: US 8713073 B2. http://www.google.com/advanced_patent_search.
The second patent by myself, and my *Managing Time in Relational Databases* co-author, in which we describe software that provides a semantically integrated implementation of nontemporal, unitemporal, and bitemporal data by using a universal ("canonical") schema to persist these temporally different kinds of data. (This is a continuation-in-part of our first patent, and includes the full text of the first patent.)

These patents may be useful for providing additional detail on how the concepts in *BDTP* can be implemented. One requirement for a patent is that it describe an "invention" in enough detail that "one skilled in the art" could build that invention from that description. Consequently, these patents are written at a level of detail, supplemented with appropriately detailed diagrams, from which program specifications could be written. Those interested in the implementation details of these extensions to standard bitemporal theory may find these two patents of interest.

These patents also describe more than our extensions to standard bitemporal theory, extensions which are, of course, patent-protected. Of necessity, they also describe implementation details which are part of that standard theory, and which therefore are not patent-protected. For those interested in developing their own implementations of standard bitemporal theory, this material in these patents may be of interest.

Kempson, R., 1977. Semantic Theory. Cambridge University Press.
A balanced presentation of (i) philosophical and logical, (ii) behavioristic (since Chomsky, of course, deprecated, albeit prematurely, in my opinion), (iii) linguistic, and (iv) pragmatic (speech act) approaches to the study of semantics.

Kimball, R., 1996. The Data Warehouse Toolkit: Practical Techniques for Building Dimensional Data Warehouses. John Wiley.
This book, and later "data warehouse toolkit" books, introduced and developed Kimball's transaction-centric approach to managing historical data. Concepts such as star schemas, dimensional data marts, the fact vs. dimension distinction, and slowly-changing dimensions, are all grounded in Kimball's work, as is the entire range of OLAP and business intelligence software.

Kimball, R., Ross, M., 2013. The Data Warehouse Toolkit. *Third edition.* John Wiley.
The authoritative statement of the Kimball approach to data warehousing, co-authored by Kimball himself and by the president of the Kimball Group, Margy Ross. Besides being that authoritative statement, this book is also valuable for its case studies in a wide number of subject areas, including retail sales, inventory management, procurement, order management, accounting, customer relationship management, human

resources management, financial services, telecommunications, transportation, education, healthcare, electronic commerce, and insurance.

But see also my comment to (Adamson, 2006).

Kimball Group. Design Tip #152 Slowly Changing Dimension Types 0, 4, 5, 6 and 7. February 5, 2013. © Kimball Group. All rights reserved. http://www.kimballgroup.com/2013/02/05/design-tip-152-slowly-changing-dimension-types-0-4-5-6-7/.

Another recent description of slowly-changing dimensions, by the president of the Kimball Group.

Knowles, C., 2012. 6NF Conceptual Models and Data Warehousing 2.0. *Proceedings of the Southern Association for Information Systems Conference, Atlanta, GA*. March 23rd-24th. http://sais.aisnet.org/2012/Knowles.pdf.

Knowles discusses 6NF, DW2.0, bitemporal data, Anchor Modeling, and XML. In his article, Knowles explicitly states that bitemporal data should be incorporated into Inmon's DW2.0. I agree.

Kulkarni, K., Michels, J.E., 2012. Temporal Features in SQL:2011. ACM Sigmod Record 41 (No. 3), 34—43.

This is the article in which the temporal features defined in the 2011 release of the ISO SQL standard were first summarized for the academic community. This article is well-written, and could serve as an introduction to the IT professional community as well, so it is unfortunate that the article is (currently) only available in a journal that is not easily accessible to the non-academic reader.

Liddell, H., Scott, R., 1994. An Intermediate Greek-English Lexicon. Oxford University Press.

The authoritative standard among Greek-English lexicons.

Lipschutz, S., 1998. Set Theory and Related Topics. McGraw-Hill.

There are countless introductions to set theory, many by more prominent authors than Lipschutz. But of the half-dozen or so that I have read, this is the clearest. My recommendation for gaining an IT professional's working knowledge of set theory is to read Appendix A in (Sowa, 1984), and then read this book and work the exercises.

Lyons, J., 1995. Linguistic Semantics: an Introduction. Cambridge University Press.

An introduction by a prominent linguist. Best read after reading (Saeed, 2003). For a comprehensive overview, I recommend reading Lyons together with (Chierchia and McConnell-Ginet, 1990), who provide a formal logic approach to semantics.

Mates, B., 1953. Stoic Logic. University of California Press.

A brilliant reconstruction and analysis of the work done in logic after Aristotle and prior to the early medieval period.

Pagin, P., 2012. Assertion. The Stanford Encyclopedia of Philosophy (Winter 2012 Edition), Edward N. Zalta (ed.), URL = http://plato.stanford.edu/archives/win2012/entries/assertion/.

Usefully read in conjunction with (Winograd and Flores, 1986).

Rockmore, D., 2006. Stalking the Riemann Hypothesis. Vintage Books.

Included for the quotation from Gauss used in the Preface to *BDTP*, this book is a fascinating account of the search for a pattern among the prime numbers, and is entirely accessible to non-mathematicians.

Saeed, J.I., 2003. Semantics. Second ed. Blackwell.

If the role of the data modeler is the most natural one, within IT, to evolve into that of a business ontologist (as I believe it is), then a basic knowledge of semantics will be essential for the data modeler. This is the best recent introduction to semantics that I know of. Of particular interest will be the discussions of semantic issues that can interfere with the objective of establishing a one-to-one correlation between data in databases, and the facts described by that data, issues involving homonyms, synonyms, ambiguity and vagueness.

Searle, J., 1969. Speech Acts. Cambridge University Press.

I confess to not having read this seminal book, although I must have read a few dozen articles and chapters on Searle's work. Nonetheless, following on Austin's work, Searle has done more than anyone else to develop reflections on how to do things with words into the formal pragmatics known as speech act theory.

For an important attempt to apply speech act theory to data management, see (Winograd and Flores, 1986).

Sellars, W., 1962. Philosophy and the Scientific Image of Man. Colodny, pp. 35−78

This is the article in which Sellars offered his famous definition of "philosophy" as the study of how "'things', in the widest possible sense of the term, 'hang together' in the widest possible sense of the term." This definition, and Gruber's definition of "ontology", are birds of a feather. Both are uncontroversial and satisfyingly terse to experts, but uninformative to everyone else.

Snodgrass, R.T., Ahn, I., Ariav, G., Batory, D.S., Clifford, J., Dyreson, C.E., et al. 1994. TSQL2 Language Specification. ACM Sigmod Record, vol. 23, #1, (March), pp. 65−86.

Although never formally approved by the ISO, I consider TSQL2 to be an alternative standard to the ISO standard. ISO 9075:2011 is the standard on which IBM's DB2 10 temporal features are based. TSQL2 is the standard on which Teradata 13's temporal features are based.

Snodgrass, R.T., 1998. Managing Temporal Data: A Five-Part Series. (1998, TIMECENTER Technical Report TR-28). (Originally published in Database Programming and Design, June − October, 1998.).

These are the first articles, to the best of my knowledge, to introduce computer science work on bitemporal data to IT professionals. Snodgrass is arguably the leading researcher in the field of bitemporal data, and also one of the very few academics to attempt to explain his work to those of us who have the job of applying theory to the practice of managing real-world data.

Snodgrass, R.T., 1999. Developing Time-Oriented Database Applications in SQL. Morgan-Kaufmann.

This book is concerned with explaining how to support bitemporal data using then-current DBMSs and then-current SQL. The extensive selection of SQL code snippets help illustrate the many technical concepts involved, and are still of practical use to developers attempting to write their own bitemporal code. This book is available in PDF form, at no cost, at Dr. Snodgrass' website: http://www.cs.arizona.edu/people/rts/publications.html.

Sowa, J.F., 1984. Conceptual Structures: Information Processing in Mind and Machine. Addison-Wesley.

Although this book is thirty years old, I still refer to it frequently. Its discussions of basic concepts in philosophy, psychology, linguistics and knowledge representation are still well worth reading. Its Conceptual Catalog (Appendix B, especially B.2) is what we would today call a formal ontology, one which expresses definitions of important concepts in a graph-like representation of predicate logic. Sections in the Mathematical Background appendix (Appendix A) include excellent brief introductions to sets, functions, logic, formal grammars and algorithms.

Sowa, J.F., 2000. Knowledge Representation: Logical, Philosophical, and Computational Foundations. Brooks/Cole.

This book is about ontologies. Appendix B contains a sample ontology which is more comprehensive than the Relational Paradigm Ontology, because the Relational Paradigm Ontology is a high-level ontology specifically for relational databases. Another point of difference is that Sowa's sample ontology could not be called a folk ontology, as I have said that the Relational Paradigm Ontology is.

Because of Sowa's background in both Philosophy and computer science, this book discusses ontologies in a way which makes it clear how much formal ontologies owe to classical ontology. A good way to begin extending the Relational Paradigm Ontology would be to work on integrating it with many of the key concepts described here in Sowa's book, as well as in Davis' book (Davis, 1990).

Spade, P.V., 1996. Thoughts, Words and Things: an Introduction to Late Mediaeval (sic) Logic and Semantic Theory. (Self-published. (c) 1996, Paul Vincent Spade.) pv**spade**.com/Logic/docs/**thoughts**1_1a.pdf.
A masterly work by a leading authority. (His spelling of the word we normally spell "medieval" is intentional.) Discussions of logic and semantics by the late medieval philosophers still appear quite sophisticated by today's standards, and can still provide insight to those working with current issues in these fields.

W3C. RDF 1.1 Semantics. W3C Last Call Working Draft 23 July 2013. This version: http://www.w3.org/TR/2013/WD-rdf11-mt-20130723/.
"This document describes a precise semantics for the Resource Description Framework 1.1 [RDF11-CONCEPTS] and RDF Schema [RDF-SCHEMA]. It defines a number of distinct entailment regimes and corresponding patterns of entailment. It is part of a suite of documents which comprise the full specification of RDF 1.1." (From the Abstract to this document.)

W3C The Organization Ontology. W3C Proposed Recommendation 17 December 2013. This version: http://www.w3.org/TR/2013/PR-vocab-org-20131217/.
"This ontology is designed to enable publication of information on organizations and organizational structures including governmental organizations. It is intended to provide a generic, reusable core ontology that can be extended or specialized for use in particular situations." (From the Introduction to this document.)
This document is a good introduction to the basic concepts of formal ontology, and provides extensive examples of supporting such an ontology in RDF. An Organization ontology is an example of what I call a "mid-level ontology" in *BDTP*.

Winograd, T., Flores, F., 1986. Understanding Computers and Cognition. Addison-Wesley.
Winograd and Flores discuss a "basic conversation for action", shown as a diagram on their p.65. It includes asserting and withdrawing statements as two of nine different speech acts that are involved in any linguistic exchange whose point is to reach an agreement about what to do.
I believe that the Extended Relational Paradigm Metamodel described in Chapter 19, and the tritemporal theory of data also described there, can serve to formalize Winograd and Flores' basic conversation for action. That metamodel provides a framework for relating speech acts to statements, and statements to their inscriptions.
See also (Grandy and Warner, 2009) and (Pagin, 2012).

PHILOSOPHICAL CONCEPTS

The best internet source for an introduction to philosophical concepts, including those used in this book, is the Stanford Encyclopedia of Philosophy, at http://plato.stanford.edu/.

Unfortunately, while each entry is individually excellent, the choice of which concepts to include seems somewhat idiosyncratic. For example, although there is an entry on logic and ontology, there is (currently) no entry for ontology itself. Nonetheless, I recommend the following entries there, as relevant to the concepts used in *BDTP*: assertion, change, epistemology, facts, Arthur Prior, propositional attitude reports, speech acts, temporal logic, temporal parts.

There are, of course, numerous other excellent introductions to philosophical concepts available on the web. The problem is that there are also numerous other very poor ones! Philosophy is a topic that seems to lend itself to this kind of variety. I recommend to those interested, that as a general rule, sources at dot-edu domains can be presumed reliable, while sources at other domains should be treated with caution.

THE COMPUTER SCIENCE LITERATURE

The computer science literature on bitemporal data is vast, certainly numbering many hundreds of publications. For those who wish to investigate that literature further, I recommend getting a membership in the ACM, and subscribing to the ACM Digital Library. PDF copies of thousands of articles published in ACM journals are available for download from that source, at no cost beyond the cost of the annual membership and the digital library option. References to academic articles published in non-ACM journals are also available, although there is usually a fee to download those articles. The url is http://www.acm.org/.

Another invaluable − and free! − source of information on temporal databases, with many links to other resources, can be found on Dr. Snodgrass' website, specifically at http://www.cs.arizona.edu/people/rts/publications.html.

Index

Note: Page numbers followed by "*f*" refer to figures.

Printed and bound by CPI Group (UK) Ltd, Croydon, CR0 4YY

03/10/2024

01040327-0005